VLADIMIR AND NADYA

NADYA, Early 1890's

Vladimir and Nadya

The Lenin Story

Mary Hamilton-Dann

INTERNATIONAL PUBLISHERS, New York

Library of Congress Cataloging–in–Publication Data

Hamilton–Dann, Mary.
　　Vladimir and Nadya / Mary Hamilton–Dann.
　　　p. cm.
　　Includes bibliographical references and index.
　　ISBN 0-7178–0712–6 (pbk. : alk. paper)
　　1. Lenin, Vladimir Il'ich, 1870–1924.　2. Krupskaya, Nadezhda Kon-
stantinovna, 1869–1939.　3. Heads of state—Soviet Union—Biography.　4.
Spouses of heads of state—Soviet Union—Biography.　5. Revolutionaries—
Soviet Union—Biography.　6. Russia—History—Nicholas II, 1894—1917.
7. Soviet Union—History—1917–1936.
I. Title.
DK254.L45H36　1998
947.084'1'0922--dc21
[B]　　　　　　　　　　　　　　　　　　　　　　　　　　　97-5843
　　　　　　　　　　　　　　　　　　　　　　　　　　　　　　CIP

Printed in Canada

Contents

Author's Foreword   vii

Preface. . .*Olga Dmitrievna Ulyanova*   ix

1. St. Petersburg, Imperial Russia, cir. 1895   1
2. Prison and Exile to Siberia   19
3. Life on the Border of Outer Mongolia   35
4. Return to Russia   57
5. The First Migration and *Iskra*   70
6. The Stalin Connection   88
7. Switzerland 1903 and Lenin's Break with *Iskra*   94
8. The First Russian Revolution 1905–07   105
9. The Second Emigration   123
10. Revolutionary Revival   134
11. Longjumeau, France 1911   140
12. World War—Trapped in Switzerland   146
13. The Inessa Letters   162
14. End of an Era—the Death of Two Mothers   171
15. Portrait of Russian Aristocracy   179
16. Abdication of Tsar Nicholas II— the Emigrés Return to Russia, April 1917   183
17. The Finland Station, July 1917   209
18. Revolution, October 1917   223
19. "Soviet Power"   235
20. Counterrevolution and Invasion   243
21. Peace and Transition   253
22. Final Journey—January 21, 1924   265
23. The Succession in Jeopardy   279
24. Nadya, Legatee of the Socialist Ideal   283

Reference Notes   297

Bibliography   298

Chronology of Lenin's writings   300

Biographical Index   301

Illustrations

  ii Nadya, early 1890s

 xii Lenin, 1897

   9 Building where Sunday evening school met

  20 Nadya, prison photos; Georgi Plekhanov; Vera Zasulich

  21 Lenin, prison photo when released into exile

  41 Shushenskoye scenes

  58 Nadya; Anna and Maria; House at Ufa

  69 Tsarist police interrogating *Iskra* readers; *Iskra*, No. 1, 1900

  88 Joseph Stalin

122 Lenin and Maxim Gorky

131 Laura Marx and Paul Lafargue

135 Covers, two of Lenin's books

138 Lenin

140 Alexandra Kollontai

142 Inessa Armand

159 Klara Zetkin and Rosa Luxemburg

164 Inessa Armand

172 Nadya, 1915–16; Yelizaveta as a young woman

193 Émigrés in Stockholm, 1917

203 Lenin reading *Pravda*

212 Lenin, passport photo as fireman

215 Railway diagram

227 Lenin chairing a meeting

234 Lenin, Nadya and Maria in car after military parade, Moscow, May 1, 1918

245 Lenin visits soldiers and nurses

249 Lenin and Bonch–Bruyevich

251 Lenin and Nadya w/peasants at Kashino

259 Lenin, 1920

263 John Reed's comment on Lenin; Lenin and Sverdlov watching airplanes

266 The house in Gorki

269 Lenin at Gorki, summer 1922

277 Funeral procession, Gorki, 1924; Lenin's bier

285 Nadya, soon after Lenin's death

287 Klara Zetkin and Nadya, Moscow, ca. 1929

Author's Foreword

Research for the present work involved several trips to Russia undertaken as an independent traveller. One purpose was to follow in the footsteps of Lenin and his wife before, during and after their 17-year emigration.

My previous familiarity with England, France, Belgium, Scandinavia and Russia narrowed the unfamiliar locales to Finland and Siberia. (The exception was Switzerland, which I did not visit.)

The following is a condensation of multiple journeys in connection with this book. My trips were during the 1980's, the last one in 1989.

Preparation proved to be complicated. Repeated letters to the Soviet Embassy in Washington, phone calls to New York, and the efforts of a determined travel agent at AAA finally resulted in permission for entry to Russia and Siberia via Finland.

Time spent at the Lenin-museo in Tampere, Finland brought me in touch with the Finnish period of Lenin's flight from tsarist (and later "bourgeois government") police. I visited the Rovio apartment in Hakaneimi Square, Helsinki, where Lenin took refuge; rode a bus to Oulunkala, the village where he lived with the Vinsten Sisters. Curators at the Tampere museum provided me with a valuable primary source book—a compendium by Finnish authors—detailing Lenin's experience during his many sojourns in Finland.

On the train from Helsinki to Leningrad/St. Petersburg I followed the same route and passed the same tiny, weathered depots that Lenin and Nadya saw on their repeated journeys between the Capital's Finland and Udelnaya railway stations and Helsinki, including several small villages along the way.

Days in Leningrad included an introduction to the V.I. Lenin Museum and Library, visits to the Kshesinskaya Palace, the Field of Mars, Volkhov Cemetery, and a long afternoon at Smolny, which contains Lenin's first office. These were interspersed with walks along Bolshaya Neva and the numerous canals.

In Moscow I stayed at the National Hotel on the floor above where Lenin and Nadya lived for a period after moving from Petrograd. Many days were spent in the Central V.I. Lenin Museum and Library near Red Square. I was privileged to hold the wedding rings of Vladimir and Nadya. "You are the first American to do so," I was told. My interest in Vladimir and Nadya as subjects for an original book led to my treatment as a kind of celebrity and brought me in touch with persons and places not accessible to an ordinary tourist. One of my contacts led to Olga Ulyanova, Lenin's niece.

Extensive research in Moscow was occasionally relieved by trips beyond the city, among them a rail journey to Gorki-Leninskiye. At Gorki I climbed a hill to the Great House where Lenin spent his last days. One memorable October day with the sun glistening on immense trees and warming the polished interior of the

Italianate mansion, I stood at a window in Lenin's bedroom looking down at the park and leaf-strewn paths. Later on I returned to Gorki and photographed the miniature Gerasimovo railway depot where Lenin's coffin was lifted aboard a train for Moscow.

A longtime interest in steam railroads led me to Moscow's Paveletskii Railway Station beside which stands a museum building housing the entire train—including the mammoth locomotive. Festooned in red and black bunting, the train is a reminder of that day in 1924 when a grieving populace bade farewell to their leader.

My departure for Siberia was marked by witty comments from fellow-Americans: "We hope you make it back" as I took off for the land of banishment.

A twin-engine jet departed Moscow at midnight for Sverdlovsk (Yekaterinburg). After a brief stop to refuel and exchange passengers, we continued to Abakan, Siberia where I was greeted warmly by my guide, Natasha Glukhova. From Abakan—a charming mid-sized city—we drove 60 miles south to the village of Shushenskoye near the border of Outer Mongolia

It was at Shushenskoye that Lenin and Nadya spent their exile years under tsarism. The village is a museum-preserve with everything as it was during that earlier time. The Petrova House where Vladimir and Nadya lived is a typical Siberian izba, beside the somnolent River Shush. I arrived three days after a visit by Michail Gorbachev, the first Soviet leader to go there. His bouquet of red roses, placed at a Lenin statue beside the house, was still fresh.

I walked through the three-room izba, visited a nearby izba where Oskar Engberg had lived, and inhaled the aroma of an exile environment. The weather was benign—warm and sunny. Once I rode a horsedrawn wagon loaded with hay. The driver lifted me to the high seat and we clopped along in the quiet Siberian twilight past fields of stubble.

In concluding this brief summary, I should speak of the countless persons abroad who generously provided historical information, materials, and valuable assistance. I wish to thank Paavo Jokela, Ph.D., of Tampere, Finland, whose letter of introduction with embossed heading opened many doors for me in Russia.

Regarding the bibliography: of primary value were the writings of Nadya and the Collected Works of Lenin which contain personal letters and recollections of those who worked with him. Likewise important were the memoirs of contemporaries whose perspectives on Lenin, and his wife were more broadly based.

Mary Hamilton-Dann
October 1996

Preface

The following biography of Vladimir Ilyich Lenin and Nadezhda Konstanti-novna Krupskaya is an extraordinary work in the world of documentary literature. For a long time the author pondered the idea of a life of Nadezhda, amazed at the image of this woman—wife of Lenin, revolutionary and educator. The original draft was entitled *Nadya*. But later, during the process of working on the manu-script, the author realized that to write about Krupskaya apart from Lenin was impossible, since their lives were closely bound together. Thus evolved the biogra-phy *Vladimir and Nadya*.

The appearance of such a book is a rare occurrence. As a rule, information about Nadezhda is limited to three words: wife, friend and companion of V.I. Lenin. But this unlooked-for work from the U.S.A. presents the subjects from a totally different perspective—depicting their life together, the amazing interaction between them, their deep love for each other, all of which remained steadfast throughout their difficult lives.

Noteworthy as well is the author's refutation of the myths and fables about Lenin's relationship to Inessa Armand.

The noted French author, Henri Barbusse, wrote of Lenin as follows:

The unshakable love he bore for the companion of his life is, without doubt, a rare phenomenon in the destiny of "great men," and particularly astonishing during the course of a professional revolutionary's life under constantly changing exter-nal conditions. In this brief memorandum, we underscore this, showing what an unusual example it is of an almost perfect union of a man and a woman, two beings so congenial. But even more working side by side on a foundation of mutuality, each with specific personal resources, yet always together in heart for the realiza-tion of a great common goal.*

The death of Vladimir Ilyich Lenin was, for his wife, an enormous, irreplace-able loss. Yet notwithstanding her gentleness, she was a strong and durable person. She began devoting herself wholly to writing her *Reminiscences of Lenin*. The work is a complete and valid biography.

Nadezhda Konstantinovna made a great contribution to popular education. A specialist in the field of pedagogy, she wrote many thoroughgoing and serious works. Officially, she was people's deputy in the Soviet Commissariat of Education,

---

*"L'amour inébranlable qu'il a porté à la compagne da sa vie est un phénomène sans doute rare dans la destinée des 'grands hommes' et particulièrement étonnant au cours de l'existence d'un révolutionnaire professionnel soumis à des changements inattendus et perpétuels quant aux conditions extérieures. Si, dans ces notes, strictements et sévèrement résumées, nous pouvions nous étendre sur ces considérations, nous montrerions quel bel exemple ce fut là, quasi parfait, de l'union d'un homme et d'une femme: deux êtres se plaisant personnellement mais, de plus, collaborant côte à côte et sur pied d'égalité, chacun avec ses ressources spécifiques, mais tous deux avec tout leur esprit et tout leur coeur, à la réalisation passionnee d'une grande idée com-mune."[1] -trans. MHD

became Doctor of Pedagogical Science and was named Academician. Elected member of the Party's Central Committee and deputy to the Supreme Soviet, she followed Lenin's direction and legacy in all her pursuits.

After Lenin's death, she directed an appeal to the people: "Comrades, men and women workers, peasant men and women! I have an earnest request to make of you. Do not grieve for Ilyich or extend honors to his memory. Do not raise statues or name palaces for him, or hold splendid celebrations to his memory. In life, all this meant nothing to him—was a burden. Instead, remember the destitution and disasters in our country . . ."[1]

The author describes Nadya in her youth, an attractive and even beautiful young woman. Also noted is Nadya's hard-working day, which often began at 5 a.m. and continued far into the night. This accounts for the extent of her accomplishments. In addition to her *Reminiscences of Lenin*, she wrote many basic works on pedagogy. At the time of their production, almost none existed.

Only on Sundays did she manage to accompany family members to Gorki, or join friends for occasional trips to Arkangelsk. All my life I have remembered the two occasions when I went with her to Gorki. Such times!

It is important to note the following: Aunt Nadya's secretary (Vera) Dridzo, made erroneous claims, in writings and anecdotes, some of which the author has included in the present biography. Dridzo aired her alleged close ties to Nadezhda only after the latter's death. She stated that only she herself was at Nadya's side. In fact, Dridzo was merely a personal secretary. Aunt Nadya's family and friends were always with her, among them Maria Ilyinichna, Dmitri Ilyich, my mother Alexandra Fedorovna, I myself, Gleb and Zinaida Krzhizhanovsky. Gleb Krzhizhanovsky was a friend of Lenin and his wife during their younger years, and in Soviet times was an important academic.

Also at Nadya's side was a dearly-loved woman, Valya Kurnikova who lived in the apartment and assisted with housekeeping. Aunt Nadya remembered only too well how Dridzo took everything upon herself: "My Cerberus" she characterized her with a rueful smile.* Dridzo followed her everywhere. One final note on Dridzo: nearly resorting to force, she kept me and my mother from Aunt Nadya's sickbed. My Aunt had called for us, wishing to bid us farewell . . . but during the final moments of her life, she was shadowed by this crude person.

N.K. Krupskaya was interred in the Kremlin Wall beside the mausoleum of Vladimir Ilyich. There are always red roses on her grave.

Olga Dmitrievna Ulyanova**
January 16, 1993

---

* In mythology, Cerberus guarded the entrance to Hades. (MHD)
** Olga Ulyanova was born after Lenin's death, thus she has no personal memories of her uncle.

VLADIMIR AND NADYA

LENIN, 1897 [Prior to Exile]

1. St. Petersburg, Imperial Russia, cir. 1895

Andrei Mitrich Kleshtch by trade a locksmith, by circumstance near destitution, sat on a wooden block scraping away at his keys, pushing them into locks and withdrawing them to continue his scraping. In a curtained alcove his wife was coughing away her life—tuberculosis. "You think I won't get away from here? "he cried to his companions-in-misery, who were lounging about in various attitudes of dejection. "I'll crawl out of here even if I have to leave my skin behind!"

"Here" was a damp cellar which served as a night shelter for prostitutes, thieves, drunks, vagabonds, the homeless. The moldy quarters were located on one of the islands of the city of Peter — he who was called The Great. Andrei represents the Russian Everyman at the turn of the century; although he is fictional, his living counterparts were legion.

Russia, land of the Tsars—of Ivan the Terrible and Boris Godunov, of Mikhail Romanov, of Peter the Great and Catherine the Great, of others neither so terrible nor so great. Before Mikhail none of them had managed to control this leviathan of a country. After Mikhail some of them tried, by means of desultory reforms, to harness an enormous and benighted peasantry to the Imperial chariot. It was also necessary to curb the ambition of relatives and great-landowners. Peter used force plus persuasion; with Catherine the order was reversed, but force nevertheless. Other rulers contrived, through assumed passivity, to ride out the gathering storm of popular discontent. A few failed utterly, and the result was a knife or a gun or a bomb.

Mikhail's last heir, Tsar Nicholas II, had the misfortune to rule over an awakened proletariat: city laborers—that phenomenon of the Industrial Revolution—whose awakening minds were stirred to action by the frightful conditions of life and work. By 1890, after nearly a century of terrorist activity on the part of a minority intelligentsia dedicated to social reform, Nicholas was enmeshed in a problem of colossal proportions. If the peasantry had by now succumbed to a state of numb lethargy, the proletariat was aroused and ready for the message of Marxism or any other that would lift them from the depths of degradation. Starvation wages, filthy living conditions, conscription into the sub-human bowels of the Imperial Navy and onto the battlefield massacres of the Imperial Army, the ever-present knout with which they were flogged—these and all the barriers of class which separated mere existence from human well-being—were beginning to reap a harvest of strikes, insubordination, sabotage. The huge army of urban downtrodden was ready for battle. Medieval, autocratic Russia had become ripe for transformation into a modern state.

1

The Tsar knew it, his imperial relatives knew it. It was felt by the elitist Imperial Guard, by officers of army and navy, by rich merchants and landed gentry.

Restiveness characterized the larger industrial centers, and the most turbulent was the Imperial Capital itself, St. Petersburg. Under the nose of the Tsar, meetings were held in factory halls, people marched in the streets, secret Marxist circles went about their business of propaganda, a compassionate intelligentsia donated their brains and money to the cause of social reform.

Maxim Gorky, creator of Andrei Kleshtch, was among the *avantgarde* intelligentsia. He contributed more than half his royalties from *The Lower Depths*, a drama about the underprivileged of St. Petersburg, to the Cause. The play was enormously successful, both in Russia and Germany, and its propaganda value, while ostensibly subliminal, was nevertheless considerable.

Nicholas II continued to observe the manifestations of civil unrest with cold, unblinking eyes, and finding them distasteful, removed himself a few miles away to the seclusion of a village palace, leaving his ministers to deal with the simmering Capital.

In this milieu a young woman, who lived with her widowed mother in a small apartment on the "Old Nevsky," went to work each morning as secretary at the railway company. On the way she met the flotsam and jetsam of a city at the crossroads of Russia and the West. Sad-faced peasant types, whose shapeless garments exaggerated their age, peddled household items in the streets: thread and yarn, leather, shoelaces, pencils. Women, old before their time, scurried about with pails for scrounging milk and kerosene. Among them walked the vagabonds who begged from farm to village to city, and the "holy men" with flowing beard and staff whose bare feet were bound in rags only in cold weather. Beggars, all of them, searching for crumbs of life with which to sustain themselves in a city of wealth and privilege.

For the young woman working at the railway company, her job was a kind of middle-class *lèse majesté*, since she had been born to parents of high social rank. As the daughter of an army officer, she seemed destined for a modicum of education and perhaps early marriage.

However, her fate was determined by her father's involvement in a revolutionary movement, *Land and Freedom*, which flourished during the mid-19th Century. While stationed in Russian Poland, Konstantin Krupskii was arrested, convicted of sedition by a Warsaw court and deprived of the right to work as a government official. In search of employment, he moved his family from place to place, finally settling them in the city of Uglich where he was given a job as inspector in a paper-making factory. His sudden death in 1883 left his family destitute. His wife went to work as a governess and his daughter, at age fourteen, found sporadic employment at "two-penny tasks."

"I wanted to become a village school-mistress," she said, "but could not find a place. Then I wanted to go to the provinces." Finding that her gymnasium (high school) education was deficient for the purposes she envisioned, the girl enrolled in the Bestuzhev Courses for Women, a substitute for higher education during an era when females were denied admission to the University.

"I started there," she continued, "expecting to be told everything I was interested in, but when they began to talk about something quite different, I left. I don't think it is worthwhile learning how to 'make a living.' If one needs money, then find a job at the railway company where hours can be put in and then you are as free as a bird. It is a pity to waste time on special training when there is so much you need to know and should know."

To close friends she was N.K.; to acquaintances and others she was Nadezhda Konstantinovna; at home she was Nadya. Her surname, Krupskaya, indicated her father's Polish origin.

Nadya was a petite young woman with large, slanting gray-green eyes, up-tilted nose and full lips. Her regular features were framed by dark red hair—long and fine, easily ruffled by the wind, which in St. Petersburg was perpetual; an instinctive and nearly automatic gesture was to smooth it back from her forehead. Later in life she became addicted to hats, mostly unbecoming, merely to keep her hair under control.

By nature extremely shy, she admitted to being tongue-tied when faced with certain persons and situations. "I can understand your shyness," she wrote to one close to her. "Sometimes my own comes over me in a wave and I cannot utter a word."

Thus Nadya often gave the impression of being a nonentity to those who didn't know her personally. Close associates, on the other hand, found her a sensitive, warm-hearted person who gave little thought to herself, traits which assured her a host of friends. Unfortunately, those who give freely of themselves find many takers, although the truly selfless do not examine the results of their largesse.

Since her affection for others was controlled, she avoided the pitfall of the spiritually lonely who lean upon outsiders for emotional support. Her friends and colleagues found her a source of strength, little guessing that her calm demeanor was less innate than it appeared. Behind her unruffled exterior lay all the uncertainties that afflict most people: nerves, things deeply felt, the everyday hurts and frustrations which are a part of life. If she failed to react outwardly to happenings that would have elicited screams of protest from the more articulate, it was not from emotional poverty.

Whether by nature or from practice, she was immune to snubs. Meanness she repaid with kindness, coldness with love, which is not to say that she neither recognized nor understood an affront. Was it merely inability to defend herself? Or was she the sort who find pettiness a waste of emotion? Whatever its source, this quality served her well, and if at times she gave vent to irritation, it was generally in private and quickly forgotten. She left to others the luxury of bearing a grudge.

Nevertheless, her self-image may have been a poor one. Glancing in the mirror, did she conclude that fine eyes were poor compensation for a thick neck? Did she consider her low speaking voice uninteresting? Her wit less than scintillating? Her manner, when being introduced, too retiring for effectiveness?

Since physical beauty or innate charm determines personality, one who possesses neither suffers from the daily humiliation of being ignored. A reading of boredom or indifference in another's eyes can easily demolish a feeling of worth. Thus, while the world may be an oyster waiting to be opened by the self-assured, its pearl is forever withheld from the shy. They are driven to find other ways.

While enduring with stoicism her days at the railway company, Nadya was looking forward to the "something more" of which she spoke. But rather than mere diversion as a means of escape from her rather colorless existence, she reached out for self-realization through the kind of education which had thus far eluded her. Evidently she had decided that plodding ahead on the road she had chosen for herself was preferable to falling into a ditch of fruitless discontent.

On Vasilyevsky Island, Marxist study circles were springing up like mushrooms, and Nadya turned to them with the passion of one earnestly seeking enlightenment. Her choice of a particular circle turned out to be fortuitous, since the leader was a man of superior intelligence and deeply grounded in Marxism, a combination which blended naturally with her desire to learn—and to exercise that learning in meaningful ways.

Did the unacquainted ones brush her aside as a school-ma'm type, intellectual and cold? She seemed to conform to this latter-day derogation. But they would have been surprised at the flood of unselfconscious affection she would soon bestow upon those for whom it was fitting, those close to her: an extended family—and one person in particular.

The place where Nadya did her Marxist homework was an unlikely setting for such activity. Called the *Neva Society for the Organization of Popular Entertainment*, the group had its own theaters, concert halls and sports premises, presumably for the better class if not the upper class. The Society's headquarters were located beyond the Neva Tollgate, where most of the factories lay, and its members conceded space and organizational assistance for workers' choirs, reading rooms and kindergartens. One of the reading rooms was used by members of Marxist study circles for meetings and talks with workers. Both meetings and talks were assuredly low key—theoretical rather than activist—

and it was here that Nadya established close ties with individual laboring people.

From her apartment on the Old Nevsky it was a long walk to Vasilyevsky Island. A horse-tram took her as far as the river, passing exclusive shops and theaters and restaurants, places she never visited. To her left was *Kazansky Sobor*—Cathedral of Our Lady of Kazan—where children played in the park before its colonnaded wings, chasing each other, rolling in the grass.

On a bench sits an elderly couple holding hands. The woman is turned toward her mate, speaking earnestly, but he seems scarcely to listen; instead, he stares before him at nothing in particular. Nadya gazes past them at the massive doors, her mind envisioning the scene within: the ikonostasis, the humble, kneeling supplicants crossing themselves. "Neither God nor his vassal the Tsar..." she is thinking. At the river she descends to cross the bridge, pausing midway for a glance at the Winter Palace, extending its elegance along the embankment of Bolshaya Neva.

> The Winter Palace—a world of its own. Like a ship floating on the surface of the ocean, it has no real connection with the inhabitants of the deep. It has forgotten the people.
>
> —Alexander Herzen
> London, November 15, 1859.

Great works of art lie within, but Nadya and her kind know them only by hearsay. Bending her head against the wind, she hurries on, chilled by the spiritual coldness of this granite city and its wintry palace. Only on Vasilyevsky does she feel at home, warmed by the prospect of meeting with congenial spirits in the Society's reading room. She opens the door. "Tovarishchi! Comrades!" Her greeting is echoed with enthusiasm by those awaiting her.

The River Neva, a watery serpent gliding to the Baltic from its source in Lake Ladoga, was parent of myriad canals and small rivers washing the clay mounds that supported the city. The largest of Bolshaya Neva's offspring, Bolshaya Nevska, flowed between two halves of the old city: one called the Viborg Side, the other the Petersburg Side. When urban decay began spreading from industrial Viborg to its neighbor across the Nevska, royalty and its satellite aristocracy and well-to-do fled across Bolshaya Neva to its eastern shore. A third city arose which turned its back upon the squalor it had created. The old tar shops and timber works of St. Petersburg's shipbuilding industry were moved across the river and out of sight, replaced by palaces and town-houses, and the institutions of a country's government, including the military.

Its bridges were to Petersburg what streets are to other cities: Dvortzovi Most (Palace Bridge), Nikolaevsky, Troitsky, Anichkov, Alexandrovsky, Berzhevoi; Pyevtchesky near the house where the poet Pushkin died after his duel with a calumniator; Moika and Fontanka across which Dostoyevsky was taken to Semyonovsky Square where a firing-squad awaited him. Some of the smaller ones were constructed of wood with a lift section in the middle. Each had a story to tell. Over them had walked two centuries of the laboring, the poor, the adventurers, the condemned. Over them, riding in carriages, passed the Tsars, the Grand Dukes, the great landowners and their ladies, the wealthy merchants on a visit from Moscow, the elite of music and literature and science.

Human history, epic and commonplace, breathed from wood, stone and steel, tales as numerous as the bridges themselves—over six hundred of them.

With the selfishness born of wealth, Royalty and its friends set about refashioning Neva's opposite bank in order to spare themselves unpleasant reminders of how the other side lived. From his windows in the Winter Palace, for example, the Tsar could look across the river to a scene of reassuring splendor. To the privileged, Viborg was not even a memory; for them it simply didn't exist.

A broad avenue lined with shops—for the rich; houses—for the rich; restaurants and hotels—for the rich; schools—for offspring of the rich; theaters—for the rich; churches—for the rich, bisected new St. Petersburg east of Bolshaya Neva. Most of its inhabitants never penetrated the purlieus of Viborg. Those few who did, however, returned with an emotional hangover unrelated to vodka.

In search of diversion one evening, Prince Felix Youssoupov (who later murdered Rasputin) and his friends went slumming:

> At a night shelter we hired three sordid pallets and lay down, pretending to sleep, but furtively surveyed our surroundings. What we saw was frightful. All around us the dregs of humanity, both men and women, lay half-naked, drunk and filthy. The popping of corks could be heard as they drained bottles of vodka at a gulp and threw the empty bottles at their neighbors. The unfortunate wretches quarreled, copulated, used the filthiest language and vomited all over each other. The stench of the place was beyond description. Sickened by the revolting spectacle, we fled.*

Dostoyevsky, with the insight of his art and the compassion of his soul, looked upon Viborg and sorrowed. Through his fictional works he became an advocate for those whom life had abandoned.

> A young man, crushed by poverty, descended from his attic room to walk the streets. The terrible heat, the aimlessness, the bustle and the plaster, scaffolding, bricks and dust, and that special Petersburg stench from the pot-houses, all worked painfully on the young man's nerves.**

Count Leo Tolstoy, relinquishing all but his particular and private religious faith, walked among the poor as one with them, wrote with passion and spoke with the fire of a great mind finally awakened to the misery beyond his aristocratic gate:

---

* *Lost Splendor*
** *Crime and Punishment*

You women out there (complains an old laborer), you're like beasts. You grow up and then you die. Men, now, they learn something going about the villages. But ask a woman anything and she don't know. They crawl around like blind pups and stick their noses in manure. Your kind is the stupidest that's made. Your kind is just hopeless.*

(Lenin: "Our backward women, psychically deprived, the intellect dulled, the will enfeebled—products of a backward society.")

Nor was this outpouring, and the conditions from which it arose, limited to Russia. Victor Hugo exploded with social consciousness in *Les Miserables*. D.H. Lawrence's *Lady Chatterley's Lover* is less pornography than an outraged cry against the industrial horrors of the English Midlands. In far-off America, Thomas Hood memorialized the sweat-shops of his native land: "... Sewing at once, with a double thread, a shroud as well as a shirt!"

These were but a few of the vanguard, some of them giants, others merely tall men rising above the company of intellectuals and enlightened upper-class involved with the cause of downtrodden humanity. It seemed that the entire world trembled with sympathy. Sentimental? Perhaps. Sincere? Undoubtedly. But writing books and plays never brought the poor to un-poverty.

If the 19th Century unrolled as an age of social protest, it was also one of intense idealism. The enlightened believed that unbounded faith in the Ideal backed up by words—oral or written—would effect social change. Speeches and paper gushed from them in a torrent of protest against the Establishment. Pushkin's poetic ridicule, the gentle fatalism of Chekov underscored the "red plague" of socialism, Marxist communism, all the "isms" named for masters of oratory and pen.

And exactly there it stopped.

The masses, as a result of all this, were supposed to rise in behalf of their own deliverance. Karl Marx aside, history itself taught that all proletarian revolutions had eventually failed through lack of organization. Despots were overthrown only to be replaced by money-tyrants in starched collars and business suits. Any military dictator knew instinctively that his days were numbered and clung to the coattails of money until the moment of his inevitable demise—political or physical.

Reality trampled theory into the dust when sporadic outbursts of popular wrath were quickly subdued by the authorities, when individual acts of terrorism against the ruling class brought its perpetrators to the gallows. Although trade unionism was flexing its muscles, the goals were purely economic, leaving the populace to deal with widespread social degradation on a one-to-one basis. The very poor, far from aspiring to political power, were content merely to survive—one day at a time.

Although Russia was not alone with her social and economic ills, there was

---

* *The Power of Darkness*

more of her, and far from being merely a late-bloomer on the social vine, hers
was a retrograde society. On paper the Imperial "Government," wrung from a
succession of Tsars terrified by the spectre of revolution, appeared as a horizontal replica of the U.S.A: executive, legislative, judicial. But in practice it was
a pyramid topped by the Autocrat. Russia's so-called representative bodies
were merely consultative. Absolutism controlled the machinery which by no
stretch of imagination could be called democratic, since it represented privilege, and privilege accrued from ownership of land. He who was without land
was without voice, even a consultative one, and that meant roughly 90% of the
population.

Viborg was, among other things, a community of factories: textile, gun-
powder, wagon and carriage repair, carriage manufacture, a boot factory,
Laferme's tobacco, Semyannikov's, the giant Putilov Works, various others
connected with Petersburg's shipbuilding industry.

The entire city, both old and new, was one of low buildings hugging the flat
landscape of a sea-level delta. Only the gilded dome of St. Isaac's Cathedral and
the needle-spires of the Admiralty and Peter-Paul Cathedral broke the skyline.
At least three of the factories—Maxwell's, Thornton's and Laferme's—
belonged to foreign investors. The larger concerns maintained their own "barracks" for workers, places notorious for substandard living conditions.
Underpaid, undernourished, illiterate, ill-housed—labor sweated out its days.
Occasional strikes resulted in lockouts or other punitive measures against the
strikers. Factory laws were harsh, fines for every breach of the rules, however
small, leaving the workers on Saturday night with little to show for a week on
the treadmill of industry. The eight-hour day and a five-day week were either
a mirage, or something reserved for the millennium of socialism about which
the intelligentsia talked while generations of the laboring wore themselves out
at the benches and looms and wheels and blast furnaces. With a huge labor
force at its disposal, management was in control.

When economic disturbances began to exude the odor of politics, there
was Peter-Paul Fortress, a walled bastion at the confluence of Bolshaya Neva,
Malaya Neva and Bolshaya Nevska. The enclave was and is a small community,
including a cathedral which houses the remains of Peter the Great. Today, its
prison cells might pass for a row of one-story garden apartments, but at the
turn of the century their appearance was more sinister. Those who didn't die
inside could, at a directive from across the river, be led at night to Commandant's Wharf, placed in a boat and taken up river to Schüsselburg Fortress and
the hangman's noose. Peter-Paul was a reminder, a warning. Not all, of course,
walked the causeway to its dungeons. There were other places, such as the
remand prisons where disturbers of the tsarist peace awaited a trip to Siberia.

In Viborg's Smolenski District, a narrow brick building that resembled a
factory had been taken over for educational purposes. On Sunday evenings the

unwashed laborers of Viborg crowded into its dingy, barrack-like rooms for instruction in the three R's, taught by a group of women who, as non-professionals, donated their time and talent. That many of them lived in the still-respectable neighborhoods of Vasilyevsky Island on the Petersburg Side indicated that they were lower middle class rather than idle rich dabbling in philanthropy.

Since no one had any money, the problem of study materials was acute.

Slates and chalk were substituted for paper and pencil. Nadya was among those who volunteered to teach, and she often brought armloads of books borrowed from the city library. Use of the building? It was probably donated by a sympathetic landlord. If a sum was offered by a factory owner, it was a case of self-interest, since literate workers were presumed to be more productive. At the height of its activity, Sunday Evening School numbered 600 pupils consisting of mature men and women, younger workers, and older children whose parents attended the classes.

Building where Sun. evening school met

A few of the school mistresses, however, had greater aspirations than merely those of traditional education. They belonged to one or another of the Marxist study circles whose leaders and members, naively trusting in tsarist tolerance, met openly in someone's apartment. When curious neighbors began reporting to the authorities, meetings were held on a rotating basis, first here, then there. Occasionally a police spy managed to infiltrate one of the circles, and its leader then faced imprisonment and eventual exile to Siberia.

Some of the groups elected to "go legal"; that is—to camouflage incendiary ideas with vague theoretical terminology which beguiled the Tsar into believing in postponed socialism; someday, perhaps, but not in his lifetime or that of his heirs. He was providing these trouble-makers with a platform for letting off steam, not unlike London's Hyde Park Corner where scruffy orators held forth. But Authority little reckoned on the ingenuity of the participants. Sly references during discussion, made in the context of future realization, were understood by the initiated as immediate. A befuddled police spy would report that nothing untoward was going on in such-and-such a group.

Many of the circles began with only vague ideas about Marxism, but all available literature was copied by hand and passed around. Circle leaders considered themselves experts in Marxism, and some of them undoubtedly were. Generally speaking, circle regulars were members of the intelligentsia—fairly well educated and of moderate financial means. A few of the leaders had well-to-do sponsors whose interest may not have been totally philanthropic. With a nose for business and an eye on social unrest, they were covering future exigencies.

Active Marxism and concentrated industry with its attendant abuses would soon turn St. Petersburg into a cauldron of incipient revolution.

Nadya's involvement with the Marxist circle, and her discussions with laboring people in the reading room beyond the Neva Tollgate, had led to her volunteering as an instructor in Sunday Evening School, a fulfillment of her desire to teach. How much more rewarding than filling out forms at the railway company, to be the means whereby others learned to write their names, even read a book! Unpaid, her compensation resulted from a carefully scribed name, or a few halting sentences emitted by a middle-aged woman from the textile factory as she carefully followed a sentence, word by word.

Regularly on Sunday evenings, Nadya put on a fresh dress, smoothed her hair, kissed her mother goodbye and started for Smolenski—the district of tar shops. From "Old Nevsky" the journey was pleasant in summer but one of nature's horrors during the winter, with Bolshaya Neva a convulsed mass of ice and Baltic winds blasting the face and frosting the eyebrows. Teachers and pupils stumbled through snowdrifts into the building's half-warmed corridors. Often it was too cold for snow, and ice crystals, hanging suspended in the air, turned the building's windows into yellow smears, barely visible from below.

At that time there was no tram on the Schüsselburg Highway; teachers and pupils either walked from the city or rode the train. One particular episode was typical. Nadya and a colleague emerged from Smolenski to board the train—a decrepit locomotive towing three ancient wooden coaches. Halfway to Petersburg, the train was stopped by piled-up snowdrifts. After shivering for an hour in the unheated coach, the pair crawled out, and taking each other by the hand, made their way to the city on foot. "We laughed and joked all the way," noted Nadya's companion. "It was after midnight when we reached home, working our way through the dark city streets lit only be an occasional dim lantern."

Nadya's shyness was not evident while teaching at Smolenski or participating in small group discussions. Strong-minded, possessed with the keen eyes of a reporter, she observed everything that went on around her, and the Marxist studies opened to her a world view. "I was twenty-one," she said, "before I knew there was such a thing as social sciences." The Marxist discussions also gave her a new perspective on the influence of the Russian Orthodox Church on society, particularly its stultifying effect on the lower classes. In writing about it, she spoke with understated humor:

> A Methodist workman who had spent his whole life seeking God, wrote to me with satisfaction that only on Passion Sunday had he learned from one of my students that there was no God at all. And how easy things had now become, for there was nothing worse than being a slave to God, as you couldn't do anything about it. But to be a slave to a human was much easier, as there a fight was possible.

"In class, we were allowed to talk about anything to our students," Nadya said, "provided we didn't use the terrible words 'Tsar,' 'strike,' etc. But the pupils soon learned which teacher was 'one of them.'" By subtle hints in her discourse, a teacher could impart the message that she belonged to The Movement. Sunday Evening School was a recruiting ground for new members.

Nadya and two of her close friends, Apollinariya Yakubova and Lydia Knippovich, were among the leaders of an embryo workers' movement whose continuing existence depended upon giving the impression of non-existence. By means of a grapevine, links were maintained between Viborg workers, Marxist groups and Smolenski's Sunday Evening School. News passing along the underground might concern an anticipated police raid, the arrest of one who had been politically indiscreet, or circulation of a tract.

> One day someone brought me a notebook containing an article *On Markets*— neatly written and with no crossings-out, produced by a newcomer from the Volga Region. The article was being passed around. At this time we were beginning to learn that the question of markets was closely connected to understanding Marxism. Formerly the subject had seemed dry, mechanical. But the newcomer's article explained everything in a concrete manner. One wanted to know this man better and learn his views at closer range.

A small group, including Nadya, arranged to meet with him in the apartment of one Klasson. In order to mislead the authorities, they called it a pancake supper. "The newcomer was introduced—V.I. Ulyanov—and then we all sat around discussing what we should do. Someone remarked, quite seriously, that the way to proceed was through the Committee for Illiteracy."

V.I. laughed, rather unpleasantly, Nadya thought. "Well," he said, "if anyone wants to save the Fatherland in the Committee for Illiteracy, we won't hinder him."

Nadya looked closely at the man whose sarcastic laugh dropped like a rock on the heretofore lively conversation, bringing it to a temporary halt. He was of medium height and sturdily built, with broad shoulders and strong, well-shaped hands. His hair, receding from a wide forehead, was dark reddish-brown, as were his small beard and moustache. The eyes suggested some remote oriental ancestor. The mouth? What she could see of it conveyed a sense of humor not necessarily ironic. But for the moment his demeanor, apart from serious and lucid remarks, was that of an unhappy man beset by ill health. Despite the growing baldness, he appeared to be in his early twenties.

Was Nadya shy that night, deferring to others? If so, the newcomer was not. His steady gaze as he listened to the opinions of others was self-assured, although Nadya didn't consider him arrogant. And so, at some point during the evening when his eyes met hers over a plate of pancakes, one might say that the future Soviet Union was "born."

There were other meetings in other places, and after one of them V.I. followed her out. As a native Petersburger, Nadya had much to say about local conditions among the laboring class, about the work at Smolenski and in the Movement. He listened without comment, meanwhile observing her dedication and enthusiasm.

He had already learned about her before the meeting in Klasson's apartment; several of her Smolenski pupils belonged to the study group he was conducting in the Neva Society reading room. After another Marxist meeting, he escorted her home, talking about social injustice and revealing to her his own dedication to Marxism. It was Nadya's turn to listen; and she continued to listen as the Petersburg early darkness (they met in winter 1894) turned to gray and then to blue, and finally to the white nights of summer.

Occasionally he came in for a glass of tea after the meeting. Nor was he disconcerted by the simplicity of Nadya's abode. Through a gate one entered a large building, climbed the dark, steep, narrow staircase to a second floor landing, pulled on a metal "pear" to jangle the bell. Inside one discovered a modestly furnished room which served as a bed-chamber (for Nadya's mother), and dining room with high-backed divan, round table, several chairs, dish cupboard and chiffonier—the gloomy interior lit by a single window.

Nadya's room resembled a long, narrow hallway. Along one side stood an iron bed (similar to a cot), a chest of drawers, wall-hooks for clothing, two tall bookcases and two chairs. At one end beside a single window stood a tiny chancellor table covered with dark-raspberry blotting paper; on it neatly stacked books and student exercise pads lay beside a glass ink stand and framed picture of Nadya's father.

The most pleasant room was the kitchen, but unfortunately for the occupants, it could be entered only from outdoors. It was necessary to traverse a courtyard and tap on the door. In this way V.I. came to drink tea and converse with his new-found friend. Nadya and her mother thought he was beginning to look less unhappy, and they welcomed him in the simple ways that made a man feel at home.

To each other, Vladimir Ilyich and Nadezhda Konstantinovna were on the point of becoming Volodya and Nadya, although he was finding N.K. more convenient, since her name kept turning up in his conversation with others. Before long he would be calling her by her pet name, "Nadyusha."

Nadya learned that he had come to St. Petersburg to take what was called the "external" examination at the University in the field of jurisprudence. She assumed that he intended to remain in the Capital and enter law practice, and at first she was right.

On October 5, 1893, he had written his mother: "I have been promised a job in a consulting lawyer's office here, but when it will be arranged (or whether it will be arranged) I do not know." The position did not materialize, perhaps a result of his having been an external graduate. Those who were in political trouble with the authorities were barred from classroom participation.

Little by little he told Nadya about his background: how he had been expelled from Kazan University for taking part in a revolutionary student meeting; that he had spent time in a prison at the foot of University Hill and was subsequently sent into exile under police escort; that he had pleaded for another chance at the law exams and had finally been permitted to matriculate at the University of St. Petersburg. What he didn't mention was the loneliness of his first days in the Capital, which he spent wandering about the streets in search of friends as well as an outlet for his intellectual and Marxist interests. "No, I have not been to the Hermitage Museum," he had written to his sister during that time. "I somehow do not want to go alone. Later, when I come to Moscow, I'll be happy to go to the Tretyakov Gallery with you."

Nor did he say anything to Nadya about his financial straits. She knew that he was living in one room and taking his meals with an acquaintance, but that his mother was supporting him was an embarrassment.

"One evening, while we were walking on the Okhta Bridge, he told me about his elder brother, Alexander," Nadya remembered. "'He was hanged for his part in an attempt on the life of Tsar Alexander III,' V.I. said. 'My mother is very strong-minded; Lord only knows what she might have done if my father had been alive. But my brother was wrong, you know. He belonged to the *Narodnaya Volya*, a terrorist organization. Terrorism by the few is a mistake. You kill one despot and another takes his place. Only the people themselves—the masses—can effect social change. The present régime has to go; it cannot be reformed.'"

V. was suspicious of liberals, those who spoke "with a forked tongue" about social reform, and now Nadya was to learn the reason. "When my brother was arrested," he told her,

> our "liberal" acquaintances shunned us. Even an aged teacher, who had formerly come every evening for chess, left off calling. There was no railway at Simbirsk at

that time, and my mother had to go on horseback to Suzran in order to go to St. Petersburg where my brother was imprisoned. I was sent to find a companion for her, but no one wanted to travel with the mother of an arrested man.

He told her, too, about his sister Olga, who died at age 17 and lay buried in Petersburg's Volkhov Cemetery. "My mother lives in Moscow," he said, "and she wanted me to visit the grave. I wrote her that the cross and wreath are still there and in good order. Olga died quite a while ago of typhoid fever." Nadya learned that he also had a younger brother and two sisters. "My older sister Anna is married to Mark Yelizarov. He works for the railway company and they move around quite a lot. Maria, the younger one, is still in school; she wants to become a teacher of French." V.'s brother Dmitri was training as a doctor. "Mitya is somewhat of a bookworm, but he plays a good game of chess. So does Mark." He likewise mentioned numerous aunts and cousins, relatives on his mother's side. Nadya would soon meet members of his immediate family. Was she slightly envious of his large number of relatives? Nadya could count only her mother, an aunt who taught school, a niece and one cousin.

Generally, however, she found V. reluctant to talk about personal matters. "We were now well acquainted," she recalled,

and it was his habit to stop in at my apartment after the meetings. At that time I was wedded to the school and would go without food rather than miss a chance of talking about the pupils or about Semyannikov's, Thornton's, Maxwell's, and the other factories around the Neva. Vladimir Ilyich was interested in the minutest detail describing conditions and life of the workers. Few intellectuals of that day really understood the workers; they came to workers' groups and read them a lecture. But V. explained Marxism to them, and then listened to their own questions about their work and labor conditions, endeavoring to answer, but mostly he listened and took note of everything they said.

Evenings in Nadya's flat, "talking endlessly," they began to formulate a plan for refashioning the loosely organized activity in Viborg. "We'll call it The St. Petersburg League of Struggle for the Emancipation of the Working-Class," V. said. The first order of business, as he saw it, was to collect data on actual conditions in the factory district. He drew up a plan of reportage which was to be carried out by an emissary to the shops. "Then I and Apollinariya put kerchiefs over our heads and made ourselves look like women factory workers, and went personally to the Thornton factory barracks, visiting both the single and married quarters. Conditions were most appalling. It was on the basis of material gathered in this manner that V. wrote his leaflets."

More specific about appalling conditions was Nadya's account of a particular episode: "Came a one-legged soldier and said 'Mikhail, whom you taught to read and write last year died at work from exhaustion; while dying he remembered you, told me to give you his best regards and wished you a long life!'"

There was a consumptive textile worker who wanted Nadya to teach her enterprising suitor to read and write. And the tobacco worker "who used to drink every Sunday until he lost all human semblance. He was so saturated with the smell of tobacco that one could not bend over his exercise book without one's head beginning to swim. He wrote (using pot-hooks and hangers), leaving out the vowels."

The idea of approaching the Movement's work through printed material seems to have been new to those involved. Henceforth, it was to be the *modus operandi*. "Although some thought the leaflets dry and uninteresting, the workers eagerly read them, since they contained material related to the workers themselves." Money for paper and copying on a hand-operated duplicator was supplied by Marxist group leaders, some of whom were financially well-off.

V.'s superior understanding of Marxism quickly placed him in the forefront of leadership. Slowly he began edging the Movement toward a more militant approach to emancipation which, he thought, must be achieved by the workers themselves: by patiently educating them to understand the nature of the régime under which they toiled, and by leading them toward more widespread goals than token economic concessions wrested from management. Educate them, yes, but with more than the three R's.

"I'm going abroad," he told Nadya. "I want to study western economy." With funds supplied by the St. Petersburg Marxists, he left Russia in the spring of 1895.

While Nadya moved efficiently through her days at the railway company in happy anticipation of Sunday evenings at Smolenski, V. was in Switzerland meeting with Marxist Russian émigrés and Swiss laboring people. Among the former were Georgii Plekhanov—called "The Father of Russian Marxism"— Paul Axelrod and Vera Zasulich, leaders of the Russian Marxist group abroad, *Emancipation of Labor*. All of them would play a fateful and negative role in V.'s future. By the first week in June he was in Paris, finding the lodgings "very cheap." But digestive trouble drove him back to Switzerland where he located a spa and settled down for treatment. "Please send me 100 rubles," he wrote his mother. "It is expensive here and I have already exceeded my budget."

The next letter to his mother was postmarked Berlin where he was "seeing the sights." "Visiting is all very well," he told her, "but there is no place like home." Because of censorship, he was unable to inform her about his meeting with Wilhelm Liebknecht, leader of the German Social-Democratic Party, nor of his time spent in German factories talking with workers. Classroom French had served him well in the French-speaking Canton of Switzerland, but in Berlin "the pronunciation of the Germans is so unlike what I am accustomed to that I do not even understand public speeches, although in France I understood practically everything in such speeches." Liebknecht provided him with an interpreter for his discussions with laborers.

At the end of September he returned to Petersburg with a trunk full of illegal literature hidden in a double lining.

"No sooner had he returned," related Nadya, "than the police were hot on his trail. They followed him and they followed his trunk. A cousin of mine was working at the address bureau, and she told me that a policeman had come and looked over the address list. 'We'll get him,' the policeman boasted, 'he's an important state criminal. His brother was hanged.' Of course I immediately warned Vladimir Ilyich."

Undaunted, V. managed to elude the police while dispatching the girls — Nadya, Apollinariya and Zinaida Nevzorova—with leaflets to be distributed in the factories. "We rolled them up as small tubes and hid them in our aprons. When people came out of the factories at closing time, we ran among them and scattered leaflets into the hands of perplexed workers."

An illegal press was now operating full time under V.'s direction. When it became evident that some better means of manifolding was needed, he located a printing press, found a compositor, and began turning out class-oriented educational material in quantity. Thus began a career in journalism that would place his life—and that of his associates—in jeopardy for years to come. Meanwhile, someone turned traitor. The compositor?

"At night on December 8/9, 1895, Ulyanov was arrested and incarcerated in a remand prison where he was kept in solitary confinement." The details behind this official statement were complex. It had been arranged that should anything go wrong, Nadya was to ask for him at a certain address. When neither V. nor the addressee were to be found, "it was obvious to me that they had been arrested." They had indeed, along with many others of "our group."

Immediately upon learning of her son's arrest, V.'s mother and sisters Anna and Maria came to St. Petersburg where they rented an apartment and settled down for a long stay. Anna, at her brother's direction, contacted Nadya. It may not have been their first meeting, since Anna's husband Mark often came to St. Petersburg in connection with his business on the railway; Anna frequently accompanied him on his travels.

Prisoners were allowed to receive books and writing materials, and on her weekly visits to the prison, Anna came armed with these as well as clothing and items of food to supplement the prison diet. "I now have everything I need," V. wrote her in a note conveyed by the warder. "In fact, I have enough tea to go into business and give the shop here real competition. I got your parcel yesterday, and just before yours someone else brought me food of all kinds." Was it Nadya? She was now working closely with Anna in carrying messages from him to the Viborg people.

By means of barely visible dots inside the printed letters of books, V. was sending a stream of messages to the outside; return communications, written with milk, were hidden in books delivered to him. When hot water was brought for tea, he tore the messages into strips and "developed" them in the tea water, a method he later used himself in preference to the dots.

By the end of his first month in prison, the "catarrh" (digestive trouble) was bothering him again, and he sent a request to Anna: "I should like to get the enema in an oval box that is in the drawer of my wardrobe (or perhaps I should say 'was'). That should not be impossible, even without a letter of attorney. Push 25 kopecks into the landlady's hand and tell her to take a cab and come here and deliver it and ask for a *receipt*. Unfortunately, that highly respected matron is stubborn."

Having supplied himself with mineral water regularly delivered by a chemist, and as his next letter indicated, the oval box, he began devoting himself to a writing project which had long been forming in his mind. "I sleep nine hours a night," he reported, "and dream of the chapters of my book."

Meanwhile, the law was taking its time. How long before sentencing? It was anyone's guess. By midsummer the St. Petersburg heat had become unbearable, and V.'s mother suggested moving to a cooler place outside the city. Anna found lodgings at Beloostrov near the Finnish border, a small town located on the main railway line between Helsingfors (Helsinki) and Petersburg, thus facilitating her periodic trips to the prison. Nadya was invited to join them. Vacation from her job was due, and work in the Movement had slowed to a halt as one after another of the leaders ended up in jail. Apparently unaware that she was next on the list of suspects, Nadya boarded the train at Finlandski Station for Beloostrov.

During the following days, conversation was largely devoted to the prisoner—his present health and future fate. Nevertheless, the family and their guest contrived a holiday atmosphere, with Anna and Nadya going bathing in the Gulf and taking hikes along country paths. Maria, prone to various ailments which left her disinclined to participate in physical activity, remained at home with her mother, the two of them assisted by a day-servant who helped with meals and cleaning.

Now temporarily free of recent tensions, friendship quickly developed through their common interest in the remand prison. Nadya was finding V.'s mother, Maria Alexandrovna, a warm and motherly person, uncritical of others, emotionally balanced, strong in the ways of one who had experienced most of what life had to offer of joy and sorrow. In young Maria, Nadya discovered a congenial spirit, but her feelings about Anna were ambivalent. For the moment, Nadya was withholding an opinion, content to accept her as a friend and trusting that Anna would reciprocate. The latter, six years older than Vladimir, exuded an air of intellectual sophistication which tended to intimidate others less well equipped.

The sisters were quite unlike, both in appearance and temperament. Anna, while not beautiful, was aristocratic in bearing. A photograph shows her wearing a stylish, flowing gown of chiffon and lace, her dark hair tastefully dressed, piled high in the fashion of the day; she might have been a princess—graceful, sure of herself, even appealing. Maria, on the other hand, was short and rather lumpy, with a broad face and high cheekbones and dark oriental eyes like her brother. Her nose was a bit too long, her lips full but lacking the humorous tilt of Vladimir's. However, these physical liabilities were balanced by an expression of benevolence. Why are the less than beautiful and brainy often such nice people? Maria, although far from being dull-witted, was what might be called a "hard sell" in the realm of intellect. French came only with difficulty, other studies caused her nervous tremors, and life in general seemed hostile, creating for her many obstacles to be overcome. Whether a cause or a result, illness laid her low from time to time, and once she was nearly carried off by the same disease that had killed her sister Olga.

Anna was the bright one, and she had attracted a husband of considerable quality. Quiet, shy Maria, with the instinct of one who perceived her own future only too clearly, was planning to be a French teacher.

From time to time, small details of the family's earlier home life drifted in and out of the conversation. Nadya listened with interest, since V. had told her little; he considered autobiography boring and in bad taste. She gathered that the family's life style had been formal. There was a servant, and the Ulyanov children had a "nanny." There were private lessons in music and French and German. Dress was likewise formal. Anna laughingly referred to her brother's recent comment, delivered from prison: "The waistcoat, frock coat and traveling rug can be taken back. They have ended up in the prison storeroom."

The entire family was well-read, and serious reading resulted in occasional literary allusions. Here, Nadya was in deep water. Recognizing that she could easily flounder, if not sink, in an attempt to keep up with them, she remained silent. In addition, they all played chess, and Nadya didn't know a bishop from a pawn. There was, however, one area she could share with them—Marxism— although here, too, she was at a slight disadvantage, having, as she said, discovered the social sciences fairly late in life, at age 21! The others appeared to have imbibed it with their milk and crackers during childhood in Simbirsk, their birthplace. Only when conversation turned to Petersburg's labor problems did Nadya feel confident. What did Anna or Maria (or Mark either, for that matter) know about the life of factory workers in Viborg? Nothing, beyond hearsay. They listened, however, and their attention would later bear fruit, not all of it palatable.

By the time Nadya left for home, she was calling Anna by her pet name: Anya or Anyuta. Maria was Manyasha or Manya.

2. Prison and Exile to Siberia

On August 12, 1896, shortly after returning from Beloostrov, Nadya was arrested and consigned to prison. Henceforth, she was dependent upon Anna for communication with V. More significant, however, than present contact with him was a mutual understanding reached during his imprisonment while Nadya was still free.

At the moment of his arrest the preceding December, whatever had been unresolved between them came into focus. His eventual fate was in question. Long imprisonment? Exile? Both? And what about Nadya? How long would her activities go undetected? Not long, as it turned out, but meanwhile she continued to distribute leaflets while awaiting a coded message from cell No. 193.

Communication continued, and later there was a request. V. had become affected by what Nadya called "prison melancholy" and he was asking that she and Apollinariya stand in a certain spot near the prison which he could see from a window when he was taken out for exercise. "For some reason, Apollinariya was unable to go," Nadya recalled. "I went for several days and stood a long time at that place, but something went wrong with the plan."

Another message may have contained something more personal than this or directives to the Viborg people.

How much did Volodya's family know about his relationship with Nadya? His mother, at least, understood that her son and this young woman had arrived at some kind of understanding, albeit complicated by his sudden imprisonment. He may have told his mother about Nadya during a Monday visiting hour (Anna's day was Thursday). Maria Alexandrovna's invitation for Nadya to visit her at Beloostrov was more than casual.

In addition to Nadya and Apollinariya, there were several "girls" involved with the League of Struggle; among them Lydia, Tonechka, Zinaida, Dominika. Lydia was already forty years old and in possession of her own family estate in Finland; she was imprisoned before the summer of 1896. Tonechka had an "understanding" with Basil Starkov, and Zinaida with Gleb Krzhizhanovsky. Dominika was already married. There remained Apollinariya and Nadya. One surmises that the former was interested in Volodya. It was a time of pairing off, and in the existing ratio of two to one, Apollinariya lost to Nadya. This interesting situation provided a sequel. More of Apollinariya later.

When V.'s case was finally resolved, Nadya was still in the limbo of preliminary detention.

On February 26, 1897, the grill on cell door No.193 slid open and a voice

Georgi Plekhanov

Vera Zasulich

Крупская   163 Надежда

Nadya, prison photos, 1896

announced: "Get your things together, you're being released. Three years in Siberia for you."

According to Nadya's mother, he had grown fat in prison and was a "terrible weight." But Nadya would have been shocked by other changes in him. His hair, which had receded even further, was long and unkempt as were his beard and moustache. On the day of his release, hunched in a winter coat with collar up to his ears, he resembled a derelict revolutionary—or nondescript hippie lacking only a guitar. Fortunately, his sense of humor had not suffered. "They should have kept me in longer," he remarked. "I could have finished my book." He avoided mentioning his chronic insomnia of recent months.

In the few days at his disposal before departing St. Petersburg, he met with Viborg people, afterward gathering up his clothing and books for the long journey east. Meanwhile, his mother and sister Maria returned to Moscow; Anna remained in the Capital to help her brother wind up his affairs and see him off to exile. The day he left Petersburg (early March 1897), several comrades were on the station platform, standing a little apart with studied indifference. As the train moved away, V. met their eyes through the coach window with a meaningful expression as if to say: "Carry on. We've only begun."

At the time of Volodya's release to exile, Nadya could expect several more months of prison before her case was adjudged. However, a horrifying event took place in Peter-Paul Fortress which altered her situation. An attractive young political prisoner, Maria Vetrova, after being raped by a male inter-

Prison photo when Lenin was released into exile

rogator, doused herself with kerosene from the lamp illuminating her cell and burned herself to death. "Several of the women prisoners were immediately released," Nadya stated, "but two policemen were assigned to each, who followed our every step."

Recent experiences, compounded of fright and uncertainty, had taken their toll. Nadya, like Volodya, came out of prison with impaired health. Now plagued with thyroid trouble and heart palpitations, her formerly attractive eyes were beginning to protrude, and the enforced inactivity of prison life had added weight to her diminutive figure. V.'s stylish sister Anna, surveying her brother's friend, cattily reported to him that she "looked like a herring" and was "sly." Nadya—sly? It was probably self-defense. She may have gathered that Anna didn't approve of her relationship with Volodya. This elder sister maintained a proprietary attitude toward him which would have included a choice of fiancée. Anna's tentative friendship for Nadya appears to have turned sour when she suspected that her brother was serious about Nadya.

Although dismissing her imprisonment offhandedly—at the time of Volodya's release, she merely remarked "I was still inside"—Nadya had reacted in ways that she concealed from others. It was her habit to spare her mother, her women friends, the pupils and Viborg laborers who looked to her for guidance and strength. Her innate psychic energy provided the necessary drive for activities whose strenuous demands would have discouraged many. Nor was she unique in such qualities—several women, who have survived only as names in Nadya's *Memoir* and letters, displayed unusual fortitude under trying circumstances.

Now released on good behavior, as it were, Nadya was making regular visits to the police commissioner in search of information concerning her eventual fate. When at length sentence was passed, she was exiled to the small city of Ufa on the main rail line between Moscow and Siberia. It lay in European Russia in the Ural Mountain region bordering West Siberia. Immediately, she requested a transfer to Shushenskoye in southern Siberia where V. was living.

At the same time, Zinaida asked to be sent to the village of Tesinskoye where her fiancé Gleb had been exiled. Gleb's sister Tonechka (a non-exile), asked permission to join Basil, her exile-betrothed in Tesinskoye. (Gleb's mother, Elvira Ernestovna, was to be a fifth in that communal household; a non-exile, she wished to be with her son.) Poor Dominika, sentenced to three months in a Petersburg jail, pleaded to serve her brief prison term in Siberia in order to be near her ailing husband, Anatoly Vaneyev. Only Apollinariya, tossed here and there by an arbitrary authority, requested nothing; there was no fiancé, nor indeed anyone else, for her to join.

Legally, the women were on their own, but in Nadya's case her plea was being reinforced from Shushenskoye.

From Siberia, soon after arriving at his destination the second week of May, Volodya ended a letter to his sister Anna: "I have given up all hope of hearing from St. Petersburg. When you write to the Bulochkins, send them my regards. They should send me their photographs in exchange for mine. How are their affairs going?"

"Bulochkin," meaning "bread roll," was the Party (secret) name of Zinaida Nevzorova (she was chubby). But he wrote "Bulochkins" in the plural. Zinaida, imprisoned along with Nadya, had two sisters. Was he planning to send his photo to each of the three Nevzorovas, or to one of them, or one to all three? And was he expecting a single or collective photo in return? He was hardly the type to be distributing photographs of himself from the distance of Siberia. The message was, of course, for Nadya. Its meaning would have been understood by Anna. By "'affairs," he meant Nadya's legal case.

On December 10th of his first Siberian winter, a letter to his mother included the following: "Someone has written that Zinaida, sentenced to three years' exile, has asked to be sent to this district. I believe Nadezhda Konstantinovna intends to do the same, although her sentence is not yet properly known." For the first time in corresponding with his mother, he closed with "I kiss you warmly," an indication of personal and private happiness. In a letter to Anna that same day: "I am writing to N.K."

December 21st to Anna in St. Petersburg: "I have written to Nadezhda Konstantinovna but have received no reply. The photos have not arrived."

December 27th to his mother in Moscow: "It is quite possible that Nadezhda Konstantinovna will come to me; the matter will probably be settled soon, and may even have been settled by the time you are reading this letter."

January 4, 1898 to his mother: "I think I have already written that Nadezhda Konstantinovna intended asking to be sent here."

On January 8, 1898, Lenin sent a telegram to the Director of Police asking permission for his fiancée, Nadezhda Krupskaya, to spend her period of exile in the village of Shushenskoye. Krupskaya sent a request to the Minister of the Interior to be allowed to spend her term of exile with her betrothed, and to have her sentence reduced from three to two years. She was given permission to spend her period of exile in Shushenskoye instead of Ufa where she had formerly been ordered to go, but the sentence was not reduced.[1]

January 24th, Volodya to his mother: "No, don't wish me comrades among the intelligentsia here—I'd rather not! When N.K. arrives, there will be a whole colony anyway."

February 7th to Moscow: "Yesterday, Mother dearest, I received letters from you and from all the family and was glad to get them; I send you my thanks for all the good wishes. I guessed, of course, that you would write to Nadezhda Konstantinovna and invite her to visit you; it is to be hoped that she will be allowed to. I still know nothing about her transfer to Shu-Shu; she keeps writing that it will be settled 'in a day or two'; but it is still dragging on. Now, however, we shall probably not have to wait long for a final decision . . . If we have any children's books let N.K. bring them for Prominsky's children."

On February 15th Nadya wrote to Maria Alexandrovna: "I still do not know when sentence will be pronounced. They said . . . that the Department can, on its own authority, permit me to spend the time I am under surveillance in Shushenskoye . . . I think I shall be allowed to go to Shusha—what do they care?" She mentioned leaving St. Petersburg during the third or fourth week of Lent. "We shall stay in Moscow two or three days, and I shall write and let you know the day of our arrival as soon as I know it."

This letter is of particular interest. In it Nadya spoke repeatedly of "Volodya," a term of familiarity hardly acceptable to a woman who was addressed as Her Excellency—unless the latter had earlier accepted Nadya as family. In extending an invitation for Nadya to visit her, Maria Alexandrovna was observing the traditional amenities of courtship . But most interesting is Nadya's subscription to that letter: "Many kisses—your loving Nadya." Taken together with the substance of V.'s letters home from December 10th, the above hardly suggests "free love" or a business arrangement. The good wishes of V.'s family referred not to a relationship, but to a marriage.

On February 24th V. wrote his mother: "N.K.'s case is still dragging on. She will probably have to drop the claim for a shortened term, but they do promise to permit her to come here. I am enclosing a letter to her because she may be now in Moscow. If not, send it on."

March 1st to his mother: "I am enclosing a letter for N.K. in case she has not yet left."

March 8th to his mother: "I am enclosing a letter to Nadezhda Konstantinovna. Please send me as much money as possible with her. There may be fairly heavy expenses, especially if we have to set up house for ourselves, so I am going to make my debt a good round sum. By autumn I shall probably receive enough for my translation* to cover my debts—*I believe more than five hundred.*"**

In considering an exchange of his present abode—which consisted of a single room and full board—for a house, he was anticipating the arrival of Nadya's mother, Yelizaveta Vasilyevna, an arrangement that paralleled that of Gleb in Tesinskoye whose mother and fiancée Zinaida were to share exile with him. Likewise, Volodya expected that his own mother would, at some future time, visit him.

March 14th to his mother: "I am not thinking of being transferred from here [from Shushenskoye to another place of exile.] I shall wait until Nadezhda

---

* *The History Of Trade Unionism* - Beatrice and Sidney Webb
** This last phrase in English

Konstantinovna arrives and see how things turn out. I am not writing to her today because I hope that she will have left Moscow by the time this letter arrives. If, despite my hopes, she is still there, please tell her that I received the German translation of Webb . . . there is no need to worry about my health— I am now quite well."

The foregoing chronology of a courtship, one that through circumstance was outwardly unconventional but in substance traditional, is significant for a number of reasons. Most notably, it refutes the premises of successive western historians who, as the result of a single enigmatic statement by Nadya, written in her old age concerning exile in Siberia—" . . . for this purpose I described myself as his fiancée"—have maintained first, that an aggressive woman imposed her presence upon a reluctant male; second, that affection and love played no part in a union which, these historians say, was predicated solely upon the business of revolution; third, that these two, scorning the institution of marriage, had espoused the cult of free love; and finally, that Nadya fulfilled the role of mother rather than wife. These diverse allegations often occur in the same opus.

Volodya's letters to his wife-to-be would, of course, make interesting reading, but the fact that they have not survived is merely unfortunate rather than crucial for the historical record. (Nadya was a prisoner of the State and subject to police harassment. She destroyed all correspondence from Volodya to avoid having it end up in police files. In later years, as a result of habit, she also destroyed any correspondence that passed between them.) This deficiency is balanced by the fact Nadya, however she "described" herself, was following the practice of those couples *forcibly separated before they had time to conclude a formal understanding, an engagement.* (The League of Struggle, which had brought them together, was of fairly recent date.) Did Zinaida and Tonechka, certain of their men's commitment, similarly describe themselves? Did Dominika describe herself as Anatoly's wife? It would be helpful to study the fastidious wording of the officials.

For instance, did the form read: Describe your relationship to this man. Check one of the following:

a) Relative? Give specific connection.

b) Fiancée? When, where, how long?

c) Wife? When married, where, for how long?

The State would not subsidize relatives nor give additional funds to a man for support of a wife to whom he had not been affianced prior to exile. In any case, the sum allotted for legal relationships was negligible, too small to serve as an incentive to wed. A man who married his fiancée during exile expected to support her.

Was Nadya, in "describing" herself as V's fiancée, merely adopting the terminology of the form she was required to submit? Or was she, in order to formalize a betrothal by her presence in Shushenskoye, of necessity required to claim beforehand that which distance and circumstance had prevented her— as well as Volodya—from verifying in normal ways? For V. to prove, from the distance of Siberia, a betrothal which was *de facto*, if not *de jure*, would have been impossible. He could only ask permission — politely.

This writer, lacking access to the Russian of Nadya's remark, is dependent upon an English translation. Could the Russian word have been 'indicated' (ukazala) or 'said' (skazala)? Even 'said' can be deliberately misconstrued: i.e., "I said that I was his fiancée (but really I wasn't)." Obviously, Nadya had to say something. Did she use the reflexive pronoun? Interesting questions. A change of verb modifies her statement as understood by English-speaking readers.

There is also the matter of semantic inference which arises from usage in a particular locality.

A final question: was her manuscript edited by the Soviet publisher?

Had Vladimir Ilyich Ulyanov not become Lenin, a world figure, Nadya's *Memoir* of her husband with its word "described" would have been insignificant. Except for a quirk of history, these two persons would have passed from the scene as an ordinary married couple who trudged to obscurity as political émigrés in Europe—by way of Siberia.

Nadya's husband, for as long as he lived, never called her "Krupskaya." In private she was Nadya or Nadyusha; in referring to her publicly, she was Nadezhda Konstantinovna; his letters and telegrams were addressed to Nadezhda Ulyanova-Lenina. Nadya signed herself N.U. or Nadezhda Ulyanova.[2] It could have been a typical, old-fashioned, bourgeois marriage. Only during the Stalin years of her old age did Nadya become "Krupskaya"; and so she has remained in Soviet historiography and western commentary. This became another seed planted in the field of rumor and speculation concerning the formal nature of their relationship: free love, or merely a business partnership. Some western historians have even gone so far as to declare that Lenin was impotent and therefore immune to sex—or vice versa.

These matters are not insignificant, since they relate to the character of a man—and equally to that of his wife—who have made a lasting imprint on human history. Superseding ideological differences between East and West is the matter of historical accuracy.

As this chronicle of courtship, marriage and two lives unfolds, let the reader draw his or her own conclusions. The nature, and indeed the quality of their relationship as man and wife would have a profound effect upon the world.

For Nadya, to the worrisome delay of her case was added the problem of her mother. Unable to find a relative willing or able to care for her for three years, the alternative was to take her along. Yelizaveta Vasilevna was an occasionally cranky woman who appeared too old and frail for Siberia, but appearances were misleading.

The climate of St. Petersburg and environs afflicted the natives with many ills accruing from dampness—influenza, sinus trouble, aches and pains and colds followed each other with predictable regularity. It was not necessarily weakness of character that prompted Tsar Nicholas II to write endlessly to his wife and mother about the weather. Amid world-shattering events—war, famine, political crises—the personal correspondence of public figures abounded with petty details about their own sniffles as a result of the climate.

Throughout her preparations for a journey that would take them five thousand miles from home, Nadya was driven to distraction by her bedridden mother, who was suffering from an attack of pleurisy. Advice was the extent of the invalid's contribution: what clothing to take, which books should be packed, exactly how many dishes and pots and pans would fit into the crate someone had brought from a warehouse. And what about money? The pair combined their meager resources—Y.V.'s small pension and Nadya's savings—unaware that part of the money Volodya had begged from his mother was intended for traveling expenses. By paying their own way, exiles were spared a police escort and transit prisons, being required only to report to the *volost* (district) commissioner upon arrival in Siberia.

Near the moment of departure, Yelizaveta arose from her bed, dressed herself and went to the kitchen to pack a lunch for the day-long journey to Moscow.

Foremost in her daughter's mind was last-minute instruction to the Viborg people—all three of them, since Nadya's departure would decrease by one the remaining four leaders.

It was time to leave. While youth looks ahead, the elderly look back. As the train lumbered out of Nikolaievski Station, Yelizaveta Krupskaya watched silently while the city where she had resided for most of her adult life began sliding away. She must have wondered if she would ever see it again. Nadya's thoughts were in Shushenskoye. On just such an icy day a year before, Volodya had left for Siberia on the same train.

The swaying coaches rolled leisurely over snow-covered flatlands to the wooded areas of the interior, through birch groves sheltering tombstones of the long-departed, past sleepy hamlets and isolated *dachas*, at length coming to a halt in the heart of a city quite unlike St. Petersburg.

Volodya's mother and sister Maria are waiting on the station platform. Maria Alexandrovna comes forward, extending her arms to embrace the travelers. "Dobrui vyecher," she says warmly. "Kak vui pozhivaete?" with the characteristic Russian falling inflection. "How are you, my dears?" Nadya is thinking how frail she looks, this mother who has lived many sorrows. The older woman observes Nadya with the keen eyes of experience. Her eyes are dark, even a little sad, or perhaps they express resignation. But she smiles winningly, her small face with its old-lady chin breaking into wrinkles when she speaks—briskly, matter-of-factly. Maria shyly waits her turn to greet them. Nadya turns to her. "Dear Manyasha," she exclaims, hugging her. They enter a waiting cab.

While driving through the city to the small apartment she shares with her daughter, Maria Alexandrovna points to some of the landmarks. In Nadya's eyes the city looks old and decrepit compared to the Capital. Here in Moscow, ornately decorated wooden dwellings rub elbows with immense stone or brick edifices, dark and uncompromising. Streets are narrow, and the Moskva seems more like a canal than a river, lying smooth and unruffled beneath the skating figures of children and their elders. Over there is the Kremlin with its impregnable walls and crenellated towers, its cluster of gilded domes rising from within the fortress.

"Have you ever been inside?" Nadya queries. Maria Alexandrovna shakes her head. "No," she replies, "people don't go there. It belongs to the Tsar. He has a palace, but you can't see it from outside. There are a lot of government buildings, too, and I've heard there's a park. The entrance gate is always closely guarded, so people never get any closer than the Red Square."

Like many first-time visitors to Moscow, Nadya's curiosity is aroused at the sight of the Kremlin. She wishes to know more about it, to feel the weight of centuries resting on that mound of history and legend. But Yelizaveta is impatient with all this. "I'm cold," she wheezes, breaking into a spasm of coughing.

By the time they reach the apartment, it is already dusk, and the city's gloomy aspect is now less evident under the glow of lights. Nadya is surprised at the suddenness of nightfall. "No winter fading," she thinks, "here it is either daylight or darkness."

At home, Volodya's mother sheds her fur coat to reveal a black, full-skirted dress with fitted bodice and high neck piped in white. Maria places a small widow's cap on her mother's white hair, and Nadya notices the girl's slender, elegant fingers.

From this moment and for the following three days, the women converse animatedly, not "woman talk" but politics and world affairs. Above all, Maria Alexandrovna wants exact details about her son: his work in St. Petersburg, his health, how he looked when Yelizaveta last saw him.

One envisions the scene at parting: a station platform, blowing snow. The elderly woman embraces Nadya, kisses her. "Promise me something," M.A. says to the small young woman who will share life with her son. "Promise that you'll take care of him." As the train begins to move, Nadya presses her face to the window, smiling reassuringly. "Perhaps someone should look after her as well," M.A. says to herself, observing the pallor of her departing guest.

Only the well-to-do traveled first class. Those of modest means took for granted the inconveniences of second class where one remained fully clothed for the entire journey, settling for a cold water wash and unspeakable toilet facilities. Knowledgeable travelers carried a small blanket and pillow, hoping for an unshared compartment where one could stretch out on the seat at night. Because of the distance between stations and the cost of depot meals, many carried their own food in a hamper—bread, cheese, smoked meat. The sole luxury was hot tea which might or might not be served on board; otherwise, one obtained it at a station stop. At journey's end Nadya would write appreciatively to her Moscow hostess: "Thank you for the food. It lasted us for three days and it was much nicer than railway station meals."

Nadya and her mother were seeing eastern Russia for the first time, and their preoccupation with new landscapes offset the limitations of second class. Wheels clicked away the miles: Nizhny-Novgorod, Kazan, Perm, Yekaterinburg. As they approached the boundary of Siberia, mountains loomed ahead, the Urals and below them the forests dark and mysterious against the snow. Across the mountains at Chelyabinsk, they boarded the West-Siberian Railway, an express that would take them to Krasnoyarsk on the Yenisei River. Like a black dragon breathing fire and steam, the train crawled over the white, frozen waste. Treeless, shrubless, flat as far as the eye could see, the steppe was an endless and icy desert. From time to time Nadya scratched a small circle on the frosted window to look out, but what she saw has hardly reassuring.

Upon approaching the newly completed bridge over the Ob River, the train slowed, and passengers knew that they were now more than halfway across the steppe.

Because letters from N.K. would have been traveling on the same train with her, Volodya was living in a news blackout. The Siberian winter lasted until the end of April; it froze the Yenisei and its steamer traffic. Thus telegrams dispatched along the way would have halted at Krasnoyarsk awaiting transportation by sledge and horse to his village, nearly 400 miles south.

Upon arriving at Krasnoyarsk, the women found the Yenisei still frozen, so were forced to remain a week while awaiting the resumption of steamer service, a week of hot food, baths and horizontal sleep. There was time also to browse in the shops and discover the post office whose clerk had become the harassed agent for book deliveries to the exile in Shushenskoye. When at length the ice broke up, Nadya and her mother went by steamer only as far as Sorokino below the town of Minusinsk. Because of low water, the remaining 55 "versts" were overland. Did they travel to Shusha by horse cart, or was it by sledge? Neither V. nor N.K. explained how she and her mother managed those last miles, weighed down as they were with trunks, boxes and crates. Among Nadya's hand luggage was a basket containing jeweler's instruments.

Their arrival May 7, 1898 was hardly a gala. Volodya was out hunting small game, and the peasant landlord, together with curious neighbors, formed the welcoming committee. But his surprise and pleasure upon returning home was compensation for the recent letdown. Characteristically, Yelizaveta's first remark to him was: "My, how fat you've grown!"

Thus ended a *mezhdugorodnaya*—long distance—courtship whose tentative beginning had been rudely interrupted by the secret police of Tsar Nicholas II. Thus began a muted love affair between Volodya and Nadya— *bessmyertnui*—without end.

Volodya's arrival at Krasnoyarsk the year before had been like old home week or a class reunion. This small city, which would later become the terminus of the West Siberian* Express, served as a gathering place for the distribution of exiles to various towns and villages along the northerly flowing Yenisei River. Because the League of Struggle had grown to considerable size, V. found a number of comrades in Krasnoyarsk who were awaiting assignment to this or that community.

At Ob Station, where he was obliged to cross the Ob River by sleigh because of the then unfinished bridge, he had written his family a description of the steppe.

"It is astonishingly monotonous—bare, bleak, no sign of life, very rarely a village or patch of forest. Snow, sky, and nothing else for the whole time. But even now at 20° below, the air is wonderful, what the Siberians call soft which, they say, makes it easier to bear the frost. I am not tired, quite surprising when I remember being exhausted after a three-day trip from Samara to St. Petersburg."

Subsequently, in a letter written from Krasnoyarsk, he included an interesting comment: "have heard that no more columns are to come here on foot but that exiles will come by rail." Presumably he was referring to those traveling at State expense. But on foot?—all the way from Krivoshchovo on the west bank of the Ob? So the State had been hoarding its resources, and legends about exiles being chained together and led on foot across the frozen waste were true!

Gleb Krzhizhanovsky and Basil Starkov had shared an apartment in Petersburg, and like many others prior to imprisonment, were engaged to young women with whom they worked in the League of Struggle. Zinaida Nevzorova, the other "bulochkin," was affianced to Gleb, and his sister Tonechka to Basil. The League was more like family than a mere political alliance, and this relationship extended to Siberia. For example, Gleb and Basil planned marriage and a communal household; Gleb's mother E.E. and his sister were non-exiles who had come to Krasnoyarsk to await the arrival of their men.

---

* West Siberia was a territorial designation similar to that of "state." At the time of V.'s passage, the Express ended at the River Ob. From its east bank a local continued across the steppe to Krasnoyarsk on the border of East Siberia.

Finding the two women was easy: those who arrived earlier often came to the station platform looking for a familiar face to emerge from the train, and information was quickly transmitted. Since the depot was a considerable distance from town, it entailed a long walk and an even longer wait for the train, which never arrived on schedule—if indeed there was a schedule. V. reported home: "The way the trains run here is beyond all bounds; the farther you go, the slower they crawl."

He found Tonechka and her mother in a state of nerves. As a result of bungled transport arrangements, Gleb and Basil and the group with whom they were traveling had been held up in Moscow. Since they were traveling at State expense, delay at some point along the way meant transit prison, not a hotel room.

While V. was trying to console the women—E.E. he reported as being ill all the time—a telegram arrived saying that the group was about to leave Moscow and would arrive approximately a week and a half later. The party included Dominika's husband Vaneyev, and V.'s close friend and associate in the League, Yuly Martov. Dominika had hurried to Siberia in order to begin serving her three months in prison, and she was now suffering from ill health in what V. described as a cold, damp cell in the town of Yeniseisk.

The exiled men already gathered in Krasnoyarsk had developed a holiday spirit, but V. rarely joined them. The book he started writing in remand prison, *The Development of Capitalism in Russia,* was monopolizing his attention. Source books, periodicals, newspapers, statistical reports needed for his research were in western libraries, and he began combing the town and environs in search of public and private collections; an effort that was marginally successful. Three years lay ahead for him in a backwater whose exact location the authorities had not yet divulged; three years of idleness unless he could obtain source material for reading and writing.

Despite walking around (which he said he enjoyed) and the company of several new-found friends, he was lonely. "Please write," he begged his family. "I am miserable without letters from home." It was at this time that his plaintive query to Anna about the "Bulochkins" was sent: "Why do you not write about them in greater detail?"

The exiles, in absence of facts, fed on rumors: some of a personal nature, others about the territory. They were particularly anxious for news about the various places to which they might be assigned. From the natives it was ascertained that the Minusinsk District was, above all others, the most desirable, both for its climate ("They call it 'Siberian Italy,'" V. informed his mother) and for its low living costs. Based upon these rumors, the exiled ones were besieging the authorities with requests for assignment to the town of Minusinsk itself, or to Tesinskoye, Shushenskoye or smaller hamlets in the vicinity. Rumor had it that Irkutsk and Verkholensk farther east were not bad, but heaven help those who were sent to Turukhansk up north.

V. was resigned, if not overjoyed, by information that someone had heard that he was being sent to Irkutsk. When he learned that his request for Shushenskoye had been approved, he succumbed to a lyrical mood and started to write a poem. "In Shusha at Sayan's* foot . . ." it began. "Unfortunately," he noted, "I got no further than the first line."

Suddenly there was good news: a train bearing the long-awaited group from Petersburg would soon arrive at Krasnoyarsk. V. rushed to inform E.E. and Tonechka and they held a celebration. But on the station platform V. embraced a pair of comrades suffering from recent experiences. Gleb and Basil looked very ill—"pale, yellow and terribly tired." Together with the rest of the group they were promptly clapped in jail. E.E. had a relapse. She spent the next days beseeching the authorities to release her son and her daughter's fiancé. Dominika's Vaneyev arrived in a terrible state that was not alleviated by learning that he would probably be sent north to Turukhansk along with Martov; Vaneyev was suffering from pleurisy.

"I hear that Fedoseyev has been sent to Kirensk in the Irkutsk District," V. reported. "NYF" as he was called in the coded list of names V. sent to his family, ended up in Verkholensk farther east. "I have written him repeatedly, but have received no reply." The reason for his silence would later become apparent. Fedoseyev, although not closely connected with the League, was a close friend. He was to be the central figure in a dramatic episode that shook the exile community.

By April 17th, ice had broken on the Yenisei, thus opening the river to traffic, but it was not until the 24th that V.'s permission for Shushenskoye was confirmed. To his great joy, Gleb and Basil, who had been in a Krasnoyarsk prison since their arrival April 3rd, were released to the village of Tesinskoye on a tributary of the Yenisei near the town of Minusinsk. The party of five, including V., Tonechka and her mother, boarded the steamer for what turned out to be a rugged journey.

On the morning of April 30th, *Svyatoi Nikolai* (St. Nicholas) headed into the current to fight its way south. St. Nicholas was patron saint of Russia. People invoked him for protection against the perils of travel, and he was said to be the special friend of scholars. But if Volodya gave Nicholas a thought, it was probably in connection with present discomforts. By May 6th, after bidding his friends farewell at Minusinsk, he continued alone by horsecart to Shushenskoye which, by this time, loomed like a mirage from the haze of speculation.

Upon finding a room with full board in a peasant household, he unpacked and settled down to study his financial condition. The Tsar's eight rubles a month would probably not arrive on schedule, and before leaving Krasnoyarsk he had wired home for money, counting on at least two weeks for a letter to arrive from Moscow; his journey had been expensive.

---

* A nearby mountain range.

To judge from his mother's peregrinations around Russia (and later in Europe), Maria Alexandrovna appears to have been fairly well-off as a result of her husband's pension and her own inheritance. Her son, however, had strong opinions about indebtedness, and his present preoccupation with acquiring books and periodicals for research and writing was motivated in part by the need to repay loans from the proceeds of publishing. This explains the substance of so many of his letters in which requests for literature predominated. That the content of his writing was intended for another purpose made the task of writing a double challenge. The actualization of his exceptional literary talent would henceforth dominate his life, as would the often successful, sometimes unproductive, pursuit of a publisher for his books and articles.

A considerable time after Volodya first learned of his place of exile, his mother received a letter: "I have left all my old nervousness behind and shall soon be in Shusha where I expect to find peace."

Peace began with a walk around the neighborhood, and he considered Shushenskoye "not a bad place to be." The village was situated on a small river connected with the Yenisei system of waterways, and from it the snow-capped Sayan Mountains were visible. Brief descriptions, however, failed to satisfy his sister Maria who wanted more.

"I thought I wrote about it," he told her.

Hm! Hm! Well, it is quite large—1500 peasant inhabitants—with several streets, rather muddy, dusty. It is surrounded by dung which the people here do not cart to the fields but dump outside the village so that if you leave the village you have to pass through quite a lot of it. This is steppe-country, no orchards or greenery of any kind. At some distance there is what the peasants quite seriously call a "pine grove" but there are scarcely any trees, since most of them have been felled.

He mentioned a stream, likewise at some distance, where he regularly went bathing. "It can be very warm here during the day and that same night you need a heavy coat."

At first, he was the only exile in Shushenskoye; later two others arrived, men unconnected with the League of Struggle who had been banished for political activities: inciting to riot, participating in strikes, membership in subversive organizations.

Prominsky was a bootmaker from Russian Poland* who had become a Social Democrat and confirmed revolutionary. Exiled for his political activism, he brought his wife and five children to Shusha where he planned to re-establish his business. A quiet man, "solid," competent at his trade, Prominsky typified the worker/peasant disgusted with tsarism. Although limited intellectually, he had definite opinions about fighting at the barricades. His only liability was a wife who was skeptical of his ideas and often derided him.

---

* At that time, part of Poland—called "Congress Poland"—belonged to the Russian Empire.

Oskar Engberg was quite a different type. A Finnish national born in the city of Viborg, he had been brought as a youth to St. Petersburg when his father went to work at the Putilov Factory. After graduating from a Swedish elementary school in Viborg, Oskar became an oiler in the steel-rolling section of Putilov where he lost a finger in an industrial accident. There was no workers' compensation, and upon returning to the factory he was given the job of apprentice lathe-turner. The callous treatment by his employer converted him into a confirmed revolutionary. At first he engaged in distributing Marxist literature; later, after being accused of instigating strikes, he was arrested and sent to Shushenskoye.

Partly as a hobby and otherwise to supplement his government allowance, Engberg fashioned jewelry with the instruments that Nadya (at Volodya's request) had brought from Russia; a pastime that brought pleasure not only to the artisan but to many young village girls who proudly wore his distinctive ornaments.

V.'s investigation of what he jokingly called "the joys of Shu-shu-shu" lasted through the summer, enlivened by shooting expeditions with the other two exiles. These hunting enthusiasts were sometimes joined by two local peasants: Zhuravliev, a thirty-year-old consumptive, and a "muzhik" (poor peasant) named Sosipatuch.

Evidently the market for boots was limited, since Prominsky soon turned to hat-making. "I need a hat," Volodya informed his mother, "Mine came from Paris—the devil take it. But Prominsky's hats look like felt boots."

By the middle of August, however, the novelty of exile gave way to boredom and even to melancholy. Volodya was excusing the tone of his letters home:

> There is nothing I can write about myself. The letters are short because life is very monotonous. Outwardly, I have described everything. Inwardly, day differs from day only because today you are reading one book, tomorrow you will read another; today you take a walk to the right of the village, tomorrow to the left; today you write one article, tomorrow another. The weather is nasty—wind, cold, autumn rain, so I stay at home most of the time. I intend to go to Minusinsk to buy myself a few things, a lamp, some things for winter, etc. I may go with Prominsky. Kisses for you, Mother dearest, and my sisters.

He asked that a catalogue of secondhand books be sent to him.

3. Life on the Border
of Outer Mongolia

Exile was imposed less for punishment than for removal of political troublemakers from circulation. Punishment was reserved for the politically violent and they were sent to labor camps.

League of Struggle people belonged to what was considered the relatively harmless category of propagandists. The banished ones roamed about quite freely, finding a variety of reasons for visiting a neighboring village or town, ostensibly for medical or shopping purposes; and on the street a greeting was usually "What! You too?" Like genuine émigrés, they formed their own society amid an alien culture, and if the police nullified visiting privileges, contact was maintained through correspondence. Writing letters and watching for the postman were major activities, and it was a depressing day when there were no letters, either from home or from fellow-exiles.

As for fraternizing, the natives accepted exiles with the equanimity of those who saw a profit to be made from supplying them with the necessities of food, clothing (particularly sheepskin coats, boots and *shapkas*—fur hats), as well as rental for a room or house. Those local authorities who engaged in private business were more interested in sales than in supervision of their charges.

Despite their common plight, the exiles had a number of diverse reactions to their new lifestyle. For some it was a respite from the necessity to earn a living; content with the subsistence level of support provided by the State, they settled in for a three-year vacation from responsibility. Some quickly became bored and sought work on a local construction project. Others succumbed to mental depression which often assumed the form of erratic behavior, leading to quarrels with fellow-exiles or even suicide. Most unhappy of all was that person who was the sole exile in a given village, cut off from friends or loved ones and from the opportunity of sharing frustrations.

Often an exile became seriously ill, the result of long detention in remand prison and the vicissitudes of travel to Siberia. More fortunate were those with means to travel at their own expense, relieving them of police and the horrors of transit prison.

There were also extremes of response. At the positive end a small minority—those with highly developed intellectual interests who welcomed the balance of recreation and mental activity denied them in Petersburg—immersed themselves in study and creative writing. An equally small minority managed to escape to freedom, and the ideological *volte face* of some of the escapees was shared by those who, although passively enduring exile, nevertheless became embittered. Upon release, the latter defected to conservatism, forsaking the ideals which had earlier motivated their lives.

Generally, however, a sense of comradeship prevailed in which mutual support, both spiritual and material, was the norm.

No small part was played by women in maintaining the mental stability of their partners. However, there is no evidence of "shacking up." A woman of camp-follower mentality would hardly choose the worst of Siberia— nor, one might add, would she have chosen to become a member of the League of Struggle, or commitment to a man of the League type.

Commitment applied equally to exiled and "voluntary" women; for example Olga, a "voluntary" who left security and comfort to follow Volodya's friend Silvin to Siberia, only to find that he had been drafted into the army, thus extending his term of banishment. She remained alone in Krasnoyarsk while he was being moved about locally, finally being sent to Riga, Latvia.

Exiled women faced a different problem, since the State assigned them to larger towns in order to spare them the primitive conditions of village life. It required a strong-minded and loyal woman to relinquish this relative security in favor of the rugged "outback" where exiled husband or betrothed might be living.

Sexual activity for unattached men was probably minimal, given the nature of Siberian morality which was bourgeois-conservative. But even had they been so inclined, it is improbable that they would have risked local scandals, thereby jeopardizing their eventual release, as well as blacklisting themselves among fellow exiles. Communal living was fraternal; single as well as betrothed men and women lived together in the same relationship they had maintained at home which was, by choice, conservative. The communes were formed for convenience and economy, not for the practice of free love or group sex. So-and-so was living with so-and-so, but not necessarily in the same room or sleeping in the same bed.

Just as historical inquiry should limit itself to available evidence rather than embrace a peeping-tom approach leading to prurient guesswork, it must responsibly analyze the personalities of those it would investigate. Then, based upon a fair degree of perception, it should credit them with the consistency of lifestyle to which they are entitled.

Olga's story had a happy ending. However, not all the women who journeyed east were so fortunate. For some it was not only the terminus of the West Siberian Railway but the end of life.

Volodya's shopping expedition to Minusinsk was extended to include Tesinskoye where he found a flock of newly arrived exiles. Upon inspecting the lodgings of Gleb, Basil and E.E., he concluded that they were excellent—the entire top floor of a two-story house "with rooms light, clean and spacious." But the two men, he reported, were in poor condition. "Gleb is often quite ill, quite despondent. Basil, too, it seems, is not so 'flourishing' after all, though he is the most balanced of the Tes crowd. E.E. does the housekeeping, enjoys life at Tesinskoye, but is often quite ill."

Gleb and Basil had found jobs— "They could not live without work, for the allowance they receive is only 24 rubles." Because Tonechka's mother, E.E., was not considered family, Gleb received no allowance for her, and Tonechka was obliged to find work as a nurse in some distant village. "She won't remain there long," V. conjectured, "because of her poor health."

From several days of happy fraternizing, "after my Shushenskoye solitude," V. returned home to prepare himself mentally for the approaching winter. It had been a good autumn, but with hunting the only diversion during the months ahead, he was not looking forward to sallying forth "in snow up to your knees and spoiling the gun."

From time to time he looked lovingly at the manuscript of his unfinished book, and once or twice he attempted to write. But restlessness drove him out into the snow with his gun and what he called "my Pegasus," a creature of uncertain breed he acquired in hope of training it as a gun dog. Between times he sought the company of Prominsky and Engberg, but by December whatever had been "the joys of Shu-shu-shu" evaporated into the Siberian murk.

He began preparing for hibernation with an attempt to educate Prominsky and Engberg in the rudiments of Marxism. These two, with dropped jaw and glazed eye, listened with abject desire to please, read what he gave them, and returned later for a "quiz" by the instructor. Their naive responses caused Volodya considerable amusement, but he kept trying. Patience was the answer.

In the meantime, his harassed relatives in St. Petersburg and elsewhere were busy attempting to fill orders for books, etc. which were, nevertheless, arriving at Krasnoyarsk with commendable regularity, only to be stalled there pending transportation south. There were endless complaints from V., as well as lengthy explanations about the problem. Letters were devoted to such crucial matters as Achinsk and the post road to Shusha; the slowness of trains and the slowness of people to answer his letters; the waywardness of the postman and who was to pay for what; how long it was going to take to unsnarl all this, and please would Anna or his mother or Maria or Mark or SOMEBODY look up such-and-such and let him know *immediately* whether the books were available or out of print or in some foreign language or had fallen afoul of the tsarist censor. And please would they remember that the Yenisei was now frozen and all this stuff had to be contracted to some delivery person who would probably need "palm oil" in addition to his fee; and would someone please get in touch with publisher ABC in St. Petersburg to find out what happened to the manuscript he sent because they said it was received but he had no further word from them; and please try to find out from publisher XYZ if they would be interested in his article on economics which he didn't want to send until he was sure they were going to publish it because you "never knew if these things were lost in the mail or just being ignored by the publisher."

Frustration and impatience breathed from every line. The longer the delays, the more vehement his complaints. One can only marvel at the apparent equanimity of his long-suffering family. But bear it they did, and the result of their diligence was to bring Volodya a desperately needed income and the ability to repay his mother and whoever else had loaned him money. He was meticulous about repayment, even going so far as to berate—albeit kindly— one of his sisters for not providing an exact account of what he owed and to whom.

Whether an asset or liability, there was now an abundance of time to think. As the days grew shorter and the nights longer, he thought about Nadya, more often than he divulged to anyone, including his mother. Said Nadya about those months when Volodya was alone in exile: "We wrote each other regularly." What he wrote to her may have been deceptively objective. Was he uncertain about the degree of her commitment to him? After all, he had nothing to offer her beyond himself; neither financial security nor a decent place to live. He was, perhaps, waiting for a signal from Nadya that nothing had changed.

And that moment seems to have arrived on the day he wrote the letter to his mother which concluded with, "I kiss you warmly." Shortly before December 10th, he must have received a letter from Nadya informing him of her wish to exchange Ufa—a city with lighted streets and shops and apartments and even a local newspaper—for Shushenskoye's drabness and dung.

In January he wrote to his mother and sister Anna in regard to the expected arrival of Nadya and her mother: "I am even getting lodgings ready; the next room in the same house. But an amusing situation is going on with the local parson, who is also asking the landlady for a room. I still don't know whether I shall be able to get rid of my rival."

February brought good news in the form of promised financial solvency. V. had a contract for translating the Webbs' book (two volumes) from English into Russian with the aid of a German version; and additionally his group of articles was to be published in book form. He requested a "Hardmuth" pencil ("my own has served its time"), a penwiper ("the skirt of my jacket I have inked up beautifully") and an English language dictionary. "The scissors I get from the landlord—sheep shears. Their advantage is that they always arouse laughter." His weather reports were as frequent and detailed as those of Tsar Nicholas.

The preceding summer Volodya had served as best man at Basil's marriage to Tonechka. Now, instead of the small pang of a "have not" among the "haves"—he was actually looking forward to another wedding in Tesinskoye; Gleb had already begun making plans for the arrival of Zinaida.

It was not Volodya's style to write with solemnity about those matters closest to him. Although in relations with his family he was entirely ingenuous and open (there were no secrets), letters to family members, including his brother-in-law Mark, were frequently passed around; reason enough to write with tasteful reticence. But these factors notwithstanding, one can nevertheless gauge the depth of his emotional involvement by noting what seems to be a deliberate reversal; viz., by noting his bantering references to matters which were, in fact, of vital and intimate concern to him. For example, he remarked to Maria Alexandrovna that at the time of Nadya's arrival in Shushenskoye: "I was clever enough to be out shooting." This breezy observation is outweighed by the amount of ink and paper he would henceforth devote to "N.K." and "Nadezhda Konstantinovna" in communications to his family.

On February 7, 1898 he wrote to his mother:

Anyuta asks when the wedding is to be and who we are "inviting"! Isn't she in a hurry! First of all, Nadezhda Konstantinovna has to get here, and then we have to get permission from the authorities to marry—we are people without any rights at all, so how can I do any inviting?

Shortly after Nadya's arrival, again referring to Anna's query about invitations to the wedding, he wrote his mother: "I invite all of you, only perhaps it would be better to telegraph the invitations!"

Meanwhile, a Catch-22 situation had arisen: the authorities had not yet granted permission for them to wed but were insisting that the marriage take place immediately. "Otherwise, it's back to Ufa for Nadya. Since I am not at all disposed to allow that, we have already begun 'bothering' the authorities."

Without identification papers, marriage was impossible, and Volodya was "afraid the police chief in Krasnoyarsk will not hurry with these." He had been an exile in Shushenskoye for over a year, and the authorities had no record of his existence. Added to this bureaucratic oversight was a stricture of the Russian Orthodox Church which prohibited marriage during the Fast of St. Peter (in June).

So, what were Volodya's intentions? Certainly not to live with Nadya "in sin" with her mother a compliant witness. Also, he expected his own family, including his mother, to visit them. It is probable that he was, as he said, "waiting to see how things turn out," to make leisurely plans for their wedding after his fiancée had ample time to recover from her recent experiences. "She does not look well and must take better care of her health while she is here." And in addition, to resolve the housing situation.

As anticipated, St. Peter's Fast and desultory Krasnoyarsk conspired to delay the wedding. "The way things are, we shall probably not be able to marry before July. We permit ourselves to hope that these strict authorities will consider this a sufficiently 'immediate' marriage?!" The exclamation marks of this period of his writing indicate a state of mind that was atypical of him.

He was planning to invite the Tes people to his wedding and "I hope they will be allowed to come" he wrote his mother. "I hope I shall get a telegram from you saying that you have decided to come to us." Unfortunately, neither plan materialized. Complications arose for his mother (Dmitri was imprisoned for subversive activity), and the police refused permission for Basil, Gleb, Tonechka and E.E. on grounds that they might try to escape. "My arguments that there was no reason to fear that the Tes people would disappear had no effect."

It was not until July 10th that Nadya and Volodya exchanged vows in Shusha's tiny parish church. Nadya's mother was the only guest. Oskar Engberg served as best man. "They decided that at age 24," Oskar noted, "I was a suitable best man for the 28-year-old bridegroom." During the elaborate Orthodox ceremony, Oskar held the bridal wreath above Nadya's head and handed the couple wedding rings he had fashioned from coins. "Then," he concluded "they bowed three times before the alter, which fulfilled all the rules of the Orthodox Church."* After the ceremony, Nadya moved into her husband's bedroom, but otherwise life went on as before.

"Fedoseyev shot himself with a revolver. He was buried on June 23rd." The story was pieced together from scraps of information: a fellow-exile of low character, while Fedoseyev was in transit prison, accused him of embezzling money collected for the needs of exiles; continuing persecution after they had reached Verkholensk; depression and hurt. Already in poor health, NYF had been without sufficient funds to sustain himself, and comrades were providing support. When the scandal erupted, he refused these offerings and suffered extreme poverty. Unable to work, he no longer desired to live. "They say he asked that I be given a message," V. wrote his sister, "to the effect that he died full of faith in life and not from disappointment. I did not expect such a sad ending." Comrades were presently collecting money to pay his debts and provide a memorial.

In Tesinskoye, a comrade had gone mad and Gleb had taken him to hospital. In Turukhansk, Martov parted company with a troublesome fellow exile and was now ill and living alone. "His nerves are all to pieces," V. reported, "and he cannot work. Yuly (Martov) has asked his father to try to get him transferred somewhere else, no matter where; God save us from these 'exile colonies' and exile 'scandals'!"

One colony was enjoying a period of tranquillity. Zinaida was now happily married to Gleb, and Tonechka was "expecting." But their contentment was short-lived. Tonechka's newborn infant died, and she herself was ill. Then E.E. fell out of a wagon and injured her liver. Except for Zinaida's cheerful dispo-

---

* In tsarist Russia, civil or Protestant marriage was neither recognized nor legal. Thus, couples disavowing the State Church either lived in common-law or acceded to a lip service ceremony.

sition, the group might have succumbed to despair. As it was, they decided to leave Tesinskoye and were petitioning the authorities for permission to move to Minusinsk where medical help, albeit inadequate, was at least close at hand.

Apollinariya was among the last of the League people to leave St. Petersburg. "We were sent a photograph taken the day after she was released from prison, and she looks simply terrible. Can she have changed so much?" Nadya

"Main Street" toward Petrova House

River Shush

Petrova House, the Lenin's abode

"Holy Door" of House, used only during Orthodox ceremonies

thought she might be sent to Shushenskoye and "that would be fine; in Shusha she might recover a little."

The next word of her came from Kazachinskoye, another village in the area, where she was reported to be "in a state of nerves and irritable, lives in a commune and does the cooking every other week." A member of the commune, Lepeshinskaya, who reported Apollinariya's nerves, was the wife of a non-League exile. V. met them both for the first time in Siberia, and a lasting association was formed. In a letter to Nadya, Apollinariya indicated that she was fed up with communal life and longed to be alone so that she could "do something."

Thus, one by one, the League detainees were finding their places in Siberia. Finally relieved of the tension of recent months, Nadya and Volodya began life together in an atmosphere of mutual contentment, the only carefree times they were ever to know. Shushenskoye was idyllic. They took long walks, bathed at scenic spots, and enjoyed the summer weather. Nothing marred these days except the Siberian mosquitoes which, Nadya said, "go out of their way to bite Volodya."

With the exception of V.'s letter about Fedoseyev written five days after his own marriage, nothing traveled west until August—neither demands nor reports. In August the pair resumed their letter writing, and Nadya was adding weather bulletins to those of her husband, between them outdoing the Tsar. But she included newsy tidbits of their domestic life: "We are pickling cucumbers"—details which V. found trivial and left for his wife to convey to the family. But their physical isolation from "exile scandals" did not rule out mental shock upon hearing the final chapter of Fedoseyev's story. His fiancée Maria, on her way to join him after a harrowing journey by way of Arkangelsk, shot herself two days after news reached her of his suicide.

Shortly after the wedding Volodya found it necessary to move his family to other lodgings; the peasants with whom they were boarding held drinking parties which lasted well into the night. Weekend mornings found the lodgers red-eyed from loss of sleep. Some of the houses in Shushenskoye were duplexes, and in half of one of these the three set up housekeeping, not an easy task. "Mother and I fought with the Russian stove," Nadya said. "At first I knocked over the soup and dumpling with the oven-hook and then scattered them all over the hearth. But afterwards I got used to it." Rent for the *izba* (a house of logs adapted to the Siberian climate) was four rubles a month.

Nadya reported that they were all flourishing on the large amounts of milk provided. "I cannot get used to seeing Volodya look so well, remembering how he was in St. Petersburg—in a permanently out-of-sorts condition." Both of them were turning into "bulochkins." Even a sharp note from Anna failed to disturb Nadya: "It gave Volodya great satisfaction," Nadya wrote back, "to read out to me all the reproaches that you had written about me. Well, I admit I am guilty but deserving of leniency." Was she speaking in jest of something inconsequential, or merely practicing her characteristic forbearance? She ended the letter with "many kisses for you, Manya and Maria Alexandrovna."

It was now time to get down to the business of translating the Webbs: no translation meant no money from the publisher. Wagonloads of interesting books were arriving, but the pair bent their heads over language dictionaries, determined to complete the task. "We are heartily sick of the Webbs," complained Nadya. As the work dragged on, Volodya occasionally turned to his unfinished book *(Development of Capitalism in Russia)*. The *ennui* of his first year in exile had dissipated, replaced by an eagerness to engross himself in creative writing, a mood now reawakened in the conditions of a good home life. Henceforth and for the remainder of his life, Volodya's demeanor was that of a happy man; one emotionally as well intellectually fulfilled by the presence of a woman who truly loved him, who understood his every nuance of feeling, and who, to a remarkable degree, shared life with him on all levels.

The founder of the Soviet Union ended his honeymoon summer by digging in the Siberian earth to prepare a seed bed for his wife's vegetables and flowers.

Nadya had described her first days in Shusha:

Spring is in the air. The ice on the river is covered with water all the time and sparrows in the willow trees are chirping furiously; the bullocks low as they pass up and down the street and the landlady's hen under the stove clucks loudly in the morning, waking everyone up.

The following year she became lyrical, her prose gaining in imagery what it lacked in artistry:

After the winter frosts, Nature burst tempestuously into spring. Her power became mighty. Sunset. In the great springtime pools in the fields, wild swans were swimming. We stood at the edge of a wood and listened to a rivulet burbling, or woodcocks clucking.

The past year had been a good one. The kitchen garden produced an abundance of cucumbers, carrots, beet roots, pumpkins. "We put up fruit preserves and vegetable relishes."

Responding to a query from home, Nadya wrote: "What do I do all day? I sew on buttons, think about a popular booklet I would like to write *(The Working Woman)* but do not know how it will turn out, and take an interest in Volodya's work." She was busy making nightshirts for her husband, but complained that he hadn't found time to try them on.

While Nadya sewed or wrote letters, the men talked endlessly about ducks and hares. At first their enthusiasm for hunting left her frustrated. "Prominsky would come in with a joyful smile, exclaim: 'I've seen them—the ducks have flown over.' Then Oskar would enter—also full of ducks. Finally I also became capable of conversing about ducks—who had seen them, and where, and when." As a huntsman, Volodya was hardly a success. Perhaps it was the dog's fault? Pegasus was replaced by another, "but unfortunately," commented V., "it is of the female estate." Zhenka, however, quickly became adept, although the same could not be said of her master.

Oskar was equally unskilled. "One day we (the Shusha colony) were all riding in a cart and we saw about twenty partridges. Volodya actually groaned. Still he managed to take aim, but the partridge simply walked away without even bothering to fly. Altogether it was a sorrowful shoot; we didn't kill anything, but Oskar shot Zhenka in the eyes and we thought the dog was blinded, but she recovered."

Volodya was also a fishing enthusiast. At the general store in Minusinsk he bought a pair of waders and fishing equipment, and during the ensuing days conversation centered around burbot.

Recently he had been suffering from a toothache, but since the nearest dentist was in Krasnoyarsk, he postponed treatment. When the pain became acute he tried pulling it himself, but Nadya protested. His reluctance to make the journey stemmed from worry about leaving Nadya and her mother alone. "It will do him good to get away," his wife thought. "He has been vegetating here in Shusha, so I am urging him to go. He already has a pass. It came earlier, but then the toothache went away. Yesterday he borrowed a saw and has been working on our door to make it latch properly. Then he showed me how to use a gun. He has arranged for Oskar to come here to sleep."

After reassuring himself that the family would be safe during his two-week absence, V. left by horse cart for Minusinsk to join Tonechka and E.E. for the steamer journey north. The women were likewise on a medical pass; Tonechka's mother had suffered a relapse of her liver ailment and was going into hospital. "I am very sorry for Tonechka," he wrote his mother from Krasnoyarsk.

> She has not yet recovered from the death of her child and her own illness; she becomes so agitated at times that she almost has nervous fits. I would rather not leave her here alone, but my time is up and I must leave. I am asking the local comrades to look after her. As a result of my trip and the need to help her, my finances are in a sorry state. Please send Yelizaveta Vasilyevna (from whom I have received a loan) about half of the sum that should be sent you from the (whole) Webb translation.

The offending tooth, he learned, was adjacent to the one he had been trying to pull, and the dentist duly extracted it. Because the steamer was delayed, he used the time at his disposal to meet with comrades. The meetings were political in nature, devoted to discussion of new socialist literature, and to mapping future strategy. Some of the League core had been settled in Krasnoyarsk, and because contact with their southern colleagues was complicated by postal surveillance, these meetings had a particular advantage. Once out of Siberia and scattered about European Russia, the League people would be in need of codes, and alternative pseudonyms for keeping in touch with each other in order to be *au courant* with tsarist politics and with socialist activity. The likelihood of future personal contact would diminish the day each of them boarded the train for Chelyabinsk and "freedom."

Meanwhile, the weather had turned foul. Armed with a supply of candles and the hitherto unopened books he had brought from Shusha, he stowed himself in the steamer and immediately descended below deck for a boring five-day journey. He was so eager to get home that he waived the stopover in Minusinsk to which his pass entitled him.

In October, Pasha, a skinny 13-year-old peasant girl "with pointed elbows," for 2-1/2 rubles a month plus boots, began to help with the chores. Unlettered but willing, she learned not to spill the tea, etc., and under Nadya's tutelage she also learned to read and write. In October Volodya piled stable manure around the foundation of their house and installed double windows. In October the temperature dipped to below zero.

The Ulyanov *izba* now became the gathering-place for what V. jokingly called the "Shushenskoye intelligentsia," meaning Oskar Engberg, Prominsky and a couple of peasants. Evening discussion about ducks frequently ended with lusty singing of Siberian folksongs, or witty recitals of the day's happenings. Yelizaveta adapted well and seems to have taken all this goodnaturedly. During these potpourri gatherings the older woman, with motherly tolerance, would enter into the discussion from time to time; and if the conviviality began to pall, she could always retire to her room.

With the coming of winter, Volodya took up skating. The men cleared a place on Shusha's frozen river, and the entire community gathered to watch the performance. V. was better at skating than hunting, a result of youthful practice at home in Simbirsk. With Prominsky's help, he learned to do "Spanish leaps" and before long he was sailing around the improvised rink with hands in pockets and air of a professional. Poor Nadya! "I've bought her a pair of skates," reported her husband, "but I don't know if she will be able to manage it." Someone brought a chair with which she was expected to perform. And since Oskar's skill matched that of his hunting, "together we provided the villagers with real comedy," remarked Nadya ruefully. Then the villagers began cracking nuts and throwing them on the ice.

If a description of their days gave the impression of a perpetual holiday, the reality was quite different. With the desperation of those who throw themselves into language study only to meet with the hopelessness of textbook French or German or English as a means to proficiency, Nadya and Volodya nevertheless worked doggedly. Nadya thought the results were "pitiful." Her own chore for the moment was English. She would memorize twelve pages of a text and then attempt to practice, from written directions, the pronunciation. Volodya's assessment was unpleasantly candid: "My sister once had an English teacher," he said, "but it didn't sound like that!" Nadya was accustomed to his bluntness. She understood that it was part of his nature, and even his teasing failed to ruffle her since she often laughed at herself.

The teasing was not one-sided. Anna wrote indignantly about Nadya allowing V. to edit her letters. "I describe Shusha life in humorous terms," Nadya responded, "and in them Volodya comes in for a lot of badinage; I would not write such letters if I did not give them to him to read before I send them off."

Nadya viewed her husband with unromantic realism. Neither then nor later did she look upon him as "a great man." Although she admired his intellectual capabilities, on other levels he was merely the man she had accepted "for better or worse." Her comment that "Volodya is soaking up so much philosophy that one will be afraid to talk to him" was mildly bantering. This did not, of course, dilute her affection for him. To his sister she wrote:

> You think "markets" are finished, do you? Nothing of the sort. Volodya writes and has no time for anything else. He asks me to wake him at 7:30 or 8 in the morning, but my efforts are usually fruitless; he gives a couple of grunts, pulls the clothes over his head and goes to sleep again. Last night he argued in his sleep about some Mr. N. and natural economy.

Yelizaveta was even less impressed. She did not hesitate to find fault with her son-in-law when the occasion arose. "Mother is displeased with Volodya." More than once Y.V. berated him for wasting money on nonessentials and making what she considered to be unnecessary trips.

There were times of depression, "that unpleasant feeling we all get when there are no letters." Even though he now had companionship, for Volodya it was sometimes a replay of his first year in Siberia. But the loudest complaints emerged from Yelizaveta. She was certain the postman was hiding the letters, or that they weren't tipping him enough. Nadya described one of these letter-less periods to Maria:

> You see what nonsense I am writing because there is nothing to write about. When things are so monotonous, one completely loses one's sense of time. Volodya and I got to a state where we could not remember whether Basil had visited us three days or ten days before. We had to adduce a whole series of arguments to settle the issue.

Suddenly, 'twas the season to be jolly. Volodya's negative view of religion had shifted the focus to New Year's, but Nadya was filled with nostalgic thoughts of childhood; of Christmas trees and midnight church services with their color and incense and deepthroated chanting. And this Christmas, her first in a real home, however primitive, with an extended family rather than merely an ailing mother, thinking that perhaps she would bear children, all made the holidays more meaningful than she dared to admit.

The Tes crowd (Basil and company) were now settled in Minusinsk, and it was decided to hold a New Year's get-together of all the district exiles. Bundled in sheepskin, Nadya and Volodya set out by sleigh the day before Christmas ("Mother didn't go and was pretty miserable").

Although the ensuing festivities were hardly rowdy, the participants wore themselves out with talk, singing and eating. V. brought along some chess men he had carved from bark and "battled on the chess-board from morning until night." "We mulled some wine, and when it was ready we set the hands of the clock at twelve and saw the old year out in style. Toasts were drunk to 'absent mothers,' 'absent friends,' and in the end we danced to a guitar." The next day the party moved outdoors. There was a troika ride and, to Nadya's embarrassment, skating. "I have some new skates, but I do as badly on these as on the old ones, or rather I do not skate but strut like a chicken!"

When it was time to leave, the hosts admitted that another day of this and they would have taken to their beds. Although they entered into the festivities with enthusiasm, it was obvious to Nadya that the stresses of exile had overtaken them.

Tonechka looks particularly bad—she suffers from anemia and eczema. Even Zinaida has grown thin and nervous. The male side is also weak. Gleb kept lying down, first on the sofa, then on the bed. We wore our hosts out completely. Toward the end of the holiday they were having ten to sixteen people to dinner every day. However, E.E. looks better than she did in St. Petersburg, although she cannot eat meat or bread at all.

The latter thought Nadya even fatter than Zinaida had formerly been.

Barely warmed by the afterglow of recent jollity, post-holiday doldrums now set in with a vengeance. Mercury froze in the thermometer, "but we have a stove in every room and manage to keep warm." Meanwhile, time was running out for *The Development of Capitalism in Russia*, and Volodya, determined to have it completed and in the hands of a publisher by spring, went to work. He had exactly two months before his waders and a new gun would lure him to Shusha's swampy hinterland with its network of streams and patchwork islands alive with small game.

Nadya was requisitioned as critic: "I am supposed to be an 'un-understanding' reader and judge whether the exposition is sufficiently clear; I try to be as 'un-understanding' as possible, but there is not much I can find fault with." She found the first chapter "very interesting." During January and February they did not see Oskar and Prominsky, sparing Nadya a preview of ducks, and relieving Volodya of interruptions.

Occasionally, however, there were other visitors. V.'s easy camaraderie with children earned him several young friends. Among them was little Minka, a peasant boy living next door who became a member of the family and burst in upon them at odd hours. V. bought Minka a horse; and although the animal didn't cost much and was worth even less, the boy was ecstatic. "Vladimir Ilyich likes me!" he cried when his mother admonished him for bothering the Ulyanovs. Yelizaveta adored him, and she was "grandma" to Minka and any other youngster Volodya "adopted."

Women, of course, didn't toss children in the air or roll on the floor with them, but Nadya too had her little friends. Prominsky's daughter became a regular visitor. "I planned to make her a blouse," Nadya said, "but when I heard Volodya asking my mother how many pounds of cloth he should buy in Minusinsk, I knew it was hopeless."

Meanwhile, Volodya's mother had been counting on her fingers. Her younger daughter Maria was barely twenty and unmarried. Dmitri, who at twenty-four was attempting (between sessions in prison and exile) to acquire a college education, was hardly thinking about marriage. Anna and Mark had thus far produced no children, probably a result of their disorganized lifestyle; Anna, not long married to Mark, was in her thirty-fifth year. As a family-oriented lady of the old school, Maria Alexandrovna yearned to be a grandmother. A discreet inquiry arrived at Shushenskoye.

"As far as my health is concerned, I am quite well," Nadya assured her, "but as far as concerns the arrival of a little bird—there the situation is, unfortunately, bad; somehow no little bird wants to come,"—meaning "we have been trying but without success," The shortcoming appears to have been Nadya's, a health problem that would make its appearance not long afterward.

The most unmistakable sign of spring was talk about a visit from Volodya's mother. This was the third year of such discussion, and now the trip seemed about to materialize. Letters traveled between Shushenskoye and various towns in European Russia where the older woman happened to be at the moment. She might come second class, which her son thought would not be too tiring.

Nadya, to reassure her mother-in-law about accommodations, provided a description of the *izba*:

> It consists of three rooms, one with four windows, one with three, and the other with one. We have one disadvantage—the rooms are all adjoining. Volodya and I are now thinking of giving you our room (the one with the three windows) and we will move into the middle one; our present room has the advantage that no one has to go through it to get to another room. The main thing, my dear, is that you should be well enough to travel here. We shall always be able to find room for you.

Nadya thought it unnecessary to mention the outdoor privy and the "nochnoi gorshok" under the bed. M.A. often spent holidays in what the family called a summer cottage and was undoubtedly familiar with primitive facilities.

In Nadya's letters there were recurring complaints about the postman:

He's an awful muddler—loses a newspaper, forgets to hand over a receipt or takes the letters to the wrong address. I am always cursing him under my breath with all the Siberian swear words. After a long wait we finally received *Nachalo*, and Volodya is indignant about a certain article. He is already thinking out a reply to it.

Lively and often vitriolic attacks on each other's views were carried on by socialists in the press.

If celebration of New Year's had compensated for a December without Christmas, there was no substitute for the approaching Easter, and Nadya was deliberating a way to circumvent Volodya.

For Russians, Easter was traditionally the great festival of the Orthodox year; a time for coloring eggs by ordinary folk, a time for royalty to commission the jeweled creations of Faubergé. In spite of Volodya's objections, Nadya intended to color some eggs and make an Easter cake of curds. "It is the custom here at Easter to decorate the rooms with spruce boughs," she observed, "a pretty custom and we intend to keep it"—an expression of yearning for the comforting traditions already fading into what would soon be called "the trash-bin of history." Volodya's disapproval, however, was good-naturedly mild; he may have been remembering his sister Olga beneath a cross in Volkhov Cemetery.

In late spring the Lepeshinskys came to visit, bringing their infant daughter. "Our apartment was filled with hubbub. The two parents are so fond of her they don't give her a moment's rest—they sing, dance and pester her all the time." Nadya welcomed the peace that followed their departure. Volodya finished his writing projects, and he and Nadya whiled away the days with long walks and bathing in their favorite spot beyond the village. Maria Alexandrovna decided not to travel to Shusha. "But it is not long before we will be returning to Russia," Nadya reminded her. "If we get away from here at the proper time, we shall be home by February."

By the time of their final summer in exile, memory of the turmoil and tensions of St. Petersburg had faded, giving way to the serenity of domestic life with its unstructured days. "You will see how Volodya's health has improved," Nadya told her mother-in-law. "You cannot compare him with what he was in St. Petersburg."

However, another exile tragedy intruded on their happiness—("the flower garden is in bloom with mignonette and pansies and phlox"). There had been visitors. "Anatoly looks bad," observed Nadya. "He is not likely to get better and his wife is completely broken, such a quiet little thing." Anatoly, after rescuing Dominika from Yeniseisk prison, had taken her to his lodgings in the village of Yermanovskoye. "Lepeshinsky's wife is a nurse and she thinks the end is not far off, although the doctor is a great optimist and assures Dominika that there is still hope."

As if to protest his illness, the weather, in Nadya's words, "has been like nothing on earth; it rains constantly and there is wind every day that makes the shutters rattle."

Volodya's frequent and detailed account of the illness indicated deep sorrow at the plight of his friend, a frail, scholarly man who was dedicated to the League. He had been a leader in the Marxist study circles, in charge of technical preparations for the publication of a new socialist. newspaper *Rabocheye Delo* (The Workers' Task). To his mother V. wrote:

> A big *merci* for carrying out my request with regard to Anatoly (the nature of the request is not known). I hope to see him again in a few days; they say that he is very bad, the blood is flowing from his throat and he even coughs up pieces of lung. The Governor was in Yermanovskoye and gave Anatoly permission to go to Krasnoyarsk, but now he himself doesn't want to go.

Anatoly had arrived in exile with pleurisy and was immediately assigned to Turukhansk—in the frigid north—along with Martov. The exiles petitioned the authorities to have him moved south, but not soon enough. Pleurisy gave way to typhus and finally to tuberculosis. Volodya: "I have very sad news for you, Mother dearest. Yesterday we buried Anatoly in Yermanovskoye."

Like Anatoly, the wind has died. Sunlight floods the scene with beneficent warmth. Around the open coffin stand his friends and comrades, mute with grief. No priest intones the litany. Dominika looks down upon her husband's emaciated features, white amid the richly colored autumn blooms that smother his pillow. Awareness of the bitter-sweet paradox of death amid life caresses the group like a gentle hand on its shoulder. It is done. *Requiescat in pace.*

The feverish pursuit of language study had a threefold purpose. Its primary one, at least for the moment, was translation of foreign books into Russian, lucrative for both translator and publisher. Particularly in St. Petersburg and to a lesser degree in Moscow, there were publishers of socialist literature: books, periodicals, pamphlets. These enterprises were tolerated by the tsarist régime as long as their output was limited to purely theoretical material. Any suggestion of revolutionary activism would encounter censorship. Likewise, there was a market for translations of foreign classics. Several exiles supplemented their income in this manner.

For a considerable period during exile, Volodya earned a fair if intermittent income from translating. The money, arriving in lump sums, was deposited in his sister Anna's bank account, and amounts were withdrawn to pay V.'s debts—what he called "internal" (family) loans. The remainder was sent to Shushenskoye. At one time, 100 rubles were forwarded to Yelizaveta for money her son-in-law had borrowed. There was a reason for laundering the money. Volodya was writing under the pseudonym "V. Ilyin" in order to avoid jeopardizing his chances for a timely release. (Martov was doing the same; his real name was Zederbaum.) Most, if not all of the socialist writers at that time practiced this procedure; their survival depended upon political anonymity.

Since the "fair copy" of a manuscript was, of necessity, handwritten, the first step in publishing was to have it printed, the author's responsibility. The first printing then had to be proofread, often several times. One can understand the difficulty for Volodya, such as long delays in sending and receiving manuscripts and printings, and then sections that might be lost in the post. Only after surmounting the problems imposed by distance did the actual work of publishing begin. First one must make the rounds of publishers to obtain a commitment; and then wait—and wait. Initially, Nadya and Volodya undertook the proof-reading themselves, but eventually they were forced to turn it over to Anna because of endless delays caused by the Siberian postal service, as well as equivocation by publishers.

These conditions pertained also to V.'s original work, which occupied at least half his work time; the other half devoted to the pedestrian chore of translation. During his relatively brief sojourn in St. Petersburg (1893-97), he was fortunate to have established associations with several publishers. Anna, although not a resident of the Capital, was able to take advantage of these contacts, and through them to discover others in Moscow.

Many of Volodya's colleagues in the League and among Marxist leaders, were similarly engaged in writing. Martov, languishing in icy Turukhansk, spent his days producing articles for socialist periodicals. And there were others, including a number of women, some of whom collaborated with their husbands, or at least listened to a reading of material, suggested improvements and helped with the mechanics of reproduction.

Nadya's participation in these activities was extensive, but her subsidiary role was occasionally a source of frustration; she longed for Volodya's background and talent. However, she knew that she was a better critic, translator and secretary. These activities were necessarily interspersed with domestic routine, but she would have had it no other way. As for Volodya, he could have found a business partner in other places had he so desired. He did not "use" her; they worked together on projects which concerned them both—financially as well as ideologically.

Another reason for language study was, for practical reasons, far from secondary. V. knew that upon release he and Nadya would undoubtedly emigrate from Russia.

Prominsky's term of exile would expire in mid-autumn, and in preparation for the journey home he killed a large number of hares in order to provide skins for his children's coats. He and his wife, now parents of six children, were wondering how to finance their journey. Since his hat-making business had barely sustained the family (their allowance from the State had been reduced), he considered traveling at State expense. For reasons unknown, he and his family got only as far as Krasnoyarsk. After remaining in Siberia until 1923, they once again started for Poland, but on the way Prominsky was stricken with typhus and died.

"In the time we have been here," said Nadya, "we have got quite used to our Shushenskoye comrades, and if for any reason a day passes without Oskar and Prominsky coming, we feel there is something missing." Nadya's mood, a sense that all of them would soon be "ejected from Eden," found expression in her signature: N. Ulyanova, In a previous letter she was, for the first time, "N.U." Did this indicate a feeling of insecurity? Was she attempting to reassure herself? Volodya's term was due to expire in approximately three and a half months. She was dreading the farewell to friends, realizing that they would probably not meet again.

Life for other exiles was also about to climax in release. Meanwhile, there were developments which would complicate their departure. Tonechka was expecting another child. A baby born to Dominika shortly before her husband's death was thought to be consumptive, and she herself "is ill all the time and very miserable." Silvin and Olga were married in late summer, but his departure for army service left her "rather poorly." "She is miserable and amuses herself by taking walks in the vegetable garden with a calf and her dog."

Since the beginning of exile, Nadya had been concerned about Apollinariya. The few letters from Kazachinskoye had ceased for a time, "and now she only writes to clear her conscience." After several months of cooking for the commune, Apollinariya complained of having to get up at 5 or 6 in the morning to get everything done. "Her work gives her little satisfaction," Nadya observed, "but that is something she cannot change. Kazachinskoye is no worse than any other place." Her friend's moods were changeable as winds over the steppe. "Why is she so bored?" Nadya wondered. Then came word that she had disappeared. Inquiries were being made everywhere, and the Yermanovskoye people reported that she was there the week before but had once again vanished. There were rumors that she had escaped abroad; someone had seen her in Berlin. "So that's that," concluded Nadya. But Apollinariya had not escaped; she was wandering in Siberia—on whose money and by what authority remained a mystery. Of all the League exiles, she was the most restless and unhappy.

Yuly (Martov), on the other hand, had managed to survive the Turukhansk winters (morning temperature in his room was 20 below!), and he wrote V. that he was now in good health.

Leo Tolstoi observed that in traveling the first part of a journey, one thought about what was left behind, but during the second half, about what lay waiting ahead.

November and December passed without incident. "I don't do anything," said Nadya, "and wonder where the time goes." Suspended as they were in a vacuum of uncertainty, she watched her husband grow thin. His nights were sleepless, and often he wakened her to talk about plans for the future. Departure from Russia was taken for granted. But a year of exile still remained for Nadya; and her husband, upon release, would be confined to the city of Pskov* and its environs. Although they considered a plan to escape, it was discarded. Nadya's request for transfer to Pskov was submitted and rejected; she was directed to proceed to Ufa pending further instructions.

While awaiting the day of Volodya's release at the end of February, it became clear that since they would be forcibly separated, there was no reason for him to delay his own emigration. Nadya would finish her term and follow him to Europe. Meanwhile, it was imperative to utilize the present relative freedom for constructing a literary base that would assure the League's future survival. This would be *Iskra*, "The Spark," a newspaper for laborers and a medium for unifying the League's ideological foundation. With the formulation of the project, V. reached the turning point in both his personal and political life. He discussed the plan with Gleb Krzhizhanovsky, carried on a lengthy correspondence with Martov (in code or invisible ink), considered ways to raise money and gain editorial support. When contacting potential supporters, they would have to circumvent the police. The Siberian locale was temporarily useful, since the League people were concentrated there; but once they were scattered, V.'s chances of finding them without being himself apprehended, were slim. His hopes centered on Krzhizhanovsky and Martov, men of superior intellect and education. Martov was also a distinguished journalist. V. wondered how many of the others had wavered in their views since coming to exile.

From the moment of V.'s arrival in Siberia, he had begun to build a network of relationships. He seemed to know everyone: exiled intelligentsia as well as peasants, railwaymen, postal clerks, factory workers, all of whom would remember him with comradely affection after he had left for Russia.

Nadya, if not the co-founder of *Iskra*, was her husband's "listener" and consultant as well as one of its most skillful staff members. As V.'s enthusiasm grew, so did his impatience. Anticipation of the obstacles ahead merely reinforced his conviction that only through *Iskra* could the League—now referred to as "The Party"—weld together the disparate elements of ideology. Back in St. Petersburg the faint-hearted were defecting to Economism, having concluded that under present conditions only limited reforms were possible, and those confined to shop/factory working environment. They felt that it was preferable to work openly for these rather than court tsarist persecution by clinging to all-or-nothing Marxism.

---

* In western Russia near the Latvian border.

The Petersburg Social-Democrats, by going "Economist"—reasoned the Marxists—were abrogating their commitment to general social reform.

The New Year passed without celebration. Nadya and Volodya were busy cataloguing books and packing them for shipment. Clothing was sorted, decisions were made about what to leave behind. Nadya's letters to V.'s family ceased and were replaced by queries to Krasnoyarsk about her eventual fate. The family was apprehensive about the forthcoming journey by sleigh. Yelizaveta, at best unwell, suffered intensely from the cold. They were attempting to obtain a hooded sleigh, and even considered having one made.

As day followed day without word from the authorities, it appeared that Nadya and her mother would be left behind. Another official snag developed concerning permission for Volodya to accompany the women to their new place of exile in order to help them settle. Technically, he was not permitted to dawdle on his way to Pskov, and any stop along the way had to receive official sanction.

Feverishly, Volodya checked off the days on the calendar. Nadya's final letter from Shushenskoye to her mother-in-law was dated January 19, 1900. The books weighed 15 poods (540 pounds), and together with certain personal effects would be shipped by carrier. They had been unsuccessful in regard to the hooded sleigh, "but we have plenty of warm clothes so I don't suppose we shall freeze, and the weather seems to be getting warmer; yesterday Oskar saw a cloud somewhere and the temperature this morning was only 28° below. The worst of it is that Mother keeps catching cold and is coughing again," Because they planned to travel day and night the matter of food was crucial. Yelizaveta began making *pelmeni*—tiny meat dumplings without fat or onions "because everything else spoils in the frost."

In the absence of official confirmation of travel technicalities, they telegraphed the family of Lydia Knippovich in Petersburg to exert pressure on the authorities. Rumors had come to Nadya that she might be shipped from Ufa to Sterlitamak or Belebei, unfamiliar names that suggested *Ultima Thule*, "edge of the world." Volodya was directed to leave on February 29 (old style). And since the authorities in Pskov had already been notified of his imminent arrival, excessive delay would entail not only the red tape of permission but the possibility of incarceration at journey's end. When by the 28th Nadya's pass had still not arrived, Volodya determined that she and her mother must leave with him. They would deal with the problem later. (Nadya's delinquent pass was awaiting her at Minusinsk through which they would pass on their way north.)

The evening before their departure was a mixture of sadness and elation. Pasha, who in those two years had become a real beauty, shed torrents of tears. Minka was fidgety and carried home all the paper, pencils and stationery we were leaving behind. Oskar, who came and sat on the edge of a chair, was evidently deeply moved. He brought me a present, a handmade brooch in the form of a book, inscribed "Karl Marx" in memory of his studies of *Kapital*.

The brooch, fashioned from the cover of a silver watch, was a work of art. "She was astonished," Engberg later recalled, "that I was able to make such lovely things." Meanwhile, neighbors kept looking into the room to see what was going on. "Our dog," said Nadya, "wondered what all this hubbub meant and kept opening doors with her nose to see if everything was still in its place. Mother busied herself with packing, coughing from the dust."

Characteristically, as he tied up books "in a businesslike manner," Volodya disguised his emotion.

At dawn the following morning, clad in felt boots and elkskin coats, the family—including Zhenka the dog—stowed themselves in a sleigh. They were stopping at Minusinsk to pick up Basil Starkov and Olga. The Lepeshinskys had intended to join the group returning to Russia, but they failed to make adequate preparations. Basil's wife Tonechka and her mother were delayed because of the latter's illness.

All the Minusinsk people were gathered to see us off. everybody was thinking about Russia—yet we talked about all kinds of trivialities. Someone attempted to feed Zhenka sandwiches, but she took no notice, instead lying at Mother's feet, not taking her eyes off her and following her every movement. (Zhenka was bequeathed to one of the remaining exiles.)

Two troikas with their passengers departed Minusinsk and followed the post road north, the horses proceeding at a steady canter over the wind-driven snow. Sleigh bells jingled merrily. The drivers gently flicked the reins from time to time, but the horses needed little urging. Their flying feet threw up clouds of snow, their eagerness for the race reminiscent of fire-horses on their way to a conflagration. It was almost a scene from *Dr. Zhivago.* Traveling by day, and by night with a full moon to illumine their path, they were following the Yenisei, whose turbulence was still frozen to immobility. Occasionally they stopped at some village inn to change horses and acquire boiling water for tea and for heating the frozen balls of *pelmeni.* When Olga complained of the cold, Volodya gave her his elkskin coat, claiming it was too warm, but Nadya observed that he continued the journey with his hands buried in her mother's muff. "At every stopping place, he carefully wrapped us all up, checking to see that we had left nothing behind." Olga called V. their "quartermaster" as he settled with the coachmen and paid the innkeepers.

Upon arrival at Achinsk, they were just in time for the mail/passenger train from Irkutsk to Moscow, which departed at 7 a.m. The steppe, although a wasteland smothered in frost, appeared less desolate to those on their way home. Even the station platform at Chelyabinsk on the border between West Siberia and Russia seemed cozily familiar. The next stop was Ufa.

In summarizing the exile years, one particular question arises: was Vladimir Ilyich Ulyanov, at this time, the "compulsive revolutionary" that western historians have declared him to be? And was Nadya, by association, a "compulsive" Marxist? Theirs was not the objectivism of true Marxist intellectuals of the type of Plekhanov; nor, conversely, were they "Narodnik" types who advocated violence as a substitute for organized reform. Since in a large measure, the Shushenskoye period shaped their future lives, the question is worthy of consideration.

Family letters provide considerable information about Nadya and Volodya. Nadya's, unlike her Memoir, are ingenuous: "My simple feminine letters," she called them, "in which I go on about this and that." These letters suggest that she was content with domestic life and found intense intellectual activity fatiguing. This is not to say that she wished to dismiss what she had learned in the Marxist study circles, nor abandon the socialist objectives.

Volodya, also, displayed an ambivalence toward both his literary and agitational activities. Although he was an assiduous taskmaster and drove himself to study and write, he succumbed easily to the blandishments of Oskar and Prominsky for a shooting expedition or fishing trip. Was he at heart also a domestic person? The last two years of exile were probably the happiest of his life, and he appeared to be one who would have preferred they be extended indefinitely. The easygoing life of Shushenskoye provided a balance between intellectual exercise and the outdoor recreation which turned him, he said, "into a real Siberian"; the books overflowing their shelves in the *izba* were there when he felt inclined to read them. Certainly it appears that he would have preferred a life of intellectual introspection and literary creativity balanced by hearth and home and hunting. But ultimately, would he have been satisfied with such a pedestrian routine? Probably not.

Because Nadya's life was inseparably bound to his, her story must concern itself with his personal inclinations and the circumstances which to a great extent controlled his life.

Although she was occasionally overcome by shyness, Nadya was, like her husband, extremely gregarious. In normal circumstances, their hunger for human intercourse might have become diffused and "revolutionary-ism" defused.

On February 28, 1900, Volodya's monthly allowance from the State was curtailed (Nadya was subsidized; her mother was not). On that day, although *Iskra* became inevitable, it was not revolution *per se* —nor for some time to come.

For the preceding two years Nadya and Volodya, working and playing together, had contrived their own special Utopia in a most unlikely setting.[1]

4. Return to Russia

At midnight 1899-1900, the ponderous boom of Big Ben echoed like a distant cannon across the Thames. Thirteen days later church bells in Russia clashed and clanged a cacophonous greeting to the New Year. People celebrated, fell into bed, and awoke red-eyed to a day no different from yesterday. As the world's clock ticked away a century, the tired old lady who ruled England was nearing the end of her long reign. But in St. Petersburg, the young Tsar slept peacefully and arose to a breakfast served by liveried footmen.

In England the royal prerogative, at most, relative, would soon be further curtailed. In Russia the anachronism of absolutism seemed destined for eternal life.

While Nadya and Volodya, oblivious to the holiday season, were brooding about their prospects for a timely release from exile, Russia's hungry people stumbled into the 20th Century with a mixture of hope and pessimism. Members of various political parties including Social-Democrats and Social Revolutionaries, undaunted by the sub-zero temperature, met clandestinely while awaiting spring thaws. The "people," they agreed, must not be allowed to dissipate their restlessness in euphoric dreams or dark despair. Unable to fathom the changing moods of Viborg and its Moscow counterpart, the secret police concentrated on real or suspected political radicals. Like most bureaucracies, they were overzealous. Many persons rounded up for interrogation were considered "guilty by association."

Upon passing through Moscow on their way to emigration, Nadya and Yelizaveta found Volodya's mother living alone. Maria was again in jail, her second incarceration. Two years earlier as she was preparing to leave for Brussels to study French, she had been arrested and sent to Nizhny-Novgorod. After three months she was returned to her mother in Moscow, forbidden to leave the country until her case was resolved (she was eventually released and permitted to go abroad).

If Maria was prototype of countless other suspects, the police were filling prisons and burdening investigative bureaus with needless work.

V.'s brother Dmitri underwent a similar experience. It is doubtful that the charges against him of passing agitational leaflets to factory workers in Kiev was a punishable offense. But for months, Volodya's letters to his mother included the query: "What about Mitya's case?" After numerous interrogations, followed by "exile" to various towns of European Russia, he was released. Thereafter he traveled about in search of a university that would accept him. Again, it was guilt by association. Handsome, bearded Dmitri—with heavy, well-groomed hair, and serious eyes that suggested a retiring personality—was the antithesis of a characteristic revolutionary. But since one brother was hanged and the other considered a serious threat to the *status quo*, the police were taking no chances.

Dmitri eventually graduated with a medical degree, found employment in the provinces, married a young woman with revolutionary sympathies, sired two children, and outlived his brother by 19 years. He died in relative obscurity, memorialized by a small street in Moscow: "Dmitri Ulyanov Ulitsa."

Nadya, late 1890s

Anna and Maria, 1912

The House at Ufa

Anna, on the other hand, merited surveillance. At age 22 she joined the revolutionary movement and subsequently became a Social Democrat. Her marriage to Mark Yelizarov, who was likewise politically active, increased the possibility of her being apprehended. Later she served as go-between for Volodya and Russian publishers of socialist literature, as well as a medium for conspiratorial correspondence and underground literature. During V.'s exile and afterwards, Anna was his principal agent in St. Petersburg and Moscow, a member of the *Iskra* organization, and a guardian of Party interests after her brother emigrated. Moving throughout Russia and Siberia, sometimes with her husband, sometimes alone, she also traveled abroad freely and returned to Russia at her own discretion.

For a time, these activities were carried on with impunity. Anna's continuing political freedom is not easily explained. Was it because she practiced
exceptional caution? At the time of her husband's first arrest (see below), she
left Russia for Germany. V. helped her find lodgings in Munich where she spent
her days studying in the municipal library. Later she went to Berlin. When
Mark was released, she returned to Russia, seemingly ignored by the police.
She was, however, under constant surveillance, although it was not until 1904
that she was arrested and imprisoned (at the same time, Mark, Dmitri and
Dmitri's new wife were arrested.) Meanwhile, she lived under a cloud. But
with selfless dedication to the Cause, she accepted its implicit perils, and her
less attractive personal qualities were counterbalanced by this commitment, as
well as her loyalty to family.

Mark Yelizarov first met Anna in 1893 when they joined the Social-Democratic Party in Moscow. Their common interests established a marital bond
which may have been more practical than romantic. Nevertheless, it was a congenial relationship. Anna's family treated him like a blood relative, and he in
turn adopted them. Seven years older than Volodya, his mature advice as well
as assistance in looking after Maria Alexandrovna, were invaluable. For example, when M.A. decided to move, it was Mark who searched for an apartment
and helped her relocate. Together with Anna, he fulfilled many of V.'s requests
while the latter was in exile. The two men shared several interests, including
chess and hunting.

During his brother-in-law's exile, Mark was a student at the Moscow Engineering Institute of the Ministry of Railways. Suddenly, on the night of February 28, 1901, he was arrested and imprisoned (at the same time as Maria).
V. wrote to him from Munich, suggesting ways of maintaining his health during solitary confinement in a cold, damp cell. "You must establish a regimen
of exercise," Volodya counseled him, repeating what he had told Maria.

After his release, Mark returned to his studies and subsequently found
employment at the railway company. As a supervisor, he was in touch with
labor unrest and thus in position to engage in political activity. Since his work
took him to outlying regions of Russia and occasionally to Siberia (at one time
he was assigned to Vladivostok), distance from the seat of authority provided
a degree of freedom from police surveillance. For a considerable time after his
first arrest and release, he eluded apprehension. Later, as the government accelerated its campaign against dissidents, Mark, together with Anna, Dmitri and
Dmitri's wife, was arrested. Thereafter, he led the precarious existence of a
marginal "state criminal" and was imprisoned several times. Deeply involved
in the Social Democratic Movement, Mark's life was divided between bread-
winning and Party work. He was also a family man. The little boy he and his
wife adopted would become one of only three Ulyanov heirs.

Of the family, only Maria Alexandrovna remained immune from the authorities. She was a frequent visitor to police headquarters and departments of inquiry, and apparently regarded as a mediator rather than an abettor of her children's activities. Dressed in a widow's gown, already over sixty years of age, her demeanor commanded respect. And thus she was treated.

Affection and concern for the family were her priorities.

But as a political person, Volodya's mother was hardly a nonentity. She understood the issues, was conversant with Marxism, and knew personally the individuals whose names recur in the correspondence with Volodya and his wife. She offered constructive listening to all—whether friends or comrades— who stopped by her apartment.

Some of her qualities were bequeathed to her children, but sentimentality was not among them. That she was warmly affectionate is evidenced by Nadya's manner of addressing her mother-in-law. If M.A. gave the impression of hardness, it was partly the mantle of old age, and otherwise a result of native and cultivated intelligence. A woman who had borne six children and buried two of them was, of necessity, a realist.

Since there are no references to church attendance or religious faith in extant letters, one assumes that Maria Alexandrovna was an atheist. For most of the 19th Century, the *avantgarde* intelligentsia was anti-clerical. Although historians attribute this to the spread of Marxism, it stemmed from wider concerns relating to abuses of the Russian Orthodox Church. Unaffected by the Reformation or the Roman Catholic reforming Council of Trent, it had deteriorated both morally and spiritually. If Volodya's mother was a latterday convert to atheism *per se,* nevertheless it is probable that she had, for a considerable time, been in harmony with the prevailing trend.

Although it is unfruitful to speculate about another's emotions, one may nevertheless conjecture the following: Three years earlier, while her eldest son Alexander lay in prison under sentence of death, did she pray for his deliverance? He had only to confess and plead for clemency. That he did not do so (confession meant betraying his friends), automatically condemned him. While Olga lay dying of typhoid fever in 1891, did she again pray? These unanswered prayers may have initiated a sense that Divine intervention in human affairs was either unreliable or nonexistent. Nadya's own mother underwent a similar experience: "I was religious in my youth," said Yelizaveta, "but as I lived on and learned life, I saw it was all nonsense."

In coming to terms with the material world, Maria Alexandrovna acquired a presence which spared her the indignity of persecution and prosecution by an authority that went by the book.

Ufa was founded about the time Tsar Ivan the Terrible proposed marriage to England's Queen Elizabeth I. Although not historically a medieval city, its flavor of antiquity lingered, since the Renaissance had been curbed a short distance beyond the borders of Russia. A small wooden *Kreml* survived as a reminder of the turbulent past when Russian settlers, pushing eastward, battled with primitive tribesmen. By 1900 the settlement had become an industrial center whose inhabitants numbered approximately 50,000. Most of them were laborers who resided in an agglomeration of small wooden houses.

Although mine owners, factory owners and managers, as well as merchants, enjoyed a life-style far above that of their employees, the general level was inferior to Russia's western cities of comparable size. Unpaved streets, poor lighting, and limited educational facilities indicated that it was a city dedicated to profits for the few at the expense of the many. Nor had it been different in the past when wealth from iron, copper and timber—aided by the State Church—erected several notable landmarks: two cathedrals, numerous small churches and a theological seminary.

Despite its location west of the Ural Mountains, Ufa was more Siberian than Russian; the same boxlike houses amid primitive surroundings; the same streets which became rivers of mud during spring thaws, dusty in summer, hard-frozen impassable humps in winter. The town's single gesture toward its proletariat was a small municipal library.

In response to a telegram, the Shushenskoye exiles found several comrades awaiting them on the station platform. A warm meal and beds for the night were offered by the fraternal network which provided a support system for its members throughout Russia. Volodya spent the following two days helping his family settle in a modest furnished apartment in Priyutskaya Street, "Kulikova's House." Meals were provided by the landlady. Because he was breaking his journey to Pskov without permission, the need for haste was imperative if he were to steal a few hours with his mother on the way through Moscow. It is questionable whether at this time he had finalized plans for his own future and that of his wife. Options were discussed, but the final choice was not theirs to make. Unless V. could obtain permission to leave Russia, his post-exile life, without income or prospects for regular employment, meant further dependence upon his family, hence inability to support his wife and her mother. Nor, under the circumstances, would Nadya be able to find gainful employment. Her roots were in Petersburg, the city that had expelled her and to which both she and Volodya were forbidden to return.

Soon after arriving in Pskov, Volodya petitioned to have Nadya spend her final year of exile with him. But when Maria was arrested and exiled to Nizhny-Novgorod, the possibility vanished that old transgressions would be forgiven or concessions granted.

Consistent with her usual equanimity in letters to the family, Nadya was giving the impression of contentment. But a detailed letter to Maria Alexandrovna, written soon after Volodya departed Ufa, has not survived. Did his mother destroy it because Nadya revealed too much of her personal feelings?

"Please forgive me," Nadya wrote V.'s sister Maria a week later, "somehow I could not write at that time." Alone on the station platform, she had watched the train bearing her husband disappear in the frosty gloom of a March morning. The day after he left, a cousin of his living near Ufa came over to console her. "She was very nice and awfully kind," Nadya said. "I felt a twinge of conscience—I do not know how to be nice to people. I wanted to demonstrate my kindness by offering to help her make jam, only I remembered in time that I have never made any jam and the Lord only knows what I might have made."

During the long wait for a letter telling Nadya that her husband had arrived at Pskov, she became increasingly despondent. But his first letter, which she received weeks later, was reassuring. In it he repeated what he written to his mother: "I sent an application about Nadya on the 10th and shall soon be expecting an answer. If worst come to worst, and the answer is unfavorable, I am really thinking of asking you (if you are quite well enough) to go to St. Petersburg and see about it personally."

With unexpressed relief, Nadya resumed her writing, letters filled with what she called "gossip." The Siberians (meaning Gleb and Zinaida) were doing well; he had a good job as assistant manager of a railway depot at Tomsk, Zinaida was employed at Nizhneudinsk; unfortunately the two communities were a considerable distance apart. "E.E. is in ecstasies over her granddaughter. She was quite indifferent to the first. But poor Silvin is having a bad time in Riga." His barracks were "worse than a prison," the clothes given him were so bad that he had to purchase his own. In addition, his company had a record of brutality. He wrote that soldiers received ten rubles for every worker killed, and that when on patrol the men opened fire on their own initiative. Olga, eager to join her husband, was living alone in a city of political strife.

Nadya had broken with Apollinariya: "To me she is now an X. I don't understand her any more. She is not the person I knew, and there is no use writing about the mists, the weather, and so on, and she doesn't seem to want to write about anything else." Nadya's friend had joined the disenchanted. While not severing connections with the League, Apollinariya was veering toward "Bernstein-ism," the ideology of a group that was in the process of rewriting Karl Marx. This movement embraced the same type of socio/political compromise exemplified by Economism.

A change of direction by Apollinariya was consistent with her ambition to "do something," to become an entity among the male intellectuals in the League. By taking issue with their ideological stance, she was posing as a thinker, wading beyond her intellectual capacity in areas shunned by wiser female colleagues. Nadya, on the other hand, had early accepted her own position among the men, albeit not as an intellectual inferior. But she had no desire to compete. For Apollinariya, however, compromise between active Marxism and domesticity was unthinkable. Although recently married to K.M.

Takhtariev, she maintained her independence. "To tell the truth, I cannot reconcile myself to Apollinariya's marriage. Her husband created the impression on me of a kind of narrow self-assurance." Hastily withdrawing from further criticism, Nadya concluded: "But I have said too much on this subject."

There is a suggestion that Apollinariya's marriage was an act of defiance—or self defense. Having lost out to Nadya (in relation to Volodya), was she attempting to prove something by this seeming *mésalliance*? Neither Nadya nor Volodya appears to have been aware of possible "sour grapes," on Apollinariya's side, or that her ideological estrangement was similarly motivated.

Volodya's efforts to have his wife join him in Pskov were met with official silence. "It looks as if I shall not be able to move from here for a long time," Nadya observed. "I am glad that Maria Alexandrovna may possibly go to visit Volodya. It is a pity that he has to live away from the family."

In order to reassure his mother, V.'s letters to her were optimistic. He was well, and "today I am trying to do without the mineral water." He was looking forward to a visit from Yuly (Martov) on the latter's way from exile. On the whole, Volodya gave the impression of being a tourist adrift in strange surroundings, one who filled the lonely hours by walking around to view the sights. Although Pskov was hardly a tourist's mecca, he was collecting postcards to send home.

But after a month's separation, both V. and N.K. became ill. Nadya was stricken with a serious gynecological ailment. "I am sending her some more money," V. wrote his mother. "I received 100 rubles from the publisher. Her treatment will be expensive. The doctor says possibly *six weeks* in bed, so she could not come to me now, even if she had permission." He had given up hope that permission would be granted.

In order to disguise their melancholy from each other and the family, Nadya and Volodya adopted what would become a rhetorical formula; "rather" lonely, "thinking of doing." It was their way of denying reality, even to themselves. In Volodya's case, such deliberate denial implied a sense of vagueness—unless compared with his personality *in toto*. If his personal relationships were conducted with tact, in business and professional matters he was exacting to a degree that could be exasperating.

He wrote to his mother: "I am thinking of asking permission to spend six weeks in Ufa with my wife." In fact, he was thinking about nothing else and, permission or not, would go on foot if necessary. Meanwhile, he was taking German lessons at 50 kopeks each, "but there is not much progress." The index to his Webb translation remained unfinished, and letters from comrades unanswered. His 'catarrh' and insomnia had become chronic; he continued to lose weight. And Nadya wrote nothing concerning her illness except to her husband.

By the time V. received word that his wife was recovering, he had been given permission to emigrate. However, there was still no reply to his request about Ufa. To his mother he wrote: "I am awaiting an answer. But whether I shall be allowed to live with Nadya for six weeks is questionable. I may have to make do with a shorter period." Then a P.S.: "I have been refused permission to go to Ufa! I am at a loss what to do!" Several days later he received permission to visit his mother. "Please tell me how to find you in Podolsk"—a town near Moscow which was used as a summer residence by the family.

Meanwhile, Maria Alexandrovna had apparently gone to Petersburg with a plea, since permission was eventually granted for her son to visit his ailing wife.

Elated at the resolution of his various permissions, Volodya busied himself with preparations for the forthcoming journeys, both within the country and beyond. Personal belongings, principally books, had to be disposed of, as well as financial settlement with publishers. Above all was the need to establish a means of communication with Social Democrats after he left Russia. For this purpose, he made an illegal trip to Petersburg where he was promptly arrested. After ten days in jail on flimsy charges, he was released and sent under police escort to his mother in Podolsk.

Happy at being brought nearer to Ufa, Volodya, together with his mother and sister Anna, embarked on a cruise down the Volga with Ufa as their destination. It turned out to be a veritable holiday they would remember for years afterward. On the meandering river under cloudless skies, the trip was idyllic. A short distance south of Kazan, their steamer entered the Kama River flowing east where it joined the Belaya which would take them to Ufa.

Although Nadya had prepared for their arrival, she was disappointed in the way things turned out. "I was so distracted that my thoughts all flew away. There was so much I wanted to say. But there were other visitors and I did not have a real talk at all. And I don't know when I shall see them again." It was not the first time that her anticipation of a quiet discussion dissolved in confusion. Once before, under similar conditions, she had mentioned a feeling of frustration.

In a subsequent letter she apologized to V.'s mother: "I am sorry you and Anyuta got such a poor impression of Ufa; the weather was very muggy at the time, and our place was all higgledy-piggledy." Bourgeois habits prevailed. Despite pecuniary or other liabilities, no respectable person dreamed of spending winter and summer in the same location. Nadya and her mother, having earlier moved to summer quarters, were now preparing to return to Priyutskaya Street. The summer flat was in disarray. Never an exemplary housekeeper, Nadya was further encumbered by her illness; she had not yet fully recovered.

The apartment to which they returned, although in the same house, was not the one they had occupied earlier. It consisted of two rooms and a kitchen, newly decorated, and located on the ground floor with a garden under the windows. With cooking facilities, they would now "eat in," thereby saving money and providing Yelizaveta with more to do than being sick and home-sick—not that her ill health was psychosomatic. Nadya found pupils to teach and was studying German with a native Berliner. "I had some difficulty per-suading him to take me twice a week. He is a real chatterbox, so I may get something out of it." She was too busy with German to go anywhere and felt herself becoming unsociable.

No longer counting the days until her release, she found it unnecessary to simulate calm. Routine brought a semblance of normalcy, and by autumn Ufa had become home. Her pupils provided a small income, and language study was a link with the future; V.'s first letter from Europe was postmarked Munich. The only drawback was Ufa's mud. "You could drown in it," she said. Evenings when there was supposed to be a moon, streets were unlit and "'you are quite likely to fall into a ditch." One of her lessons was given in a pupil's home at night.

Before long, however, again there was turmoil. Ufa was to European Rus-sia what Krasnoyarsk was to Siberia: a collecting point for exiles. In addition to those being sent eastward, a steady flow of returnees stopped off in Ufa on their way home. Nadya's apartment began to serve as a halfway house, and before long it resembled a miniature railway depot. Luggage piled up in the entry, soiled dishes overflowed the sink, cigarette smoke smudged the walls and clogged the stale, heavy air. The excitement of release acted as a stimulant; comrades were loathe to go to bed. Some of them slept on the floor, others retired to another comrade's apartment in early morning hours. Nadya was exhausted. Forced to abandon her German lessons, she complained that although a certain amount of turmoil was natural, "when there is turmoil in Ufa, it is like nothing on earth."

Returning exiles brought word of those they had left behind. Zinaida, usu-ally healthy and ebullient, was thin and pale, a shadow of her former self. Although she was eager to return to Russia, her husband liked his work in Tomsk and was content to remain in Siberia. They were making no plans to leave. Silvin had reportedly been through a bad time. After being transferred from Riga to a Krasnoyarsk regiment, he had immediately been marched off to an unknown destination. His wife Olga, having followed him to Siberia, found herself alone in Krasnoyarsk and was seeking a means of support.

In a letter from Lydia Knippovich, still being detained in a Petersburg jail, Nadya learned that she was asking to be sent to Ufa. "I should like very much to see her before I leave," N.K. noted, "but I wonder if she will be able to get transferred."

With the coming of winter—an early arrival at that latitude—a decreasing flow of exiles lessened the tension. Nadya resumed her German studies and waded through snow on her way to teach. It was not unlike her dream of becoming a village schoolmistress. Recovered from her illness, she embraced this seemingly mundane existence with enthusiasm. "I like teaching," she said, "and do not find it tiring." The pupils gave her pleasure, and one in particular she found captivating. "This little girl waits for me on the stairway every time and is simply 'longing' to read, write and do arithmetic. Such wonderful children do exist!" Among her pupils were five children of a millionaire merchant.

Nadya was extremely interested in the children's family life. In particular, she admired the methods of her merchant family. "The parents do not dress them up, they have very few toys, no nursemaids, plenty of freedom, the youngsters are in the street all day, the children clean their own boots (even wash clothes). In general there is nothing aristocratic about them and they are not spoiled." But she added that her favorite pupil had not been "drilled." "She sometimes wipes her nose on her frock." Nadya's only complaint was of too much time wasted in going about Ufa to give lessons which she felt were "foolishly arranged."

Days were busy and full. French had been added to German studies, and there were suggestions from Munich that she resume her study of English, "but I don't suppose I shall follow his advice; Volodya has an *idée fixé* about languages." As in Shusha, proficiency in a foreign tongue continued to elude her. "Nobody here knows any languages, so I with my half-baked knowledge am considered a specialist in this field." Her day ended at 8 p.m., but rarely an evening passed without someone stopping by. She had little opportunity to be considered anti-social.

Although several months of exile still remained, Nadya summarized her current feelings with the simplicity of one who chose to accept each day on its own terms

> There is nothing so very bad about Ufa except the mud, and I have long since become an Ufa patriot. We have adapted ourselves to provincial life. Five months and eleven days—I no longer know whether that is much or little. Time goes like a machine that has been wound up.

Often life resembled a carousel. Round and round it went. Zinaida had again grown fat and happy, while her husband became thin and despondent. Silvin was back in Krasnoyarsk after his army trek in the Siberian wilds. Yelizaveta was well for a while, but then became ill: "First she has palpitations, then she catches cold." Nadya herself was well, although her next letter revealed that she was recovering from influenza. The German lessons were going well, but a few days later, "I am making little progress." "Volodya seldom writes." But soon afterward a batch of letters arrived—some chronologically out of order. Passage down the highway of time was beset by twists and turns that frequently reversed direction.

As Christmas approached, Nadya prepared to celebrate without constraint.

If not religious, it would at least be festive. Her pupils were given a fortnight's leave, the French teacher went on holiday, German lessons were suspended until after the New Year. "I began today by cleaning up the house," announced her letter of December 22nd to Volodya's mother and sister Maria, "and finishing all kinds of unfinished jobs. I am in a real holiday-eve mood. This letter will not reach you in time for the holidays, but I wish you, dear people, a Happy New Year. I send you many kisses and wish you everything, everything that is good."

Notwithstanding a daily temperature of 30° below and frequent snowstorms, Nadya bundled up in her mother's fur coat and felt boots and went shopping for Christmas treats. Like a child let out of school, she abandoned herself to the highly charged atmosphere generated by the season. But there was more. "I get lost in wild ideas if I think of spring and my journey." She noted that her friends were all "nervous wrecks," subject to moods, "but why let oneself go—that I cannot understand." Thereafter, she proceeded to "let herself go," preaching to them the necessity of remaining even-tempered. "But I got so angry that I proved brilliantly that I was not even-tempered." Her sermon elicited a burst of laughter.

There were no post-holiday blues this year. "Today the sun is shining in a joyful, spring-like way, and I just dream of spring, I keep returning to the idea that there are only six weeks left and then . . . then I shall be quite crazy with joy, especially when I have traveled to where Volodya is." Nadya felt herself growing lazy, and instead of the regimen of early rising and structured days, she was lounging about in a dressing-gown after breakfast, reading silly novels. A spring mood of *ennui* sent her out to wander about the streets.

During more sober moments, she worked on a translation of French into Russian to which she mysteriously alluded. When "our people" began contributing articles to the Samara* *Gazette*, Nadya emulated them. "I would like to get into the literary world, but I just hate the stuff I write." Nevertheless, she attained a measure of success with publication of her article, *The School and Life*.

Temporarily, she was more successful than Volodya. His articles sent to *Nauchnoye Obozreniye* ("Scientific Review," Petersburg) had not been rejected but merely ignored, and he was asking Nadya to retrieve them on her way through Russia to emigration (she called the editor a blockhead). And after reading V.'s *Development of Capitalism*, Mark Yelizarov found it "dry",—too scholarly—and "nobody" was going to digest the statistical tables upon which V. had lavished painstaking work. Recently, Nadya had received a letter from comrades begging to know where they might obtain V.'s *Essays and Studies*; it

---

* A city 275 miles southwest of Ufa, a center of Social Democrat activity.

was not on sale "anywhere." (The vicissitudes of creative writers are not limited to time and place!).

"Just one month left. Wonderful, isn't it? The time will come when there is just one day left! Yes, everything will come!" Nadya's joyous anticipation was echoed from Munich, less emotional but nevertheless intense: "Fewer than two months remain to the end of Nadya's term of exile. In summer I hope that we shall be together."

Last-minute requests from Ufa to Moscow included a capitalist item. Yelizaveta had purchased a lottery ticket, but the drawing would take place in April after she had left Ufa. N.K. wrote Maria Alexandrovna: "Please insure it. The fee will be three rubles, and keep the receipt yourself. Hoping to see you soon..."

However, Nadya was suddenly beset by fears that her departure from Russia would be delayed by red tape, or worse, that she would be denied permission. For a married woman, emigration depended upon her husband's consent. But Volodya was in Europe. Official delay or silence? V. informed his mother: "I am in Vienna to arrange for Nadya's passport. I think there should be no hitch with it now, and I hope she will soon be seeing you." His letter was dated seven days before Nadya's scheduled release. The Russian Consul in Vienna must have been Europeanized, moving with celerity. His telegram to St. Petersburg prodded the sluggish bureaucracy to affirmative action. The Day was at hand.

Although the future was still uncharted, a footnote to Nadya's life in Ufa carries a moral. After Christmas, her French class was disbanded, and "the Frenchman teaches me very perfunctorily when I go alone." With the aid of a crystal ball, that gentleman might have been more diligent. If he was still alive in 1918, what must have been his thoughts! The pupil who had bored him in Ufa was living in Moscow—in the Kremlin.

Early morning, March 11, 1901. The train for Moscow is about to leave. Nadya and her mother bid their friends a tearful farewell on the station platform. Helped aboard with their luggage and a hamper of sandwiches, they settle in a compartment. Ghosts from another life—prison, Shushenskoye, Ufa—ride with them for a time, fading at last as the train steams westward through those places whose names spell Russia and home.

No. 1, Dec., 1900

Tsarist police interrogating *Iskra* readers

5. The First Emigration and *Iskra*

In 1902, "Ulyanov" became "Lenin." After experimenting with numerous pseudonyms, he had chosen "Ilyin," his father's given name, but later decided that it was euphonically awkward. In contrast to Ilyin, "Lenin" was easily transliterated to foreign languages, and the initial consonant gave it force and character. With the establishment of *Iskra,* he began writing editorials under the name by which he would henceforth be known. (There was a rumor that "Lenin" derived from the River Lena.)

When V. was arrested in St. Petersburg on his way from Pskov to Ufa, he was carrying two thousand rubles donated by Kalmukova, owner of a book warehouse in the Capital. Her code name was "Auntie." Now 52 years old, she had long been a political activist—first in the *Narodnaya Volya* movement, later an adherent of Plekhanov's Emancipation of Labor. When the latter moved its headquarters to Switzerland, she joined the Petersburg League of Struggle whose leaders often held meetings in her warehouse. Her contribution was earmarked for *Iskra.*

During exile in Siberia, V. had obtained financial commitments from several individuals; later in Ufa, while visiting Nadya, he made contacts which led to support for his projected publication. With the help of Martov, after the latter's arrival in Pskov, he acquired additional financial backing, and upon leaving Russia, he possessed sufficient funds to establish the newspaper. Temporarily, he was self-supporting. From Germany he wrote his mother: "There is no need to worry about my finances; I have received 250 rubles from the publisher, and Mark sent me 75 rubles from the sale of my gun. In case of need, I will let you know in advance."

Iskra, printed abroad, was to be shipped by clandestine routes for distribution in Russia. But since kopeks from the sale of the periodical would not cover its cost, much of V.'s time, in addition to writing articles and supervising production, was devoted to acquiring additional financial support.

Editorial policy was directed by a joint board comprised of Georgii Plekhanov, Paul Axelrod and Vera Zasulich—from the Emancipation of Labor group—and three from Germany: Lenin, Martov and A.N. Potressov, a publisher, journalist and bookseller who had been exiled for participating in the League of Struggle. Potressov was an indifferent journalist, but a valuable addition to the team for his expertise in the mechanics of publishing. Thus an editorial balance of forces existed between Munich and Switzerland.

Compared to Russia, Germany's political climate was laissez-faire, but tsarist spies were active abroad, and continuing secrecy was necessary if *Iskra*'s

Russian contacts—persons delegated to distribute the journal and maintain lines of communication with Germany—were not to be jeopardized. Moreover, *Iskra* was designed as an organization that would have agents throughout Europe as well as in Russia to promote its objectives and direct their implementation.

The Russian October Revolution of 1917 began with *Iskra*, but at the time of the paper's founding, Lenin was not speculating on the future. The present task, as he perceived it, was to awaken the proletariat. Circumstances alone would determine the fate of *Iskra* and prospects for salvation of the Fatherland. Whether "The Spark" would ignite a flame was problematical.

After spending several days with Maria Alexandrovna in Moscow, Nadya went to Petersburg where she made temporary arrangements for the care of her mother. The ensuing journey to join her husband was a nightmare. Never having been outside the borders of her native land, Nadya "made her way" as she aptly described it, across the frontier and boarded a train for Prague. How she coped with the Czech language is a mystery.

Having sent a telegram, she expected to be met at the depot, but no one appeared. Disconcerted, she hailed a cabby and directed him to the address of a Czech who, as it turned out, had merely provided a forwarding address for V.'s letters to Ufa. After being fed "klosse" by the man's little white-haired wife, she was given an address in Munich. Since by April the weather had turned warm, she checked her fur coat and luggage at the Munich railway station and took a tram for the house of a certain "Herr Rittmeyer." It turned out to be a beer shop.

"I went to the counter, behind which stood a plump German, and timidly asked for Herr Rittmeyer. 'That's me,' he said. 'No. it's my husband,' I faltered. We stood staring at one another like a couple of idiots, until Rittmeyer's wife walked in and, looking at me, guessed what was the matter. 'Ach, you must be the wife of Herr Meyer; he is expecting his wife from Siberia. I'll take you to him.' I followed Frau Rittmeyer through the backyard of a big house into a kind of uninhabited apartment. The door opened, and there at a table sat Volodya, his sister Anna, and Martov. Forgetting to thank the landlady, I cried: 'Why the devil didn't you write and tell me where I could find you?'

"'Didn't write you!' exclaimed V. 'Why, I've been going three times a day to meet you. Where have you sprung from?'" Later they discovered that a friend to whom a book had been sent—in which was concealed the Munich address—kept the book to read! (Similar episodes bedeviled the émigrés. One Russian was sent to Genoa instead of Geneva; another, instead of going to London, had been about to start for America.)

Nadya stayed with her husband for several days, during which he complained about the Swiss contingent. He had locked horns with Plekhanov—via the post—on organizational matters. The latter, a tall, middle-aged man with large head and prominent features, was a gifted though pompous intellectual. Peering through glasses, he easily intimidated the young socialists who sought him out in his Swiss retreat. He was now demanding that publication of *Iskra* be moved to Switzerland, apparently with intent to dominate its editorial policy. Although V. was personally fond of him, to relinquish control of the project was unthinkable. This preliminary skirmish was followed by ideological disagreements.

In contrast to Plekhanov, who confined himself to pontification, Axelrod was an organizer through whose hands passed whatever correspondence *Emancipation* carried on with Russia. It was Axelrod who interviewed occasional socialist pilgrims after they had been rebuffed by Plekhanov. Unfortunately, his energy became diffused, driving him first in one direction, then another, to the detriment of his health. V., reading the disjointed scrawl of an Axelrod letter, observed: "It's simply awful to get in such a state as Pavel Borisich."

There was a parallel with Munich, where Martov was the talker and Lenin the doer. Matters reached a point where Lenin had to ask Martov to keep his distance; the talk was driving him to distraction.

When Nadya arrived in Munich, she found Volodya living in a small, poorly-furnished room at Herr Rittmeyer's and taking his meals with a German woman who fed him on *mehlspeisse*. "Morning and evening he drank tea out of a tin mug which he washed thoroughly and hung on a nail by the tap."

Soon afterward, they went to live with a German working-class family whose six members lived in the kitchen. "I decided to put Volodya on home-cooked food, so I organized the cookery. Although using the landlady's kitchen, I had to prepare everything in our room. I tried to make as little noise as possible, as V. was then beginning to write his pamphlet *What Is To Be Done?*" When composing a literary work, it was his habit to walk briskly up and down the room, whispering the projected text to himself. Once he had mentally assembled his ideas, he and Nadya would take a walk together and discuss these ideas.

For Nadya, housekeeping in a single room was difficult, and it became necessary to find more spacious quarters. They rented a small house in the new development of Schwabing, a Munich suburb and, as Nadya described it, "lived in our own fashion."

Their first visitor was Martov, "who talked interminably, and kept switching from one subject to another." Subsequent board meetings with Martov and Vera Zasulich (in Munich as representative of *Emancipation*) lasted far into the night, leaving V. exhausted. Eventually he asked to be excused. "But Martov could not exist without these talks. After leaving us, he would go with Vera to some café where they sat for hours." He began to attach himself to each newly arrived émigré.

At age 29, Martov was hardly a dotty old man, but he was already displaying characteristics that eventually contributed to the break-up of *Iskra's* editorial board. This dissension in turn precipitated a division in the Russian Social-Democratic Party.

But it was Paul Axelrod who became a greater impediment to the smooth administration of *Iskra*. "Pavel had lost three-quarters of his working capacity," noted N.K. "He did not sleep for nights at a stretch and wrote with extreme intensity for months on end, without being able to finish the articles he had started." (Axelrod was in his 50th year.) He now insisted that all communications with Russia pass through his hands. In short, he was demanding to be secretary of *Iskra*. This, together with Plekhanov's request that the newspaper's headquarters be moved to Switzerland, posed a dilemma.

To counter it, V. appointed Nadya secretary. Since both he and his wife had already done the leg work for *Iskra*, this move was not unreasonable. Their experience with codes, false-bottomed trunks, in addition to the hundreds of contacts they had developed on both sides of the Russian border, justified V.'s desire not to lose control of the publication. Nor could he imagine the wives of Plekhanov and Axelrod dressing up as workers and distributing leaflets in the factories. Henceforth, Nadya would be key for sending and receiving communications. With her impeccable handwriting and experience in the Movement, she was a logical choice. V. was accused of usurping authority, but the same could have been leveled against Plekhanov and Axelrod.

The balance of power was upset by Vera Zasulich. A nervous, feverishly active woman who chain-smoked, Vera was a talented journalist and Marxist scholar, a dedicated socialist whose loyalties were about to shift. V. wrote to his wife in Ufa: "Wait till you see Vera; there's a person as clear as crystal" In the beginning, Vera told him bluntly: "Your *Iskra* is silly." Later, she modified her opinion, with doubtful benefit to Plekhanov and Axelrod. V. liked and admired her, but nevertheless was amused by her ways. "Vera doesn't write an article, she constructs a mosaic—painfully, piece by piece."

Despite their obvious character differences, Nadya and Vera became close friends. Vera described to her the long, cold years of emigration when the Swiss group had been isolated from contact with Russia. She believed that Plekhanov's imperiousness resulted from lack of information concerning political developments at home, causing him to retreat into subjective speculation.

"Of the *Emancipation of Labor* group, Vera was the most lonely," observed Nadya. Both Plekhanov and Axelrod had families, and Vera often spoke about her loneliness: "I have nobody close to me," she said. Then immediately trying to hide her feelings, she bantered, "but you love me, I know. And when I die you'll say—'dear me, we're drinking one cup of tea less.'" Nadya thought how greatly she needed a family. N.K.'s *Memoir* includes a vignette of Zasulich:

Nobody guessed the qualities Vera possessed as family woman and housekeeper. She lived in nihilist fashion—dressed carelessly, smoked incessantly, and extraordinary disorder reigned in her room. She never allowed anyone else to tidy it up. She also ate in a rather fantastic fashion. Once she cooked herself some meat on an oil stove, clipping off pieces to eat with a pair of scissors.

When Vera was writing, she shut herself in her room and fed on strong coffee alone. But later, after joining a commune, she became a good housekeeper, carefully purchasing the provisions when her turn came to cook dinner. This woman, who had been raised in a foster home, loved children. One had only to see how tenderly she treated the pale little son of a comrade.

When Nadya first met her, Vera was 53 years old, but she resembled the beautiful young girl whose exceptional intellect had alienated her from the traditional feminine role.

In founding *Iskra*, one of Lenin's objectives was to unify the splinter Russian socialist groups abroad and integrate them with those of Russia. He could not have foreseen that joining forces with Plekhanov and Axelrod would prove to be a tactical error. Meanwhile, Vera acted as mediator.

Lenin, while avoiding contact with rank-and-file German socialists, sought the company of their leaders. In anticipating world unity of the proletariat, he was likewise in touch with their counterparts in France, England, Belgium, Holland, Switzerland, Austria, Austrian Poland, German Poland, and countries of the Balkans. These international leaders, including several women, were engaged in political activities which ranged from so-called "legal" socialism—i.e., permission by the authorities to publish and distribute innocuous literature—to "illegal" underground Marxism. Whatever their status, whether legal or illegal, they maintained a mutual solidarity *contra* the police; thus Lenin's anonymity was rarely in jeopardy (both he and Nadya were registered with Bulgarian passports under assumed names).

Rosa Luxemburg came to Munich where Lenin met and conferred with her. A Polish Social Democrat, brilliant Marxist, theoretician and talented speaker, Rosa easily dominated left-wing factions in both her native land and Germany. Lenin called her "an eagle soaring above the chickens"—referring to her intellectual superiority. She was a small, dynamic woman with expressive black eyes and dark, glossy hair. Despite a childhood injury to her hip which caused her to limp, she exuded irresistible charm. What V. thought about her liaison with Leo Jogiches, another Polish S-D, he kept to himself.

However, Vladimir and Rosa, two stubborn individualists, soon found themselves at odds ideologically; for the time being, their primary area of agreement was activism.

Through Rosa, Lenin met Klara Zetkin, a German national who lived in Stuttgart but traveled around Europe in connection with the Socialist Women's Movement that she had helped to establish. Klara had been a close friend of Frederick Engels.

Although hardly in a class with Rosa intellectually, Klara was able to hold her own with European Marxist scholars. Her marriages—first to a man considerably older, and later as a widow married to one much younger—were not happy, but this did not affect her relations with other persons. Upon first meeting her, they instantly responded to her warm smile and outgoing manner. She gave the impression of clasping all humanity in a loving embrace. Among her assets were enthusiasm, and an unusual gift of perception.

No two women could have more physically dissimilar than Rosa and Klara. In contrast to small, dark, Jewish Rosa, Klara was a statuesque blond. Emotionally, they shared an ideal and a friendship. But Klara was not an ideologue like Rosa. Consequently, Lenin's earthy approach to social reform appealed to her, and she became his faithful ally. Nadya didn't meet either Rosa or Klara at this time. However, many years later the tall, stylish German woman became a cherished friend.

Why Munich? It was not happenstance that exactly twenty years after the founding of *Iskra*, Hitler stood on the table of a Munich beer hall expounding National Socialism (a contradiction in terms).

Historiography has often been carried away by events in Russia, neglecting the early socialist movement in Germany, one that became firmly rooted in Munich long before the turn of the century. In short, Munich was, and continued to remain, a leading center of socialist activity. In order to float his publication, Lenin needed a printing press as well as a compositor—and secrecy—all of which he expected to find in Munich. He had only to strike a bargain with a congenial publisher of socialist literature. However, the first issue of *Iskra* was printed in Leipzig, where Lenin traveled to supervise the editing. Subsequent issues were printed in Munich.

Lenin was impressed with the vigor of German Social Democracy. Although he did not consider its current leaders intellectually superior to Plekhanov and certain other Russians, he was aware of their numerical superiority. But he was skeptical of the German trend toward revising Marxism. Not only in Germany but all over Europe, what Lenin called "pseudo-Marxists" were beginning to preach a new doctrine and calling upon the befuddled proletariat to follow. It was like re-writing the Bible—omitting what seemed irrelevant, outmoded or merely distasteful.

However, theoreticians alone—whether Marxists or not—could not lead the masses. Between them and an enormous laboring class stood the shop foremen, trade union leaders, secondstring organizers, politicians, all of whom benefited, however marginally, from the *status quo*. In order to prevail, the ideologues would have to win the allegiance of this group who constituted actual leadership of the laboring classes. Heretofore, history had not provided a single example of spontaneously generated social change that had been leaderless at the grassroots level.

But to win lower-echelon leaders, theoreticians would have to arrive at an ideological consensus. At least some of the theorists agreed that unless unity could be achieved among themselves, the cause of socialism was doomed.

Lenin, although not originally a Marxist "purist" would, by gradual stages, become one, thereby saying: "You are a Marxist or you are not; there can be no quasi-Marxists." In short, he believed that to reject part of the basic Marxist program was to shred its entire fabric. His ideological position resulted from intensive study of alternative theories of social transformation, causing him to conclude that Marx had created a workable blueprint, and that it rested with the present generation of socialist leaders to interpret it with precision and act upon it decisively.

But in assuming that international unity was achievable, Lenin failed to take full account of the vacillating moods of proletarian Europe. The mere existence of militant Social Democracy seemed to indicate an impending crisis in which members of national movements would join forces with their proletarian brothers everywhere.

Likewise, he concluded that a socialist Russia could not survive in a vacuum, economically isolated among capitalist countries and thus without trading partners. These economic concerns did not, however, supersede his purely social goals, both for Russia and the world.

Once he had clarified his own thinking through study, not only of Marxism but of alternative theories of social reorganization, he began to formulate the program to which he would later adhere. It was not, however mere infatuation with Marxism, nor was he an ivory tower intellectual. He had mingled with the oppressed classes. In his view, social betterment could only be achieved by bridging the gap between theory and implementation. There were other areas of disagreement among Social Democrats, but the primary one was of talk versus action.

Whether Marx had offered revolution as a mere alternative was being debated both in Russia and Europe. Marx's abstruse language and reasoning made it difficult to extract the essence of his thought, and this was further complicated by Marx himself. When he died, his unfinished work passed to his colleague and successor, Frederick Engels. Engels was closer in thought and time to the 20th Century, but his influence on the divergent trend was negligible. The revisionists were either ignoring or discarding what Lenin considered the foundation-stone of Marxism, and were edging toward gradualism, or accommodation with the existing order, thereby creating a schism in the Socialist Movement as a whole, and Russian Marxism in particular. All that Lenin said, wrote and did was rooted in his homeland. He perceived Marxism as relevant to conditions in Russia.

Henceforth, most ideological as well as tactical disagreements between Lenin and other socialists stemmed from his rejection of Marxist revisionism. Subsequent historical development would either confirm or invalidate Lenin's conclusions.

Nadya described her first summer in Munich: "We go for walks in the countryside. Yesterday, for instance, we went on a marvelous road lined with poplars and with fields and orchards on all sides. There is a park nearby and a place to bathe." With the exception of occasional tram rides and a visit to one of the picture galleries, she and Volodya lived quietly.

From her description of Munich, it might have been an average provincial city with pleasant suburbs and a sprinkling of cultural institutions. The reality was a metropolis of imposing architecture and a tradition both rich and varied. As capital of Catholic Bavaria, it enjoyed the beneficence of kings and Church. Among its cultural assets was the Royal Library, repository of a million-plus books and rare manuscripts; its numerous art museums were among the best in Europe.

But Nadya and Volodya were in no mood for sightseeing or mere browsing. If, as they expected, Munich was henceforth to be their home, they would need to become part of the social fabric. They were well aware that linguistic facility, familiarity with new ways of shopping and preparing food, and the countless subtleties of human intercourse which characterize any given society, were not easily acquired. Meanwhile, they felt like the outsiders they were, merely two among countless unassimilated Russian émigrés who flocked to Europe in search of a better life.

Many, if not all the émigrés became bitterly disillusioned. They found adjustment difficult, and their discontent and homesickness led to quarrels with fellow émigrés. Idleness was their enemy. The unskilled suffered economically, and even those with a trade or profession found it difficult to find employment. As a result, they banded together in colonies or in communes where they shared expenses and chores. Those with more financial means supported their less fortunate compatriots, to the latters' chagrin and resentment.

Having learned the value of privacy from his experience with Siberian "exile scandals,"* V. shunned the émigré colonies. Likewise, and for reasons of secrecy, he avoided contact with the garrulous Russian "politicos" outside his small circle of confrères. Thus he and Nadya suffered a dual estrangement; apart from the activity of establishing *Iskra*, their social contacts were narrowly restricted. "We have become terrible homebirds," Nadya reported to her husband's family. As in Shushenskoye, they waited hungrily for letters, "but our friends in Russia seem to have forgotten that we exist."

---

* The Russian word "skandal" means "row" or "quarrel" rather than moral offense, as in English.

Like many intelligent women, Nadya's inclinations were a counterpoint of domesticity, social concern, pedagogy and friendship, all of which she endeavored to reconcile harmonically. If one or another tended to dominate the melodic strands, she became vaguely unhappy. Whenever she found herself drifting toward either the purely feminine or vocational, she had only to think of Volodya in order to bring her life into balance.

> In general, life here is gradually beginning to conform to a pattern and Volodya is getting along better with his work ... As far as I am concerned, I work very little so far, or, to tell the truth, I do not work at all. Time passes, but where it goes I just don't know.
>
> I intend to visit the local schools. This place is a sort of child's kingdom. Everybody pays so much attention to them and the children are so nice and healthy. I have been to our city schools and cannot help drawing comparisons; I find that the children here live a lot better. My intentions will probably remain only intentions.

Nadya's urge to write was intermittent. In her reticence about minor successes, she neglected to mention the nature of an article for which a Petersburg woman publisher promised to pay her 600 marks.

Yelizaveta, only recently arrived from Russia, was already talking of returning home. "She is bored with our life here," reported Nadya to Maria Alexandrovna, "but I am not." Volodya thought her mood of boredom would pass: "I am trying to dissuade Y.V. from going back to St. Petersburg," he wrote, "I have told her that she will miss us."

Toward the end of summer, Plekhanov and Axelrod came to Munich to confer about *Iskra*, and one evening they all went to a café. In a gymnasium next door, fencing was in progress. "Under the new order," said Plekhanov laughingly, "we also will fight with wooden swords." On the way home, Nadya walked beside Axelrod who commented dryly: "Under the new order, there won't be any fights at all—only deadly boredom." Nadya was too shy to respond, but she was "amazed" at such a statement.

Although the meetings began with apparent equanimity, they quickly dissolved into verbal sparring. When Vera attempted to defend one of Lenin's proposals, "Plekhanov took up an intransigent pose, and, folding his arms, gave her such a look that she became quite confused; V. was greatly pained at any difference with Plekhanov. He grew restless and did not sleep at night. And Plekhanov was angry and peevish." As the "elder statesman" of Russian Marxism, Plekhanov's attitude was one of lofty disdain for those who presumed to disagree with him.

At this time, Lenin still considered Plekhanov his superior, which put him at a disadvantage in the editorial policy of *Iskra*. It was not a question of revising Marx, but of bringing theory into line with present conditions and expectations for the future. "Tactic" meant *What Is To Be Done?* (Shto Delat)—the title and substance of Lenin's tract. He was also writing a pamphlet, *Where To Begin?*

Autumn quickly dispelled the languorous mood of summer. With *Iskra* firmly established, and with Plekhanov and Axelrod back in Switzerland, "Volodya is now working quite hard and I am glad for his sake; when he throws himself completely into some task he feels well and strong—that is one of his natural qualities; he is in very good health, there does not seem to be a trace of the catarrh left and no insomnia, either. Every day he takes a cold rubdown and we go bathing almost every day, too."

For Nadya it was a time of apprenticeship. Now entrusted with full responsibility for international communications, she had little time for introspection or day-dreaming. All personal matters were preempted by *Iskra*. She understood that her life was in peril. One indiscreet move could bring an ominous knock at the door; any day her husband might not return home. Whatever hardihood she already possessed was further tempered by the Munich experience when, for the first time, she was fully exposed to the enemies of socialism.

However, life was not totally infused with "conspiratorial" fever. Quite the contrary. Like everyone else, Nadya and Volodya put on their shoes each morning and prepared to deal with the petty details of existence in which personal satisfactions were often outflanked by monotony. Nevertheless, a small happiness crept in by the back door, hardly noticed. As a consequence of dealing with tradespeople, they were beginning to use their textbook German and to develop skill that now accelerated their integration into a foreign culture.

Although they always considered themselves wholly Russian, N.K. and V. were on the threshold of becoming internationalists—in a real as opposed to a theoretical sense—thus inadvertently conforming to the socialist ideal.

In 1878, Bismarck's (German) government had passed the Exceptional Powers Act, directed specifically against the German Social Democratic Movement whose influence was spreading. The Act prohibited the right of public assembly and a free socialist press. However, Bismarck was unable to curb the prerogatives of socialist deputies in the Reichstag, and in 1890 the Assembly voted against renewing the Act. Nevertheless, repression continued. It was not until 1902 that the ban on peaceful demonstrations was lifted.

Nadya and Volodya witnessed the first German May Day* parade. She was amazed at the lack of enthusiasm. Forbidden to assemble in the streets of Munich, socialists repaired to the countryside where columns of men, their wives and children marched silently and with regimental precision, their faces deadly serious, their pockets bulging with radishes. "It did not at all resemble a demonstration of working-class triumph," Nadya concluded.

As their second year in Munich drew to a close, she would later remember

---

* May Day celebration of working-class unity originated in Chicago in 1886.

it as "a particularly bright period." "There was not yet such a deep gulf between
V., Martov, Potressov and Zasulich. All forces were concentrated on one
object—the creation of an all-Russian newspaper. These were extraordinarily
good-humored days."

Precisely at the time when many difficulties appeared to have been sur-
mounted, the socialist publisher, fearing arrest, declined to lend his printing
press. It was obvious that the project would have to be removed from Germany. The Munich group was in a quandary.

The last place V. wanted to go was Switzerland; so, after consultation, they
chose England. The nation that tolerated Hyde Park Corner might be expected
to turn a blind eye toward yet another manifestation of socialist dementia.

Regretfully, Nadya and Volodya sold the used furniture they had "bought
cheap," and shipped their books to a comrade who resided in London. On
April 10, 1902, Lenin wrote his sister Anna in Berlin:

> I am being run off my feet! We are leaving on the 12th. For the time being, in case
> anything is urgent, write to this address.
>
> > Mr. Alexejeff,
> > 14, Frederick Street
> > Gray's Inn Road,
> > London, W.C.
> > (for Lenin—inside).
>
> The address of the local doctor* is in any case valid; he will always forward let-
> ters.
>
> Thank Auntie** for the letter, which I received today (and for the books).
>
> > All the best,
> > Lenin.

Travel plans were as follows: Yelizaveta, by her own wish, would return to
St. Petersburg; Martov, Potressov and Zasulich would go to London at some
later date. When Volodya and Nadya left Munich, their immediate destination—via Stuttgart, Frankfort, Cologne—was Liège (Belgium) where, according to Nadya, "M- and his wife, old Sunday-school friends of mine, were living;
M- was knowledgeable about the Social-Democratic Movement in Belgium."
However, V. wanted to visit the Cologne Cathedral, so the journey was broken
for a few days of sightseeing.

In Liège, they found the atmosphere tense. Shortly before their arrival,
there had been a violent confrontation between police and strikers during
which the latter were fired upon. "We went to look at the House of the People.
It stood on a very unsuitable site. The crowd could easily be trapped in the
square facing the house."

From conversation with Nadya's friends, V. learned that Belgian Social-

---

* Refers to Alexeyev who was trained as a physician.
** A.M.Kalmukova, the Petersburg publisher.

Democratic leaders were mistrusted by the workers: "Troops fired on the crowd, while the labor leaders sought a pretext for pacifying them."

They departed Liège with a discomforting awareness of the widening rift in Social Democracy.

On the pier at Calais, passengers are waiting to go aboard the Channel steamer. A musty odor of timber, water-soaked and rotting, mingles with the wind. From an open grill nearby, the greasy stench of frying fish adds flavor to the last port of call before England. As the émigrés inch toward passport control, they try to conceal their nervousness, but the official merely glances at them as he stamps their papers and waves them aboard. Nadya and Volodya stand at the rail, watching the coast of France diminish to a slim wedge floating on the Channel's restless expanse. "I look at the little black dots on the map of Europe," he had once said, "and wonder if I shall ever visit those places."

Thus far the pilgrims had crossed two language zones (Belgium was not yet bilingual). They were now entering a third. During the Channel crossing, Nadya and Volodya rehearsed the textbook phrases they trusted would facilitate communication at Dover, although experiments with the crew of their English steamer—whose accent befuddled even the educated natives—were not reassuring.

The wharf at Dover was a mediocre gateway to the Empire: spars and gravel, the odor of tar and fish. From a rocky cliff rising sheer above the harbor, Dover Castle stood guard, a relic from medieval times.

When asking directions, V. found his English unintelligible. But Dover was a small town, and the pair had only to follow their fellow-passengers to the railway depot where, aided by sign language and a handful of money, they purchased tickets for London.

After the monochrome landscape of Belgium and France, they were struck by England's lush green vegetation. But as the train plunged through the Kentish countryside, their view was limited to steep banks on either side. Except for a ribbon of sky and an occasional bridge overhead, they might have been passing through a tunnel. (The railway ditches, called "cuttings," were said to have resulted from a stipulation by lordly landowners that the trains be kept out of sight.)

Upon approaching London, the right-of-way emerged into open country and gradually ascended a trestle. Below lay Southwark with its lumpy cathedral tower and rusty docks. After crossing the Thames, the train coasted eye-level with a forest of chimneypots and the upper-story windows of rowhouses, brown as mud. Charing Cross Station was a cavernous barn of steel whose lofty glass roof was obscured by grime. Belching steam, the locomotive slowed to a halt, emitting a whistle which echoed shrilly above the hum of human traffic milling about the platforms. Nadya described the weather as "dismal."

We were met by Nikolai Alexeyev, a comrade living in emigration who had a fine knowledge of English. He acted as our guide, as we were in rather a helpless position. We thought we knew English, but we could not understand a single word and nobody understood us.

For several weeks they lived in a furnished room under the name of Richter: "To English people, all foreigners looked the same, and our landlady took us for Germans. Another advantage was that no identification documents were needed." Between sight-seeing from atop the omnibuses and walking about the Inner City, they applied themselves to language.

> We started going to meetings and carefully studied the orator's mouth. We went frequently to Hyde Park where speakers harangued the passing crowd on diverse themes. An atheist, standing among the group of curious listeners, proved there was no God. We were particularly keen on listening to one speaker of this kind. He spoke with an Irish accent, which was easier for us to understand. Nearby, a Salvation Army officer uttered shouts in appeal to God Almighty, while a little further on a shop assistant was holding forth on the long hours of servitude of assistants in the big stores.

Nadya and Volodya were fascinated by London—its size and diversity, especially its antiquity; in contrast to St. Petersburg, barely two centuries old, London seemed to personify the whole of England's thousand-year civilization and before. "Volodya cast curious glances at this stronghold of capitalism, forgetting for the while Plekhanov and the editorial conflicts."

In answer to an ad, he exchanged Russian lessons for English with two natives, and by autumn was spending each forenoon in the library of the British Museum, a library Nadya called "the richest in the world." To be near the library, they were now occupying two rooms in Finsbury (#30 Holford Square). The neighborhood abutted Holborn, an industrial area with dreary slums where the workers lived. Nearby in the shadow of St. Paul's Cathedral, pigeons strutted and pecked among the litter. Just as the serpentine Thames was reminiscent of Bolshaya Neva, Holborn reminded Nadya of the Viborg District of Petersburg.

> In slum areas we went on foot, observing these howling contrasts to the shining windows adorned with greenery, the separate entrances, the drives frequented only by polished broughams, which we had seen from the tops of busses. "Two nations!" muttered Volodya between clenched teeth.

London was further confirmation that capitalism—whether tsarist or democratic—had not taken a step toward narrowing or eliminating the gap between rich and poor.

Nadya described with humor one facet of London socialism:

> There is no recounting the strange variety of meetings we attended at one time or another. We once wandered into a socialist church. The socialist in charge first read aloud, his nose glued to a Bible, and then preached a gospel something like this: The exodus of the Jews from Egypt symbolized the exodus of the workers from the

Kingdom of Capitalism into the Kingdom of Socialism. Everyone stood up and sang from a socialist hymn book: "Lead us, 0 Lord, from the Kingdom of Capitalism into the Kingdom of Socialism."

In a letter of May 8, 1902, V. wrote his mother: "I am hoping to see you soon, my dear. I hope the journey will not tire you too much. You absolutely must take day trains and spend the nights in hotels. I advise you to take express trains in Germany and Austria (the extra fare in third class is small but the time gained is tremendous)." A month later he wrote: "We are all expecting you, and are making arrangements for you to stay."

However, the plan was altered by Anna, who still lived abroad. Instead of London, Volodya, his mother and sister spent a month together in a small fishing village on the Brittany Coast of France. V.'s traveling expenses, and all others connected with the vacation, were paid by Maria Alexandrovna and her daughter.

Anna, who was fond of resorts and had been living in a tourist area of Switzerland, undoubtedly considered Brittany preferable to a dingy flat in London. But was she also seeking to re-establish the close family circle which had prevailed before her brother's marriage? Nadya, on the other hand, was glad of her husband's respite from *Iskra*. Besides, her own mother was about to leave Russia for London; as predicted, Yelizaveta had been unhappy in St. Petersburg.

An episode described by Nadya in her *Memoir* is at variance with the evidence of a letter she had written from Siberia: "Apollinariya, after escaping from exile, came to London where she married Takhtariev." More surprising was the *Memoir* statement: "Apollinariya was overjoyed at our arrival. The Takhtarievs took us under their guardianship and helped us get fixed up in cheap quarters." Nadya, admitted, however, that there were occasional tensions between them, and once or twice ruptures occurred, followed by reconciliation. Apollinariya's husband was editor of *The Workers' Thought*, and V. disagreed with this journal's editorial policy. "But finally the Takhtarievs officially announced their sympathy with the *Iskra* tendency." The latter statement may be taken with reservation. Nadya's *Memoir* occasionally bent the truth.

The next to arrive in London were Martov and Zasulich who set up a communal household with Alexeyev in what Nadya described as "one of the big continental-looking houses not far away from us." Potressov arrived later. It was here that Vera became a good housekeeper. Otherwise, she remained in character. When asked by a curious Englishwoman how long she cooked her meat, Vera replied: "If I am hungry, ten minutes; if I am not hungry, three hours."

Because V.'s personal resources were now exhausted, he was forced to accept a small salary from the *Iskra* organization, "so we had to look after every penny, and live as cheaply as possible." Recreation was limited to visiting Primrose Hill, a trip costing sixpence. "From the hill we could see the whole of London—a vast, smoke-wreathed city receding in the distance. Here we got close to nature, penetrating the parks nearby and along green paths." A further attraction of Primrose Hill was its proximity to the cemetery where Karl Marx was buried.

The pattern of life in Munich was re-established: V.'s days in the library, work on *Iskra*, walks in the countryside, family solidarity. Taking advantage of the mild English winter—"very little rain or fog"—they attended a concert and, in V.'s words, "were very pleased with it, especially Chaikowsky's (sic) latest symphony, the Pathétique." But occasional theater performances were less inspiring: "What we should like," declared Nadya, "would be to visit the Russian Art Theater and see Gorky's play, *The Lower Depths*."

However, when spring ushered in their second London year, Nadya was overcome by lassitude and apparent boredom. Disinclined to write letters, she complained to Maria Alexandrovna: "It requires quite a lot of willpower to take up the pen . . . Once I start to write, however, the letter writes itself, I even begin to like it, but it is very difficult to start." This, her only surviving letter of the year 1903, with its homely details, summarizes the London experience from a personal standpoint. In some respects, it characterizes Nadya herself more completely than her other writings, including the *Memoir*.

It is doubtful, despite what she wrote to M.A., that they attended the theater frequently or went somewhere almost every evening; rather, it suggests an attempt to reassure her mother-in-law that all was well. On the other hand, "there does not seem to be anything to write; life drags on very monotonously, the same impressions and the same people every day." Yelizaveta, conforming to her own wretched pattern of existence, had just recovered from a bad case of flu. "At first the doctor thought it was typhus. She is now recovered, but the weakness remains." They talked of going into the country, "but Volodya is not keen on it, he is very fond of Prague; I also have got used to Prague but shall nevertheless be glad to get away from here." Like an imprisoned creature of the wild, she cried: "Give me the wings of a swallow . . . But now I am beginning to ramble. Sometimes I feel terribly homesick, today especially. By the way, that is how I am, I am always feeling drawn to somewhere else." Affection permeated the letter: "How I should like to stay with you now! I embrace you and Manya fondly, my dear ones."

"Prague" meant London. In view of what was actually transpiring, the letter's non-political flavor is understandable. Plans for a Congress, to be held in Brussels of representatives of all the Russian Social-Democratic Parties abroad and at home, were being directed by the London *Iskra* Organization. The undertaking involved fake passports, accelerated communications, setting agenda—in short, a plethora of organizational details that depended upon minimal friction and maximum secrecy. In all this, Nadya played a leading role. "A table in the commune was turned upside down to serve as a press for passports. Our methods were primitive; we were naive, but in that day there was not such danger of spies or provocateurs."

As secretary of *Iskra*, Nadya was charged not only with letter writing, but familiarity with code names for hundreds of people working for the organization, as well as those of cities and towns throughout Russia. Activity itself was coded: "handkerchief" for passports, "warm fur" for illegal literature. From the jargon of secrecy a new vocabulary developed.

Her responsibilities also included tracking literature after it had left the editorial office. For example, trunkloads sent by way of Marseilles, bundles sewed into jackets or hidden in luggage. During the Munich period, letters from Russia were addressed to comrades in various towns of Germany to be forwarded to a Dr. Leman who in turn sent them to Munich. The sheer complexity of these operations needed a full-time staff of considerable size. That Nadya, with V.'s help, handled them efficiently, is testimony to a good memory and unflagging energy.

Lenin was deeply concerned about the activities of the Social Revolutionary Party in Russia. A non-Marxist group which commanded a large following among the peasantry, it was numerically superior to the Social Democrats. One aim of *Iskra* was to attract the peasantry to Social Democracy. Planners agreed that this should be a priority on the agenda of the forthcoming Congress.

Nadya explained her husband's desire to form a solid, united Party into which would be merged all the individual groupings whose present attitude toward the Party was based upon personal sympathies or antipathies. Unfortunately, he was having little success in modifying or eradicating the egocentric proclivities of his fellow-countrymen. Their preoccupation with details of procedure, or their own personal prerogatives, was weakening the Cause.

One morning at 6 o'clock there was a violent rap on the door. Aroused from sleep, Nadya hastily donned a robe and went downstairs. "I knew that if the knock was unusual, it must be for us." She opened the door to be confronted by a tall, somewhat disheveled young man with a small, pointed beard and sparkling blue eyes. A pince-nez clinging precariously to his nose gave him an owlish expression. His manner was expectant. "May I come in?" he queried in cultivated Russian. "I realize it is early, but I have just arrived in London and am anxious to talk with Lenin." Nadya led him upstairs to the bedroom. Her husband was awake, and she left the men alone while she went to prepare coffee. When she returned, V. was still in his night-shirt, sitting on the edge of the bed conversing animatedly with the newcomer.

From hearsay, Lenin already knew about him. Word had come from Russia that a certain exile, distinguished for his political activism, was about to escape. In the bedroom that morning, Lenin questioned him about his background and political views. Satisfied that he was "one of us," and impressed by his keen mind, he wrote to Plekhanov suggesting that the man be co-opted to the editorial board of *Iskra*. Enclosed was an article by "The Pen," code name of its author. Plekhanov snapped back: "I don't like the 'pen' of your 'Pen.'" His letter criticized the man's literary style. Nadya, however, believed there was a deeper reason; that Plekhanov feared competition from one who represented a younger constituency of the Party.

His name was Lev Bronstein, but the world would later know him as Leon Trotsky, the pseudonym on his passport.

He remained in London for a time, during which he began to write for *Iskra*. Later, in a hired auditorium in the Whitechapel District, he delivered his first speech abroad, which took the form of a debate with two Russians of opposing views. Whitechapel adjoined Stepney, which included the notorious Limehouse District, setting for many fictional tales of degradation and murder. The ambiance of poverty provided a suitable environment for ideas being propounded by socialist speakers; from the factories and docks, men and women crowded into the hall, filling it with the stench of unwashed flesh.

As a frequent visitor to the "commune," Trotsky has left a memorable description of Vera Zasulich. After quoting what Lenin had said about Vera's "mosaics," he added:

> She did, indeed, put down one sentence at a time, pacing up and down her room, shuffling in her slippers, chain smoking cigarettes which she rolled herself, throwing butts in all corners of the room, on the windowsills, on the table, scattering ashes on her blouse, on her arms, her manuscript, her tea, and incidentally also over her interlocutor. An old-type radical intellectual with Marxism grafted on to her by fate.

He thought her an "exceptional person. . . .She was also charming in a peculiar manner."

Autumn and winter were times of frenetic activity. New faces and controversial personalities were converging on London, all of whom added confusion to the over-strained resources of *Iskra's* small staff. When Plekhanov suggested that a man named Deutsch be added to the editorial board as representative from the Emancipation of Labor group, Lenin readily assented. Since Trotsky had been accepted, albeit provisionally, Deutsch would restore the balance of forces between Switzerland and London.

By spring, however the enterprise was verging on collapse. First, Potressov fell ill, victim of a pulmonary ailment exacerbated by the London fog. His departure for the better climate of Paris was followed by that of Martov; Yuly had become bored by what he called the "inactivity" in London. And when urgent requests for Trotsky's return began arriving from *Iskra* representatives in Russia, he departed for Paris and points east. To make matters worse,

Deutsch and Zasulich proved wholly inadequate for the practical side of publishing and distributing literature, as well as preparing for the forthcoming Congress. Thus the entire burden of communications and planning were left to V. and Nadya.

"Volodya would spend sleepless nights after receiving letters with such news as: 'Sonya' is as silent as the grave, or 'Zarin' did not come to the Committee in time, or, no contact with 'the old woman.' Those sleepless nights remain engraved on my memory." V.'s letters to Russia were filled with requests for news: "We beseech and demand that you write us more often and in greater detail, *at once*, without fail, the very same day you receive this letter."

Because of the precarious state of *Iskra* in London, Plekhanov and Axelrod were again urging a relocation to Switzerland, whereat a vote was taken in which Lenin was the only dissenter. Under mounting pressures, his health broke down. "He became so overwrought that he developed a nervous illness called shingles. We could not think of going to an English doctor, as it would have cost a guinea." After consulting a medical handbook, Nadya followed the example of English workers and applied a home remedy. "I painted Volodya with iodine, which caused him agonizing pain."

While he was recuperating, Nadya and her mother packed up and made arrangements for the journey to Switzerland. Among V.'s personal belongings was one of particular value. Anna had sent a letter before leaving Russia containing photographs of Alexander Ulyanov, which had been taken at the request of his mother while he was in prison awaiting execution. Anna had been afraid to carry them on her person when she crossed the frontier.

Déjà vu began at Charing Cross, continued through the dripping countryside of Kent, waited on the pier at Dover, rode the Channel steamer to Calais, where the odor of fish was unpleasantly familiar. During the journey across France, Lenin became increasingly restless, and upon arrival at Geneva he collapsed.

They had come to London in April 1902, and exactly a year later, they departed for Switzerland. On April 22nd, Lenin, abed in a Swiss boarding house, observed his thirty-third birthday. The month of rain, of hope and disappointment, of fresh initiatives ending in failure, once again inaugurated a new phase.

6. The Stalin Connection

One spring evening in 1897, a young man named Viktor K. Kurnatovsky stepped off the train at Krasnoyarsk. Because he had made the journey from St. Petersburg alone, no one met him, nor did he expect to find a familiar face in town. As a member of the Emancipation of Labor group, he had been living abroad. Immediately upon returning to Petersburg, he was arrested and exiled to Siberia. Since the mass arrest of members of the League of Struggle was still underway in the Capital (they had not yet arrived in Siberia), he was without the companionship and support they would have provided. He was fortunate to be assigned to Kuraginskoye in the Minusinsk District which was known for its desirable climate. However, he was the only exile in that village. Later, when League members began arriving, he was joined by the Lepeshinskys. Meanwhile, to amuse himself he went hunting.

Josef Stalin

Whether from boredom or financial need, he eventually went to work in a sugar refinery where, for a meager wage, he put in a 12-hour-a-day, seven-day week.

Once the League people arrived and were settled in various communities, word spread that an *Emancipation* man was among them, and he quickly became known.

Historically, Kurnatovsky is a man of mystery. Because of his affiliation with the Swiss rather than the Petersburg group, he has fallen through the cracks of history. But this elusive man was destined to be the vital link in a chain of relationships that would have worldwide consequences, the knowledge of which, ironically, he himself was denied.

Volodya and Nadya first met him at the New Year's party in the town of Minusinsk. Immediately upon returning to Kuraginskoye, he petitioned for transfer to Shusha, an indication of instant rapport with V. and his wife. Instead, the authorities—suspicious of his motives and desirous of keeping V. isolated—sent him to Yermakovskoye "where," said V., "he will be quite alone."

Occasional references to him appear in subsequent letters from Shushenskoye to Maria Alexandrovna: "Kurnatovsky may come to visit us," or "Kurnatovsky stayed with us for two days." Through correspondence and visits, a friendship developed, although it never reached the stage of first-name familiarity; both Nadya and Volodya referred to him by his surname.

V.'s interest in Kurnatovsky was both personal and political. In addition to becoming better acquainted with a fellow-exile, Kurnatovsky's work at the refinery afforded V. an opportunity to study labor conditions in that area of Siberia. With these ideas in mind, he wrote Kurnatovsky, expressing a wish that they again meet. One Sunday morning in October, having hired a cart, he and Nadya set out for Kuraginskoye. She described their visit:

> We looked over the refinery; the director was unusually attentive to the "important foreigners" (although Volodya in his felt boots and quilted trousers looked like a giant from Hop-o-My-Thumb, and the wind had made my hair stand on end); he tried to justify the rotten conditions in which the workers have to work, turned the talk to that subject himself and extended his kindness so far that, despite his elegant and prosperous appearance, he rushed to give Volodya a stool to sit on and himself brushed the dust from it. I almost burst out laughing.

Upon their return, Yelizaveta berated them for wasting their host's time and eating his food—"which we did," confessed Nadya, "but respite from work was good for him."

A final reference to Kurnatovsky appeared in Nadya's letter of October 1899 to her mother-in-law. "A few days ago Kurnatovsky visited us. The men all went out shooting first thing in the morning; Kurnatovsky is fanatically keen on this sport."

What sort of man was he? A revolutionary-minded drifter of indifferent character and habits?—A Party hack?—an intellectual?—well-to-do, or impoverished and supported by the Party while he was abroad? In absence of description, he remains a faceless blur. Nothing can be learned from the fact of his employment at the refinery, since many "upper class" exiles worked at menial jobs. All that can be deduced from the record is that he had means, from whatever source, to live abroad, that he was an occasional visitor to Shushenskoye, and that he was 33 years old when he left Siberia. There is no evidence pro or con on his closeness to Plekhanov.

One thing, however, is certain. Following his first meeting with Lenin at the Minusinsk holiday gathering, he was converted to Social Democracy as spelled out in the program then evolving to *Iskra*-ism.

Viktor's term of exile ended in 1900, at which time he started back to Russia. But instead of continuing west from Ufa, he headed south. His train, following the Volga, passed through Samara and Saratov to Tsaritsyn where it turned southeast to Rostov on the Sea of Azov. A few miles away lay Georgia. After continuing across the frontier, he changed trains at the small junction of Desiant where he left the Russian railway system for that of Georgia.

Thereafter, via the circuitous route of Petrovsk and Baku on the Caspian

Sea, he reached Tiflis (now Tblisi), the Georgian capital. In physical appearance and climate, Tiflis might have been a city in Persia (Iran) or Turkey, both of which shared borders with Georgia. Historically and culturally, Georgia had close ties with Armenia and was thus "rescued" from Islam. Neither Russian nor Arabic, Georgians were unique. Through the centuries, as a result of military invasions and human infiltration from south and east, the people of Georgia had developed racial characteristics more oriental than European. Georgia was a part of the Russian Empire, but it maintained an autonomous relationship with Russia which was more fundamental and subjective than one that could have been imposed by geopolitical boundaries.

Marxism had come to Tiflis two years before Kurnatovsky's arrival when a man named Noah Jordania took over publication of *The Furrow*, a periodical of Georgian intellectuals. Kurnatovsky's objective in Tiflis was to organize a Social-Democratic committee and promote *Iskra*-ism. Ground had already been prepared by Jordania, but the latter's Marxism held the same ambiguous approach to social change that characterized Plekhanov and his *Emancipation of Labor*, to wit: a union of the proletariat (workers) and the bourgeoisie (the middle class, dominated by commercial and industrial interests) to overthrow the Tsar and establish constitutional government. What then, distinguished Lenin's Marxism? He stated it with simplicity: "Every solution that offers a middle path is either deception of the people or an expression of dull-wittedness." By "middle path" he meant that historically, the bourgeoisie always dominated any constituent body in which they participated, and there was no reason to assume they would act differently in the future. "Would a polite request from us suffice for the bourgeoisie to give up their privileges? It's like preaching chastity to a brothel keeper. Mankind has passed from one exploiter to another."

The role of the peasantry in effecting social change was likewise disputed between the two Marxist factions. Whereas a simple class division existed in the cities—proletariat (hired labor) and large and petty bourgeoisie (owners of large and small enterprises, including landed estates)—the peasantry did not constitute a third and monolithic social stratum. There were rich, middle and poor peasants. Because of economic diversity, the peasantry, solely concerned with its own problems—specifically land—remained aloof. In joining together to form a so-called peasants party (the Social Revolutionaries) they were defiantly independent and indifferent to urban socio/economic problems. With an enormous numerical superiority, they were in a position to overwhelm the voting blocs of other parties elected to a representative assembly envisioned by both die-hard and revisionist Marxists. At this stage, Lenin believed in the principle of a representative assembly.

The overriding question was how to win the S-Rs to Social Democracy, and what to do with them afterward. Would they (the S-Rs) break up into constituent parts, with rich and middle peasants aligning themselves with their large and petty bourgeois counterparts in the cities, leaving poor peasants to hang on the coattails of the urban proletariat? Lenin felt that reliance on the support of a *united* Social-Revolutionary Party was unrealistic. History proved him correct. He further believed that the peasantry, despite overwhelming numbers, was incapable of leading any social movement to victory; that its lack of internal unity would, under stress, fracture the S-R bloc and render it useless for the Cause (history vindicated this perception). It was his desire to win the poor peasants to Social Democracy, to ignore the enticing prospect of a coalition between the Social Revolutionary Party as a whole, and Social Democracy. Others in his Party disagreed.

One of the recruits to Jordania's Marxism was a nineteen-year-old theological student named Iosef Djugashvili. Born in Gori, a small town near Tiflis, the fourth child of a twenty-year-old woman and her shoemaker husband, the boy was raised by his pious mother with expectation of his becoming a priest. Historical speculation about the conditions of his childhood is inconclusive. Rumor postulated a drunken father, and a mother of peasant stock worn down by child-bearing. The facts suggest poverty unameliorated by family unity.

By the time Iosef was enrolled in Tiflis Theological Seminary, he was a tousle-haired youth with an enigmatic, "closed" expression of countenance. Short of stature, hesitant of speech, afflicted with a slightly deformed arm, he was already the epitome of a young rebel alienated from mainstream society. During his student years, first at Gori Theological School, later at Tiflis Seminary, he imbibed the terminology and thinking of his chosen vocation; but the indoctrination was superficial. Shortly before graduation, he was apprehended and expelled for the possession of Marxist literature, and for a short time thereafter, he became a drifter. Eventually he found employment, including lodging, at the Tiflis Geophysical Observatory.

Now liberated from academic restraint, Iosef was a ready candidate for Marxist indoctrination which would transform him from theorist to political activist. Jordania's organization, on the lookout for recruits, invited him to join.

Iosef's enigmatic demeanor made him relatively inconspicuous among the group with which he was now associated. Members found him a plodder willing to assume routine tasks, a loner in spirit as well as in fact, who emerged from his room to blend with the crowd, and just as unobtrusively disappeared again into the Observatory. Whether or not Iosef was a typical Georgian, nevertheless his personal traits were more Asiatic than European. His stolid personality was underscored by a habit of remaining silent among his articulate associates; that he was watchful and alert did not strike them as sinister. He himself was becoming aware that silence, if employed skillfully, was a weapon of power. Likewise, it was a means of camouflaging his own inadequacies.

On May Day 1900, Iosef made his first public speech. But his innocuous demeanor and presentation failed to attract the police, and he continued unmolested in his job at the Observatory.

If Jordania "discovered" Iosef, the same was not true of Kurnatovsky. Noah's recruit was drawn to Kurnatovsky's Social Democratic group like iron filings to a magnet. Rather than time-serving at the editorial office of *The Furrow, Iskra* promised the action for which Iosef was temperamentally suited. Action came sooner than he expected. When Kurnatovsky and his fellow Iskrists were arrested,[1] a search of Iosef's room at the Observatory lost him his job, and he was forced to go into hiding. But hiding was not hibernating; remnants of the group went underground. Work for the cause intensified, and Iosef emerged from his cellar to organize and lead a street demonstration. Two thousand people marched, the police fired, blood stained the pavement, jails filled to bursting. Iosef fled to his widowed mother's house in Gori.

During the following months, Tiflis Social Democrats regrouped, and by November 1901 they had organized a committee under new leadership to which Iosef was elected. He returned to Tiflis and soon afterward was dispatched to organize an S-D Committee in Batum, a town on the Black Sea coast 160 miles away. At a New Year's Eve party in Batum, a Tiflis branch of the Social-Democratic Party was formed under the leadership of Iosef and an associate. Three months later they were arrested, and during the following year Iosef was shuttled between prisons in Batum and Kutais, the latter on the main railway line to Tiflis.

Removal from circulation afforded him leisure to contemplate the past and relate it to the future—his own future. With activity temporarily in abeyance, he began to envision himself as a journalist in the Marxian tradition of his predecessors and contemporaries in the revolutionary movement; an aspiration not without substance. *The Furrow* had given him practical experience in the mechanics of publishing. Exposure to the journalistic side whetted his appetite for recognition beyond that of rabble-rousing—however worthy he considered its objectives. In short, he perceived himself as a potential interpreter of Marx—as a writer for Social Democracy. Years in theological institutions had educated him, but a *Molitva Gospodnya* (Pater Noster) education was a poor substitute for that of a university. His specialization did not prepare him for critical analysis. Likewise, while its curriculum included Greek and Latin, it left him with the Georgian language as a sole means of communication with Russians. In addition to his education, one should speculate about the depth of his exposure to contemporary socialist trends. How much of Marxism did he really understand? How much of *Iskra*-ism?

In 1903, a wave of political strikes, emanating from Rostov, spread to Baku and Batum, followed by others in Kiev, Odessa and Yelizavetgrad. Iosef, recently released from prison, was again arrested and this time sentenced to three years in Siberia. A pattern of arrest, exile, and escape continued for ten years, during which he assumed no less that sixteen aliases, not including the one he finally adopted. To credit him with implication in all the political disturbances in southern Russia during those years would be an exaggeration of his influence. There were many others whose stature in the Party was greater, men and women who were raising a political firestorm in southern Russia.

Iosef's career as an agitator ended abruptly in 1913 when he was called to military service in the tsarist army. Meanwhile, his first pamphlet, with the ungrammatical title "Slightly About Party Differences," was followed by translations of Lenin's current writings into Georgian (linguistic differences were reconciled with the use of a dictionary). There was a meeting between the two men in 1907, but it was not until 1912 that Lenin officially recognized him, suggesting his name for a Party post. By that time, much had transpired both within the Social-Democratic Party and on the world scene. Still, Iosef remained relatively unknown outside his native Georgia.

Iosef first entered the Batum prison while Lenin and his wife were on their way from Munich to London (April 1902). Many years would elapse before he gained Lenin's attention. Meanwhile, their destinies were joined through *Iskra*, with Kurnatovsky as catalyst. The fact of Lenin's physical distance from Russia (after he emigrated), as well as desultory communications between *Iskra* abroad and Georgian political cadres—hence ignorance of the personal characteristics of a certain Iskraite operating in his native territory under minimal supervision from senior members of the Tiflis Organization—had fateful consequences. The unprepossessing revolutionary from Georgia was Josef Stalin.

7. Switzerland 1903
and Lenin's Break with *Iskra*

After two weeks in bed, V. recovered sufficiently to undertake the project he had formulated in London; all activity in Geneva was addressed to the forthcoming Party Congress.

In the kitchen of their small rented house on the outskirts of the city, Volodya and Nadya conferred with arriving delegates, among them the former defectors Martov and Potressov. Trotsky came from Paris, Krzhizhanovsky was on his way from Siberia. But upon returning to *Emancipation* territory, Zasulich forsook her tentative alliance with Lenin. "A damned fine state of affairs," he complained. "Look at Vera. Nobody has the courage to reply to Plekhanov. He trounces Trotsky, and Vera merely says: 'Just look at our Georgii. All he does is shout. 'I can't go on like this'." Plekhanov was continuing to protest the co-option of Trotsky to the editorial board.

The house was located in Séchéron, Chemin privé du Foyer, 10, a working-class district near the lake, and when these kitchen arguments became untenable, comrades went to the shore for a quiet discussion.

Once again Nadya was confronted with language problems and cultural idiosyncrasies. This time, however, she had recourse to comrade women who had been living in Switzerland's French-speaking Canton. Not wishing to encumber themselves with possessions, she and Volodya had purchased a few essential items of furniture in secondhand shops. Packing cases were used for storing books and crockery, causing one visitor to observe that the place looked like a smuggler's den. Fortunately, their living quarters were above rather than adjacent to the kitchen. But Nadya had little time to establish a domestic routine; barely three months after arriving in Switzerland, she accompanied her husband to Brussels for the Party Congress.

Her account of that event is both humorous and candid. Comrade Koltsov, a longtime resident of Brussels, had been entrusted with arrangements. Sessions were to be held in a large flour warehouse, "where our advent not only disturbed the rats, but also the police; the rumor went around that Russian revolutionaries were assembling for some mysterious conclave." There were other difficulties. As delegates began arriving at the Koltsov apartment, his landlady told him either to stop the visits or clear out. Consequently, Mrs. Koltsov (Comrade Koltsova) had to stand on a street corner and shoo the newly arrived delegates into a socialist hotel—"Coq d'Or, I believe it was called," Nadya stated. The hotel erupted in conviviality. One Gussev, holding a glass of brandy, sang operatic arias every night with such effect that crowds gathered beneath the windows to listen. "Volodya liked to hear Gussev singing, especially 'We Were Wedded out of Church' . . ."

Lenin, deferring to Plekhanov, suggested that he open the Congress. Elated at perceiving himself in a position of authority, he became Lenin's enthusiastic ally. On an improvised platform beside a huge window draped with red material, he made what Nadya described as "a solemn speech filled with deep emotion." One of his statements was significant: "The well-being of the Revolution is the supreme law." Later, at a moment of crisis, Lenin would remember it.

After months of discussion, the editorial board of *Iskra* had finally reached agreement on a Party Program which was now submitted to the Congress. Fifty-seven delegates hotly debated the precise wording of the Program. Nadya, listening from the sidelines, made a cogent observation:

> Many practical-minded people considered that these disputes were of a purely armchair nature, and that it didn't matter a fig whether such phrases as "more or less" remained in the Program or not . . . Heard from outside, theoretical controversies do not seem worthwhile quarreling about, but once their gist is grasped, it is realized that the matter is of the most importance.

She was stating that, for a considerable time thereafter, problems of semantics would place the Party in an equivocal position. Who, at this point, knew how long it would be before another Congress was convened?

Just when it seemed that delegates were about to reach a consensus favorable to the Program, the police moved in. Noisy sessions had not only disturbed the peace but reverberated in the chambers of government. Under increased police harassment, delegates packed up and moved to London.

Had the Brussels conference continued, it is possible that unity would have eventually resulted, but interruption of the proceedings had unfortunate consequences. In London, differences about ideology and organization, exacerbated by private animosities, once again flared. Nadya remembered a scene just before the voting: "Axelrod was reproaching a comrade for what seemed to him to be a lack of moral sense, and recalled some unpleasant gossip from exile days. The latter remained silent, and tears came to his eyes." On another occasion, "Deutsch was angrily reprimanding Glebov about something. The latter raised his head, and with gleaming eyes said bitterly: 'You just keep your mouth shut, you old dodderer!'"

Driven to distraction by the bickering, Lenin succumbed to acute depression: "He got in such a state that he left off sleeping altogether, and was extremely restless."

Although the Program was finally accepted, factionalism among the delegates accelerated after they returned to Geneva. Friends and backers now turned away with "What was all the trouble in Brussels and London?" Non-participating émigrés, scattered in various places, added their voices of disapproval. In Geneva: "We can no longer lend you our apartment for meetings," and "We are withdrawing financial support."

Nadya was hurt by one episode involving a longtime friend.

> In our childhood we had played wonderful games together, and I was overjoyed at hearing that she would soon arrive in Geneva. Now she was by no means young, and had become quite a different person. Her family had always given us assistance, but now she viewed these personal "scandals" very unfavorably.

Lenin's break with *Iskra* was a mere breath away. When Martov refused to serve on a newly constituted editorial board, not only was a long association and deep personal friendship severed, but the entire enterprise was about to go the route of "arm-chair revolution." With issue #51 of *Iskra*, Lenin resigned. Henceforth, he became the object of intense vituperation, accused of being overbearing and of harboring a lust for power.

Trotsky continued to remain aloof from Lenin's group. Plekhanov, Axelrod, Potressov, Zasulich and the entire company of dissenters—now called Mensheviks—took control of the Organization. For Lenin, it was a question of starting over, of building a new organization with the loyal remnants of a Party now fractured beyond repair. Henceforth they would become known as "Bolsheviki." Lenin detested the word, calling it "ugly." However, it meant simply "majority," in the same way that Menshevik meant "minority."

Why "majority"? It related to popular following and the situation in Russia, not that among the hierarchy scattered in Europe. The Mensheviks constituted a majority in the conciliatory Central Committee and on the *Iskra* editorial board. But in Russia? In Viborg? In the industrial purlieus of Moscow and other large centers? Time would validate the description "Bolshevik."

Although now divorced from *Iskra*, Lenin continued for a time as an active member of the Russian Social Democratic Labor Party's Central Committee, a position to which he had been elected. But subsequently he also resigned from C.C. He wrote a special pamphlet, "One Step Forward, Two Steps Back" to explain the nature and significance of the Bolshevik-Menshevik split It served as a supplement to his earlier *What Is To Be Done?* His next independent act was to establish a new periodical—*Vperyod*, "Forward"—which was soon followed by the call for a Third Party Congress to rally the Bolshevik majority. He continued to entertain hope that some of the defectors would reconsider and rally to the new organization. Unexpected support was coming from Russia. Persons like Lydia Knippovich, unmoved by the recent émigré uproar, wrote encouraging letters.

Before long, Lenin had the support of a new core group within Russia whose relationships were relatively untainted by personal animosities. Its members were also in position to exercise considerable influence.

Russia's War with Japan

From the time they first left London for Switzerland, neither Nadya nor V. wrote to Maria Alexandrovna. Then in January 1904, having received word of the arrest of Anna, Maria, Dmitri and Dmitri's wife in Kiev, Nadya sent a commiserating letter: "Your news came as a great shock to us. I don't know what conditions in the Kiev lock-up are like now—they used to be bearable." Her mother-in-law was alone in Kiev trying to negotiate a release, and Nadya had written to a friend, asking her to visit M.A. She added: "We are not living too well in Geneva; mother is often poorly. We feel unsettled somehow and the work goes badly . . . Mother is sorry she is not in Russia with you. Wishing you health and strength."

Whatever Volodya's personal feelings, they were concealed from his mother. In a January (1904) letter, his first since the preceding March, he told her of a "wonderful outing" he had with Nadya and a friend.

> Down below in Geneva it was all mist and gloom, but up in the mountains there was glorious sunshine. And at the foot of the mountain, a veritable sea of mist and clouds, concealing everything except the mountains jutting up through it. So we are beginning to get to know Switzerland and its scenery. In the spring we intend to make a long walking tour.

For reasons of secrecy, he omitted reference to the arrests. Another letter, written several days later, referred only to the police "dragnet." This letter—the last to his mother until July of that year—was dated January 20, 1904.

Twenty days later, Russia and Japan were at war. The Russian Empire resembled a beached whale. With the Atlantic Ocean a continent, away, and a Pacific coast that was accessible by land only above the 60th parallel, Russia lay inert, a helpless bulk of maritime aspirations.

At Kronstadt in the Gulf of Finland, a few nautical miles from St. Petersburg, the Baltic Fleet lay at anchor, its crew on perpetual holiday broken by occasional sallies down the Gulf and thence around Denmark to the North Sea. Access to the Atlantic lay through the English Channel. The Black Sea Fleet was a misnomer in terms of usefulness; to reach the Atlantic, it had to inveigle its way through Turkey's Dardenelles and past Great Britain's Gibraltar—straits both figurative and actual. In the Caspian Sea, a small flotilla protected Georgia and Trans-Caucasia from southern predators. At 65° latitude north, Arkangelsk was home to ships locked in ice for most of the year.

The principle eastern port of Vladivostok, thousands of miles from industrial (European) Russia via a single-track railway, faced the Sea of Japan. With frigid climate and an ice-blocked harbor from December to April, it was hardly suitable for a naval base or that of a merchant marine.

Thus Russia's pretensions to being a maritime power, with a merchant fleet at liberty to ply world oceans, had long been the subject of extra-national levity. In order to wriggle out of a situation imposed by nature, Nicholas II struck a deal with Manchuria for lease of its warm-water port at the foot of a peninsula jutting into the Yellow Sea. To his mother he wrote:

> Of course you already know the glad news of the occupation of Port Arthur, which in time will be the terminus of the Siberian railway. At last we shall have a real port that does not freeze...Now we can feel safe out there for a long time! (March 1898)

The Port Arthur naval base was, at best, a compromise that entailed building a railway from southeastern Siberia across Manchuria to Mukden and thence south to Port Arthur on land leased from Manchuria. Life for the Pacific Fleet sailors resembled that of their Baltic brethren. The navy occasionally crept out of port on assumption that the Tsar commander-in-chief had not roiled the diplomatic waters.

Late in the evening of January 27, 1904, Nicholas was approached by an aide who handed him a telegram from the naval commander at Port Arthur stating that a Japanese squadron under Admiral Togo had, without warning, attacked the Pacific Fleet. A subsequent letter from Russian Admiral Alexeiev to Nicholas read:

> About midnight on January 26 (1904), Japanese destroyers made a sudden attack on our squadron anchored in the outer roadstead of Port Arthur. The battleships Retvizan, Tsesarevich, and the cruiser Pallada were torpedoed . . . I report further details to Your Majesty in due course.

"So war has begun," sighed the Tsar. "May God be with us."

Russian losses, while considerable, were not catastrophic. However, upon leaving port to pursue the fleeing enemy, ships of the line entered an electromagnetic minefield laid by the Japanese. The flagship Petropavlosk, pride of the fleet, went down with the Admiral and six hundred men, and another ship was badly damaged. The remainder hurried back into port, there to remain under blockade for several months.

Meanwhile, the small Vladivostok squadron, apprised of developments, had slipped anchor and was "somewhere in the Pacific." Japanese Admiral Kaimamura with seven cruisers went in search but without success. With one part of the Russian Pacific Fleet inactivated and the other playing hide-and-seek with Kaimamura on the high seas, Japan undertook the second phase of its project.

For years she had waited on the sidelines for her chance to acquire a share of the imperialist spoils. Perceiving Russia's logistical problem in defending a Pacific beachhead, she mapped a strategy of conquest while quietly building military and naval strength: first, she would invade "the effete little kingdom of Korea" whose independence had been honored by the flaccid giant that was China; then Manchuria; and finally, China itself.

Official St. Petersburg was in a quandary. To transport an army and its supplies via the Trans-Siberian Railway required months, during which Japan would benefit from proximity and preparedness. Russia's history of unpreparedness for war was legendary, a condition the West attributed to "Slavic inertia and ineptitude." But the Japanese *coup* at Pearl Harbor in 1941 was history repeating itself against a background of Anglo-Saxon efficiency.

The main division of Russia's Baltic Fleet was dispatched to the Pacific in early October 1904, and in its wake trailed a procession of slow-moving supply ships containing coal to fuel the boilers, munitions, gear—everything needed for a voyage during which there would be minimal contact with foreign ports. After putting in at Libau on the Baltic coast of Lithuania to take on additional food supplies, Admiral Rozhestvenski finally slipped anchor on the night of October 13-14. While passing through the Baltic, skirting Denmark and into the North Sea, all lookouts were on 24-hour alert. Suddenly off the English coast of Northumberland near the Dogger Banks—a sunken sand bar—one of them sighted what was in fact a small British fishing fleet. The uneasy Russians, fearing torpedo boats, gave the order to fire, provoking an international incident from which Russia extricated herself with considerable difficulty. The Tsar noted:

> I went to Kronstadt to bid farewell to the cruiser Oleg and the gigantic auxiliary Ural ... The next day we received reports of the meeting of our squadron and the English fishing fleet during the night, and the firing that occurred... The English are very angry and near the boiling point ... I sent a telegram to Uncle Bertie (King Edward VII) expressing my regret ... but I did not apologize. I do not think the English will have the cheek to go further than indulge in threats. Our own calmness will soon calm them.

Thenceforward, the voyage was uneventful. After navigating the English Channel, Rozhestvenski headed for open sea. With the passing of months, the coasts of France, Spain and Africa were no more than designations on the chartroom map. Upon rounding Africa, the fleet headed east for the Island of Madagascar where it put in for further instructions from home.

Meanwhile, frantic telegrams were being exchanged between the Pacific admirals and their high command at Petersburg. The Japanese had landed troops on the Korean Peninsula and were working their way north toward the Yalu River, where Russia had assembled a force from its Far-East division. The two armies were about to engage. Although Russian reinforcements had begun arriving from the west, the outcome of a land battle—as well as the fate of Port Arthur—was balanced on a knife edge.

Rozhestvenski reached Madagascar only to learn that Port Arthur had fallen, and he telegraphed H.Q. that he was returning to Kronstadt. The answer came back: "Stay where you are. We are sending another contingent of the Baltic Fleet by way of Suez. Will rendezvous with you, whereat proceed to Pacific as per original plans."

Britain, perennially suspicious of Russian aspirations in the Far East, never-theless was facing the present reality of Japanese aggression. As a result, the tsarist government, for an astronomical sum, was permitted the short route through Anglo-Egypt and the Red Sea to the Indian Ocean. Once joined, the combined fleet steamed out of port to pass south of India and into the Bay of Bengal, where it moved through Malacca Straits and thence north into the China Sea.

After another port of call at Camranh Bay in Cochin China (Viet Nam) for further orders, the ships started for Vladivostok. It was now May 1905, nearly seven months since Rozhestvenski had departed Libau. The sailors, accus-tomed to icy Baltic winds, were finding the tropical heat nearly unbearable. Sheepskin jackets and fur caps had long since yielded to summer wear and finally to underclothing. Officers, on the other hand, sweltered in summer uni-forms. The crew would don uniforms only when—or if—they reached Vladi-vostok. In the meantime, dysentery, malaria, and a variety of tropical diseases were taking their toll.

The lobster-claw at Korea Straits was activated and waiting. After leaving Camranh Bay in mid-May, the Russian fleet disappeared into the Pacific. Two routes were open to the Admiral: one north to the Kurile Islands, the other between the pincers of Korea and Japan. The former involved finding a pas-sage between Urop and Etorop Islands into the Sea of Okhotsk, then a run through Soyazaki Strait's narrow channel separating Japan from Sakhalin Island. To reach Vladivostok following a southwesterly direction, he would have to cross the Sea of Japan. With the enemy patrolling their own waters, both routes were hazardous and, additionally, the Sakhalin Island route meant days lost as Vladivostok awaited siege. Rozhestvenski, after considerable hesi-tation, decided to take his chances with Korea Straits, a move anticipated by Admiral Togo, whose ships were lying at anchor in the Tsushima strait where the Yellow Sea joins the Sea of Japan.

In early afternoon of the 27th, the two fleets met in a mighty battle, dur-ing which the Russian cruisers repeatedly wheeled in desperate attempts to gain fire-power advantage over the enemy.

By daybreak of the following day it was all over. The entire Russian fleet had been captured or sunk.*

As the land and sea war dragged on, a mediated cease-fire was arranged by the United States. Russian and Japanese diplomats, meeting with President Theodore Roosevelt at Portsmouth, New Hampshire, signed a peace treaty that heavily penalized the Russians.

The murky political maneuvering that led to an "unprovoked" attack was not unilaterally Japanese. But the outcome was clear. Had Russia defeated Japan, the unpopular Tsar might have been reinstated in the public mind. As

---

* Unlike the disaster at Pearl Harbor, the entire navy was destroyed along with naval personnel. The then-Capital, St. Petersburg, lay open to invasion.

it was, the hostility of a defeated people led to official reaction, to modification or withdrawal of recent reforms, to increased activity by the secret police, to the Tsar's further alienation from the people.

"Volodya and I took our rucksacks and went into the mountains for a month . . . We always selected the wildest parts and got away from human beings. Each day we never knew where we would be on the morrow; by each evening we were always so tired that we sank into bed and fell asleep immediately . . ."

Following a winter of what Nadya described as "turmoil" and "the nuisance of housekeeping," she and Volodya sublet the house in Séchéron and went to Lausanne for a short rest before starting out on a walking tour. "We are sleeping ten hours a day and go walking and swimming; we even have begun to look healthy again." To her mother-in-law she wrote: "It has been a difficult winter and our nerves have been under such a strain that we cannot be blamed for taking a holiday, although I am already beginning to feel guilty about it. Volodya and I have agreed not to talk about our work—work, he says, is not a bear and will not escape into the woods."

For the Swiss "tramps," as they described themselves in postcards dispatched along the way, worry about finances had not been left behind; V. was translating Hobson's *Imperialism,* "but I only work at it now and then." Prior to their departure, he had received 150 rubles from one of his Russian publishers.

Family letters from Russia were filled with gloom. Yelizaveta, currently visiting friends at their country house near Petersburg, was writing about "the terrible cold and rain." From Kiev where V.'s mother was still living pending the release of the four detainees, news was likewise depressing. In addition to suffering from the humidity and heat of the southern Ukraine, she was ill.

By summer's end, however, both the "tramps" and their beleaguered relatives in various parts of Russia had overcome all setbacks imposed by weather, illness, imprisonment, fatigue, depression. The prisoners were released, Maria Alexandrovna had found a summer place in the countryside. Nature compensated for its vagaries with offerings of sunshine and cooling breezes. Even water-soaked St. Petersburg was granted a reprieve.

Refreshed and happy, the pilgrims returned to Geneva. "Volodya's nerves became normal again. It was just as though the mountain streams had washed away all the cobwebs of petty intrigue."

In order to be near the Société library, they moved from Séchéron to an apartment in the center of town—No.3 Rue de Colline. Nadya has provided a description of her husband as he appeared to the librarian:

> There arrived every morning a Russian with trouser-bottoms turned up, Swiss fashion, to avoid the mud. He invariably forgot to turn them down again. He would take out books left unfinished the day before, then go to his customary place at the

little table by the window, smooth down the thin hair on his bald head with a customary gesture, and bury his nose deep in the books. Only rarely did he get up, and
then in order to take down a dictionary from the shelf and search for an explanation of some unfamiliar term. He would then stride up and down for a while,
resume his seat, and in a tense manner rapidly scrawl something in minute handwriting on little squares of paper.

Nadya mentioned that Société members were elderly professors who seldom used the library.

It was here that Lenin wrote a scathing assessment of Russia's war with
Japan, which appeared in the second issue of his newly established periodical,
Vperyod. With a blend of sarcasm, humor, literary *panache* and objectivity, he
set the tone for Bolshevik journalism.

> Why and to what extent is the fall of Port Arthur really an historic disaster? Advanc-
> ing, progressive Asia has dealt backward and reactionary Europe an irreparable
> blow. Ten years ago this reactionary Europe was perturbed by the defeat of China
> at the hands of young Japan, and it united to rob Japan of the fruits of her victory.
> Europe was protecting the established relations and privileges of the old world, its
> prerogative to exploit Asian peoples a prerogative held from time immemorial and
> sanctified by the usage of centuries.
>
> The recovery of Port Arthur by Japan is a blow struck at the whole of reac-
> tionary Europe. Russia held Port Arthur for six years and spent hundreds of mil-
> lions of rubles on the building of strategic railways, harbors, and new towns, on
> fortifying a stronghold. Military commentators (in European newspapers)
> declared these to be impregnable, as strong as six Sevastopols.
>
> And behold, little Japan captures this stronghold in eight months, when it took
> England and France together a whole year to capture Sevastopol.*
>
> The question of supremacy on the seas, the main and vital issue of the present
> war, has been settled. The Russian Pacific fleet, which at the outset was certainly not
> weaker, if actually not stronger, than the Japanese fleet, has been completely
> destroyed. The very base of naval operations has been lost, and the only thing left
> for Rozhdestvensky's (sic) naval squadron is to turn back** shamefully after a use-
> less expenditure of more millions, after a great victory of his formidable battleships
> over the English fishing smacks.
>
> Russia's loss from naval tonnage alone amounts to 300 million rubles. More
> important, however, is the loss of some ten thousand of the navy's best men, and
> the loss of an entire army. If Kuropatkin is now 'relieved' of his worries over Port
> Arthur,*** Russia has been relieved of an entire army.
>
> Japan has acquired a base of operations of incalculable importance for exert-
> ing pressure on Korea, China, and Manchuria. It has achieved complete supremacy
> of the sea (meaning in the Pacific area most vital to Russia). Now the Russians have
> to fear for Vladivostok, as well as for Sakhalin.
>
> Events have corroborated the opinion of foreigners who laughed upon seeing
> hundreds of millions squandered on the purchase and building of splendid war-

* Reference to the Crimean War.
** Reference to the Baltic Fleet still at Madagascar.
*** The Commander-in-Chief had been recalled to St. Petersburg. Above article published in
Vperyod No.2, Jan.14, 1905 (*Collected Works of Lenin*, 8:47-48. Moscow edition 1962).

ships, and who declared that those expenditures were useless if no one knew how to manipulate such modern vessels.

The generals and commanders-in-chief proved themselves incompetent nonentities, and the officers were uneducated, undeveloped and untrained. The ignorance, illiteracy, and backwardness of the peasants (sailors and soldiers) became appallingly obvious when they came up against a progressive nation.

Never before has the military organization of a country had such a close bearing on its entire economic and cultural system.

Lenin included a prophecy: "The debacle has deeper implications; it signifies the collapse of our entire political system." It was, he stated, the inevitable consequence of imperialistic adventurism in which "people had to pay for autocracy with their life-blood." "War opens the eyes of millions to the disparity between peoples and governments."

Nadya's reaction to the war was one of simplistic outrage which was shared by her fellow-countrymen: "Russia had commenced the Japanese War, which brought out particularly the whole rottenness of the Tsarist Monarchy. In the Japanese War the defeatists* included not only the Bolsheviks but also the Mensheviks, and even the Liberals. A wave of popular indignation surged up from below. The working-class movement entered a new phase. News came more and more frequently about mass public meetings held in defiance of the police, and direct fights between police and workers."

War had activated the Russian people. Aroused from the lethargy that had overtaken them during the recent years of suppression, their restiveness stirred the somnambulant Tsar and his beleaguered ministers to renewed attempts at appeasement. But "bad government is never so vulnerable as when it attempts to reform itself," observed British historian James Anthony Froude. The writer was alluding to those reforms which, rather than being offered on principle, instead result from the pressure of long-standing popular grievances. In the latter case, the current régime is perceived as weak, and the moment ripe for its overthrow. Reform-minded tsars of the 19th Century reverted to tyranny when their moves toward liberalization opened the floodgates of revolution. Russia's bad government was vulnerable at the point where longevity became senile, and with Nicholas II, the senility of tsarism climaxed. Lenin called him "that idiot, Romanov."

In Russia, the poor of city and countryside, whose sons were being sent to die in the Far East, became "political" with a fervor that pamphleteering had failed to arouse. The moribund correspondence that Lenin and his wife had complained about now sprang to life, and they were receiving more than three hundred letters a month. Nadya read, sorted and passed them to her husband. Although many were illiterate, he found them valuable for their unvarnished

---

* Defeatism – active promotion of military defeat of the Fatherland with the objective of removing the government responsible for the war.

expression of the popular mood. "Volodya really knew how to read workers' letters," she observed. "I remember one letter, written by workers of the Odessa stone quarries. It was a collective essay, written in several primitive-looking hands, devoid of subjects and predicates, innocent of stops and commas . . . I do not remember what the letter referred to, but I remember what it looked like—paper and red ink."

How many letters of a similar nature were, immediately upon arrival, trashed by the Tsar's staff? . . . hundreds? . . . thousands? Lenin read them all, pacing up and down in thoughtful reflection. "Don't send resumés," he directed others who received correspondence from Russian workers. "Send me the originals."

Contact with individuals in Russia on a personal basis—heeding their opinions, responding to their grievances—was building an organization that surpassed in numbers and strength the original *Iskra*. Lenin was particularly concerned that the *Vperyod* organization should not become a perquisite of the Party's "elder statesmen." There exists among us," he said, "a kind of idiotic, philistine, spineless fear of youth,"—a backhanded rebuke to Plekhanov.

Nadya closed this phase of émigré life with the ominous remark: "We were already on the threshold of Nineteen 'Five [1905]."

8. The First Russian Revolution 1905–07

In St. Petersburg, following the League's collapse, Father Georgii Gapon, a priest of the Orthodox Church, became active among the workers. Unhampered by the presence of Marxists, most of whom were either in Siberian exile or had fled to Europe, Gapon was able to achieve unprecedented popularity. Neither his motives nor his methods aroused any suspicion in proletarian minds. As a "man of the cloth" he appealed to those in whom Marxist atheism had not matured, and before long he commanded a following that numbered thousands.

It is possible that his original intent, with its emphasis on passive resistance, was genuine. But at some point, impressed with his own success, he succumbed to an urge for power. As an *agent-provocateur* for the government, his rewards would be temporal rather than spiritual.

On Sunday January 9, 1905, thousands of workers rallied to form a procession with Father Gapon at their head. Streaming across Palace Bridge from Viborg, the crowd, chanting fervently, followed the priest's elevated banner— an ikon, symbolizing respect for Tsar and Church. Long before the procession wheeled left into Palace Square, the Imperial Guard, smartly at attention in ankle-length great coats and "kepis," were standing with rifles cocked. At one of the Palace windows directly above, someone with a camera waited expectantly. As the Square filled and Gapon prepared to offer a petition to "Our Little Father, the Tsar," several volleys of shot exploded into the crowd. From his vantage point, the mystery witness captured on film a horrifying spectacle: people running or in the act of falling, others prone on the stone pavement.

An expensive camera with rare, high-speed film? Was it Nicholas himself, a photography buff? Although his officials reported that he was not in residence, they had reason to protect their patron's reputation.

Gapon fled the Square, which was littered with 200 dead and over a thousand wounded. Somewhat later, he turned up in Switzerland where, for several months, he lived the life of a country squire.

Meanwhile, St. Petersburg erupted in protest. Fighting broke out in various parts of the city, and before long the entire country was paralyzed by strikes. "Bloody Sunday" became the rallying cry of revolution.

News of the Petersburg event reached Geneva that same night, and by morning of the 10th, telegrams from Swiss correspondents in Russia appeared under banner headlines in the Geneva *Tribune*. In the apartment on Rue de Colline, Monday began like any other day. Nadya and Volodya ate an early breakfast and started for the Société library. "On the way we met the

Lunacharskys* who were on their way to us," Nadya said. "I remember the figure of Lunacharsky's wife. Anne was so excited that she could not speak, but only helplessly waved her muff."

Lepeshinsky** had opened an émigré restaurant in Geneva, and the Bolsheviks immediately gathered there to digest the news.

> We had been living from one issue of the *Tribune* to the next, and now we were stunned. The atmosphere was so tense that we scarcely spoke to one another. We were overwhelmed with the thought that the revolution had already started, that the bonds of faith in the Tsar were broken, that the time was quite near when "tyranny will fall, and the people will rise up—great, mighty and free!"

Upon arrival in Geneva, Gapon first contacted the Social Revolutionaries, who immediately claimed him as "their man," and through him, responsibility for the Petersburg workers' movement. Their support gave him enormous prestige, and soon London newspapers were paying him large sums for journalist contributions. Elated at finding himself an international celebrity, the Priest told a woman S-R that he wanted to meet Lenin. Having previously been brushed off by Plekhanov, Gapon's presence at Rue Colline seemed undesirable, so the two men agreed to meet in a café.

Prior to the rendezvous, Lenin was extremely nervous, but curiosity overcame his scruples. From Nadya's description of the meeting, gleaned from her husband, Gapon appears to have put on a superlative performance of Tsar-hating. V. reacted cooly to this revolutionary fervor, but if Nadya's chronicle is to be credited, he was not suspicious. "We'll have to teach him," she quoted V. as saying. "I said to him: 'Don't you listen to flattery, little father: study, or that's where you'll find yourself'—and I pointed under the table."

This handsome, bearded young man, son of a wealthy Ukrainian peasant, did in fact end up "under the table." An active member of the Zubatov group, he was later exposed as an *agent provocateur* and killed by the S.R.s.*** Nadya's conclusion: once a priest, always a priest. "It would be difficult to meet anyone so thoroughly permeated with a priest's psychology as Gapon," she wrote.

Lenin's encounter with him, while of negligible significance, nevertheless brought him *au courant* with conditions then existing in Russia: i.e., the S.R. apparent takeover of Viborg. The Social Revolutionary Party was predicated on terrorism. And what, historically had been the result? In terms of social progress—nothing. An individual or group, employing guns and bombs, could not substitute for an enlightened, organized proletariat.

The Narodniks and other organizations from which the S.R.s sprang, had no program beyond acquisition of land; "Kill the Tsar," they said, "'take the land, and let the future take care of itself." After wedding terrorism to their par-

---

* A.V.Lunacharsky was one of the editors of *Vperyod.*
** Lenin's friend from exile days in Siberia.
*** The Zubatov society was created to exalt the tsar and tell the people he would ease their economic hardship. Zubatovs blamed the bureaucrats for social ills.

ticular need, the S.R.s were amenable to any form of government that would concede land.

"Revolution is an art," wrote Karl Marx. Lenin considered terrorism—as part of ideology—a form of insanity. In order for revolution to succeed, it depended upon what Lenin called "the balance of forces": a confluence of several specific conditions and events, one of which could be war, with its socio/economic dislocation leading to consolidation of the various social groups for revolution. To subjoin a program of reorganization to the primary task of overthrowing the Tsar was, he declared, the task of Social Democracy. And in this, both Mensheviks and Bolsheviks were agreed. Where they differed—and this was crucial—concerned the form of post-revolution government.

Act Two of the Russian Revolution was delayed for more than a decade. Meanwhile, Father Gapon's role in producing Bloody Sunday was that of catalyst for a dress rehearsal. In 1905-07, Lenin's balance of forces did not prevail. This he understood, hence his optimism, despite overwhelming setbacks, during the years to follow.

The uprising of recent days, quickly subdued by the authorities, was an object lesson showing all revolutionary factions that attempts to compromise with the *status quo* were futile; that Gapon's ikon had failed to protect a peaceful demonstration from rifle fire. It also taught the folly of unpreparedness. The balance of forces was notably absent when an unarmed crowd came within range of the Imperial Guard.

Before Gapon met his end, Lenin engaged him for gun-running into Russia. "The proletariat must be armed," V. said. Plekhanov and the armchair theorists raised a storm of protest, further distancing themselves from Lenin whom they now accused of being a quasi-terrorist.

The business of supplying weapons, purchased in England and transported in a leaky ship or smuggled across borders, was both complex and inadequate, and when the "Little Father" complained about having to hide out in Viborg under an assumed name, it became evident that this haphazard procedure would have to be restructured. Many émigrés were returning to Russia, and Volodya and Nadya decided to join them. Before leaving, Lenin discussed with colleagues the need for convening another Party Congress; events in Russia appeared to be moving toward revolution.

The staff of *Vperyod* had grown and, in addition, a new publication—*Proletary*—had been launched. Among those who labored in the editorial office on Rue de Carouge, two would become memorable. Vladimir Dmitrievich Bonch-Bruyevich was a bear of a man; energetic, loyal to Lenin and, above all, practical. Leo Kamenev, on the other hand, was a slender, scholarly type with pince-nez, a short pointed beard, and tidy starched collar; subsequently, he became "Castor" to a "Pollux" named Zinoviev. These "heavenly twins" later attempted to dominate the socialist firmament.

Lenin went alone from Switzerland to Stockholm where a man was to provide him with documents under an assumed name. However, the man failed to appear. V. waited two weeks before favorable weather allowed him to board a steamer for Hanko in Finland. From there he went by rail to Helsingfors (Helsinki) where he changed trains for St. Petersburg. Ten days later, after settling affairs in Geneva, Nadya followed him.

Finland, at that time part of the Russian Empire, was in the throes of revolution, and Nadya's account of the journey was humorously off-handed:

> A police spy fastened himself on me at Stockholm and afterwards on the train from Hanko to Helsingfors. In the railway carriages everyone was talking loudly. I got into conversation with a Finnish Party-worker who described the successes of the revolution. "Spies," he said "why we've arrested 'em all and shoved 'em. in jail." My glance fell on the spy who was accompanying me.
>
> "But new ones can arrive," I said, beginning to laugh, and looking expressively at my detective. The Finn grasped the situation. "Oh!" he cried, "you have only to say the word if you notice anybody, and we'll immediately arrest him!"

When the train paused briefly at the next small wayside station, the spy got out, and that was the last she saw of him.

At Finland Station in St. Petersburg, there was no evidence of a city seething with revolution. A comrade with whom V. was staying met her and conducted her to his apartment. "Volodya was extremely embarrassed when living in other people's quarters. It hindered his capacity for work. When I arrived, he hastened to find a place where we could be together."

Since Nadya was able to move about more freely than her husband, she went apartment hunting and eventually located furnished rooms on the Nevsky. But living independently was hazardous. Upon registering for legal residence, they moved in with friends in the Gretechevsky Prospekt.

> Immediately the house was surrounded by police spies. Our terrified host did not sleep the whole night, and walked around with a revolver in his pocket. "Oh, devil take him," said Volodya, "he will get us into a scrape." So we went to live illegally again, and apart from each other.

Nadya was given a passport with the name of Prascovia Onegina; her husband changed his passport several times.

A "legal" periodical called *Novaya Zhizn*—"New Life"—was circulating in Moscow and Petersburg. Its nominal publisher was Maria Andreyeva who, gossip said, was "living in sin" with Maxim Gorky, now divorced from his first wife. Whether or not theirs was a common-law marriage, nevertheless the relationship was both close and durable (Nadya referred to her as Gorky's wife). Andreyeva, a comely woman of matronly dimensions and pleasant expression, had starred in early productions of Gorky's play *The Lower Depths*. It is probable that her position with the newspaper was a cover for her husband, whose political views would have curtailed the life of *Novaya Zhizn.*

The Bolsheviks were invited to contribute editorials. Lenin's first article was a businesslike essay on the Party's "new line." Boldly discarding the idea of revolution instigated by small circles within the Party, he postulated the necessity for basing the Party program on worker initiative; a stand that was anathema to some of the Marxist elite who considered themselves the custodians of revolution.

Soon after arrival, Nadya had gone to the Smolenski Sunday Evening classes.

> No longer were geography and natural history taught. Propaganda was now conducted in classes crammed full of working men and women. They sat there listening to the orators, not winking an eyelid. Nobody asked any questions. The currents of Party work and that of the activities of the workers themselves somehow did not seem to converge.

From chance encounters on the street with her former Sunday School pupils, she learned that the workers had developed tremendous initiative. It appeared to her that they had outstripped their instructors, whose pedantic approach to Socialism was at variance with its dynamic substance.

While living apart, Nadya and Volodya met in secret at the *New Life* office. His move to an apartment at the corner of Besseunaya and Nadezhdinskaya Streets now made it possible for Nadya to visit her husband. "I had to enter through the kitchen and speak in undertones, but we were nevertheless able to discuss everything."

As in Geneva, Lenin' s independent views were opposed by the Mensheviks, and before long the latter withdrew, leaving the Bolsheviks in control of the newspaper. Gorky, as a journalist-contributor to the paper and his wife as publisher, found themselves in the awkward position of having to choose sides. Although they did not break with Lenin at this time, the recent editorial rift prevented a close relationship with Lenin.

But what the Opposition considered to be obstinacy was, in reality, Lenin's extraordinary identification with The People. Only with them did he feel ideologically at ease. This willingness to forego Marxist dignity and mingle with the laborers of factory and field resulted in comic situations to which no other leader of modern times would have subjected himself.

After returning from a Moscow conference with Party members, Nadya visited him. Police spies were lurking about, but V. had not left the house since moving in, and consequently was unaware of them. While unpacking his trunk, Nadya discovered a pair of large, round, blue glasses. "What on earth are these?" she queried, to which he responded that comrades in Moscow had provided him with a disguise before putting him aboard a non-stop train moments before it left the station. "Our job now was to get out as soon as possible," she noted. "We emerged arm in arm, which was a thing we never usually did, walked in the opposite direction to that we needed, took three cabs one after another, traversed several courtyards and arrived at a comrade's house, having shaken off our followers."

They stayed overnight with one of Nadya's friends, and in the morning hired a cab and drove past the house where V. had been living. Spies were still outside the house, so V. did not return. Instead, he sent someone to collect his things and settle with the landlady.

Despite constant police surveillance, the Petersburg Bolsheviks were feverishly active. Nadya was in charge of appointments and communications. Ciphered addresses were kept in matchboxes or inside book bindings; committee meetings were held of which no record was kept. "Everything depended upon memory." People flocked to the *New Life* office for fake passports, literature, instructions, advice. "It is difficult to imagine how we coped. Nobody was in charge."

But while St. Petersburg was attempting to break the police stranglehold, Moscow workers and their leaders grasped the initiative.

On February 17, 1905, the Tsaritsa's brother-in-law, hated Governor-General of Moscow, was murdered by a Social Revolutionary. A month later, the peasants, awakened from their recent slumbers, rose in the countryside. In May, Admiral Togo sank the Russian Fleet. In June, the first Soviet (Council) was formed at Lodz, an industrial city of Russian Poland—a spontaneous move to organize a local workers' government. That same month, sailors of the battle cruiser *Potemkin* mutinied. In July, a Soviet was organized in Kostroma, a mill town 230 miles from Moscow. In October, all railways of the Empire (except Finland) were on strike. October through December witnessed a series of political strikes which culminated in Moscow with a walkout of 150,000 workers. Russia's second city now assumed the lead: barricades were erected in the streets and guerrilla warfare sent the inhabitants scurrying for cover during a six-day siege of The Establishment.

The immobilized hands of a giant clock, lubricated by Bloody Sunday, had finally begun to move.

> In the beginning of December 1905, there took place
> the Tammerfors Conference. What a pity the min-
> utes of this Conference were not preserved!—N.K.

The Finnish city of Tammerfors (now Tampere), second only to Helsingfors in size and importance, developed as an industrial center under the aegis of Tsar Alexander I. In 1900, its proletarian inhabitants, like those of other western European cities, established a People's House where Social Democratic leaders and workers met to discuss ways for improving conditions in shops and factories. The building contained a meeting hall, an office for Party business, a library of Socialist literature, and a college for workers.

Since the recent ferment in Moscow indicated a resurgence of revolution-ary spirit, the Bolshevik wing of Russia's S-D Labor Party moved quickly to support what appeared to be the beginning of a general uprising. Forty-one representatives from all over Russia, including Lenin and his wife, converged on Tammerfors, 125 miles north of Helsingfors, for a meeting to formulate strategy. Upon emerging from the railway station, many of the delegates walked or rode by horsecab down the city's main street, Hameenkatu, to the Hotel Baier. The Lenins stayed at the Pelleri tourist home.

Early on the bitterly cold morning of December 11, delegates made their way through snowdrifts to the People's House at No.19 Hallituskatu, a broad avenue crossing Hameenkatu at its far end from the railway depot. In a sec-ond-floor meeting hall belonging to the college, they sat on wooden benches behind long tables supplied with pen, ink and paper for recording the resolu-tions to be propounded. Among the delegates were many women—vigorous in appearance, with plainly dressed hair and clad in long, bulky, woolen gar-ments.

"It is hardly likely that any of the delegates to that conference could ever forget it," Nadya said.

> Among those present, were Lozovsky, Baransky, and Yaroslavsky. I remember those comrades because their reports from the localities were so enthrallingly interesting . . . We passed a resolution on the necessity for the immediate preparation and organization of the armed insurrection. . . . In the intervals between sessions, we learned to shoot.

During the deliberations, which lasted until the 17th, Lenin presented the Party's agrarian program. When a delegation of Finnish workers visited the conference, Lenin promised them Finland's independence after the Russian Revolution, "provided our Party has enough influence."

The event was noteworthy for being the first formal conference of Russia's Social Democratic Labor Party conducted by the Bolsheviks independent of the Party's other factions. The conference was likewise significant for another reason: it was here that Lenin first met Stalin, a delegate from the Caucusus. That neither Stalin's presence nor his report is mentioned in Nadya's account, written many years later under the Stalin régime, indicated that she refused to be coerced into placing him among the leaders at Tammerfors. This omission was later "rectified" when Soviet artists began painting Stalin into the Tam-merfors canvas, side by side with Lenin and Yaroslavsky!

"We returned to Petersburg," Nadya concluded,

> on the very eve of the Semenov Regiment's departure to quell the Moscow insur-rection. While walking near Trinity Church, I observed one of the soldiers and a young worker in heated conversation. The faces were so expressive that it was clear

that the worker was asking the soldier not to take action against the workers, and it was also clear that the Semenov man would not agree to this.

Regardless of proletarian solidarity, however, Social Democrats were unable to rally Petersburg workers for support of the rebel workers of Moscow. "Our leaders were frustrated, but they had not taken into consideration how fatigued the Petersburg workers were from the preceding series of strikes and, what was most important, that they felt how badly they were organized for a decisive fight with Tsardom, how poorly they were armed."

In Moscow it was a life and death struggle. Inadequately armed workers were slaughtered by the Tsar's crack regiment, and those taken prisoner were subjected to gross cruelty. By December 30th, all hope of a genuine revolution had faded. At the railway station in Moscow, Lenin's sister Anna was met by a working woman who spoke bitterly of Petersburg's quiescence: "Thank you, Petersburgers, for your support, for sending the Semenov Regiment."

After studying conditions surrounding the recent debacle, Lenin observed prophetically:

> It would be greatly to the advantage of the government to suppress isolated action of the proletarians as it has been doing. The government would like to challenge the workers of St. Petersburg to go into battle at once under circumstances that would be most unfavorable for them. But the workers will not allow themselves to be provoked and will be able to continue their path of independent preparation for the next all-Russian action.

For the next several months, Finland supplanted Petersburg as the hothouse of revolution. Through the Capital's Finland station passed conspirators looking anxiously over their shoulders for the omnipresent police. As a historical landmark, the depot ranked high among relics of the Revolution, and its demise under German guns during World War II must have saddened those inclined to nostalgia. How many foreigners—or even natives—sensed the ambiance of revolution lingering in a modern glass oblong that is today's "Finlandski Vokzal"? Who among them feels stirred upon beholding this functional successor to a gateway for baroque emotions?

"With autocracy restored, we went underground." Nadya became liaison for the Organization, arranging places for rendezvous with comrades arriving from all parts of the Empire. At first she met them in a back room of the *New Life* office (it included a book shop where illegal literature was sold). "One day the door burst open and a police inspector poked his head in. 'Aha', he said, and locked us all in. We could not climb through the window, so we just sat looking at each other."

When he returned, they blandly lied about the nature of the literature, which meanwhile had been destroyed. "He looked at us mockingly, but did not arrest us, merely took our names and addresses—which were, of course, fictitious."

Another port of call was the office of a dentist on Nikolayevskaya street. The door was opened by a servant, and Nadya, carrying armloads of illegal material, "sailed headlong down the corridor."

> On my track, ghastly pale and trembling all over, pounced the servant. "The Colonel is not at home." "What Colonel?" "Colonel Riman." I had stumbled into the flat of Riman, Colonel of the Semenov Regiment which had quelled the Moscow rising. His servant thought I had come to assassinate his master.

After camouflaging her blunder with vague words about a toothache and having expected to find a dentist at No. 33, she hastily departed.

Although near-misses occurred frequently, Nadya managed to elude apprehension, but the greatest impediment to her activities was that of communicating with her husband. Sometimes they met at the Vienna Restaurant; on other occasions they engaged a room at one of the hotels. Once, on their way to a hotel, their cab passed a frail, slender young man walking alone. "It's Yuzef," said V., stopping the cab. "Climb aboard," he called, "if you don't mind sitting in the driver's box."

"I was brought up in the country," the man laughingly responded, "and can even travel on the driving seat of a sleigh." As he hoisted himself up, his eyes, large and expressive, twinkled with humor—he was clean-shaven, boyish, almost aesthetic in appearance.

Henceforth, the big names of Russia's October Revolution crept into Nadya's *Memoir*. Time and circumstance would give them substance. Of all those who rose from obscurity, "Yusef"—Felix Djerzhinsky—is perhaps the least known or understood.

V's discomfiture under the kindly but intrusive hospitality of his hosts became so acute that he and Nadya went to live together in rooms on Pantaleuymonovskaya Street. Once again the police closed in, and one evening he failed to return from a meeting. "So there sat I (sic), at the window, all night long, and when morning came I concluded that he had been arrested." Word reached her that he had escaped to Finland and was living in a dacha (country house) called "Vasa" near the town of Kuokkala.

The house was a rambling wooden structure reminiscent of Swedish rural, which belonged to G.D. Leyteysen, loyal Bolshevik and financial contributor to *Vperyod* and *Proletary*. More like a hotel than a residence, "Vasa" housed some of the editorial staff of numerous Social-Democrat periodicals that appeared in rapid succession; as each was closed down by the authorities, another took its place. Lenin was given a private room where he spent his days writing. His presence attracted many rank-and-file Party members and before long, "Vasa" became the revolution's headquarters. Self-appointed couriers daily rode the train between Finland Station and Kuokkala, bringing letters and newspapers from the Capital, and returning there with messages and V's articles.

Only once during this period did he travel to Petersburg, where he addressed a meeting and conferred with the Party faithful. While he was absent from the city, Nadya served as his deputy.

The "Vasa" group, in conjunction with the Mensheviks, convened a Congress in Stockholm for the purpose of unifying the Party's two wings, and Nadya was given a mandate from Kazan to be a voting delegate. "I arrived at the Congress rather late, accompanied by T- and by Claudia Sverdlova. Claudia's husband (Yakov Sverdlov, a future leader of the October Revolution) had intended to come, but the Ural workers were reluctant to part with him."

In St. Petersburg, meanwhile, the first Imperial Duma was formed, a landmark in the history of Russian absolutism. Unfortunately for democracy, the Tsar retained his authority at the apex of an administrative/legislative/judicial pyramid. A new party, the Constitutional. Democrats had just taken shape, thus dividing the revolutionary pie into three mutually antagonistic segments. The C-D's, abbreviated "Cadets," were against the Tsar but pro-bourgeoisie; some of them were in favor of a constitutional monarchy. The burning issue now was: should Social Democrats participate in the Duma? Lenin said they should (and eventually they did, but not without internecine controversy). Most of his colleagues disagreed with his opinion that it would benefit the Cause if S-D's were to utilize this all-Russian platform for airing their views.

He was aware that the Party would be a voting minority, but he anticipated an eventual union between Social Democrats and Social Revolutionaries to form a bloc whose sheer weight of numbers would relegate the upper-class Cadets to a minority position. First, however, was the primary task of unifying the Social Democratic Party itself; the Mensheviks were now advocating a bloc with the Cadets.

When the Stockholm Congress adjourned, having achieved a nominal truce between Bolsheviks and Mensheviks, Nadya and Volodya returned to Petersburg.

> We took quarters on Zabalkanskoya Street, I with the name of Prascovia Onegina and V. under the name of Tchkheidze. There was a through courtyard, and living there was extremely peaceful save for the fact that our neighbor, some military man, engaged in deadly fights with his wife, beating her and dragging her up and down the corridor by her hair. Save also for the amiability of the landlady, who would ask continually after Volodya's relatives, assuring us that she knew him when he was a four-year-old youngster.

Lenin's only public speech during this period was delivered on May 9th— "one of those exhilarating white Petersburg nights" Nadya recalled. A large crowd of workers jammed the Panina Hall, and among them stalked two police inspectors. Suddenly they disappeared, and Nadya, standing in the back of the hall, overheard a waggish remark: "Someone must have sprinkled them with insect powder." The meeting was called to order by the Cadet chairman who introduced "Karpov." A smattering of applause broke the silence as Party members recognized Lenin. Nadya observed with apprehension her husband's demeanor as he mounted the platform. Pale and obviously nervous, he began to speak, his voice low and at first barely audible; but as he continued, a wave of enthusiasm swept the audience: "Who is it, who is it?" At the conclusion, he mopped his brow and retired unobtrusively, to the cheers of sweaty laborers who began tearing up red shirts for banners. Revolutionary songs joined the shuffle of bodies inching their way out of the hall.

Lenin didn't return home that night but stayed with a friend; as "Karpov," he understood that another meeting of this dimension could land him back in Siberia.

Lenin has been accused of cowardice, of remaining in the background while goading others to man the battle-line. Although a general may win adulation for front-line heroism, martyrdom does little to advance a cause in its embryonic stage. Being alive for the revolution, he reasoned, was preferable to wasting away in prison or in some frozen outpost beyond the Urals.

Barely two months after convening the Duma, Tsar Nicholas, alarmed at its aggressive character, ordered it dissolved. All socialist newspapers were closed down, and the police began hounding suspects. Arrest followed arrest. Frustrated hopes gave way to rebellion; first the Kronstadt sailors, then those of Sveaborg at the Russian naval base in Helsingfors harbor. "We sat in Menzhinsky's flat, waiting for news on the progress of the uprising." At length Nadya sallied forth in search of information. Upon approaching a certain house in Gussevsky Street, she met two women walking arm in arm. "If you are going to number so-and-so," they cautioned her, "don't go in. There's a raid going on and they're arresting everybody."

The next day, Lenin left for Kuokkala. "After a while, I also went to live there." Each morning Nadya took the early train to Petersburg and returned late at night. Every time she passed safely through Finland Station was considered a gratuitous act of Fate. Unquestionably her regular arrivals and departures were stretching the laws of chance. One evening might she, too, fail to return home?

She found living at Vasa uncomfortable. Eventually the Leyteysens went away, leaving the big, drafty house to their Bolshevik friends, and V. immediately arranged for his sister Maria and Nadya's mother to join them. With the entire lower floor at their disposal, the family kept open house for the stream of political visitors passing through Kuokkala on their way to and from St. Petersburg. The Bogdanov family moved in upstairs followed by one Dubrovinsky. "At that time," Nadya observed, "the Russian police had decided not to meddle in Finland, and we had considerable freedom there. The door of the house was never bolted, a jug of milk and a loaf of broad were left in the dining room over night, and bedding spread on the divan, so that in the event of anyone coming on the night train they could enter without waking anybody, have some refreshment, and lie down to sleep. In the morning we often found comrades in the dining room who had come in the night."

Nadya and a woman friend spent their days in Petersburg interviewing comrades in the dining room of the Technological Institute where, because of the large number of diners, "no one took any notice of us." One day, however, a man named Kamo arrived for an interview. Dressed in Caucasian costume, with rows of white-tipped cartridges adorning the pockets of his tunic, he was a sensation. Everyone stopped eating, all eyes were fastened on a large round object he was carrying wrapped in a napkin. "A bomb"! they conjectured. Instead, he unwrapped a huge watermelon. "For you and your husband," he said to Nadya, shyly. "My aunt sent it." Kamo was a frequent visitor to Vasa, where he arrived fully armed. "He and my mother became friends," said Nadya, "and she used to strap his revolvers on his back with particular care."

Under Lenin's direction, a "samizdat"—privately printed, illegal—edition of *Proletary* was distributed in Viborg by a fearless woman named Lydia Gobi. But she needed an assistant, so comrade Komissarov suggested his wife Katya, "a modest-looking woman with short hair and a businesslike manner." Nadya's suspicions were aroused. "I immediately felt an acute mistrust of this woman; I could not understand where the feeling came from, and it soon disappeared." Too soon, as it turned out. All contacts entrusted to the Komissarovs came to grief. The pair was spying for the police, "but they never found out where Volodya was living; in 1905 and 1906 the police apparatus was still considerably disorganized."

A second *Duma* was called for February 1907, and Lenin, having won in his bid for Bolshevik participation delegated Bogdanov to supervise the work of Bolshevik deputies. But this seemingly direct line of communication between Social Democracy and the State Organization was immediately complicated by factionalism. On the train one night while returning to Kuokkala, Nadya encountered Axelrod who—true to his Menshevik inclinations—talked of converting Social Democracy to a labor organization.

However, plans were already afoot to convene a united-Party Congress in London. "The delegates arrived in St. Petersburg in throngs, coming before the credentials committee in a long file." Nadya, as a member of the four-person committee, was kept busy screening delegates and eluding the police. Since tracking individuals in a large industrial city was inefficient, the authorities concentrated on Finland Station, where several delegates were arrested on their way out of the country. That most escaped detection was due in part to Nadya's personal experience with the conduit to Finland, as well as her expertise in conspiratorial techniques.

"I did not hurry back to Kuokkala," she noted. "I did not arrive home until Sunday evening—and what did I find? Seventeen delegates were sitting in our place, cold and hungry, having eaten and drunk nothing. Our domestic worker had Sundays off, so it took me a considerable time before I could provide them all with food and drink."

Lenin and Bogdanov had already left for London when she arrived home, and after bidding the seventeen comrades *bon voyage*, she returned to the Capital. "I did not go to the Congress myself; there was no one to whom I could hand over the secretarial work. Those were difficult times. The police were getting more and more impudent. People began to be afraid to put Bolsheviks up for the night, or to let them use their houses for appointments." She was particularly hurt by one erstwhile supporter who sent word by an emissary that his premises would no longer be available for interviews: "I was vexed that he had not told me himself."

London, May 1907. Maxim Gorky attended the Party Congress as a "free-lance socialist." More an observer than participant, his perceptions as a creative writer were focused on personalities rather than events. "I had never met Lenin before this," he stated, "but what I had heard from the enthusiastic account of those who knew him personally had attracted me strongly toward him."

Their meeting-place was the Brotherhood Church in Southgate Road, a wooden building whose interior had been stripped of ecclesiastical ornament to a degree that Gorky found "absurd." While the delegates milled about prior to the opening session, someone brought the two men together. "Upon being introduced, Lenin shook me heartily by the hand and scrutinizing me with his keen eyes and speaking in the tone of an old acquaintance, he said jocularly; 'So glad you've come. I believe you're fond of a scrap? There's going to be a fine old scuffle here'."

Gorky was taken aback by Lenin's appearance. "Standing there jauntily with his hands somehow poked up under his armpits, he seemed too ordinary, did not give the impression of being a leader. Something was lacking in him. I had expected someone quite different, and before me now stood a bald-headed, stocky, sturdy person, speaking with a guttural roll of his r's, and holding my hand in one of his while with the other he wiped his forehead. He was beaming affectionately at me with his strangely bright eyes."

Mentally contrasting Lenin with Plekhanov, whom likewise he had just met for the first time, Gorky replicated Vera Zasulich's description of "The Father of Russian Marxism": "He stood with folded arms, looking at me with the severe slightly bored expression with which an overworked teacher regards an additional pupil. Nothing that he said has remained in my memory except the extremely trite remark: 'I am an admirer of your work,' and neither of us during the whole time of the Congress felt any desire for a heart-to-heart talk."

Obversely, Lenin, in the brief moments before the meeting was called to order, spoke knowledgeably with Gorky about the latter's recent book *Mother*.

How would Gorky have described Nadya . . . a short, somewhat pudgy woman with no taste in clothes? . . . A "bulochkin" with prominent eyes and straight, pulled-back hair? With an occasional sweet smile that erased the twin furrows between her brows? Would he have noticed her beautiful, expressive hands, through which had passed so much of the Party's business? Or would he, too, have ignored her, as others so often did?

To Lenin, Gorky* also seemed ordinary. There was nothing about him to suggest the artist. With his bushy moustache and tousled hair, with unpressed suit of indifferent cut and fabric, the author of widely acclaimed plays, children's books and novels might have been a Yankee farmer. But his facial expression was that of one who had seen the best and the worst of life— contemplative, receptive to impressions, compassionate, yet slightly quizzical. Upon first meeting him, one would have said: "He is a person I would confide in." Even now, a slight flush on his cheeks betrayed the tuberculosis that later caused him to remark almost casually: "I can't undertake anything at the moment because I am spitting blood."

As the Congress opened, three hundred delegates representing 150,000 organized workers sat at attention, a bizarre "congregation" in that sanctuary of London sectarians. Plekhanov delivered the first speech. Gorky, sitting beside the pulpit, watched rather than listened.

> Plekhanov, in a frock coat, closely buttoned up like a Protestant pastor, spoke like a preacher confident that his ideas are incontrovertible. Way above the heads of the delegates he skillfully weighed out his beautifully rounded phrases, and whenever anyone on the Bolshevik benches uttered a sound or whispered to a comrade, the venerable orator made a slight pause and sent his glance into him like a needle. One of the buttons of his frock coat was a great favorite with Plekhanov; he stroked it caressingly, pressed it like an electric bell—it seemed to be this pressure which interrupted the flowing current of his speech. The person who did the most fidgeting on the Bolshevik benches was Lenin.

Martov "did not argue but implored; at times he seemed almost hysterical." "Little Theodore Dan spoke like a man whose relation to the authentic truth is one of father to daughter—he has begotten and fostered it. He is Karl Marx incarnate, and the Bolsheviks—half-educated, ill-mannered children." Rosa Luxemburg spoke "eloquently, passionately, using irony with great effect."

> Then came Lenin. "Comrades!" he said in his guttural way. He seemed to me to speak badly, but after a minute, we were all absorbed in his speech . . . The unity, directness, simplicity of his speech, his whole appearance in the pulpit, was a work of classic art; everything was there, and yet there was nothing superfluous . . . he gave a shorter speech than the orators before him, but he made a much greater impression.

Gorky was appalled by the subsequent wrangling over "order of the day" which soon threatened to disrupt the proceedings. "But more than that," he said, "was the hostile attitude of the Reformers (Marxist revisionists) toward

---

* Gorky's real name was Alexei Maximovich Pyeshkov. Lenin referred to him as "A.M.".

Lenin. It oozed and spouted out of their speeches like water under pressure from an old hosepipe."

The first session adjourned and the delegates drifted toward the canteen organized by Gorky's wife, Maria. In their wake was Lenin. To Maria Andreyeva he queried: "What do you think? Are the workers getting enough to eat? No? H'm! Perhaps we can get more sandwiches?"

A comical episode took place in the inn where Gorky was staying. On a visit to Gorky's room, Lenin began feeling the bedding with a preoccupied air. "What are you doing?" Gorky asked. "I'm just looking to see if the sheets are well aired," came the reply. What difference did it make what the sheets were like in London? "You must take care of yourself," Lenin explained. In Russia there were often bedbugs, and travelers contracted a variety of diseases from slovenly conditions in public hostels.

Substantively, the Congress was a disaster. "Volodya returned later than the rest," his wife reported. "His appearance was most extraordinary; moustache clipped short, beard shaved off, and wearing a huge straw hat. He was exhausted by the Congress, overwrought and could not eat." To further complicate matters, the second *Duma* had just been dissolved, and the entire Bolshevik contingent descended on Vasa late that same night.

While feeding and housing a veritable army of callers, Nadya tried unsuccessfully to shield her husband from emotional encounters. Finally, "I prepared his things and packed him off to Stirsuden in the heart of Finland."

Like many well-to-do Petersburgers, the family of Lydia Knippovich owned a country house in Finland. At Stirsuden, a short distance from the Russian Capital, their rural retreat was an island of hospitality maintained by a small staff of servants. Lydia's father was a prominent biologist and university professor who became involved in the revolutionary movement; her mother, independently wealthy, had been contributing money to the Cause. Their daughter, raised in this atmosphere of social concern, joined the *Narodnaya Volya* Group* in Helsingfors as a young girl. When the group disbanded, she transferred her allegiance to the League of Struggle and, as previously noted, suffered for it in a Petersburg jail.

After "settling our affairs," Nadya and her mother went to Stirsuden where they found V. somewhat recovered from recent stresses. "They told me that during the first few days he would sit down under a fir tree and immediately drop off to sleep. The children called him "old drowsy." Lydia fed him on reindeer ham and omelettes, and by the time I arrived, he was becoming his old self again. Those were wonderful days at Stirsuden; the woods, the sea, wildest of the wild.

The only surviving letter of this period—a joint epistle written to Maria

---

* The organization to which Lenin's executed brother, Alexander, belonged.

Alexandrovna—confirms Nadya's later recollection. Postmarked "Stjernsund," it identifies more precisely the Stirsuden of Nadya's *Memoir* as a bay in the Gulf of Finland. V.'s brief paragraph noted that he came back from London "terribly tired, but I have now completely recovered; here you can have a wonderful rest, swimming, walking, no people and no work. No people and no work— that is the best thing for me. I expect to be here another fortnight or so and then return to work. Nadya and her mother are well and are having a good holiday." Nadya's portion of the letter noted that "we have all put on so much weight it's not decent to show ourselves in public."

Unfortunately, their desire for solitude was thwarted by some Russian neighbors who were housing two prominent Petersburg Bolsheviks; the latter became offended at V.'s efforts to avoid them. Bicycle rides, days spent by the sea, visits to Zenia—a Knippovich relative who was a professional singer and treated them to a private concert—hours of blissful indolence that ended when V. and Nadya left for nearby Terijoki and another contentious conference. At issue was Bolshevik participation in the third Duma. "Boycottists did not wish to reckon with grim realities, but were intoxicated by their own high-sounding phrases." Nadya describe how comrade K- rode up on a bicycle and stood outside the open window of a house where the meeting took place, listening to Lenin's speech in defense of participation in the *Duma*. "Afterwards he did not come in, but walked away deep in thought. Indeed, there was plenty to think about."

Because of rumor about an impending police raid on Vasa, Lenin did not return there; instead, he went further west into Finland, leaving Nadya and her mother to terminate their residency with the Leyteysens. By this time, living out of a suitcase had become a way of life, but the simple routine of packing was followed by a task of greater importance. Nadya and Natalya Bogdanov spent days sorting the Party archives, burning some and entrusting the remainder to a Finnish comrade for safekeeping. "We burned so energetically that one morning I noticed that the snow all around Vasa was strewn with ashes. If the gendarmes had come, they would have found plenty of evidence." When word came that the police were in Kuokkala, Natalya's husband and Dubrovinsky hid in the woods, leaving the women to deal with an eventuality which, fortunately, did not transpire.

But if the police neglected Vasa they were diligent elsewhere in Finland, interrupting V.'s link with St. Petersburg and eventually driving him from the country.

While Nadya was in the Capital making arrangements for the care of her mother before joining V. abroad, he nearly met his end on an ice-floe in the Gulf of Finland. The final leg of his journey to the safety of Stockholm began at a place Nadya called Oglbu.

Äggleby, then known by its Swedish name, was a small village near Helsingfors served by local railway. Now a part of Helsinki and called Oulunkala, it is little changed except for a highrise encroaching on the original wooden dwellings. It was (and is) an agglomeration of houses clinging to undulating terrain and surrounded by trees. Instead of a grid of streets, the village straggled in disarray over its bumpy, ungraceful underpinning. The effect was that of houses planted in a forest—cozy, quiet, secluded, ideal for those in hiding.

In a large house on the outskirts, two young women, sisters named Vinsten, took in boarders. However, income from their remote *pension* was insufficient to sustain them, and each morning they commuted a fifteen-minute ride to the city where they worked.

"One day in 1907," the sisters remembered, "a certain influential person, instructor at the University of Helsingfors, telephoned to ask we could give refuge to one of the Russian émigrés. Since we were against tsarism, we readily agreed. Then this gentleman appeared. He was of medium stature, ruddy-faced, not very good looking. Speaking in German, he explained exactly what he wanted."

After showing him through the house, the stranger chose a room from which he could observe any suspicious activity outside. "Our home was ideal," the sisters noted. "We were near a railway station in case he had to leave in a hurry; and a nearby woods could, if necessary, serve as hiding-place." Their only contact with him was at mealtime. "He spoke very little, was quiet and reserved and rarely left his room where he assiduously wrote. Now and then he went to Helsingfors. One time an attractive Russian woman came to see him, and later we learned that she was his wife. Soon afterward he disappeared. We concluded that he had fled from the gendarmes."

Not until many years later did the now-elderly sisters learn the identity of their boarder. "We happened to see his photograph in the newspaper. There was no mistaking it; Lenin had been our guest!"

Nadya described "a formidably clean, cold room with lace curtains and everything neatly in place. While his hostesses socialized in the next room—there was a continual sound of laughter, a piano, and the chattering of Finnish language—Volodya tiptoed about his room while composing the text of a book begun at Vasa: *The Agrarian Program of Social Democracy.*"

The usual route to Sweden was by steamer from the port of Åbo (Turku), the sea-lane kept open in winter by icebreakers. But with all departure points under police surveillance, a Finnish comrade suggested that V. cross the ice to an island beyond the harbor where a steamer would pick him up after leaving Åbo (the Gulf Islands were outside Russian jurisdiction).

"Although it was December," Nadya reported, "the ice was still unsafe in some parts." Unsuccessful in obtaining a guide for this hazardous undertaking, he found two tipsy Finns willing to lead him "three versts" across the ice at night. "In one place the ice began to move away beneath their feet, and they only just managed to extricate themselves. Volodya told me he thought, 'Oh, what a silly way to have to die.'"

The recent influx of émigrés back to their Russian homeland was now flowing in the opposite direction, and by traveling singly and taking the late night train from Finland Station, most of them escaped the police dragnet. Nadya's journey to Sweden was uneventful, having been arranged by one Borgo, a Finnish comrade whose loyalty to the Revolution later cost him his life. On the steamer she encountered several compatriots who were likewise on their way to emigration via Stockholm, a reunion with gloomy overtones; all of them wondered when, or if, they would return home.

Lenin and Maxim Gorky

9. The Second Emigration

As a result of the Industrial Revolution, Socialist ideas flourished in the north of England where distortion of human existence, and exploitation, was exemplified by the cities of Birmingham, Liverpool and Sheffield. Industrialization, superimposed upon English class stratification, transformed a poor but self-sufficient agrarian population into dependency upon a wage-based economic system. As the rich prospered, their workforce sank lower on the economic scale, spreading the slum disease of despair, whose only cure lay in restructuring of the political status quo.

Karl Marx and England's industrial woes found each other at a critical moment in history. His towering intellect was devoted to codifying the prevailing human condition in terms of historical perspective and, in the process, distilling what he considered to be the remedy for class disparity.

When industrial blight began spreading to continental Europe, it spawned a new social class referred to as the intelligentsia. These persons were regarded by many as utopian dreamers, as liberal bourgeoisie who had nothing better to do with their educated, comfortable lives than preach equality among those who were trapped in non-egalitarian rigidity.

The inevitable spin-off from theorizing was a small but dedicated group of men and women who believed in actualizing their commitment to the exploited. Their degree of commitment ranged from terrorism and anarchism to various forms of compromise with the existing order.

If at least some of the socialist programs appear to have been requisites for effecting social betterment, at the same time spiritual lethargy among the Socialist Parties' large following—often but not always a result of official repression—kept them from exercising the power implicit in their numbers.

In Germany during the last quarter of the 19th Century, the activist movement was spearheaded by William Liebknecht and later by his son Karl. The latter became one of the triumvirate composed of fellow-countryman Franz Mehring, and Rosa Luxemburg—a native of Poland who settled in Germany and devoted her life to Social Democracy.

Germany's intellectual climate produced a number of outstanding Marxists, men of brilliant intellect and selfless dedication. But they were contending with a national temperament that favored orderliness and regimentation. Emotional display was taboo. The German working class, and a reasonably prosperous agrarian population, could not easily perceive their oppression. They needed to be reminded by intellectuals that conditions were ripe for radical change. Therefore, it is not surprising that reformist socialism enjoyed more widespread support than the minority activists. While maintaining a discreet distance from the Party's left wing, the former conducted themselves as gentlemen-reformers and stable members of society; a state of affairs that also prevailed in France, Belgium and Holland. À propos of this emasculated socialism, an exasperated Karl Marx had written: "I sowed the dragon's teeth and harvested fleas."

On the other hand, the emotional Italians embraced a more radical approach to social reform. Conservative Austria was disturbed by political ferment among its Slavic neighbors, including its Hungarian appendage. Of the remainder, Spain was feudal and isolated; Switzerland a relatively passive bystander.

But if the socialist presence in Germany's Reichstag was reassuringly docile, nevertheless Kaiser William II began to react to the large number of Russian revolutionaries turning up in his realm. By the time Lenin, his wife, and their Swiss-bound comrades arrived for a stopover in Berlin, they might as well have been in St. Petersburg; the local police were staked out around every residence suspected of harboring a Russian.

After spending a few days in Stockholm, Volodya and Nadya traveled by rail to Trelleborg on Sweden's south coast where they boarded a steamer for the German port of Sassnitz on the Baltic Sea. In Berlin they were met by comrade A-, "a member of the Berlin group," who warned them not to call on Russians at home. Instead, he led them around all day from one café to another. They spent the evening with Rosa Luxemburg and, according to Nadya, the discussion centered on the socialist, revolutionary approach to war. Since the Stuttgart Congress of 1907, V. and Rosa were in agreement that the struggle against war should aim not only at peace, but also at the replacement of capitalism by socialism. As internationalists, Marxist Social-Democrats were anti-war but not pacifist. They advocated the utilization of an international war, and its attendant suffering for the working population, as a means for replacing the war-making political system with one predicated on socialism and peace.

Nadya felt that this particular meeting of V. and Rosa helped consolidate the forces "of the left," an achievement that would be tested under fire some years later.

When Nadya and her husband returned to the hotel that evening, both were taken ill: "In going from one restaurant to another, we got fish poisoning." Because Nadya was registered as an American citizen, the chambermaid called an American doctor who, "suspecting that all was not quite in order, charged us an outrageous fee." V. was diagnosed as seriously ill, but the doctor looked at Nadya and said: "Well, you'll live!" "We hung about for a couple of days, and then dragged ourselves, only half cured, to Geneva where we arrived on January 20, 1908."

Another dismal journey, plagued by illness—similar to their retreat from London—brought them to the German town of Gottmadingen where they crossed the Swiss frontier at Thengen and a change of trains. Upon arrival in Geneva they sought comrade T- "who lived in a tiny room, and with difficulty roused himself from bed when we arrived; we talked little here." In another house they found Karpinsky who was suffering from a bad headache which made him blink all the time. "The shutters were drawn as the light irritated him." The only other comrade then living in Geneva was K-'s wife (or companion), a capricious young woman with liberated habits.

Winter in Geneva was gray and cheerless, without snow but raked by chilling winds. Along the embankment of the lake, picture postcards of avalanches were displayed for sale, reminding Nadya—homesick and physically debilitated—of Russia's blue-white fields under a dazzling winter sun. She wrote:

> When we left the Karpinskys, we walked along the empty Geneva streets which had turned so friendless. Volodya murmured: "I feel just as if I'd come here to be buried." Our second period of emigration had started. It was very much harder than the first.

The second Geneva period was noteworthy for acrid polemics between Bolsheviks and Mensheviks, both in person and in the editorials of their rival publications. To the serious-minded, these inner-party squabbles were a poor substitute for the high purpose of Social Democracy, representing as they did consolidation on opposing sides of a rift that would soon become a chasm.

Tsarist persecution was driving hordes of dissidents from their homeland. The same people whose expectations had been raised by the revolutionary events of 1905-07, now found themselves once more in a trough of depression; isolated, many living in extreme poverty, with no other outlet for their frustrations than that of belaboring theoretical issues. However petty this now seems, at the time it was vital to participants as a proving ground for the giant upheaval of 1917.

Since few of the émigrés kept a journal, Nadya's *Memoir* has become a primary source for the so-called 1908-11 "period of reaction." Unfortunately, she said nothing to explain Zinoviev's sudden appearance in the Bolshevik ranks. We learn only that "Zinoviev and Lilina arrived from Russia; Lilina gave birth to a son, and she and Zinoviev settled down in their little household." She added that Kamenev and his family arrived (Kamenev was married to Trotsky's sister). The ubiquitous *Proletary's* editorial board was now composed of Lenin, Kamenev, Zinoviev and Dubrovinsky.

But if affairs in Geneva were besmogged by the verbal climate, Tiflis erupted in an explosion that dazzled both the Party and the world in general. Bolsheviks had sounded the depths of financial support and found them deficient. Suddenly came word that Stalin and his Georgian comrades had robbed the State Treasury in Tiflis's Yerevan Square. When shock waves from this well-publicized incident reached Switzerland, Nadya reported: "The good Swiss burghers were frightened to death. The only thing one heard talked about was the Russian 'expropriators.' They were discussed with horror around the dining table, in the boarding house where Volodya and I usually dined."

Their horror would have been even greater had they known that a non-committal Russian tablemate was the intended recipient of some of those funds! "When comrade T-, dressed in his Caucasian costume, came to see us, he so frightened the landlady that, with a shriek, she slammed the door in his face."

Lenin was among the few who were not embarrassed by this seamy caper. "I would accept money from the Devil himself," he observed, "if it would further the Revolution." Nevertheless, it became a stain on the Party's reputation, and useful for Menshevik finger-pointing. As for the money, it followed a tortuous route after leaving Tiflis. The "take" was in 500-ruble notes, which posed a dilemma for seedy-looking Russians attempting to exchange them at foreign banks (the serial numbers were recorded), and several comrades—at the behest of the Russian Imperial Government which was demanding their extradition—were arrested.

In general, however, dramatic highs like the Tiflis affair were extremely rare; Party activities were mostly limited to the daily task of grinding out the newspaper, on an antiquated printing press, and devising innovative methods for its distribution. Once again Nadya was in charge of correspondence, "but we waited for letters more than we received them."

Meanwhile, Gorky and his wife Maria had retreated to idyllic Capri where they established a splinter group of Social Democrats gathered around a Party school. Trotsky, likewise distancing himself from Bolshevik "violence," was currently in Vienna as Bolshevik representative on the editorial board of Austrian *Pravda*; he politely declined to contribute editorials to *Proletary*. Dubrovinsky, unable to clarify his own allegiance, veered between Menshevism and Bolshevism. And with bewildering frequency, editorial boards shifted personnel until it became a matter of daily concern to both factions whether comrade X was "with us" or had gone over to "them."

Although the intricacies of Party affairs during this period were admirably detailed by Nadya and are therefore valuable to historians, they hold little interest for general readers. It is necessary to eschew the specifics and yield to generalities, except where they provide insight into future developments. One of the most interesting was an attempt by one group of Marxist revisionists to turn "Scientific Materialism" into a religion. The leader of this movement was Bogdanov, the upstairs boarder at "Vasa." To Lenin's disgust, this gentleman proposed that Social Democrats substitute a new "God" for the old one. And if this were not enough, to the recurring bogey of Economism (emphasis upon shop/factory reform only) was added a variety of alternatives: bizarre alliances with this or that faction; even the suggestion that all S-D Parties should be dissolved.

The period 1908-11 was a test of personal fortitude. Those who survived it with principles intact and optimism undimmed, would become the eventual leaders of a movement which, for the time being, appeared headed for oblivion. The gray-black years of reaction were summarized by Nadya in a brief paragraph:

> After the revolution, we found it difficult to get accustomed to life in exile again. Volodya spent his days in the library, but in the evenings we did not know what to do with ourselves. We did not feel like sitting in the cold cheerless room we had rented; we longed to be among people, and every evening we would go to the cinema or to the theater, although Volodya rarely stayed to the end, but usually left in the middle of the performance and would go wandering somewhere, most often to the lake.

Lenin's first letter home from Switzerland, written to his sister Maria, was undisguisedly pessimistic: "We have been hanging about in this damned Geneva for several days now. It is an awful hole, but there is nothing we can do. We shall get used to it." That he and Nadya considered it temporary is indicated by the rented room "Chez Küpfer" at Rue de deux Ponts, 17. Although he was expecting payment from a Petersburg publisher (for translating Vol.1 of the Webbs, and for editing Vol.2 which had been translated by someone else), this may also have been dictated by poverty. When the money arrived, and when it became evident that Geneva was no worse than other Swiss cities, they moved to permanent quarters and prepared for a long sojourn.

The dreary routine of days in the library, of sending to Russia for books and periodicals, of walks along the lakes was temporarily alleviated by an invitation from Gorky to visit him in Capri.

It is difficult to account for a contradiction between the penury in which Lenin and his wife lived, and their occasional expensive trips and holidays. One explanation may be the *largesse* of friends; Gorky, for example, whose affluence resulted from his enormous literary successes, may have offered to pay for the current trip. Lenin welcomed the idea, "But not," he informed Gorky, "until we have become settled here." Always loathe to accept charity, in this instance he may have rationalized the trip as affording opportunity to discuss Party matters with Gorky.

The establishing of permanent residency abroad, even in liberal Switzerland, was beset by legal redtape. The Swiss may have been tolerant politically, but their moral standards were Victorian. "Shacking up" was definitely out, and even if no one went to prison for practicing free love, Swiss landladies were known to eject boarders for suspected loose living. But V.'s and N.K.'s marriage certificate was in Siberia!

"I had a talk with the Director of the Police Department yesterday about my *Acte de mariage*," V. informed his sister Maria.

> It seems it is necessary. Ask some lawyer of your acquaintance to think of some way of getting a copy (because probably no great hopes are to be placed in "palm oil"). Cannot Yelizaveta apply to some authority in Petersburg and demand from him an *instruction* to issue a certificate to her requiring the Krasnoyarsk church authorities to supply her with a copy of the marriage license?"

Three days later, in a letter to Maria asking for numerous books and periodicals, he referred to Karl Kautsky, the German socialist-ideologue who would later become the *bête noire* to orthodox Marxism.

Lydia Knippovich was currently in Petersburg nursing Maria, who was recovering from typhus. Otherwise, the news from home was as colorless as that emanating from Geneva. Even word that Lenin's *Development of Capitalism in Russia* was going into a second edition failed to interest him beyond the promise of more money.

By the time Yelizaveta came to live in Geneva, his recurring attacks of abdominal catarrh had begun to subside, and with the establishment of normal family life, he reported to his mother that he was in good health. "I now expect to earn a lot of money,* he wrote her in autumn 1908, suggesting that family members come to Geneva for a visit. However, only Maria made the journey. But immediately upon arrival she developed a serious ear infection which seemed to demand an operation. Lodged in a room above "where a stove has been put," she was studying Latin in order to prepare for university examinations that would lead to a degree in French.

Lenin's increasing adjustment to émigré life was evidenced by the large number of optimistic letters written to his family during this time. Nadya, on the other hand, was strangely silent. Her reservoir of good humor in the face of adversity apparently dried up, for—in addition to a letterless period covering nearly three years—her *Memoir* is often devoid of personal information. Was she unhappy in her marriage? Frustrated at having little or no involvement in Party work? Discouraged with life in general? Ill? Or was it homesickness? This curious lapse cannot be explained from the evidence. Her long silence was punctuated by a single letter of December 1909 to Maria Alexandrovna, and she did not write again until autumn two years later. The earlier letter was postmarked "Paris":

> "Dear M.A.,
>   To begin with, let me embrace you fondly. This letter is written mainly to tell you that, because actually there is nothing much to write about. Our way of life differs from last year only in the apartment being very warm and Volodya having become a stick-at-home. To think we have been living in Paris (actually Geneva)

---

* From his new book *Materialism and Emperio-criticism* which his friend Bonch-Bruyevich was undertaking to publish in Petersburg.

for a whole year already! We have become fairly used to it, but it's a pity we see so little of the real local life.

From Geneva, Lenin had written his mother: "As regards this move of ours, it is almost fully decided; we are tired of staying in this provincial backwater."

Proletary had recently been moved to Paris, and Lenin's improved financial position enabled him to resettle in an environment that provided both anonymity and access to mainstream activity. After shipping their furniture by slow freight, the family left for Paris where they stayed in a hotel prior to moving into an apartment in Rue Beaunier (Bonier), 24. "It is very elegant and expensive," he noted. Four rooms + kitchen + storerooms, water and gas (sic)." The cost was around 1,000 francs per annum. "Yesterday we bought furniture for Manyasha (Maria)."

The apartment was located on the outskirts of Paris near Montsouri Park, and Lenin found it "quiet as a provincial town." According to Nadya, their sole diversion was that of attending a small theater nearby where working-class people applauded "not good or bad acting, but good or bad actions."

At first, she had been enchanted with the apartment—mirrors over the fireplace, large and pleasant rooms, a concierge! She and Maria immediately set to work embellishing it, "but Volodya was not at all interested in our fixing up the place; he had more important things to do." The flat was well suited to family living, with separate bedrooms for Yelizaveta, Maria and "Volodya and I," but Nadya complained about the redtape of housekeeping in Paris; it had been simpler in Geneva, principally because they had frequently taken their meals out. Likewise, she noted the inadequacy of their second-hand furniture:

> The contempt with which the *concierge* looked upon our white deal tables, common chairs and stools was worth seeing. In our "parlor" we had only a couple of chairs and a small table. It was not cozy by any means. This luxurious apartment did not at all suit our mode of life.

Unlike Geneva, Paris was, in Nadya's words, "all hustle and bustle." Exposed to Parisian night-life, comrades were spending their evenings in various cafés where they discussed, planned, argued. To the Bolsheviks' delight, Yuly (Martov) apparently mellowed by the *bonhommie* of sidewalk cafés and French wine, temporarily forsook his Menshevism and joined the editorial board of *Proletary*. And with the establishment of a daily schedule of study at the Bibliothèque Nationale, V.'s lifestyle resumed the pattern of Munich/London/Geneva—a union of domesticity, Party work, publishing, study, creative writing. Compared to his former life, it seemed relatively ideal.

Before long, however, he began to have second thoughts about Paris. First, he became exasperated with the Bibliothèque: "Poorly organized", he thought, "and a lot of bother about borrowing books." Then the bicycle upon which he traveled to the library was stolen. Soon after acquiring another one, he collided with an automobile and totaled his own conveyance. "Paris is a rotten hole in

many respects," he informed his sister Anna. "I am still unable to adapt myself
fully to it (after living *here* for a year!) but I nevertheless feel that only extraordinary circumstances could drive me back to Geneva!"

Among encounters of purely human interest was that with Dubrovinsky
(the other upstairs boarder at Vasa) upon his first coming to Paris. Like many
comrades shuttling between Europe and St. Petersburg on Party business, he
was arrested and exiled to Siberia. After escaping, he became extremely ill
upon arriving at Paris. Nadya related how, on his way to exile, the iron fetters
had so chafed his legs that deep wounds were caused. "Our doctors were called,
but could do nothing." Subsequently, a French doctor who treated him jeered
at the queer remedies prescribed by the Russians. "Your Russian physicians
may be very good revolutionaries," he said, "but as doctors they are jackasses."

Volodya roared with laughter," said Nadya, "and on many occasions afterwards repeated the story. However, Dubrovinsky had to have medical treatment for a long time."

Another League of Struggle comrade was living in Paris. "I sometimes see
Augusta Pavlovna here," V. wrote his mother. "Her relatives are in Moscow—
do you ever see them? She is very nice." Augusta, the third Nevzorova
(Zinaida's sister), after being arrested several times in Petersburg, had escaped
abroad where she joined the Bolsheviks.

Meanwhile, the Party game of musical chairs continued unabated. Paris
had now become the center of political activity, and the growing concentra-
tion of Russians insured that factionalism would reach new heights of acri-
mony. Nadya's December letter to her mother-in-law was, for security reasons,
deliberately misleading; far from being a stick-at-home, Lenin was driven to
distraction with the demands of Party work. In the past, the remedy had been
retreat to a peaceful rural spot. After scanning the newspapers, he located a
cheap boardinghouse in the village of Bombom (Bon-Bon), immediately
south of Paris, where ten francs a day provided room and board for four persons. But there was another reason for going to the country: Maria was con-
valescing from an appendectomy performed by the same French doctor who
had treated Dubrovinsky. Before leaving Paris, the family decided not to renew
their lease on the apartment. The past year had drained resources, making it
necessary to seek more modest quarters.

Nadya's account of their month at Bon-Bon was graphic, and included ill-
concealed contempt for the assorted boarding-house characters. Among mealtime companions was the valet to a Count. Others were office employees or
shop assistants.

Madame Lagourette, saleswoman in a fashionable Paris shop, was typical of the
rest. She had a great fund of suggestive stories which she would relate with gusto.
It was interesting to watch this petty-bourgeois crowd with its strongly marked

Laura Marx and Paul Lafargue

petty-bourgeois mentality. This mediocrity bored us. It was a good thing that we were able to keep aloof and live as we wanted to.

Nadya was not criticizing the boarders because they were employees, but because they pretended to be gentry—the same trait which Lenin found inimical to genuine proletarian interests.

"Living as we wanted to" included cycling to Clamart Forest, fifteen kilometers away, where they basked in the sunshine of carefree days undisturbed by Party thoughts and Party confrontations.

Upon returning to Paris, they moved to a small apartment in Rue Marie Rose.

> We had two rooms and a kitchen. our windows looked out on a garden. Our living room was now the kitchen, where all heart-to-heart talks took place. We had many visitors, crowds upon crowds. By spring, Vladimir* was eager to set to work.

One of the visitors was Maxim Gorky. "I saw Lenin in Paris in a two-room student's flat (it was a student flat only in size, not in the cleanliness and order that reigned there). Nadezhda Konstantinovna had gone out after giving us tea and we remained alone together."

A highlight of this period was a meeting with Paul Lafargue, husband of Marx's daughter Laura. The couple lived in a town near Paris, and one day, after an introduction had been arranged by a mutual acquaintance, Volodya and Nadya cycled out to visit them. "The Lafargues received us very amiably." While Lenin was telling Lafargue about his own (V.'s) book on philosophy, Laura took Nadya for a walk in the park. But conversation was stilted. Overcome by awe in the presence of the great man's daughter, Nadya's innate shy-

---

* A rare use of his first name without the patronymic "Ilyich."

ness reached new heights: "I babbled something inarticulately about the part women were playing in the revolutionary movement and about Russia." Laura, who seemed vague and preoccupied, responded politely, "but somehow or other, the conversation lagged." When they returned, the men were still discussing philosophy.

Both Lafargues were elderly and in poor health. Discouraged with their present nonproductive lives as torchbearers for the ideals of Laura's father, they eventually committed suicide. Nadya later recalled a comment of Laura's: "'Soon my husband will prove how sincere are his philosophic convictions,' she said, exchanging significant glances with him."

An ebullient letter of February 1909 from Lenin to his sister Anna included the news that "Maria was more lively today and went out walking—today is *mardi gras* and the French are on the rampage." Meanwhile, in Moscow, Anna was coping with proofs of her brother's manuscript (*Materialism,* etc.) and nursing her ailing mother. Time after time, while simultaneously bombarding her with corrections and addenda, V. apologized for burdening her with the task of the book's publication. All of those concerned, including the publisher, were heartily relieved when the book finally appeared in print. Volodya, Nadya, Yelizaveta and Maria celebrated by going to Bon-Bon. "In autumn," Lenin wrote his mother, "we shall wait for you here in Paris and we shall be beautifully provided for."

Unfortunately, money from the publication was delayed. "I am afraid the publisher will swindle us," V. informed Anna. "Please send me five hundred rubles that are in the bank, since I cannot rely on the publisher."*

To this letter Nadya added a postscript:

You ask why I do not write. All this winter I have been in a state of utter melancholy, the time has been frittered away. I could not work properly and so I was in no fit state to write. I told Volodya and Manyasha to give you my regards but I don't suppose they did.

The following spring Lenin wrote his sister:

Dear Anyuta (Anna), there is no change here at all. Nadya is feeling rather poorly— her nerves are still not quite in order . . . it is possible we shall again go to Bonbon this summer, although Nadya does not seemed inclined to go there again. Perhaps this time we shall try the socialist colony at the seaside. Y.V. was there last year and liked it.

In spring of 1910, after recovering from her appendectomy. Maria returned to Russia where she stayed for a time in a private cottage at Terijoki Station on the Finland Railway. Later, she joined her mother in Moscow and subsequently went to work at the Moscow *zemstvo* (district government headquarters).

Lenin accepted Gorky's invitation to visit Capri. But at the end of a week,

---

* Bonch-Bruyevich was in the process of establishing his own firm and had been obliged to entrust the manuscript to another publisher.

Gorky would have been happy to see him depart. Like a schoolboy on holiday, his guest turned the peaceful island retreat into a marathon celebration. With amusement, Maria Andreyeva observed the emotional arguments, battle-to-the death chess games and boisterous levity. But her tolerance was occasionally strained, and once she gently called Lenin to order.

After sub-letting the apartment, Nadya and her mother went to the Brittany Coast where they joined a Party camp of French socialists located near the village of Pornic. "But we were not happy. The French kept to themselves and were unfriendly toward Russians." When two Russian comrades arrived and immediately had a quarrel with the manager, Nadya and Y.V. packed up and moved to Pornic where they lodged with the coastguard's family in two small rooms. When V. arrived from Capri at the beginning of August, he found the arrangement congenial; even the address conformed—Rue Mon Désir, Les Roses. "Volodya bathed in the sea a great deal, and chatted cheerfully on all sorts of subjects with our hosts, enjoyed eating the crabs which the coastguard caught for us."

The stout, loud-voiced landlady, a laundress, appealed to him because of her anticlerical views. "The village priest wants my son to enter a monastery," declared the woman, "but I didn't raise the boy to be made a despicable Jesuit."

"And that was why Volodya praised the crabs so highly," added Nadya with unintentional wit.

Near the end of August, Nadya wrote a short note to her husband's sister Anna: "Shkurka left yesterday, and Mother and I are thinking of staying here in Pornic till mid-September. It's really nice here."

"Shkurka" was Volodya, and he had left for Copenhagen to attend a congress of the Socialist International. Considerably later, V.'s letter from Copenhagen to his mother stated that the congress had just ended.

> I shall be waiting for you on the wharf at Stockholm. A comrade from Stockholm will rent for me two rooms for the week of September 17-24. I embrace you fondly. Hoping to see you soon. Yours, V.U.

10. Revolutionary Revival

The year 1910 began with profound changes occurring within the Party. Lenin now believed that only reconciliation with the Mensheviks would preserve Social Democracy (Nadya said of that time: "The very existence of the Party was at stake")—a conclusion based upon several factors. Gorky's defection to Capri, Trotsky's alliance with Austrian Social-Democrat Adler, Bogdanov's "God-building," the Tiflis affair—all combined with other Party fractures to convince him that unity was more vital than ideological intransigence.

Although not disavowing Bolshevism, nevertheless he accepted the idea of compromise, at the same time hoping to move dissidents to accept his program. His particular talent was persuasion. He didn't browbeat his opponents but reasoned with them, a procedure he would adhere to for the remainder of his life.

His drive for unity had widespread support. By expelling Bogdanov from the Party and passing resolutions condemning the liquidators, conciliators and other separatists, Social Democracy hoped to preserve itself for better days, meanwhile providing leadership for the masses stranded in a Russian winter of discontent.

The initial moves toward reconciliation were hardly reassuring. Typical was an event that took place one evening in a café on the Rue d'Orléans where Bolsheviks were gathered for a peaceful discussion. Suddenly a group of Mensheviks burst in, demanding to be heard. A verbal scuffle ended with two opponents at each other's throats, whereat the proprietor—accustomed to brawls—extinguished the lights. "There was no fight," Nadya related, "but afterwards Volodya wandered the streets of Paris all night and when he returned home he could not fall asleep." In a letter to Gorky, he referred to this and similar incidents with particular bitterness:

"Well, it seems that the 'ludicrous' is the predominant note in unity and gives good grounds for sniggering, jokes, etc. It is sickening to have to live amidst this squabbling and scandal. But the development of Social Democracy will go on."

Unity was, nevertheless, finally achieved, and after expelling troublemakers from the Party, both factions patched up their differences. First on the agenda was money: whose, where it was located, and what then to do with it. In order to eradicate the stigma of Tiflis, as well as save the Bolsheviks from mass arrest, the remaining 500-ruble notes were burned, and other Bolshevik funds placed under a trusteeship composed of Karl Kautsky (later to become

Socialism and War, printed in Geneva, 1915

Materialism and Empiriocriticism
by "Vl. Ilyin"—1909

a renegade from Marxism); Franz Mehring, one of the group including Karl
Liebknecht and Rosa Luxemburg; and Klara Zetkin, whose loyalty to the Bolsheviks, and especially to Lenin, was unwavering. The trust money was to be
used for general Party purposes. Should the two factions eventually separate,
the fund would then revert to the Bolsheviks.

But there was another and more immediate need for unity. At Copen-
hagen, divergence of opinion among the Russians had been acutely manifest.
Unlike the united-party delegations* from each of the European countries,
Russia was unique in being divided into several parties. Thus the Russian S-
D's, as a voting bloc, were pitted against their own countrymen as well as for-
eigners. Besides Lenin, Kamenev, Zinoviev and Martov, their alliance included
Trotsky, Plekhanov, Lunacharsky, and Alexandra Kollontai, the only woman
delegate. The total Russian delegation of all shades numbered twenty, which
Nadya considered large in comparison with those from other countries.

The Party Congress, in bringing together disparate elements in the Socialist movement as a whole, gave rise to new initiatives. Although to outsiders it
appeared as a mere replay of the past, the scenario underwent a remarkable
transformation, with enthusiasm replacing stagnation. Which is not to say that
disputes were no longer center-stage. Within the Russian S-D Party, the total
defection of Trotsky to his Vienna *Pravda* upset Lenin's hard-won unity, but
the consequent turmoil of shifting positions began to stabilize.

"He who is not with us is against us," declared Lenin with scriptural apt-
ness. Liberal socialists, Marxist revisionists, and all the other divisive 'ists' had
no place, according to Lenin, in a movement professing revolution. It was time
for both sides to clearly define their goals and take an unequivocal stand.
"Volodya hated this vague conciliationism that was devoid of all principle,
conciliation with anybody and everybody, which was tantamount to surren-
dering the position when the battle was at its height." Thus Nadya described
her husband's frame of mind during and after the Congress. She concluded:
"To have lived another year or two in this atmosphere would have been fatal.
But the years of reaction gave way to years of revival of the revolutionary
movement."

Toward the middle of September 1910, Lenin's mother, accompanied by
Maria, left Moscow for Stockholm and a reunion with her son (the Copenhagen Conference had adjourned). After the night journey from Moscow to St.
Petersburg and a day spent visiting friends, they boarded the sleeper for Helsingfors. Except for snatches of Finnish language among those who entered the
train at various stations along the way, the two women imagined themselves
still in Russia: the same birch groves, the same pine forests, an occasional dacha
with light glimmering from a pedimented window—no sign of nationhood

---

* Despite a looming split between orthodox and revisionist Marxists in European S-D Parties—
particularly in Holland—an uneasy truce prevailed at this time.

except that imposed by man. Crossing the frontier seemed no different from traversing one's own back yard. Did Maria Alexandrovna, a seasoned traveler on the road of life, ponder the paradox of nature and politics?

At Åbo (Turku) the next day, they waited on the pier where a well-appointed steamer lay moored. "Although you will be crossing open sea," her son had written her, "the three hour journey, in fine weather, is like sailing down a river." As a commuter on that route, he was well informed. A late-summer calm prevailed on the Baltic, reminding M.A. of that long-ago journey down the Volga to Ufa.

After the austerity of Petersburg—Stockholm, another city of waterways—impressed the women with its sunny openness and cosmopolitan bustle. Lenin's first meeting with his mother in over three years was emotional. "Mother dearest" had aged. She was now 75, but her frailty only accentuated a vigor of spirit; and although her eyes were dim, they still conveyed an affection and concern that through the years had sustained and reassured him.

Ten days later they again stood on the pier. "This was the last time Volodya saw his mother. He had a premonition of that, and it was with sad and wistful eyes that he followed the departing steamer." Maria, too, sensed the meaning of this parting between her brother and his mother. She wrote:

> When we left, Vladimir Ilyich accompanied us to the boat—he could not go aboard the vessel because it belonged to a Russian company and he might have been arrested on it—and I still remember the expression on his face as he stood there looking at Mother. How much pain there was on his face! He seemed to feel that this was the last time he would see her. And so it was.

The revolutionary revival of which Nadya spoke was spontaneous, but external events may have heightened the mood. "We have had floods here such as have not been known for a long time" (water in the Seine rose 24 feet above normal). In a letter to his sister Maria, V. described "Venice in Paris": the horse-trams were running reduced services, the metro was at a standstill, many people were out of work. "I managed to get as far as the Seine on two occasions. Fortunately, the district where we live is unaffected."

Natural disasters, like war, offered relief from monotony, stirred the senses, challenged the spirit. More relevant were two other events unrelated by place or circumstance; first, the "Moroccan Affair." Recent bloody encounters between troops of European powers and natives of their African possessions had resulted in a notorious episode to which Paris reacted with vigor. To Lenin's mother Nadya wrote: "I was sorry that Manyasha was not here when we went to see a demonstration of a hundred thousand people. That created a very strong impression."

The second event occurred in Russia on the occasion of Leo Tolstoy's death. Suddenly the moribund socialist parties came to life in a demonstration that swept the populace along with them. People began remembering the old man who, for a time, had been regarded as a utopian eccentric. With his passing, all that he stood for—renunciation of wealth, anti-clericalism, humanitarianism—came into focus, illuminating the ideals and concrete objectives which the reaction had appeared to annihilate. A mood of optimism quickly spread among those whose bickering had replaced a positive outlook.

On New Year's Eve, Lenin wrote an editorial which ended:

In the first Russian Revolution, the workers taught the masses of the people to fight for liberty; in the second revolution the workers must lead them to victory.

Matters abroad, however, continued to seethe. The battle of polemics spread to *Vorwärts* and *Die Neue Zeit* in Germany, and to *Le Peuple* in France— socialist periodicals with wide circulation. Meanwhile, the Vienna *Pravda* was adding its share to dissension. It seemed that the revolution, whether French or German or Russian, would begin and end in a blizzard of ink.

Lenin's erudite literary style changed to wrath when newspapers printed a story that Gorky had been expelled from the Party:

> Some idiot heard rumors he did not understand and got everything wrong. The publication that started all this must be a shady little rag to have cooked up such a story. The Cadets (Constitutional Democrats) are, of course, happy to have something to lie and talk scandal about.

By 1911, neither Nadya nor her husband complained of stagnation. At times they even thought nostalgically about peaceful, backwater Geneva. Paris was alive with comings and goings, and scarcely a day passed without bringing someone to their door.

The financial plight of many fellow-émigrés weighed heavily upon those with means to support themselves. "Ideologically, we became stronger," Nadya said. "The only trouble was that we were so poor." Most deprived were the intellectuals who, without skills, attempted unsuccessfully to learn a trade. The humiliation of living on donations and eating in communal dining rooms at others' expense became an emotional burden that drove the proud into isolation. "One sad case," Nadya related,

> was that of a comrade who tried to become a polisher. He lived in a working class district far from the other exiles. At last he became so weak from lack of food that he could not leave his bed, and wrote us asking for money. Another giant of a man positively withered away from starvation.

Kamo had been in and out prison and exile since the day he brought a watermelon to the Petersburg dining-hall. After escaping from a Russian mental hospital where—having feigned insanity—he was confined, he stowed away on a ship bound for France. "He would sit in our kitchen/living-room eating almonds I had bought him, and tell us about his experiences. Volodya felt very sorry for this brave, childishly naive, warm-hearted man. When he made fantastic proposals, Volodya did not correct him; instead, he listened patiently and then brought him back to earth."

Kamo was cross-eyed, making him an easy target for spies, and Lenin suggested that he go to Belgium for an operation. Examining the man's coat, he asked: "Have you got a warm coat? You'll be cold on deck with this one." Their visitor left Paris wearing the gray woolen cloak that had been a mother's parting gift at Stockholm.

11. Longjumeau, France 1911

In 1910 Inessa Armand arrived from Brussels. She
was a very ardent Bolshevik and soon gathered our
Paris crowd around her.—N.K.

Two women, worlds apart in background, nationality and temperament, added titillation and color to the canvas of Social Democracy. Although united ideologically, their mutual and feminine antagonism ebbed and flowed beneath the male-dominated surface of the Party.

Alexandra Kollontai,* née Domontovich, born in St. Petersburg in 1872, was the daughter of a Polish tsarist general. As a member of the elite, she was a brilliant woman who exuded self-assurance acquired by education and opportunities for travel. Although not beautiful in a conventional sense, she had both charm and style, the latter tending to be "frou-frou" rather than chic. At odds with her fussy-looking clothes were a stentorian voice and dominating manner. This combination attracted attention wherever she went. Alternating between coyness and aggressiveness, she gave the impression of waging an inner battle between two selves. Men she found irresistible, but as a liberated woman, she scorned the traditional role of wife. "Sex," she declared, "is no different from drinking a glass of water,"** and true to her belief, she proceeded to slake her thirst. Her succession of affairs, while privately scandalizing the straight-laced Bolshevik hierarchy, had no adverse effect upon her public image. As "Alexandra," she played house with a current gentleman friend; but as "Madame Kollontai," she climbed the ladder of Party leadership without mishap.

Alexandra Kollontai

Although not a prototype feminist in the style of her austere Anglo-Saxon counterparts, Kollontai was nevertheless a whirlwind of energy in the Women's Movement. Her facility in foreign languages was extraordinary, making her

* Kollontai, a Pole, was early divorced from Alexandra.
** A simile Lenin criticized in a famous speech to the youth.

equally at home on the lecture platforms of Great Britain, Germany, Denmark, France, Belgium, Sweden, Norway and the USA. She helped found the Mutual Aid Society for Working Women, contributed to the Socialist press, and carried out assignments for the Party with consummate skill. Absence of creative talent in the ideological sphere undoubtedly contributed to her acceptance by male-chauvinist colleagues. And while practicing considerable independence of political views, she nevertheless continued to maintain her equilibrium amid the shifting sands of Party politics. Her particular talent was diplomacy, both personal and professional. Like Rosa Luxemburg and Klara Zetkin, she occupied a unique position in International Socialism.

Despite her peripatetic lifestyle, however,—her thousands of contacts with people, her exceptional talents—she failed to inspire the kind of love or even affection that moved others to speak of her as friend. The saga of her life, although sensational, is arid. Nadya, who knew her well, added nothing beyond mere references to Kollontai, and these are devoid of personal observation.

There are occasional rare persons who invite others into their private lives. One such individual was Inèsse Steffane. Two years younger than Kollontai, she was born in Paris to a theatrical family. Because of her beauty, Inésse might have become an actress. But after the death of her father while she was still a child, she was sent to Moscow to be raised by well-to-do relatives. At age 18 she left home to marry Alexander Armand, whom she had known since childhood. As a young woman, now called Inessa, she had become attracted to the Socialist Movement. An early photograph shows her sitting demurely with long braids resting on her chest amid a group of youthful males in the clowning pose of rebels figuratively thumbing their noses at the world of conformity.

Marriage and the birth of children did little to reconcile her to the milieu in which she had been reared, and she left the security of home to follow the life of a revolutionary. Armand money, together with bilingualism (French and Russian), provided a unique opportunity for her to sever connections with bourgeois society. After repeated arrests for participating in the Russian Revolution of 1905-07, she left Russia and drifted around Europe in search of a congenial Socialist faction.

There is no doubt that Lenin and his wife had known Inessa for a considerable time prior to 1910. But an unsubstantiated statement by a writer who claimed to have known Lenin during the latter's early years in Petersburg, draws an uncharacteristic portrait of him. As a so-called witness, the reporter refers to Inessa, not by name, but as "La Belle Française," who spent her evenings in various cafés in company with Lenin who "ogled her with his little Mongol eyes." The sleuth further claims that Lenin hired a boat and took Inessa rowing "on a lake," although *which* lake he failed to mention: Ladoga, that sea of trapped water? . . . The Neva? . . . the Baltic Sea?

The rumor is as preposterous as it is titillating. Lenin enjoyed being in the water, not on it. If the reporter had mentioned bicycles or walking trips, any western historian would have pounced on this as evidence of lechery. Nor was pub-hopping in company with a married woman with five children consistent with Lenin's frugal lifestyle during that time.

Inessa Armand at age 19

> Mother dearest, please send me some money, mine is nearly at an end . . . I am keeping a cash book to see how much I actually spend. From August 28 to September 27, I spent almost 54 rubles 30 kopeks . . . It is true that part of this was spent on things that do not have to be bought every month (galoshes, clothes, books, an abacus, etc.), but even discounting that, the expenditure is still excessive . . . Obviously, I have not been living carefully; in one month I have spent a ruble and 36 kopeks on the horse-trams, for instance.

Nevertheless, gossip would associate Inessa with Lenin, who hardly fitted the image of womanizer. If the reporter was certain of his facts, why "La Belle Française" for a woman with a name?

The liberal-minded would undoubtedly applaud the discovery of a crack in Lenin's moral façade, but the spreading of rumor was in line with the mode of Lenin-haters. Let the reader decide if this, together with similar rumors spread by women, is valid. The Lenin chronology shows that early in his Petersburg residency, he was sent abroad by the Party to study European economies; that soon after his return he was arrested and imprisoned and exiled. His uncommitted time was brief and fraught with financial worries.

Early in the 20th Century, Longjumeau, now a part of greater Paris, was a small storybook village of brick houses. With their steep-gabled roofs and narrow shuttered windows, they resembled the clustered, single-street miniatures reminiscent of artist Maurice Utrillo's Seine villages. Although on market day, a procession of produce wagons rumbled through on their way to the Capital, filling the air with dust, the village was otherwise an oasis of pastoral tranquillity surrounded by fields of wildflowers, and hay stacked ready for storing.

Party schools were in vogue, and like Gorky's on Capri, each faction was engaged in educating workers for the task of reforming society. Although the number of students was small, eagerness to spread the word of Social Democracy back home provided incentive to probe depths of learning that would have discouraged many a university graduate.

Lenin chose Longjumeau for its isolation and peaceful setting. "No Russians and no visitors," observed Nadya. At one end of the village Nadya and Volodya, together with Zinoviev and his wife, rented rooms. At the other end, Inessa leased an entire house, part of which served as dining hall for students renting rooms in the village. Katya Mazonova, the wife of a worker who had been exiled to Turukhansk during Martov's time there, acted as cook/housekeeper, and according to Nadya, "everything went splendidly."

That Inessa was the only woman instructor (she tutored those studying political economy) among a group of distinguished men, was the entrée in a meal of gossip upon which historians feasted. It is unlikely, however, that under the circumstances Inessa and Lenin indulged in romantic dalliance under the stars.

The school curriculum was stringent. Lenin, aided by Kamenev and others who came from Paris as visiting instructors, practiced his belief that students, however unlettered, should be exposed to serious studies presented in a learned manner; talking down to a young metal worker from Petersburg, for example, would dishonor the cause of Marxism and send him away with a smattering of everything and nothing.

The tedium of days crammed with learning was relieved by evenings of singing and chatting as they lounged beside the haystacks. The easy camaraderie and informal atmosphere that prevailed between instructors and students would, at the end of the month, send the apprentices back to Russia invigorated and—hopefully—educated in more than technique for manning the barricades in street battles, or distributing illegal literature.

Nadya enjoyed this summer of respite, affording her opportunity to observe the pattern of daily life in this typical French village.

The two rooms where she lived with her husband and mother belonged to a tanner's family.

> This man would go to work early in the morning and come back in the evening completely exhausted. There was no garden attached to the house. Sometimes, he would bring a table and chair out into the street, and would sit for hours resting his tired head on his arms. None of his fellow workers ever visited him. On Sundays he would go to church. His wife would put on her wooden shoes early in the morning, take her broom and go to the neighboring chateau where she was employed as a charwoman. Her young daughter would remain at home to look

after the house. All day long she would stay in the gloomy, damp house, taking care of her younger brothers and sisters. Her life was just one round of household drudgery on weekdays and of visits to church on Sundays and holidays. It never occurred to any of the members of the tanner's family that any change was required in the social system. Why, God created the rich and the poor, then things must be so—reasoned the tanner . . .

Among the students was a young man from Kiev named Andrei Malinovsky whom Nadya thought mediocre except for his excellent singing voice. That she regarded him with suspicion, as she later said, may have been convenient hindsight. Lenin, however, saw nothing amiss except that Andrei was a "Plekhanovist," a condition that could be remedied. Malinovsky turned up later in a role Nadya claimed to have anticipated.

When one of the students contracted typhus, the French doctor who treated him made a sly comment: "What strange teachers you have—walking around barefoot all day." The "teachers" to which he referred were actually students; in renting rooms, they represented themselves as Russian village school teachers. "It was unbearably hot that summer," Nadya observed.

True to habit, she and Volodya occasionally went cycling into the countryside. "Often we visited an aerodrome, a secluded place where we were the only visitors, and Volodya was able to watch the maneuvers of the planes to his heart's content."

Nadya's recollection of a blandly pleasant summer is at odds with her long letter written at the time to Lenin's mother:

> Our summer has not been very fortunate. Mother had pneumonia, and the doctor says her lungs are not in good condition. It is hot in the house and noisy. If we want to be outdoors, we have to go to some place, which is not the same at all.

This account was followed by a long recital of inconveniences. In the beginning, she and her mother took their meals at Inessa's communal dining room, which entailed walking a "verst" through the town. Later, Nadya carried meals home, "but there is the bother of washing dishes." More disturbing were Yelizaveta's spells of mental depression. However, Nadya was satisfied with the financial arrangements. The rooms cost only ten francs a month, and dinner and supper one franc, thirty centimes a head.

At the end of August, school disbanded. Nadya and Volodya were on the point of returning to Paris when he was called to Switzerland for a meeting of the International Socialist Bureau. "I am traveling around lecturing," he informed his mother. "Yesterday I went climbing on Pilatus—nearly 7,000 feet. The weather is wonderful." Disappointed at not being able to accompany him, Nadya decided to extend the holiday in Longjumeau until his return. Unfortunately, Inessa's dining room closed, leaving Nadya and her mother in a quandary about meals. "The restaurant here is bad and expensive." On September 21st, she reported: "Today, at long last, we moved back to Paris. When is Anya (Anna) coming to see us? I am already in the mood to go sightseeing with her."

Upon his return to Paris, Lenin observed with dismay the growing evidence of a factional split. In Nadya's words: "Party unity, which had been achieved with so much difficulty, gradually began to break up." Given the intransigence of each faction, a break was inevitable, and this realization resulted in a hardening of principles among the Paris Bolsheviks who rallied a group of loyalists numbering about forty. In addition to Inessa and Nadya, the group included several women, among them Ludmila Stahl, a friend of Nadya's from the Petersburg days. "Comrade Stahl and I tried to carry on some work among the masses of foreign women workers—milliners, dressmakers, etc. And Volodya considered this work very important, but other comrades said 'why call a women's meeting?' The work petered out."

While the Russian Party was undergoing internal convulsions, German Social Democracy was similarly afflicted. A seemingly insignificant episode involving Rosa Luxemburg and fellow-Marxist August Bebel was more than a straw in the Socialist wind of dissent. "Opportunism"—the nemesis of revolution—assumed concrete form when Bebel attacked Rosa for publishing a letter by one Molkenburg written to the Central Committee of the German S-D Party: "It would be inexpedient to criticize the German Government's colonial policy in connection with the Morocco incidents," he said. Lenin defended Luxemburg. Bebel, the "grand old man" of German Marxism was, by indirection, defending Imperialism. "Inexpediency" had been, and continued to be, the hallmark of Opportunism.

In October of that year (1911), the Lafargues committed suicide. Nadya wrote:

Vladimir Ilyich wrote out a speech and Inessa translated it into French. I remember with what deep emotion he delivered the speech at the funeral, in the name of the Russian Social Democratic Labor Party. He felt a desire to say that the cause of Marx would grow and spread even to remote Asia.

"On the eve of the New Year, the Bolsheviks called a conference of the Bolshevik groups abroad. Everyone was in good spirits, although life abroad had frayed everyone's nerves considerably." Thus Nadya wrote "finis" to Act I of a production that had managed to survive its first rehearsal.

Stage-managing the revolution would soon pass from the control of its handful of directors. Individual acts and a collective will, lashed by the whip of historical inevitability, were about to unite in a charge across the stage, knocking down props and scattering principals into the wings. That even the most canny politicos failed to read the future was due to the insidiously slow incubation period of an embryo monster—world war.

12. World War I—Trapped in Switzerland

The elements that exploded into World War I became identifiable in 962 A.D. when a German king, Otto I, united his territories under an umbrella of federation thenceforth to be known as the Holy Roman Empire. Subsequent emperors and popes ruled over a commonwealth of Europe with variously expanding and contracting boundaries. In practice, the Vatican bowed to its temporal partner.

Included in the Empire was part of a corridor extending from the Baltic Sea to the Mediterranean, separating western Europe from Russia. Bounded on the north by Poland, its southern extremity was Greece.

In 1806 when the Holy Roman Empire dissolved, a remnant survived as the Austro-Hungarian Empire. But instead of a confederation, the Empire was an absolutist monarchy held together by real or implied force imposed by the dominant Germanic Austrians.

The corridor was predominantly Slavic, but although united ethnically, albeit to varying degrees, it was nevertheless riven by national rivalries reinforced by religious differences. Originally, Eastern Europe had no enemy in common; in the north it was a Teuton, in the south a Turk. But with the emergence of the Russian Empire, a new enemy threatened both north and south. For Russia, the enemy was Teuton, Turk and its own Slavic neighbor, Poland. After the Reformation, Poland—a monolith of Roman Catholicism—was positioned between Lutheranism in northern Germany, Russia's Eastern Orthodoxy, and a Bohemia (Czechs and Slovaks) struggling for religious orientation. For all its great size and strategic position at the head of the corridor, Poland was militarily weak, and repeated incursions from west and east and south led to three partitions. During Europe's 19th Century era of colonialism *cum* imperialism, Poland was divided among Prussia, Austria and Russia.

Poles disliked and feared their neighbors, and the feeling was mutual. Balkan peoples of the southern corridor hated and feared Russia, Turkey and the Austrian Habsburgs. Among the corridor states, only Bulgaria, possibly because it shared an alphabet, linguistic similarities, religion, and ethnic ties with its giant neighbor across the Black Sea, was moderately pro-Russian. That Bulgaria had been infiltrated by the Islamic Turks, and at various times been absorbed into the Ottoman Empire, did not radically alter its Slavic complexion.

An incipient *coup de grace* against territorial sovereignty in eastern Europe materialized when Bismarck's Germany became an empire (1871). The corridor was now encircled in the iron grip of three empires, at least one of which—

Russia—coveted possession of the Dardenelle Straits, a strategic waterway controlled by Turkey. European Turkey sliced across the southern Balkans, an Islamic highway to the Mediterranean.

The Balkan Wars of 1912-14 began with an attempt by Bulgaria to drive Turkey from Europe, a unilateral move that served to polarize loyalties: Slav against Teuton, Teuton against Slav, with Turkey a predestined loser. A chance turn of events placed Lenin and his wife near the scene of conflict.

Summer, 1912: "We began to make preparations to move to Cracow." Cracow was a small city in Poland whose provincial appearance belied a historically colorful past. Its blend of Poles, Jews and Germans resulted in an atmosphere of laissez-faire that allowed newcomers to live in a manner of their own choosing, unhampered by "overseer" landladies.

> In many respects, Cracow was more convenient than Paris. In addition to lying close to the Russian border, the Polish police, unlike those of France, were hostile to the Russian police. No one would spy on us, and we would be sure that our letters would not be intercepted.

Nadya and Volodya sublet their Paris apartment to a Pole from Cracow who questioned them about household affairs. What was the price of geese, of veal?

> I could not tell him anything about geese and veal, but I could have told him the cost of horseflesh and lettuce.

Together with the Zinovievs and a Polish political exile named Bagotsky, they rented a house in the suburb of Zvezhintsa. The unpaved, muddy streets reminded Nadya of Ufa. However, the nearby Vistula was convenient for bathing, and the beautiful woods of Volsky Lyas a focal point for bicycle excursions.

> Volodya and I like Cracow; it reminds us of Russia. As a very young child I lived in Poland, and early memories of our life there remained. It reminds Mother also of her young days.

Having managed to cope with German, French and English, Nadya was now confronted with Polish. Fortunately, Lilina Zinovieva "spoke Polish better than any of us." On daily trips to market, the two women encountered local peculiarities. Mondays there was no bread at the bakery because the baker was recovering from his weekend hangover. And at the butcher shop, "the Lord God created cows with bones, so how can I sell you meat without bones?" In the open market, one haggled over prices. Upon returning home, a decrepit wood-burning stove had to be kindled. "Housekeeping was a much more serious business here than in Paris," Nadya observed. Lenin's concept of a society in which women no longer spent their days over a hot stove undoubtedly hatched from his wife's domestic problems.

In Cracow the poor were highly visible.

> I recall how peasant women, coming to the marketplace to hire themselves as ser-

vants, would crowd around the "lady" and kiss her hand. A coachman or a carpenter, upon receiving a tip, would kneel and bow his head to the ground.

Church-going was the only recreation.

A nursemaid, hired by the Zinovievs for their little boy, was emaciated from fasting and praying. But when Nadya talked to her, a litany of hate against the masters replaced this façade of piety.

> The poverty and wretchedness of the peasants and of the poor generally was evident all around and was still greater than in Russia at that time.

Polish Social Democracy was a vigorous contingent of international socialism; but as elsewhere, ideological differences were rife. Warsaw and the industrial city of Lodz were leaders in the fight to defend what Nadya called "strict principles" against the onslaught of Polish revisionists, opportunists and liquidators. An exceptionally strong bond that transcended both national antipathies and religious differences existed between Polish and Russian proletarians. It was from this background of solidarity that many Poles lent their support to the Russian Revolution.

Soon after their arrival in Cracow, the émigrés were absorbed into the Russian revolutionary community. Free at last from contentious compatriots, Nadya detailed the ease with which revolutionary work progressed. Regular border crossings were undertaken by Polish couriers and ordinary people recruited from Cracow and the countryside, who transported literature and letters to and from Bolshevik comrades in Russia.

Border crossings by Russians were likewise facilitated by partisan natives. "By this means we once got Stalin across," said Nadya in one of her scant references to Iosef Djugashvili. Among those border commuters who came to grief in St. Petersburg following a clandestine entry were Inessa and her male companion, Safarov; both were imprisoned, and it was there that Inessa suffered permanent physical impairment. Safarov, seventeen years younger than Inessa, was described by Nadya as Inessa's "close comrade" which, in the parlance of the day, meant anything from bedfellow to good friend. A 38-year-old woman, the mother of several children, may have needed Safarov as protection during her travels, but gossip called them lovers. Since neither Lenin nor his wife commented in print about the real nature of this relationship, one assumes that their attitude was indifferent. The "affair" does, however, add another dimension to the gossip about Lenin and Inessa.

"In the autumn the 'great powers' intervened in the Balkan affair, and things began to smack of war." Nadya recalled that Socialists reacted to an incipient all-European conflict with timidity. "Not now," they said. "To organize strikes and armed uprisings—even demonstrations—against war would be a mistake."

During this time, while privately agonizing over what he considered to be a retreat from manifest conditions for revolution, Lenin devoted his writing to the nationalities question. According to Nadya—and this is confirmed by her husband's numerous writings on the subject—"Since his early youth, he had hated national oppression in every form. Marx's statement that no greater misfortune can befall a nation than that it subdue another nation, was near and comprehensible to him." Similarly, Lenin repeatedly denounced what he called "Great Russian chauvinism" against the country's national minorities. Leninism emerged during the prelude to World War I.

The nationalities question continued to confound the Bolsheviks. In was one thing to look with tolerance upon the Ukraine, for example, and its history of separatist aspirations, but it was quite another to accept the idea of a large number of hostile, independent states on the southern border of Great Russia.

First of all, what constituted a nation? . . . individual nationalities within the boundary of a given state, in this case the entire southern half of Russia?

As a political unit Russia evolved thus: north, from 1533; central, from the late 1500's; south, early to middle 1800's. (Siberia's absorption into the empire began as early as the 17th Century.) At least one of the nationalities—Armenia—sued for admission as protection against the Turks. At the time of their entry into the Russian Empire, the border areas were territories rather than political entities.

In Lenin's mind, was the difference between nations and nationalities merely a question of semantics? He had no difficulty later with releasing Finland from Russian bondage. In fact, the Finns were astonished at the ease with which they gained independence after a history of subjugation, beginning with that by Sweden. Also, Lenin would later sign away the Baltic nationality/states. And except for the large Polish "bulge" into Russia, that nation, too, would be ushered out of the Empire.

He trusted that persuasion, as well as the merits of Socialism itself, would become acceptable in self-determination within the Russian nationalities and elsewhere. His objective was a supra-national confederation of Socialist peoples, and eventually a boundary-less world. Trotsky believed that a United States of Europe—including Russia—was both necessary and inevitable.

Germany' s defeat in World War I did not radically alter the prospect of future conflict on Russia's borders.

In an era of imperialism, Lenin's *credo* is remarkable when judged by the situation that would confront the new Soviet State concerning the question of nations and nationalities. How ironic that a socialist state, the first in history, later fell into the hands of Stalin, a man whom Lenin had designated as "Commissar of Nationalities."

Was Lenin sincere in what he said and wrote concerning nations and nationalities? A premature death deprived him of the opportunity for practicing to the full his stated position on this question.

During the Cracow period, Lenin began a theoretical consideration of "socialist construction": i.e. the economic and social machinery of government. There existed no precedent for establishing a socialist state; neither apparatus, nor constitution, nor record of success or failure to serve as practical guides for implementing Marxist theory. All would have to be invented. Lenin, alone among his colleagues, understood the hazards of improvising under the chaotic conditions imposed by the transition to Socialism. "Had we not experienced the Cracow period of semi-exile," Nadya observed, "it would have been difficult to deal with all the aspects of Soviet construction which arose after the October Revolution."

Lenin spent his days devising a rough draft for the future, one that included restructuring financial institutions, foreign trade, jurisprudence, transportation, industry, agriculture, education.

One of his most far-sighted projects was that of nationwide electrification. This, with universal education, he considered the priority of socialist construction. "When the Soviet Government was established, all the problems were already familiar to him; all that had to be done was to apply the solutions that he had already worked out."

The usual stream of visitors flooded the Lenins' suburban apartment. Some stayed for a day, others for a week. Among them was the peripatetic Malinovsky, who arrived with a weird and implausible tale of his adventures in Russia. At this time, no one suspected him of being an *agent provocateur*, but another comrade immediately aroused Nadya's suspicions:

> We did not like C-, and I did not even ask him to stay the night, so he was compelled to spend the night walking the streets of Cracow.

One day after moving back to the city from Zvezhintsa, Nadya and Volodya were looking through the window and observed a young man approaching the house who was carrying a large canvas bag on his back. Upon admitting him, they learned that he lived in Vienna under the name of Orlov. V. talked with him at length and finally asked him what he was carrying. "He drew a number of splendid paintings from his bag," Nadya remembered, "and we examined them with interest. Volodya liked pictures very much."

Their visitor was Nikolai Bukharin, subsequently a prominent figure of the Revolution, whose brilliant mind and independence of thought would later bring him into conflict with Stalin. Bukharin and Iosef were already acquainted through their connection with the Vienna *Pravda*, and it is probable that their paths crossed in Cracow. "Stalin also arrived," Nadya said, "and he discussed the national question with Volodya." Shortly afterward, Lenin wrote Maxim Gorky:

We have a wonderful Georgian here who is writing a long article for the press. He has collected all the Austrian material as well as other material for it.

The "wonderful Georgian" was then 33 years old, an apprentice Bolshevik whose personality was still in the formative stage.

Although setbacks occurred from time to time—arrests of "our people" in Russia, or V.'s articles gone astray or ignored by publishers—the mood in Cracow was generally one of optimism. When a packet containing salmon, sturgeon and caviar arrived from Maria Alexandrovna, Nadya consulted her mother's cookbook and prepared a feast for visiting comrades. She reported that Volodya was highly pleased with the affair, that he liked to treat friends to the best.

Occasional arid spells during which no visitors appeared depressed Nadya. She complained to her mother-in-law:

We are living here as if we were in Shusha. The coming of the postman is the greatest event to look forward to. Until eleven o'clock we try to pass the time away somehow or another. At eleven o'clock the postman comes and then he comes again at six—we can hardly wait so long.

Since V. was busy, "we" must have referred to the women. Nadya, observing her husband's intense preoccupation, declared a moratorium on study and writing, and sleepless nights. It was time for a holiday.

Poronin was a small village on the border of Austrian Poland and the Austro/Hungarian Empire; a resort area centered at Zakopane in the Tatra Mountains whose salubrious climate was compatible with rest and relaxation. Nadya wrote:

Together with the Bagotskys, the Zinovievs and their dog Zhulik, we rented a large bungalow and moved out together. The view of the mountains was extremely beautiful, the air wonderful ... The mountain air helped me a little. But my health got worse, and after consulting Bagotsky, who was a neurologist, Volodya insisted on my going to Berne (Switzerland) to be operated on by Köcher.

The thyroid condition, called Grave's Disease, which had afflicted her since the St. Petersburg days preceding and following imprisonment, was now acute. Occasional periods of regression had accustomed her to accept the illness as something to be borne with stoicism.

But Volodya gets very worked up. People are telling him all sorts of nonsense: that I will go blind, that I shall have to remain in bed for eighteen months and so on.

Nevertheless, she gave way to his urging and agreed to an operation.

On the way, they stopped in Vienna where they visited the Bukharins. Nikolai's wife, Nadezhda, was very ill, and they found him tending the house and cooking, putting sugar instead of salt into the soup while talking animatedly to V. about everything of mutual interest.

From Switzerland, a spate of cheerful letters to the family successfully disguised Volodya's panic over his wife's condition. In Berne, they sought a comrade family living in a small cottage "who fussed endlessly over us." "Mother dearest," wrote V., "Nadya and I have been in Berne for several days. Köcher has not yet received us. He is a difficult person, a celebrity and likes to be begged."

On July 26, 1913, V. reported that the operation appeared to have been successful. Convalescence, however was preceded by a period of delirium and high fever, following an operation during which "they tormented Nadya for about three hours without an anesthetic, but she bore it bravely.... On Thursday she was very bad, so I was pretty scared." He remained constantly by her side, and not until several days later did he begin dividing his time between mornings at the hospital and afternoons in the Berne libraries.

After two weeks they prepared to return to Poronin. On the way, they stopped in Munich for a glimpse of the changes that had taken place since their sojourn there eleven years earlier. An interesting episode occurred at a Munich restaurant famous for its Hofbrau beer. Mugs were inscribed with the initials H.B. which to Nadya were the Russian letters N.V. "This is the Narodnaya Volya beer house," she said in jest, a painful reminder to her husband of a brother hanged for his involvement in the Narodnaya Volya plot to assassinate Tsar Alexander III.

They returned to Poronin to be greeted by Kamenev, "the usual rain, and a great deal of news about Russia." Immediately, a Poronin conference of representatives from several leading party organizations was called, among them Bolshevik members of the Imperial Duma (St. Petersburg). A renewed outbreak of strikes in Russia, as well as other signs of social unrest, seemed to portend an upsurge of revolutionary spirit, and it was necessary for Social Democrats to map a strategy based upon ever-changing conditions.

"I remember the disputes on the national question that took place in our kitchen," said Nadya. "I remember the passions that were roused around it and the ardor with which it was discussed."

The Duma contingent included Malinovsky. "He was in a terribly nervous state," Nadya reported.

> He would get drunk night after night, would become maudlin and complain that he was mistrusted. The Moscow electors were very indignant at his behavior. They sensed a certain falseness and play-acting in his stories and conduct.

Two weeks after the conference ended, the Poronin group—Lenin's family, the Zinovievs and the Bagotskys—moved back to Cracow, and to a life that V. described as "narrow, quiet and sleepy." In late autumn, Nadya's mother underwent a severe attack of influenza. The day after Christmas, Nadya wrote: "We do a lot of walking; what else is there to do in Cracow except walk?" New Year's Eve was dismal: outside, half rain, half snow; inside, alone in the apartment with Volodya "over a plate of curds." Thus the year 1914 innocuously stole into the kitchen of a modest flat in a backwater town of Austrian Poland.

A mere 200 miles away, Emperor Franz Josef, a reticent old man of iron will, lay in bed listening to the cathedral bells of Vienna ring in the New Year. The city of Johann Strauss and Franz Lehár, of youthful exuberance and jaded sophistication, of parties, balls and festivals, no longer mattered to him. At age 84, his thoughts were elsewhere: a troublesome, overweight nephew—his heir—married to a commoner; the Balkans in ferment; his "cousin" Willi Hohenzollern, acting the buffoon in Germany; Austrian Social Democrats springing up like mushrooms, supporting the dreadful Russians with their gluey speech and bizarre ways. "Lenin" was just a name among many, most of which ended in "ski" or "ov." The Emperor, who seldom traveled, perceived "cousin" Nicky Romanov as the exemplification of Russia, when in fact the Tsar was a man of small stature and limited intellect, propped up by a strong-willed German wife. The old Emperor was thinking: "We three—either we stand together or we fall one by one." Unfortunately, the political and territorial aims of Russia did not coincide with those of the Austrian Habsburgs. Nicholas, although a brother autocrat, was first of all a Russian whose dedication to The Fatherland ranked above that of dynastic fraternity.

The midwinter hiatus ended with Lenin's departure for Paris to attend a Party conference. The Kamenevs would return to Russia.

> We all went to the station to see them off. It was a cold winter evening. We spoke very little. Only Kamenev's little son kept up a steady chatter. We all asked ourselves how long Kamenev would hold out, how soon would we meet? When would we be able to go to Russia? Each of us secretly thought about Russia. Night after night I would dream about Nevaskaya Zastava (Old Nevsky—the area of the *Lavra Gate*—home) in St. Petersburg.

March 8th was International Women's Day, and whether by coincidence or design, the first issue of *Rabotnitza* (The Woman Worker) appeared in Petersburg, selling for four kopeks a copy. "Lilina Zinovieva and I wrote articles for the paper," Nadya said. The newspaper had been started by a group of four: Nadya, Inessa Armand, Lilina and Ludmila Stahl. With limited financial support, they were able to produce seven issues. As Nadya's first serious endeavor in the field of socio-political journalism, it brought her considerable satisfaction.

Of the six letters Nadya wrote to her husband's family during the first half of 1914, only one contains personal news. Dated March 16th from Cracow, its melancholy flavor was probably a result of her physical condition. She and Volodya were "very lonely." They were arranging for a second summer at Poronin:

> Perhaps I shall recover my breath there. Again I have thyroid trouble, although not as badly as before; my eyes are almost normal and my neck swells only when I am excited, but the palpitation is rather bad. Although the disease does not yet bother me very much, it is a bore to have to start an invalid routine again.

However, the letter ended with a note of optimism: "It is very damp here in Cracow, but in Poronin I shall probably get over it all very quickly."

In May, Volodya and Nadya and her mother moved to Poronin, but it was hardly a vacation. Numerous comrades arrived to discuss plans for a Party congress in Vienna. Likewise, plans were formulated for a Russian "unity" conference to be held in Brussels. "Inessa was to go. She spoke French like a native, never got confused and had a strong will."

But in addition to the Brussels meeting, Lenin was preoccupied with the Malinovsky affair. As a member of the Bolshevik faction in the Duma, Malinovsky held an important position; the discovery that he was in the pay of the Tsar's secret police led to his resignation, but the Duma president agreed not to publish the reason, thus avoiding a grave political scandal—not only for the Bolsheviks, but for an institution struggling for credibility against insuperable difficulties.

Nadya described what followed: "Completely knocked out of action and in a state of suspense, Malinovsky idled about Poronin. No one knows what he lived through during this time. Then he disappeared, nobody knew where."

Despite continuing ill-health, Nadya devoted herself to plans for a Socialist Women's Conference to be held in Vienna. The eighth issue of *Rabotnitza*, in which the leading news would be devoted to the projected conference, was targeted for midsummer. But neither the eighth issue nor the conference materialized.

> On August 1st, Germany declared war on Russia. On August 3rd, declared war on France; on August 4th, war on Belgium and on the same day England declared war on Germany. On August 6th Austria declared war on Russia; on August 11th France and England declared war on Austria.

Thus Nadya described the birth of a monster horror striding across the map of Europe.

"The Russians are poisoning our wells!" Panic and national chauvinism erupted in Poronin with a vengeance; first a house-search, with the local gendarme poking among V.'s books and personal effects with the air of one expecting to find a bomb in what was only a jar of paste. "I'll have to arrest you," said the Inspector. "Be ready tomorrow morning to board the six o'clock train for Novy Targ" (district police headquarters).

Nadya was frightened, but her husband displayed an outward coolness. Registered in Cracow as a political exile, he was reasonably certain of being absolved of spying charges, but how long it would take was another matter. Meanwhile, his wife and her mother would be alone.

> Volodya and I stayed up all night. We could not sleep, the situation was so alarming. In the morning I saw him off and came back to an empty room.

It occurred to them how easily V. might disappear into an unmarked grave, victim of some overzealous official. However, immediately after the search, V.

activated the Socialist network in his own behalf. Telegrams, letters, personal visits to the authorities by his colleagues moved along the line of communication, at length coming to rest with Socialist Victor Adler in Vienna, a member of the Austrian Parliament.

At Novy Targ, Lenin was interrogated and placed in jail. Fortunately, Nadya was allowed to visit him, and each morning she boarded the early train for an hour's ride, afterward wandering around the station until the 11 a.m. visiting hour. To her surprise, she found her husband in good spirits. Quickly making friends with fellow inmates, he forgot his own dilemma when listening to their troubles. Some were incarcerated for petty breaches of the law, and he established a "legal-aid bureau," dispensing advice and writing petitions. The inmates nicknamed him "Sturdy Peasant." At night, when the others were asleep, he lay on his bunk figuring out ways to turn the international war into a war of liberation for the proletariat.

At Poronin "our household went to pieces." A servant girl hired for the season turned hostile, spreading gossip around the neighborhood about "the Russians." Nadya was so disturbed that she packed the girl off to Cracow, paying her train fare and wages in advance. The day of his arrest, Lenin arranged for a male comrade to stay with the women pending further developments. "Comrade T- kept smoking pensively, and packing books. It was obvious that we would have to leave after Volodya's release."

Nadya worried about her mother.

She was already 72 and very ill. She saw that something was wrong but could not understand just what it was. Although I told her that Volodya was under arrest, at times she would say that he had been drafted for the war. She became agitated every time I left the house, thinking I would disappear in the same way as Volodya.

During this time, Nadya observed the reaction of local people to the war. Most were bewildered and depressed. Having no idea what the war was about, drafted men went "as if led to the slaughter." Only the clergy glorified the war, arousing patriotic sentiment and encouraging their flock to acts of hostility against foreigners.

Once at the railway station, I heard some peasant women coming out of a Catholic church discussing aloud—apparently for my benefit—how they would deal with spies. Even if the authorities released the spy, they said, the peasants would put out his eyes, cut off his tongue, etc. I did not tell Volodya.

As a result of Adler's intercession, Lenin was released after eleven days in jail. On August 19th, Nadya was admitted to his cell to help him pack his things. But after returning to Poronin in a hired cart, they waited a week before receiving a permit to return to Cracow. Although the city was in turmoil (a battle had just been fought at Krasnik, and trains were constantly arriving with dead and wounded), they were able to rent what Nadya called "a nook" in the corner of a house.

On the next day we witnessed a horrible scene from the window of our room. A train arrived, and relatives of the men who had taken part in the battle ran after the stretcher-bearers and looked into the faces of the dead and dying, afraid to recognize their kin. Those who had been less seriously wounded came slowly from the railway station with bandaged heads and arms. One could not help thinking "Here is war!" And this was only the first battle.

Shortly afterward, Volodya and Nadya received permission to leave for neutral Switzerland. Yelizaveta's sister had recently died, and money from her estate—four thousand rubles and some valuables—was deposited in a Cracow bank. To obtain it required the assistance of a Vienna banker, who retained half for his services. Nevertheless, the balance was sufficient to sustain a modest lifestyle in Switzerland, and during the war "we lived mainly on this money." They were so frugal that, upon returning to Russia three years later, some of it still remained.

Civilian rail travel was greatly curtailed, with passenger coaches shunted onto sidings to permit passage of troop trains. The travelers observed with interest the activities on station platforms:

Nuns and other women were distributing small images, prayer books and similar articles among the soldiers. Chauvinist agitation was everywhere evident—slogans on what to do with the French and English, and "a shot for every Russian"!

The stark realities of war were symbolized by several railway cars loaded with insect powder and bound for the front.

At Vienna, they were met by comrade R- who conducted them to Victor Adler; the latter described his conversation with the Austrian Minister: "Are you certain that Ulyanov is an enemy of the Tsarist Government?" the latter queried. "Oh yes," came the reply, "a more implacable enemy than Your Excellency."

On September 5, 1914, the wanderers crossed into Switzerland. That same day Lenin telegraphed Adler:

Dear Comrade, I have arrived safely with all my family at Zurich. Papers were asked for only at Innsbruck and Feldkirche: your help was therefore extremely useful to me ... Very best wishes and deepest gratitude.

The battle near Cracow was expanding eastward toward Russia. Before long the Vistula Line would become a major proving ground for Austrian military capability against the Russian peasant-boy soldiers who straggled into a war they understood even less than their Polish brethren.

The national chauvinism Nadya observed in Poronin, Cracow and Vienna was but a microcosm of that which infected European Socialist leaders. Discarding their commitment to internationalism, they boarded the steamroller called "Defense of the Fatherland," each to his own vehicle. The centrists among them attempted to rationalize their patriotism in a curious straddle of mutually incompatible positions. "Sitting between two stools," Lenin said.

The list of waffling or renegade Socialist leaders was lengthy; it included Plekhanov and his Emancipation of Labor group; Emile Vandervelde and Camille Huysmans in Belgium; Karl Kautsky in Germany. Italian socialist Filippo Turati and his associate Angelica Balabanova—a Ukrainian—were initially anti-war but later retreated to defensism. On July 31, eve of the war, French socialist Jean Jaurès was assassinated by a fanatic, thus depriving him of the opportunity to practice his avowed "non-patriotism." But his colleagues Guèsde and Vaillant at once turned defensist (pro-war). In Great Britain, chauvinists quickly dominated the political scene, supported by Hyndman and his lukewarm socialists; the Social Democratic Labor Party, headed by Keir Hardie and Ramsey MacDonald, had been—and continued to be—pacifist. In Holland, the trend was likewise pacifist, with socialist writer Madame Henriette Roland-Holst standing aloof from both defensism and revolution; but Troelstra's Dutch S-D's, earlier pacifist, were now pro-war.

The Socialist International convoked its Second Congress for the express purpose of dealing with the present crisis. Speaking with one voice, it formulated policy vis-à-vis the war. Voting was heavily weighted on the side of participation in the war effort, whereat Vandervelde, Belgian delegate to the II International, began meddling in the affairs of Russian Social Democracy, using his considerable influence to defuse its explosive potential against the war. The Belgian leaders detested Lenin. One provided a withering description of him: "A little man with a rusty beard, patiently explaining Marxism in a flat, monotonous voice."

"The voice," meanwhile, was speaking with conviction to a small company of Bolsheviks gathered in the woods near Berne. The group passed a resolution condemning the war as imperialist and predatory.

It also formulated a Party program: struggle against the monarchy, propaganda for revolution, struggle for a republic (!), for the emancipation of nationalities oppressed by the Great Russians (inhabitants of northern European Russia), confiscation of estates of the nobility, and parochial matters like the eight-hour workday.

Lenin's proposal, "that from the standpoint of the working class and the toiling masses of all the people of Russia, by far the lesser evil would be a defeat of the tsarist monarchy and its armies which oppress Poland, the Ukraine and a number of nationalities in Russia"—was unanimously accepted.

Was he justified in condemning the war as imperialist and predatory? Kaiser Wilhelm II declared war against Russia on the grounds that Tsar Nicholas was mobilizing his forces on the Russo-German frontier. Of the remaining countries, only Belgium had a legitimate claim of self-defense; the other belligerents plunged into the fray for purely imperialistic reasons. The term "spheres of influence" was a euphemism for territorial plunder; one has only to study a pre-war map to understand that the war aim was to retain colonies and—hopefully—add to them by redistributing territory. To the victor the spoils.

Within a few days of mobilization, Germany's Social Democrats split on the war issue. A new party was in process of formation led by Rosa Luxemburg, Karl Liebknecht and Franz Mehring—and by Klara Zetkin, whose political involvement included both the German S-D Party and the International Socialist Women's Movement of which she was co-founder. The German schism was tangible evidence that anti-war sentiment had not been suppressed by the Second International.

World War I might have been halted at the outset had the majority Socialist hierarchy adhered to principles, urging the bewildered proletariat to unite against a conflict instigated by entrenched power. Proletarians of the belligerent countries possessed a powerful weapon: the political strike. But when war economy in western Europe and Britain swung into place, wages rose, particularly those of shop foremen and middle-management. Thus potential grassroots leadership, corrupted by money, became a willing tool in the hands of Socialist mentors whose former ideological equivocation suddenly hardened on the side of the political "right."

Hostility to Lenin, which had once been merely spiteful, now became virulent. His press releases were submerged in the tide of pro-war Socialist journalism that swept Europe. To this was added official propaganda in which The Enemy was depicted as a monster with bloody claws, a beast in human dress with leering countenance and fangs.

Although Nadya was not a pessimist, she must have wondered at times if her husband's attempt to prevail against the emotional *volte-face* of so many of his formerly internationalist colleagues was fruitless. Lenin, however, adopted a pragmatic attitude. With the consistency of purpose which hitherto had ordered his life (Vera Zasulich likened him to a bulldog who clamped his jaws on an idea and never let go), he settled down in Switzerland to continue theoretical work, at the same time pursuing avenues of contact with the Russian working-class movement. Communication had always been difficult, but it was now exacerbated by the war, and Lenin began a methodical search for ways of continuing the flow of information and political agitation.

His objective was twofold: to denounce the war and, by exposing its nature, to rouse proletarian sentiment to the boiling point of revolution. Because the Second International had failed him, he concentrated on Russia, leaving Europe to the ministrations of its own Socialists. "Perhaps," he was thinking, "the example of Russia, if successful, will be the spark—iskra—that ignites the flame beyond her borders." He did not, however, discontinue his journalistic and verbal battle against Kautsky, Madame Roland-Holst, and anyone else who disagreed with him.

Nor was Nadya a mere bystander. "We formed a new Committee of Organizations Abroad, consisting of the Berne comrades Shklovsky, Kaparov, Inessa, Lilina and Krupskaya. The task of the day was to rally our forces on an international scale."

Upon arrival in Switzerland, Volodya and Nadya debated a place of residency. Their rented room in Berne was a temporary expediency, with Geneva in mind as their probable destination. However, comrades who were familiar with conditions there advised against it. A large number of Russian émigrés, living in Paris, had fled to Geneva at the outbreak of war, thus creating a diverse—and to Lenin—uncongenial colony whose political views were often centrist to right-wing. Foregoing the convenience and resources of the Société de Lectures library in Geneva, he elected to remain in Berne, a more provincial city but also more peaceful.

Klara Zetkin and Rosa Luxemburg at the Congress of the Social Democratic Party, Magdeburg, Germany, 1910

"The memory of that autumn (1914) is interwoven in my mind with the autumnal scene of the forest of Berne," Nadya related.

> The weather was glorious. We lived in Berne on Distelwag, a small, tidy, quiet street adjoining Berne forest which extended several kilometers. Across the road lived Inessa, and a few minutes' walk distant the Zinovievs and the Shklovskys. We would wander for hours along the forest paths, bestrewn with fallen yellow leaves. On most occasions the three of us went together on these walks, Volodya, Inessa and myself.

Inessa's presence in this private colony led to historical gossip. Ignoring or discounting Nadya's version of that time, writers made a case for Lenin and Inessa as lovers, strolling à deux in Berne forest; or a confrontation à trois, also in Berne forest, with Nadya threatening to leave her husband, to relinquish the field to Inessa. If true, who would have told it? Nadya? And to whom? To her mother? And would Yelizaveta have revealed a daughter's unhappy plight? Inessa, bragging of her love affair to some friend? Lenin himself? None of these is likely. Nadya's description of the days in Berne forest is consistent with her husband's demeanor and practice.

> Sometimes we would sit for hours on the sunlit, wooded mountainside while Volodya jotted down outlines of his speeches and articles. I studied Italian, and Inessa sewed a skirt and basked with delight in the autumnal sun—she had not yet fully recovered from the effects of her imprisonment.

In the evening they usually visited the Zinovievs who, with their little boy Styopa, lived in one room. V. played with the child, and after he was put to bed, "made a series of concrete proposals—the main points of the line of struggle, formulated in a condensed, precise manner . . ."

Nadya said of Inessa at that time:

> She took Volodya's plan for the international struggle very much to heart. She began to take a most direct part, conducting correspondence, translating our documents into French and English, gathering materials, talking to people, etc.

Not all the Paris Bolsheviks emigrated to Switzerland; a small group remained, and it was imperative to maintain contact with them. Also crucial was the matter of unity between and among those socialists, female as well as male, who had not defected. For this purpose, plans were made for an International Socialist Women's Conference to be held in Berne. Because of her linguistic skills, as well as expertise in political matters, Inessa became the principal medium of communication, a task that brought her into active contact with, among others, Kollontai, Balabanova, Zetkin, Luxemburg, and Ludmila Stahl. As an "agent" for Lenin she was, in Nadya's opinion, "very well fitted for this work."

Was it Inessa's support for Lenin's program, her enthusiasm for him and the work itself, that engendered envy which led to gossip among the women with whom she was associated? Zetkin, Luxemburg and Stahl were above pettiness, which leaves Kollontai and Balabanova to share responsibility for rumors about Lenin and Inessa. It is significant that neither the men deeply involved with the Bolshevik Party, nor the Russian Social-Democratic Party of various "fractions," nor the Socialist Movement as a whole, concurred in the gossip. Some disliked Lenin, a few hated him, and these would gladly have used slander as a political weapon.

Thus one might conclude that Inessa herself, merely by her demeanor—however ingenuous she was, however innocent of intrigue with Lenin—was responsible. A beautiful woman is often fair game for the less well-endowed of her sex.

There was hardly a Swiss town or city that did not have its Russian colony. Here and there a future Soviet leader resided. Despite the fact that Luxemburg once called him an "idiot," Maxim Litvinov, for example, became first Soviet ambassador to the United States. Others, such as Nikolai Bukharin, were already on the road to Party fame. One of them, Olga Ravich, earned a place in revolutionary history out of proportion to her status in the Party when she elected to join Lenin's group on its final journey to Russia in 1917. She had, however, done valuable service in Switzerland by attending to the mechanics of publishing.

Neutral Switzerland, stronghold of pacifism and haven for beleaguered revolutionaries, played a leading role in preparation for the "Ten Days That Shook the World." But during the war years and before, none of the participants could have measured the value of Swiss hospitality and tolerance.

13. The Inessa Letters

My dear and dearest friend, Today at first (sic) I've got a report (very very good!)-evidently written by Kamski. I greet you thousand times!! Your task was heavy & . . . Huysmans had done all against you & our delegation . . . You have rendered a very great service to our party! I am especially thankful because you have replaced me.
P.S. Write—are you very tired, very angry?
Are you wild with me for persuading you to go?*

Unless Lenin's correspondence with Inessa Armand is considered in toto, it is possible, based upon isolated remarks lifted from context, to establish an affair between them. But a realistic appraisal of those letters should include, in addition to their contents, the circumstances under which they were written. Of the hundreds or probably thousands of letters relating to Party business that Lenin wrote between January 1914 and March 1917, ninety were addressed to Inessa.

The correspondence can be divided into four segments; some brief, others covering an extended period of time. For example, letters from the first period written from Cracow (and Brussels when he was attending an S-D conference), are few in number and concentrated within a short space. Inessa was then living in Paris.

The Poronin (2nd) period covered May-July 1914. During that time, Inessa and her children were residing in Lovran, a summer resort near Trieste, Austria. All but two of the letters were dated between July 4 and 24. On July 26, Lenin was arrested and imprisoned at Novy Targ. World War I had just begun.

Subsequently, Lenin and his family arrived in Berne where they were joined by Inessa "who lived across the street from us." She was not accompanied by her children. The Safarovs, husband and wife, were also residing in Berne.

The Berne/Sörenberg/Berne (3rd) period included only seven letters. Inessa had left Lovran for Les Avants, a small town on Lake Geneva in southwestern Switzerland. What later motivated her to move to Berne cannot be ascertained from Lenin's letters to her just prior to her arrival. From Sörenberg he wrote a single letter which included minute instructions relating to travel from Berne to Sörenberg. "Inessa came to stay with us," Nadya recorded. Lenin's letter suggested that Inessa inquire of Karl Radek if he, too, would like to come to Sörenberg: "If so, we shall extend an invitation," he added.

There was no correspondence during the latter half of 1915, because Inessa was either in Berne or Sörenberg. After returning to Berne from Sörenberg,

---

* Written by Lenin in English July 19, 1914

Lenin wrote three letters to Inessa who was once again in Paris. The letters were dated January 15, 19, and 21, 1916.

When the Ulyanovs' unpleasantness with their Berne landlady necessitated a move to Zurich (period 4), Inessa was still in Paris. Lenin wrote to her three times: February 26, March 31, July 7, 1916. In early summer she returned to Berne and soon afterward went to Hertenstein, a resort area on Lake Lucerne approximately 50 miles south of Zurich. Meanwhile, Nadya's condition had worsened, and Lenin took her to a rest home in the mountains at Flums in eastern St. Gall Canton. Two letters from Lenin, written a week apart, were addressed to Inessa at Hertenstein.

During the fourth and final period—September 1916 to April 1917—all V.'s letters to Inessa were written from Zurich. She had moved from Hertenstein to Sörenberg where she remained, apparently alone, from early autumn until late November.

"*Don't* sit in Sörenberg," Lenin admonished her, "You'll freeze and catch cold. P.S. Maybe you have no money for your fare? Mind you, let us know: we can easily get what you need." By November 30, she was residing in Clarens on Lake Geneva. From that time until the end of February 1917 when she joined the Bolshevik group returning to Russia, her address was Clarens. Some of her children were living with her.

Lenin's correspondence with Inessa was prolific during the Zurich period—fifty-four letters—and for reasons that will subsequently become apparent.

With but two exceptions, his unvarying salutation to Inessa was "Dear Friend," the same used for certain male comrades with whom he was particularly congenial.* Until January 17, 1915, his subscription was likewise uniform: "Yours, V.I. (or V.U.)." After that date, his letters to Inessa were signed "Yours, Lenin." When writing to his family, Lenin usually ended with "Nadya sends regards." This was not generally true of his letters to comrades or other Party members, including those to Inessa. In the latter case, his omission of references to his wife is not significant. **Internal evidence from Lenin's letters shows that Nadya herself was regularly corresponding with Inessa.**

His style of writing was businesslike, although occasionally he expressed exuberance resulting from a particular event that pleased him. The words "very, very, very" sometimes underscored a comment. For example, in a letter to his mother, Lenin wrote: "We thank Anyuta very, very, very much for the book." At other times he resorted to playfulness in writing to female comrades (see letters to 'Rozalia'). However, there was always an underlying reserve. Neither in letters to Inessa, nor to his family or colleagues, did he transgress the bounds of personal propriety.

---

* See letters to Shlyapnikov, Dubrovinsky, Zinoviev, Karpinsky, and occasionally to Olga Ravich.

What distinguished letters to Inessa from his correspondence with other female Party members, was the uninhibited manner in which he castigated the various pro-war factions. Indeed, his passionate denunciation of the war permeated everything he wrote from 1914 onwards. Apparently he felt that Inessa would not take offense at his unbridled language: "*Voilà*. I apologize for this long letter and for the abundance of sharp words: I can't write otherwise when I am speaking frankly. Well, after all, this is *entre nous*, and perhaps the unnecessary bad language will pass."

Inessa Armand (mature photo)

The foregoing does not necessarily infer intimacy with Inessa on another level. Lenin spoke with equal vehemence to Nadya, not only because she was his wife, but because she was an intelligent and sympathetic listener.

From his letters to Inessa, it is evident that he respected her views, sought her opinion of his ideas, entrusted her with important Party assignments, even admired her. But there is nothing in the letters to suggest that she was more than a good friend, albeit a "very, very, very" good friend. There is no doubt that he was fond of her. In fact, he said so. "I have received your story of S-'s report and the speech by Y-; frankly speaking, I was angry with you—you did-n't understand what the essence of Y-'s position was. And I again—I'm sorry—called you the Holy Virgin. Please don't be angry, it was because I'm fond of you, because we're friends, but I can't help being angry when I see 'something that recalls the Holy Virgin.'" The letter, dated April 1, 1914, ended: "All the best, Yours, V.U."

What, then, is to be understood from his occasional remarks that have unleashed such widespread gossip by historians? This speculation bears little relation to the evidence. Only by placing Lenin's personal comments within the framework of the letters, and relating them to the external events and sit-uations which prompted his writing to Inessa, do they become intelligible.

The second "Dear Friend" letter (the first is a fragment dealing with Party concerns), written from Brussels to Paris, January 26, 1914, began: "I was ter-ribly glad to receive your nice, friendly, warm, charming letter. I am inex-pressibly grateful to you for it. Things here have gone worse (sic). One has already deserted to the conciliators . . . who will now have it their own rotten way." After alluding to other matters related to the Brussels conference he was attending, Lenin concluded: "My very, very, very best regards, my dear friend. Excuse the haste and brevity. I have no time. Yours, V.U."

In a letter written two days later he reminded her of the importance of her task as unifier of the wavering Paris group. One paragraph of a letter (other-wise devoted to Party affairs) posted from Poronin two months later, would have indicated to a perceptive woman that her correspondent was not emo-tionally involved with her: "I am awfully glad that your children are coming to see you and that you will soon go off to spend the summer with them. All the very, very best. P.S. I apologize for this brief letter. I am in a great hurry." Inessa was still in Paris.

Like many of her female colleagues, she was struggling to master the com-plexities of Socialist theory. She was also attempting to formulate a theoreti-cal basis for her own emancipation from what was termed "the bourgeois tradition and practice of female subjugation by men." One of Lenin's most interesting letters concerned the analysis and criticism of a pamphlet Inessa was writing on the subject of love/sex:

> I advise you to throw out altogether paragraph 3—the "demand (women's) for freedom to love." This is not really a proletarian but bourgeois demand. What do you understand by that phrase? What *can* be understood by it? Freedom *from* mate-rial (financial) calculations in affairs of love? The same, *from* material worries? From religious prejudice? From prohibitions by Papa, etc.? From prejudices of 'society'? From the narrow circumstances of one's environment? From fetters of the law, the courts and the police? From the serious element of love? From child-birth?

Freedom from adultery? Etc. . . . The thing is not what you *subjectively* "mean" by this. . . . Friendly shake hands! (sic). V.I.

When Inessa shot back in defense of her position, Lenin replied:

So—you have undertaken to demolish me? . . . What you write is: "Even a fleeting passion and intimacy, are 'more poetic and cleaner' than 'kisses without love' of a (vulgar and shallow) married couple." That is what you write, and that is good. Is the contrast logical? Kisses without love between a vulgar couple are *dirty*? I agree. To them one should contrast . . . what . . . kisses *with* love?

This lively, handwritten discussion, a topic he would return to many years later in conversation with Klara Zetkin, covered several pages.

The excerpted letter quoted at the beginning of the chapter refers to Inessa's trip as a delegate to the Brussels Unification Conference. Anticipating that Karl Kautsky, the Belgians (Huysmans and Vandervelde), Rosa Luxemburg and others were out to "get" him in debate, Lenin decided not to attend. A few days before the conference, he wrote to Inessa: "Forgive me, please, this disjointed letter . . . I am extremely nervous, almost ill." When Zinoviev declined to attend because of his wife's severe illness, Lenin urged Inessa to substitute for him. At first she refused; it meant leaving her children in someone's care. But his stubborn insistence finally persuaded her. After the conference, he wrote her:

Your behavior at the conference was right and was a great service to the Party. Popoff writes me that you were ill, your voice was feeble. What is this illness? Please write me in more detail!! I cannot be quiet otherwise. Many kind regards and best wishes: be healthy and quiet. Yours truly . . .

Inessa's health was of frequent concern to him. Because her primary illness (tuberculosis) had been contracted in the service of the Cause, he felt particularly responsible for her. She was a person who merited compassion; but rather than seeking it, she denied her own frailty. Writing in English, early September 1914, Lenin queried:

What is the weather like in Les Avants? Do you make (sic) walks? Do you feel better now? Have you books? Papers? Please write more about yourself. Very, very kind regards and shakehands (sic) . . .

Sometimes her long silences troubled him, and he would dispatch a series of letters and postcards asking for news. "Do you go skiing? It is good for the health."

One might ask: Would Lenin have felt warmly toward her if she had been old and ugly? Nadya related,

Of the two days Volodya stayed in Ufa, only one remains in my memory, a visit to the old Narodnaya Volya member, Chetvergova, whom he had known in Kazan. She had a bookshop in Ufa. On the first day, Volodya went to see her, and his face and voice seemed to become particularly gentle as he talked with her.

A clandestine love affair has been manufactured from portions of a letter

Lenin wrote to Inessa in January 1916. After some hard words about Radek and Trotsky, he wrote:

> It is a glorious sunny day today, with light snow. After influenza, my wife and I took our first walk along the road to Frauen-Kapellen where the three of us—you remember?—had that lovely stroll one day. I kept thinking of it and was sorry you were not here.

Even when excerpted, the observation is bland. But the letter continued:

> By the way, I'm rather surprised that there is no news of you. Let me confess, while I'm at it, that the thought occurred to me that you might have "taken offense" at my not having gone to see you off the day you left (for Paris). I did think that, I must confess, but I dismiss the unworthy thought, I have driven it from my mind. This is my second postcard to you. Maybe the first one went astray?

Four days later, he wrote again:

> This is my third postcard to you . . . If you are offended with me, you would probably have written to other friends, but as far as I know, you have not written to anybody. If I don't get a letter from you within the next few days, I shall write to our friends to find out whether you are ill.

He reiterated the comment about "our walk" and concluded:

> How are you getting on? Are you content? Don't you feel lonely? Are you very busy? You are causing me great anxiety by not giving any news of yourself! . . . Where are you living? Where do you eat? At the "buffet" of the National Library? Again I ask for letters poste restante (General Delivery). Sincerely yours, Basil*. P.S. Again nothing! No letters from you.

A long-awaited reply from Inessa reached Lenin on January 21, putting his mind at rest and eliciting from him some brief news about the Trotsky-Radek controversy.

Lenin's uninterrupted series of letters written to Inessa during the final (Zurich) period, revealed his emotional stress; in Nadya's words: "He felt keenly the approach of revolution." Because Inessa was not a member of the male-dominated inner circle of the Party, his epistolary discussions with her added another dimension to his thinking. Their correspondence often took the form of debates, for Inessa was by no means a passive recipient of his opinions.

In one letter he stated flatly: "No! Engels was *not* infallible. Marx was *not* infallible." At another time he wrote: "I wanted very much to write you a long letter on pacifism (an extremely important subject in general, a basic one from the standpoint of the whole international situation today)."

His letters were replete with arguments, as much with himself as with Inessa. It was apparent that he was still wrestling with theoretical problems that were not yet fully resolved to his own satisfaction. However, Inessa was more than a sounding-board. She may have influenced him more than either

---

* For security reasons.

of them realized. In any event, hers was a separate and distinctive voice in the ongoing general debate. With only minimal support from his male colleagues, he found Inessa, if not exactly a soul mate, at least an intellectual companion for whom he had a great affection.

What did Nadya think of all this? Her husband's letters to Inessa rarely employed the first person singular. When referring to his side of the correspondence, it was almost always "we" or "us." The implied conjugal solidarity would have communicated itself to a wife who lived in close communion with her mate.

Was Inessa the aggressor? Had she "fallen" for Lenin? At all times, a number of persons knew exactly where he was and what he was doing. Following Inessa around Switzerland would not long have remained a secret. It was Inessa who followed Lenin: to Berne, Sörenberg, Poronin, and eventually to Russia. Granted that some of this was by invitation related to Party matters; at other times it was on her own initiative.

It is possible that his change of subscription to "Yours, Lenin" at the beginning of 1915 resulted from certain gossip that had come to his attention. On the other hand, Inessa may have entertained feelings for him that were not reciprocated.

Many unattached "women of the revolution" were lonely. Unlike the men, most of whom were married, these forlorn "maidens" were seeking emotional ties. Vera Zasulich was in love with Plekhanov, a married man, who appears to have treated her devotion with tolerant objectivity. Destitute since the day in 1878 when she walked into the office of General Trepov, Governor of St. Petersburg, and shot him in protest for his order to flog prisoners, she fled to Switzerland (after being acquitted by a sympathetic jury), where for the remainder of her life she was supported financially by Plekhanov and Paul Axelrod.

Olga Ravich was living with Karpinsky in what may have been a common-law marriage, despite the fact that Lenin referred to them as "the Karpinskys."

Rosa Luxemburg, on the other hand, was passionately devoted to Leo Jogiches and spent her entire adult life trying to get him to the altar. When they separated after a lovers' quarrel, she turned for solace to Klara Zetkin's twenty-two-year-old son, Kostya. But Leo continued to dominate her emotions. Her despairing letters to him often verged on hysteria.

> Our only ties are the Cause . . . When, totally exhausted by the never-ending Cause, I sat down to catch my breath, I looked back and realized that I don't have a home anywhere. I neither exist nor live as *myself.*

After the break, Jogiches, as he had from the beginning of their relationship, continued to pay her living expenses including clothing.

Unlike the League of Struggle women, Alexandra Kollontai openly consorted with lovers. Only Klara Zetkin, among leading Socialist women referred to in this narrative, looked upon men as comrades. First widowed, and subsequently involved in an unhappy marriage and divorce, she turned from love of men to love of mankind.

Angelica Balabanova's connection with the Russian revolutionary movement was limited to attacks upon Lenin and his Bolsheviks. Because of her Ukrainian heritage, she was hostile toward Great Russians. Her departure for Italy, where she dedicated her literary talents to the socialist journal *Avanti,* was a way of distancing herself from Russian Social Democracy.

Physically, she was an unattractive woman. In order to compensate, she retreated into a sanctuary of idealism in which private "ikons" substituted for marriage or a love affair. Angelica was probably one of the few genuine spinsters of International Socialism.

Like many uncompromising idealists, she spoke out against the imperfections of *realpolitik.* Subjectively, however, she envied those with charm, or charisma. or mere personal self-assurance. Whereas Rosa Luxemburg wrote: "It's a pleasure to talk to Lenin. He is sophisticated and knowledgeable, with that kind of 'ugly face' I like so much to look at . . . Balabanova saw only the 'ugly face.' And she proceeded to demolish him, both as a public figure and a private person. Nor did she spare his wife. Balabanova was one of those women who contributed to the gossip about Lenin and Inessa.

Underlying her account of the Russian endeavor was a barely concealed spite. Thus, what might have been an objective statement by a woman of intellectual talent, became instead a bitter revelation of personal loneliness and estrangement.

Emotional deprivation was the price extracted from many so-called "women of the revolution."

Although Inessa Armand had chosen to leave her husband in order to pursue the life of a professional revolutionary, the separation was amicable; Alexander Armand continued to remain her friend. Nevertheless, Inessa missed the closeness to a particular person, a void that was often filled by her children, to whom she was devoted. Under the circumstances, it is possible that her initial admiration for Lenin turned to love. If so, she found herself vulnerable in circumstances for which there was no possible resolution.

"Of course, I also want to correspond," he reassured her. "Let's continue our correspondence." The letter was signed "All the best, Lenin."

But the unhappiness Inessa imparted to him was more than that of unrequited love, or ill-health or boredom. Her depression may have been exacerbated by menopausal symptoms. At that time (1916) Inessa was in her 43rd year. "Dear Friend," he wrote, "I wish you all the very best, and ask you again to make a trip somewhere, if only for a time, if only with lectures or anything else, so as to have a change, to throw yourself into some absorbing occupation."

That same day or evening, he must have received a telephone call from her, because the next day he wrote again:

> I know how terribly bad you feel, and I am eagerly anxious to help you in any way I can. What about your trying to live at some place where there are friends and where you could have talks on Party affairs? Believe me, absorbing work is most important and soothing for health and mind!

And the following day he continued his concern. "I would dearly love to say a lot of kind words to you to make things easier for you until you get your stride with work that will engross you completely. All the very best, yours, Lenin."

Were these the words of a lover? To a woman in love, they would have been empty and disappointing. For Lenin's part, had he once led her on and then abandoned her emotionally? Or had she misinterpreted his ingenuous manner towards her?* After more than seventy years, the Inessa legend still survives. A Leningrad (Petersburg) record shop displayed an album entitled *Romantic Ballads—Inessa Armand*.

Nadya's room in the Kremlin, which served as a study, remains today as it was during her lifetime. On a small chest of drawers are three photographs of Lenin, a round photograph of Nadya and her mother, *and a small photograph of Inessa.*

---

* At the time the letters to Inessa were first published, there were persons still living who would have known the facts. If the letters were of a questionable nature, it would have been an easy matter to suppress them, or at least delete what the State Publishing House considered to be controversial passages.

14. End of an Era—
the Death of Two Mothers

"In March (1915) my mother died." Nadya has left a poignant account of her mother's last days, one familiar to any woman who has watched over the waning life of a beloved parent.

Yelizaveta Vasilyevna had once been a stylish, slender woman with delicate features and the compact look of one who had found her place in the shifting environment to which life had assigned her. Fashion-conscious, she adopted the Gibson Girl image of the early 1900's: straw sailor hat, leg-o-mutton sleeves, long full skirt below a puffy blouse and narrow waist. Unlike her "bulochkin" daughter, she displayed a grace of movement that only the small and agile can achieve. But slowly, chronic health problems reduced her to a withered caricature of her former self. Racked by a persistent cough, subject to the many ills that afflict those with a weak chest, she slid down the incline of old age.

Maria Alexandrovna received a postcard, sent from Poronin in June 1914, in which Nadya described the weather: "It is pouring rain from morning to night here . . . Mother is poorly all the time, her heart troubles her. This year she has frequently suffered from palpitation, and because of her illness and the rain, she is in a bad mood." In a November letter of that year, Lenin wrote his sister Anna: "Y.V. has aged badly." The following February he informed his sister Maria that Yelizaveta was ill with influenza.

Y.V.'s demise left a void in the family circle, the size of which can be measured even in the following brief and unpretentious description of a mother's life and death:

> The last winter was a very trying one for her. All her strength gave out. She was yearning to go to Russia, but we had no one there to care for her . . . Not long before her death mother once said to me: 'No, I won't go alone to Russia, I'll wait and go with you two.' At another time she began speaking about religion. She considered herself religious, but had not been to church for years, never observed religious feasts, never prayed, and in general religion did not play any part whatever in her life, but she never liked to discuss the subject. And now she suddenly said: "I was religious in my youth, but as I lived on and learned life, I saw it was all nonsense."

Yelizaveta was fond of Berne forest, and one day Nadya took her for a short walk. "We sat on a bench for about half an hour, but afterward she could hardly get home. Next day, she was already in her death agony."

Acceding to her mother's request, Nadya arranged for cremation. Instead of the traditional Russian funeral with its overt display of emotion, daughter and son-in-law waited quietly in the Berne crematorium. "After about two

Nadya, 1915–16, soon after her mother's death

Yelizaveta as a young woman

hours, an attendant brought us a tin box, with the ashes still warm, and showed us where they were to be buried."

It sometimes happens that a single incident, recollected in after years, may contain the essence of a life and its relationships. "Mother and Volodya often argued, but she was always solicitous about him, and Vladimir, too, was attentive to her." Yelizaveta was an inveterate smoker, and once during a period of low spirits, she found herself without cigarettes. It was a holiday and all the shops were closed. "Don't worry," said Volodya, "I'll find you some." He went searching in the cafés, found cigarettes and brought them to her.

In summarizing her mother's life, Nadya called her a "close comrade," a helper in revolutionary activities who hid illegal materials during police raids or sewed them into shirts and waistcoats of departing comrades; one who managed the household, visited comrades in prison; listened, advised, sometimes even criticized; one who complained but nevertheless contributed the stability of her presence during trying times. "The comrades loved her."

Nadya's comment, that during the war "we lived mainly on Mother's inheritance," is refuted by a statement she wrote at the time (December 1915) to V.'s sister Maria in Moscow: "We shall soon be coming to the end of our former means of subsistence, and the question of earning money will become a serious one." Apparently Lenin was reluctant to use the inheritance. Money from his article on Karl Marx, written for Granat Publishers in St. Petersburg to be included in their encyclopedia, had been given personally to his sister Maria, but it was hardly enough to sustain him for more than a limited time. As the war dragged on, prospects for a normal structured life faded. "I have to think about a literary income," Nadya added. "I don't want that side of our affairs to be Volodya's worry alone. He works a lot as it is. The question of an income troubles him greatly."

Now and then he was invited to lecture before Socialist groups in various Swiss cities for a small stipend. At other times he actively sought opportunities to speak. "Dear Comrade Olga (Ravich)—Can you arrange for me to speak at Zurich? What about the fee? Would it also cover traveling expenses and room and board? I am extremely short of money just now."

Émigrés had difficulty finding any kind of employment. So desperate was the Berne group for money, that Shklovsky organized a small chemical laboratory in which comrade K- and Zinoviev worked. "Tubes and bulbs now appeared in everyone's room," said Nadya. "I have been promised a pupil, but it is slow in materializing. I have also been promised some copying, but nothing has come of it. I shall try something else, but it is all very problematic."

Lacking the proper contact with publishers in Russia, and with only rudimentary literary skills, Nadya's chances for success in that field were minimal. In the same letter to Maria, she stated:

"I have written a pamphlet, *The Elementary School and Democracy*. Perhaps you could find a publisher? It is difficult to do anything from here. By the way, I have sent an article on Rousseau to *Svobodnoye Vospitanye* (Free Education) but have had no response, although they have begun sending me the journal." In a postscript, she inquired as to the whereabouts of Lydia Knippovich and Zinaida.

Following her mother's death, Nadya suffered a relapse of her ailment and was ordered to the mountains by her doctor. Lenin found an inexpensive hotel in the non-tourist area of Sörenberg, and "we lived there the entire summer." Whether by invitation or on her own initiative, Inessa followed them to Sörenberg. There is no clue concerning the whereabouts of her children.

After rising early, mornings were spent in the garden where Nadya and Volodya "worked," while inside, Inessa played Beethoven on the hotel piano. "It was particularly good to work to the sound of music that reached us," Nadya remembered. In Switzerland, it was customary to serve dinner at noon, and afterward the three went hiking—gathering alpine roses, berries and white mushrooms. "We argued about the many mushroom varieties until one would have thought it was a question involving important principles . . . Towards evening the view of the Alps was wonderful; down below, the fog was turning rosy." They went to bed "with the chickens." Nadya reported that she was recovering from her illness.

In Germany, the rift in Social Democracy was nearing a climax. In Switzerland, too—at Berne, Zurich, Geneva, Lausanne, Chaux-de-Fonds, Clarens, Montreux—small pockets of ideological dissension were entrenched. Swiss Socialist leader Robert Grimm called a preliminary meeting of left-wingers to arrange for an international gathering of the Left, and on September 5, 1915, the famous Zimmerwald Conference took place. Present were many leading figures of Social Democracy. In addition to some of those already mentioned were Karl Radek (Polish), and Fritz Platten, a slender handsome young man with the sensitive features of an artist who was secretary of the Swiss S-D Party and a leftist. Both physically and temperamentally these two were opposites. Radek's waspish personality was a combination of keen intellect and clever tongue. A small man, peering up through thick, round lenses, he could easily demolish with a sharp rejoinder anyone he considered dull-witted. Nor did his endless flow of humor soften the image; while original, it tended to intimidate rather than entertain.

As an expression of unity, the Conference was an abysmal failure, serving only as the penultimate arena for separating Compromisers/Opportunists from Bolsheviks. Axelrod, Balabanova,* Martov (Yuli), Trotsky, Madame Roland-Holst (who arrived late), and their fellow ideologues argued heatedly against Lenin's anti-war, pro-revolutionary position, and when the meeting

---

* One of her colleagues on the Italian Socialist journal Avanti was a brash young revolutionary named Benito Mussolini.

adjourned, only nine delegates among thirty-one were identifiable as true leftists: Lenin, Zinoviev, Platten and six others. Lenin returned to Sörenberg in a
state of nervous agitation. "It required several days of roaming over the mountains before Volodya was himself again."

The preceding spring had been a trying one. Their landlady, a pious old
laundress, had decided to evict them. "You'll have to find another place," she
said, "I prefer to rent only to believers." "So we moved to another room," Nadya
concluded without further comment. Letters from home were now directed to
"Madame Oulianoff, Seidenweg 4-a, à Berne."

In a letter to his mother (October 7, 1915), V. indicated that he was satisfied with their new room: "Nadya and I moved here a few days ago. We wanted
to stay longer in Sörenberg, but it was snowing there and the cold was just
impossible. We have found a nice room here with electricity and bath for thirty
francs. Nadya has put on quite a lot of weight; the palpitation has gone; let's
hope there is no recurrence of that thyroid trouble."

Autumn 1915 resembled the periods of depression which characteristically followed those of heightened activity. From Seidenweg to the library and
back and, weather permitting, walks in Berne forest "could not remove the
feeling of being cooped up in this democratic cage; somewhere beyond, a revolutionary struggle was mounting, life was astir, but it was all so far away."

With the aim of activating the moribund leftist movement in Switzerland,
Inessa undertook a pilgrimage to French Switzerland in search of Swiss leftists
Naine and Graber. But these gentlemen proved to be elusive. Naine was out
fishing when Inessa called, and Graber's small daughter announced primly:
"Father is busy today hanging out the wash." Upon hearing Inessa's report of
a fruitless pilgrimage, Nadya's response was caustic: "Fishing and hanging out
washing are not bad occupations. Volodya has often stood guard over a pot of
milk to keep it from boiling over, but when laundry and fishing-line interfere
with discussing important matters about organizing the Lefts . . . "

Inessa's subsequent trip to Paris to help organize the Lefts may have
increased her unpopularity in certain (female) quarters. Arguing skillfully for
Lenin's program, she succeeded in bringing unity to the Paris faction, some of
whose members had strayed so far as to enlist in the French army!

Unfortunately for Volodya and Nadya, their landlady at Seidenweg—a
Frau Schneider—proved to be even more troublesome than the previous one.
After a fruitless search for other lodgings, Lenin decided to spend a couple of
weeks in Zurich studying in the libraries. Nadya's even-tempered reaction to
this turmoil amazed V.'s sister Anna: "I have had a letter from Nadya," she
informed Maria, "who writes that their landlady drove them to desperation .
. . She wrote about this trip (to Zurich) and the shake-up as of something plea-
surable."

Attracted by the more liberal environment, as evidenced by the ease with which they secured lodgings, the pair decided to remain in Zurich. Although the Kammerer residence had certain drawbacks—a relic of bygone days located in what Nadya called a "smelly court"—its cosmopolitan atmosphere more than compensated, as did Frau Kammerer's cheerful and hospitable nature. Kitchen conferences took place in which the boarders, of diverse nationalities and professions (including a prostitute), shared their views. The group was openminded, non-chauvinist, with the landlady vehemently anti-war. "We could have found a better room for the same price, but Volodya would not listen to any suggestion about changing quarters."

The émigré community was large and varied; besides Russians, it included laborers from eastern Europe. Because so many were gainfully employed in the trades and factories, their mood of optimism set the tone for individual as well as group relationships. Some of this buoyant atmosphere may have emanated from Fritz Platten (the Swiss S-D Headquarters were in Zurich), whom Nadya described as "a simple, ardent fellow, the son of a worker, who had much influence among the people."

Repeated attempts to unify International Socialists had failed, and now even the "lefts" could not reach consensus. In May/June 1916, a final meeting of the Zimmerwald group took place in southern Berne Canton. As delegates trooped into the lobby of Hotel Kienthal, an oversized chalet rising amid the snow-capped Alps, few of them believed that prevailing differences could be resolved.

The two-year war was stalemated in the muddy trenches of France, while on the eastern front a motley Russian army fought on horseback against the guns of Krupp. In the trenches, Russian boys waited for shipments of ammunition for their frail rifles, and in some sectors there was ammunition but no rifles. Wading through mud and snow in bast (wood-fiber) shoes, they went hungry when Russia's already decrepit transportation system broke down.

By this time, Germany would have welcomed a negotiated peace with the Russians, leaving her free to concentrate forces on the Somme front. The Allies, on the other hand, were urging the Tsar to mount an offensive on a front that was already near collapse under Austro-German pressure. Even some of Russia's bourgeoisie admitted that the situation was hopeless. And at Kienthal, the "leaders" of militant Socialism were debating the fine points of its role in the present world crisis!

One more detour on the road to "Liberty, Equality and Fraternity" could be attributed to national chauvinism. To Lenin, this "hiding behind patriotism" (his own words) was an excuse for inaction, an alibi for postponing that which required not only hard decisions, but a certain recklessness of action—a willingness to gamble on the will of the proletariat to assert itself. "This war could be stopped," he said, "if we actively promoted the general strike, sabotage, insurrection." Nor was he referring only to Russia. The firms of Krupp,

Skoda and other munitions factories were obvious targets; likewise railways, bridges, communications systems. Whole armies could be persuaded to lay down their arms, fleets to mutiny, factory workers to cease producing secondary war material. The only missing ingredient was leadership.

As anticipated, the Kienthal meeting adjourned in confusion. Although Zinoviev felt that a degree of progress had been achieved, Nadya, after listening to her husband's account, wrote to Comrade S-: "There seems to have been too much rhetoric and no inner unity, the kind of unity that would be a guarantee of the solidarity of the thing. It seems that the masses are not yet 'pushing', except, perhaps, in Germany." The German masses were being pushed by Rosa Luxemburg, Karl Liebknecht and Franz Mehring, aggressive leaders who were convinced that all was not lost to the chauvinists.

But in the opinion of the Zimmerwald Left, International Socialism as a whole—including both the Zimmerwald center and right—was caving in at the historically appointed moment for seizing the initiative.

At the end of 1914, the Yelizarovs, Mark and Anna, moved from Grechesky Prospekt (in St. Petersburg) to an apartment on Shirokaya Street, Petersburg Side (Peterburgskaya storona). Mark was currently employed by the Po Volga Steamship Company with offices at No. 45 Nevsky Prospekt, and the change of residence indicated that, after a lifetime of nomadic living, they expected to remain in the Capital. Maria and her mother were still living together in Moscow.

The following summer, Maria Alexandrovna came to Petersburg for a visit, and her declining health indicated to the Yelizarovs that she should remain with them. Several items of her personal furniture and household belongings were shipped from Moscow: the family piano, with its brass candelabra on which the girls had practiced their "pieces" and M.A. herself had often played; an ornate, plush-upholstered armchair; the family cutlery and chinaware; a bedspread, and some pillow covers embroidered by Maria. All contributed to the atmosphere of home.

Although the apartment was cozy, it was oddly shaped. Located at the far end of a building that fronted two streets intersecting at an acute angle, it resembled a ship in whose prow was the living/dining-room. With windows overlooking both thoroughfares, the occupants had an interesting view of life outside. In the corridor beyond the apartment, a wrought-iron cage-lift provided a convenient alternative to several flights of stairs. When Mark and Anna first moved in, there were protests from the other tenants about the presence of revolutionaries in their midst. As a result, the family members kept to themselves.

The Shirokaya Street apartment was a supporting player in the Revolution drama.

Nadya's final (extant) letter to her mother-in-law was dated October 11, 1915:

> I very much want to write you a few lines and give you and Anya many kisses . . . How is Manyasha (Maria) getting on? Volodya is all the time expecting letters from her. Do you know her address? Again many kisses, Yours, Nadya.

In summer 1916, Anna and her mother went on holiday to the small village of Yuki near St. Petersburg. It was there, in July, that Maria Alexandrovna died. She was laid to rest in Volkhov Cemetery beside her daughter Olga. At the end of a grassy aisle, amid towering trees and the ornate, graven monuments of the Petersburg deceased, a family plot was established.

The event not only ended Nadya's correspondence with the family (with the exception of two brief notes to Maria), but likewise marked the near-termination of Lenin's letters to his relatives; only a few remain that are dated after his mother's death. But there were other letters.

Apparently the subject of Maria Alexandrovna's death was too personal for Nadya to include in the Memoir about her husband, for she didn't even allude to it. It remained for Maria to describe how it was: "We did not receive the first letter Vladimir Ilyich wrote when he had news of Mother's death. The next letter has not survived either, but from what I remember of it, it showed what a heavy loss it was to him, how much pain it caused him, and how tender he was to all of us, who were also distressed by our loss."

The death of Maria Alexandrovna brought to full circle a phase of life whose impending termination had been signaled a year earlier, when Nadya and Volodya stood by as the tin box, with its warm ashes, was laid away.

15. Portrait of Russian Aristocracy

Major-General Frederick Grant, son of President Ulysses S. Grant, together with his wealthy wife Ida, was in Europe for the wedding of their daughter Julia. Born in the White House on June 7, 1876, Julia was an attractive young lady with widely spaced, serene gray eyes and the self-assurance of one whose childhood and adolescence had been spent traveling the world in the quasi-jet-set company of the rich and famous. The bridegroom was Prince Michael Cantacuzène, a Russian nobleman whose Greek title—inherited from a relative—he preferred to that of Sperensky. As an officer of the Tsar's Imperial Guard, he shared with Julia a love of military display. And although Julia's grandfather, a famous general as well as a president, had been proletarian rather than gentry, she assumed the role of Princess Cantacuzène with the aplomb of one born to royalty.

In Russia the Cantacuzène properties were numerous. They included an estate in the Crimea, a villa on the Black Sea, a large and well-staffed town-house in St. Petersburg, a country retreat near the Capital, and richly furnished "cottages" at the various military encampments where the Prince was stationed.

Before long, Julia, like the foreign born Tsaritsa herself, became more Russian than the Russians. "Our Russia" and "our great Catherine" (German-born Catherine II) spilled from pen and conversation with the ease of a native. And because "Julia" was not sufficiently exotic, she changed it to "Joy."

Forsaking the middle class Protestant Church of the Grant family, she prayed before ikons, and reacted with emotion to the parades and official ceremonies during which the Almighty was invoked as protector of the Tsar and his Imperial relatives.

Not that Julia was particularly religious. Rather, it was a ceremonial rite connected with tsarism. Those who frequented the company of Nicholas II and his grand-ducal relatives observed the forms, if not always the spirit, of Russian orthodoxy. The color and pageantry of the Church were natural adjuncts to the opulence of the Winter Palace, Peterhof, and their counterparts in the countryside near Petersburg.

Perhaps as a result of her past and present life of privilege, Julia was protective of her social position. The workers and peasants of Russia—who in their enormous numbers were called "the masses"—Julia referred to as "rabble" and "scum." "They (the Bolsheviks) offered the scum a long holiday, and Trotzky (sic) seemed to harangue them with great success." In quoted conversations, she referred to herself by social rank: "You must take my advice,

Princess," said her banker. "Yes, Your Highness, I would like to go to America," one of her husband's military aides informed her.

Prior to August 1, 1914, Julia's existence had been one of garden parties and balls, of her children and their governesses; of frequent travels undertaken to assuage the restlessness and boredom of an aristocratic lifestyle. With the declaration of war, a new diversion was added; bittersweet, perhaps, but nevertheless challenging. Like others of her class, Julia threw herself into war work: rolling bandages, knitting socks for the soldiers, organizing charities, cheering warriors (the Imperial Guards) on their way to the front, sympathizing with those presently or soon to-be bereaved. Her concern, however, was reserved for those of her adopted class. "The rabble," regardless of how they lived or died, were perceived as objects of patronage. One passed them small gifts and religious tokens as they marched off to war. But as human beings, they hardly existed.

The Tsaritsa, too, rolled bandages. Swathed in the white habit of a Sister of Charity, Empress Alexandra mingled with the ladies of Petersburg society.

In spring of 1900, Julia had attended a military exercise on the parade ground of Petersburg's Field of Mars. Nineteen years later, when she had already fled from Russia to a comfortable home in Florida, her memory of that event was undimmed. She wrote:

> Heading the cavalry . . . all unconscious, disdaining praise, was Nicolas-Nicolaiovich, Grand Duke of Russia. Then passed the Emperor's escort: Cossacks in Circassian, scarlet dress; all trimmed with gold braid, and with black fur caps; mounted on pure white horses, with oriental saddles; truly a splendid sight. These were followed by four regiments in metal armor, worthy of "Lohengrin"; on horses dark-bay, black, chestnut, light-brown, according to the regimental law of each. Then the light cavalry, with hussars looking like empire portraits of Murat at his best; scarlet and gold their uniforms, with much braiding and embroidery, and white dolmans trimmed with sable, hanging from their backs. Great sable caps, with high white plumes. And then the lancers and dragoons, with slim lances capped with tiny pennons, and flying plumes of horsehair in their shining headgear. The grenadiers with their quaint helmets followed, and the light-horse-cavalry going full speed finished the line. All this made a great show . . . It was quite the most splendid sight I ever saw! And the Grand Duke left me with an admiration not unmixed with awe for his remarkable personality.

By Autumn 1914, little had changed; the parade ground mentality continued to grip St. Petersburg society. Insulated from battlefield horrors, and after a hard day rolling bandages, the ladies gathered for tea during which they exchanged the latest rumors drifting back from the front. "I loved St. Petersburg in those fine first weeks of the war," Julia remembered.

> I was very busy, for besides my afternoons in the palace bandage factory, my mornings were spent in the throes of settling our newly-bought house. Workmen were

hard to find—they were always being mobilized for war work, as were my servants. I had to resign myself to great waste of time and energy.

Prominent persons of wartime St. Petersburg are mentioned in Julia's chronicle with the familiarity of one who was their close friend. Conversations, minutia of daily life, descriptions of people and places flow from her recollections of life in Russia. However, her chatty style turned acid as she repeated the prevailing gossip of "Germans in the streets" who were said to be fueling revolution by underwriting the Bolsheviks.

Her version of the history of those days is inaccurate as well as biased. Although she described conditions at the Imperial Court with commendable candor, otherwise her account is often a compendium of rumor and falsehood. As a historical document, however, it is valuable for its revelation of upper-class contempt for anything that impinged upon privilege. Like many others of its kind, it is an unwitting indictment of an arrogant society whose members had not the slightest awareness of the cause for their impending fall.

The memoir contains an unmistakable flavor of anti-Semitism. One individual was described as "rather a Jewish type." On another occasion, Julia referred to "refugees and Jews." When applying at Smolny (Bolshevik Headquarters) for a passport to leave the country, her husband the Prince "found himself opposite a Jewess." Lenin, employing his characteristic reprimand, would have said "Shame! Shame!"

The Princess's estimate of Lenin is expressed in particularly vitriolic language: "Rasputin's[1] lurid depravity illustrated, in extreme form, every fault in the ancient system of government, and he was the first example of the mentality which triumphs in Russia today.[2] He was as much the instrument of the conspirators behind him, as the man of the present 'soviet', who is Bolshevik, is a tool of the infamous Hun, who has formed him to be destructive."

To whom was she referring—a humble member of one of the village soviets (councils)? Someone in the Kremlin? Later in the narrative she was more specific. "'Lenine' (sic) is a criminal leading the country to disaster." "He played his waiting game, talking, working, always especially among the poor."

Alluding to the Kshesinskaya Mansion, she wrote: "From this pulpit Lenine and his followers preached their poisonous doctrines."

Julia was unable to differentiate between nihilism[3] and anarchism.[4] "Lenine had been an exiled nihilist under the old régime and had lived in Switzerland.[5] "The Bolsheviks were avowed anarchists."[6]

Her obsession with the notion of a German role in the Russian Revolution once again surfaced: "Documents[7] were found in the house[8] which showed up the Leninists in their relationship to the enemy, and German gold was captured."[9]

The following statement by Julia summarizes the irreconcilable conflict between aristocracy/bourgeoisie and proletariat/peasantry: "Lenine's theories are a menace for the future of the country, *to those of our class who thought only of winning the war,* and of preserving Russia." (Emphasis added.)

In midwinter 1917-18, Prince and Princess Cantacuzène entrained at Petersburg's Finland Station for Tornio. Sewn into the lining of Julia's fur coat and other clothing were jewels and five hundred-ruble notes "of the old régime." Her fur muff concealed a valuable Faubergé bird to which she attached miraculous powers.

As the couple traveled north and crossed the Finnish frontier into Sweden, they were following the route of other aristocrats fleeing the Bolshevik threat to confiscate their wealth. The path around the Gulf of Bothnia was well-traveled. Both expropriators and the expropriated were familiar types to border guards, and to the drivers of sledges, or boatmen who transported them across the river between Tornio and Haparanda.

"We were in Sweden," Julia remembered,

> and I turned back to look my last at the homeland we were leaving. Three or four hours before, when we left the train at Tornio, the sky had been dark and threatening. Now there was a complete transformation, and it was hung with millions of stars, while on the horizon rose high into the heavens, the splendid halo of a magnificent aurora-borealis. Perhaps it was a promise for the future of our unhappy country.
>
> Mysterious as always, Russia stretched out her great plains towards the light. Then I faced around again, and I saw the gay lamps of Haparanda station, which were approaching; and I realized we were out of danger now, and free, though we were refugees in a strange kingdom.

Julia Grant Cantacuzène died in 1975, one year short of her hundredth birthday. Having lived through the Stalin years, did she say to her highly placed Washington friends: "I told you so?"

16. Abdication of Tsar Nicholas II—
the Émigrés Return to Russia April, 1917

> *My Beloved:*
> *The trains are all mixed up again. Your letter came,*
> *after 5 o'clock, but No. 647 arrived just before lunch . . .*
> *Yesterday I visited the ikon of the Holy Virgin and*
> *prayed fervently for you, my love, for our dear children,*
> *for our country, and also for Anya.* Tell her that I have*
> *seen her brooch, pinned to the ikon, and touched it with*
> *my nose when kissing the image.*
>
> (Letter of Tsar Nicholas II to his wife, from
> army headquarters at Moghilev, Feb. 26, 1917.)

A few hours later, Nicholas received a telegram from Rodzianko, President of the Imperial Duma, stating that revolution had broken out in Petrograd.** He added: "The army is demoralized, the government paralyzed, the dynasty in peril."

On the 27th Nicholas wrote to his wife:

> My Treasure—Tender thanks for your sweet letter. This will be my last one. After yesterday's news from town, I saw many frightened faces here. Fortunately, Alexeiev [General of the Army] is calm, but thinks it necessary to appoint a very energetic man, so as to compel the Ministers to work out a solution of the problem—supplies, railways, coal, etc. This is, of course, quite right. I have heard that the disorders among the troops are caused by the company of convalescents. I wonder what Paul [Grand Duke, uncle of the Tsar] is doing? He ought to keep them in hand.

At 3 o'clock on the 28th, Nicholas signed an act of abdication. A coat of varnish was placed over the signature, and delegates returned to Petrograd with the document. Afterwards, in a noncommittal telegram to his wife, he remarked that the weather was "wonderful." While the Tsar was preparing to abdicate, Mark Yelizarov also received a last letter:

> From the enclosed you will see that Nadya is planning the publication of a Pedagogical Dictionary. I am strongly in favor of this plan because, in my opinion, it fills a serious gap in Russian pedagogical literature; it will be a very useful work and will provide an income, *which for us is extremely important. . .*
>
> I am sure Nadya can do this because she has been working in pedagogy for years, has written about it and has undergone systematic training. Zurich is an exceptionally convenient centre for work of this kind. . . There is no doubt that such an undertaking would be profitable . . .
>
> I should very much like you to give this plan your best attention, take a look

---

* Madame Viroubova, confidante of the Tsaritsa. "Anya" had the measles.
** Change of name from German-sounding St. Petersburg.

around, talk to people, worry them, and answer me in detail. All the best, Yours, V. Ulyanov. P.S., If you are successful, send a telegram, "Encyclopedia contract concluded" and Nadya will speed up the work.

The letter was posted from Spiegelgasse 14, Zurich I, Switzerland, to Nevsky Prospekt 45, Petrograd, Russia, on or about February 19, 1917.

Revolution erupted with a suddenness that startled both Europe and Russia. The war had been going badly for the Russians, but at the beginning of 1917, no one could have foreseen that within two months the 300-year-old Romanov dynasty would fall to the ground like a collapsed parachute—softly, soundlessly.

Although the Tsar was blamed for his own downfall, many external factors were involved. Nicholas, like Russia itself, was suffering from a psychological malaise too complex for known remedies. Against the advice of his ministers and generals, he assumed command of the army at a critical time, evidence not only of flawed judgment, but of an inability to recognize that Russia had already lost the war.

It was not true, as some believed, that Russians were poor warriors; under Peter the Great, they reduced Imperial Sweden to a nonentity. Ethnic groups such as Tatars and Cossacks were renowned for their military prowess. But isolated battles of the 18th Century were a far cry from a continuous front extending the length of eastern Europe. Under conditions prevailing in 1917, Genghis Khan himself would have lost the day against Germany's enormous war machine. Inadequate transportation, lack of supplies, inept military leadership, obsolete weaponry, and 19th Century military strategy and tactics were pitted against the enemy. To these liabilities was added the common soldier's disillusion with the war's objectives.

The overthrow of any regime leaves the remnants of government in disarray. This is particularly true when the current system has been in place for hundreds of years. Institutions, like habits of mind, are slow to adjust to sudden change, and an orderly transfer of power may be subverted by a military *coup*. Fortunately for Russia's interim government, the tsarist generals were kept busy on a thousand-mile front, thus removing, at least temporarily, a threat from the political right.

But while the bourgeois ministers scrambled for answers to complex questions, they were trapped in an unpopular war and confronted with incipient revolution from the political "left." Moreover, the French and British ambassadors were clamoring for action on the Eastern front. In order to satisfy these demands, an army in retreat was now expected to launch an offensive.

Nor was there unanimity within the ministerial ranks. Resignations and new appointments followed each other in rapid succession. A government had been formed under Prince Georgii Lvov, but in frustration he soon resigned.

It was a replay of 1905 when, in the midst of revolution, the Tsar wrote his mother: "The ministers, instead of acting with quick decision, only assemble in council like a lot of frightened hens and cackle about providing united ministerial action."

Although the Russian people now believed that a genuine revolution had occurred, they were misled. Behind the scenes, a group of aristocrats and businessmen were at work fashioning a constitutional monarchy. The Tsar's brother, offered the position, declined. "Not unless the people want me," he said with extraordinary perspicacity.

The February Bourgeois Revolution had gotten off to a shaky start, and with the passage of time, the efficacy of its Provisional Government came into question. Rising to the top of the ministerial heap was a young Social Revolutionary named Alexander Kerensky whose unattractive personality was combined with a self-assurance disproportionate to his leadership ability (Lenin called him a "braggart"). Kerensky became a pawn in the hands of the bourgeoisie, who used him for their own purposes. Designated a genuine proletarian by his sponsors, he was in reality a mere figurehead of authority.

In order to retain his position, Kerensky was forced to promote the war. Regardless of his personal ideology—and no *a priori* statement of it existed—his background as a member of the Social Revolutionary Party presupposed a commitment to violence against tsarism and tsarist policies. But S-R views on the structure of a future state were ill-defined. Kerensky now found himself obliged to cooperate with the bourgeois class enemy and support a system he was presumed to oppose.

The bourgeoisie were pro-war. Under the guise of "Defense of the Fatherland," they were busily engaged in protecting their own interests. A multinational business community, including "cartelism," was the bourgeois capitalist version of internationalism.

With Western money invested in Russian enterprises, and with Russian businessmen heavily in debt to Western banks, political and military loyalties rested on mutual support of the *status quo* and maintenance of a united front against Germany and her allies. Nicholas himself, in order to finance the war, had borrowed large sums from French banks. Successful prosecution of the war insured the bourgeoisie their survival against the onslaught of the revolutionary "scum"* that was threatening to unseat them. That same "scum" was also fighting a war in which it had no vested interest.

Meanwhile, the soldiers were, to quote Lenin, "voting with their feet." Out of the trenches and off the battlefields, back to their cities and towns and villages and farms they went. In order to stabilize the faltering army, Kerensky

---

* See also letters by Nicholas to his mother, the Dowager Empress, in which the words "scum" and "riff-raff" recur.

appointed political commissars who were sent to the front to oversee officers and men, and to agitate for continuing the war.

While debates were raging over questions of the war, and of the time and place for convening a constituent (representative) assembly, Kerensky moved into the Winter Palace, where he adopted the life style of its former tenant. The tsarist ministers must have observed this sudden transformation of a proletarian rebel with amazement. In the audience chamber where formerly they had bowed their way into the Tsar's presence, they were now waiting, hat in hand, to confer with a plebeian in peasant's tunic and leather boots. The new president, elevated from his position as Minister of War, was sleeping in the Tsar's bed and dining off the Imperial tableware. Even more disconcerting, in a bearded society, was his clean-shaven face.

Generations of Socialist theoreticians had ruined their eyesight poring over Marx's spidery handwriting and convoluted sentences. But despite differing opinions concerning interpretation of Marxist theories, most agreed that he had stated unequivocally that Russia was unripe for Socialism; that after ridding itself of feudalism, a backward country like Russia must first pass through a bourgeois phase and the establishment of capitalist democracy (to amass financial reserves). In the present case, however, this metamorphosis did not depend upon economics; capitalism in Russia was already established. At issue was the political structure and, correlatively, which social class controlled the wealth, including land ownership.

Requisite conditions for Socialism would be established once feudalism was discarded and the socio-political structure stabilized on a bourgeois foundation. And revolution? Whether or not it materialized, stated the Marxists, depended largely upon the crisis factor: war, or a similar upheaval such as widespread famine, etc.

According to this formula, Russia was presently conforming to the historical process: from tsarist feudalism, to bourgeois capitalist democracy, to (sometime in the distant future) Socialism. If certain individuals were impatient, feeling that Socialism was long overdue and that the tsar-ridden populace deserved better than innumerable decades of capitalist democracy, their voices were often lost in the din of propaganda favoring a system modeled on that of Western countries. Centrist reformers likewise accepted the idea of a bourgeois state, albeit as a way-station on the road to Socialism. Bolsheviks, on the other hand, feared that the way-station might prove to be the final destination. Lenin's quarrel with fellow Marxists stemmed from his growing belief that Russia could bypass the bourgeois-capitalist stage and *start* on the road to Socialism. He did not subscribe to the idea of instantaneous transition.

In Zurich, the day began as usual. After an early breakfast, Volodya prepared to leave for the library. Nadya had just finished washing the dishes. Suddenly the door burst open. "Haven't you heard the news?" Bronsky cried excitedly. "There's a revolution in Russia!" After describing what he knew, Bronsky left, and Nadya and Volodya went to the shore where the latest newspapers were displayed on billboards. "I do not remember how the rest of the day and evening passed," she related, "but from the moment news of the February Revolution came, Volodya burned with eagerness to go to Russia."

A record of his attempts to find a way around the diplomatic barriers is contained in a series of telegrams and letters. To Kollontai in Sweden he wrote: "We fear we will not be allowed to leave this cursed Switzerland for a long time ... The British will never allow us to travel that way (via Britain)."

Initially, he was adamant against a negotiated passage through Germany: "Berlin variant is unacceptable to me," he wired Social Democrat J.S. Hanecki. "Either the Swiss Government obtains a carriage as far as Copenhagen, or the Russian (Provisional) Government reaches agreement on the exchange of all émigrés for interned Germans." A second telegram to Hanecki stated: "Your plan unacceptable. Britain will never let us through, more likely intern me. Milyukov (head of the Provisional Government's Foreign Department) will swindle us. The only hope—send someone to Petrograd and secure through the Petrograd Soviet of Workers' Deputies [bypassing the Provisional Government] exchange of interned Germans. Cable."

Night after night, while awaiting a solution, Volodya and Nadya lay awake discussing alternatives. "We made all sorts of incredible plans. We could travel by airplane. We could pass ourselves off as Swedes. But since we didn't know the language, I said to Volodya, 'you will have a nightmare and cry Scoundrels! and give the whole thing away.' Such things could be thought of only in the delirium of the night."

Lenin finally concluded that his only way out of Switzerland was to be smuggled through Germany.

Earlier, there had been rumors that Switzerland might be drawn into the war, and this may have been one cause of Swiss Socialist Robert Grimm's hostility toward the internationalists. National chauvinism divided his Party; at the Zimmerwald Conference he had been a member of the political "right."

On March 19th, all Russian political émigrés met in Zurich to consider a means for returning to Russia. Meanwhile, Grimm's ineffectual telegrams to the Russian Provisional Government remained unanswered.

It was during this gathering that Lenin uncovered an additional reason for Grimm's equivocation: Martov and Axelrod had enlisted Grimm on the side of the Mensheviks. Platten offered an interesting explanation for the latters' timidity:

> That only a small number of people undertook the journey was not due to the
> threats of the Milyukov government ... nor to the short period of time they had to
> make ready for the journey. The overwhelming majority of the émigrés were afraid

of something else; they were tormented by political doubts. The Mensheviks, more than anybody else, feared to lose their political virginity. They considered Lenin's undertaking politically inexpedient and compromising.

A German Socialist who was present described the Russians' dilemma. "One day at noon I was summoned by telephone to the Eintracht Restaurant, the place where foreign and Swiss Socialists usually met. In the first room I found a small group seated at a table; the group included Krupskaya (Nadya) and other Russian comrades. Subsequently, I was summoned to a small room of the secretariat (H.Q. of the Swiss Socialists) where I saw Lenin, Fritz Platten and others.

> It was the first time I had ever seen Lenin so excited and so furious. He was pacing up and down the room, tersely summing up the situation. He briefly informed me on the state of negotiations with the Russian Government and Grimm's talks with the German Embassy. We unanimously agreed that Grimm was deliberately hindering the return of the Bolshevik group to Russia. Lenin kept saying: "We must go at all costs, even if we go through hell."

Lenin's final telegram to Grimm was an ultimatum:

> Our Party has decided to accept without reservation the proposal that the Russian émigrés should travel through Germany, and to organize this journey at once. We already expect to have more than ten participants in the journey.
>
> We absolutely decline further responsibility for any further delays, resolutely protest against it and are going alone. We earnestly request you make arrangements immediately and, if possible, let us know the decision tomorrow.
>
> With gratitude—Lenin, Zinoviev, Ulyanova (Nadya)

When no response was forthcoming, the émigrés were now limited to the Berlin Plan (without benefit of Provisional Government approval or a deal with the Germans for exchange of an equal number of their interned nationals). However, a majority still insisted on affirmation from Petrograd. Only Lenin was willing to hazard an unauthorized trip across Germany, negotiated between Swiss Socialists and the German Government. He was fully aware of the risks involved. Not only would he be accused of collaborating with the enemy, but the possibility of physical peril threatened him and his group on the long journey through hostile territory.

Although Platten was reluctant to assume responsibility for the proposed journey, nevertheless he agreed to meet German Ambassador Romberg at Berne. "When a letter came from Berne informing us that Platten's negotiations had come to a successful conclusion," Nadya related, "Volodya said that we should go to Berne immediately. The next train left in two hours, and we had only that amount of time to liquidate our entire household, settle accounts with the landlady and return books to the library. 'You go and I'll follow tomorrow,' I suggested. 'No, he replied, we'll go together.' We needn't have hurried, though. It was Easter Sunday and the train was late departing."

Upon arriving at Berne, they went immediately to the People's House (Socialist meeting-place) where several Bolshevik émigrés had already gathered. Among them was Inessa. Eager to escape from the *ennui* of Clarens, she had made arrangements for the care of her children before hurrying to Berne.

Present was Fritz Platten, who outlined the procedure to be followed. Each passenger was required to sign the following statement:

I affirm—

1) That I have been informed of the terms of the agreement between Platten and the German Embassy.

2) That I will follow the instructions of Platten, our agreed leader for the journey.

3) That I have been informed of the note published in *Petit Parisian*, according to which the Russian Provisional Government threatens to bring the Russian émigrés returning through Germany to trial for high treason.

4) That I am taking all political responsibility for my journey upon myself.

5) That Platten guarantees my journey only as far as Stockholm.

Lenin presented his own stipulations. The carriage in which the Russians traveled should be guaranteed extraterritorial immunity; no passports were to be inspected; there should be no contacts between Russians and Germans. Platten's mission was to act as liaison with the German authorities en route. His presence would also assure that all portions of the arrangement were adhered to. These conditions were accepted, and plans for the journey went forward.

Lenin immediately sent a message to the Zurich Bolsheviks:

Dear Friends, Enclosed is a copy of our committee's decision . . . I consider the Mensheviks who have wrecked our common enterprise *scoundrels* who are afraid of "Public opinion." I am going (and Zinoviev) *in any case*. Find out who is going and how much money they have. We already have a fund of over 1,000 francs for the journey. . . P.S. I enclose the 100 francs which you asked Zinoviev to lend you.

Platten included an interesting footnote to his own account: "The émigrés later decided that in the event of arrest upon arrival in Russia and trial for high treason, the defense would have to be collective and not individual. The aim of that was to attach great political importance to the trial."

In early morning of March 27, 1917, thirty-three persons gathered in Zurich. These included Lenin and Nadya, Inessa Armand, Karl Radek, Olga Ravich (Karpinsky remained behind in Geneva), Mikha the "wild Caucasian," an un-named mother and her four-year-old son Robert, Safarov and his wife Valentina. Some had come from as far away as Lausanne, Geneva and Chaux-de-Fonds.

At the depot, after receiving special passports, checking trunks and collecting a few edibles, the pilgrims began stowing themselves in various compartments of the coach. Packages of cheese, sausage, bread and tea jostled hand luggage for space on the seats and overhead racks. At precisely 3:10 p.m. the train pulled out of Zurich station. During the two-and-a-half hour journey to Thengen on the Swiss border, quiet prevailed among the passengers; it was too early to rejoice over their impending escape from Switzerland.

At the German frontier station of Gottmadingen, they piled into the "Russian" coach that was waiting to convey them across Germany; and once settled, they began to unwind. Occasional snatches of song burst from the open doors of compartments; excited conversation and laughter mingled with the grinding click of wheels and an occasional hoot from the train's whistle. The food they had carried aboard was superfluous; meals were served from the restaurant car which Nadya considered "exceptionally big, to which our emigrant fraternity were not much accustomed."

In the gathering dusk of that first day, Nadya sat quietly beside the window of a compartment she shared with her husband, observing with interest the prosperous-looking fields and orchards of rural Germany. She was struck by the absence of adult men in the fields, on station platforms and city streets. "One observed only women and teenage young people," she said.

The train halted at Stuttgart where a bizarre episode occurred: "I was called out of the carriage," Platten related, "and was informed by the escorting officer that a Mr. Janson wanted to talk to me. Our meeting was extraordinarily unpleasant."

Janson, a representative from the German Trade Unions, wanted to speak to Lenin. This proposition was greeted with a chorus of derision inside the coach. "We'll throw him out if he dares to enter," the group shouted. For the past three years Lenin, in a series of blistering articles, had been attacking the Union leaders for their support of the war. Poor Fritz returned to Janson with a toned-down refusal, meanwhile attempting to cover his own embarrassment.

The following leg of the journey was uneventful. The cities of Frankfort, Gottingen and Hanover provided diversion from an otherwise bland landscape of forests and pastures.

As the train approached Berlin, it halted briefly at a suburban station where a group of Germans entered the coach and took possession of an empty compartment at one end of the corridor. The men were Social Democrats who had come aboard to quiz Lenin. Platten immediately confronted them, protesting that the coach was out of bounds for German nationals. "None of us spoke to them," Nadya reported, "except little Robert who ran into their compartment and queried in French 'What is a conductor for?'"

Since no further mention of the German intruders appeared in any of the accounts, one presumes that they got off at Berlin.

According to Platten—who had no reason to lie—Lenin spent the entire trip through Germany sequestered behind the closed door of his compartment. The hubbub which attended his departure from Switzerland had left him no time to develop a strategy for the immediate future. Suddenly the moment for which he had waited his entire adult life was at hand, and the knowledge must have stunned him. "I shall probably not live to see the next rise of the (revolutionary) tide," he had confided to his sister Anna one day during the years of reaction.

He now had privacy and leisure to compose his thoughts and assemble them into concrete form. With pen in hand, he developed a rough draft of the famous "April Theses," whose seven-point program was a *précis* distilled from many years of theoretical inquiry and florid verbiage. Concise and specific, it left no room for compromise or equivocal interpretation.

1) No concessions to "revolutionary defensism."

2) The Provisional Government should renounce conquests.

3) Not a parliamentary republic, but a republic of Soviets of Workers, Agricultural Laborers, Peasants, and Soldiers Deputies.

4) Specifics of propaganda, agitation and organization in the period of transition.

5) Nationalization (confiscation of all landed estates). Each large-scale estate to be turned into a "model farm."

6) A single bank under the control of the Soviets of Workers' Deputies.

6-bis) Not introduction of Socialism at once, but the immediate, systematic and gradual transition of the Soviets of Workers' Deputies to control over social production and distribution of products.

7) Congress: Change of program and name. A new International. Creation of a revolutionary international ... (end of ms.).

With the airing of this document, Lenin would be staking his own political future and that of the Bolshevik Party. From Berlin, the train took them to Sassnitz on the Baltic coast where they boarded a steamer for Sweden.

The question now arises: what motivated the German government to allow passage to the Russians? Did it truly believe that a handful of Bolsheviks were capable of overthrowing Russia's Provisional Government and removing that country from the war? Was Lenin's reputation such that he might be expected to succeed where early peace negotiations had failed?

Hindsight provided an affirmative answer. But at the time, Germany's attitude may have been: "So what? Let them pass through Germany." Another answer may lie in the nature of bureaucracy. Ambassador Romberg was merely a cog in the wheel, but his acquiescence contributed to a successful outcome for the Bolsheviks. Was his telegram to the Government in Berlin phrased in routine language? An intriguing if unlikely possibility exists that he was bribed.

A more plausible explanation is to be found in the activities of one Dr. Alexander Helphand, a wealthy German businessman of Russian extraction with close ties to the Imperial German Government. An adventurer who dabbled in international politics, Helphand invested his money and political influence on behalf of the Bolsheviks at a time when their position at home and abroad, although presently precarious, was nevertheless promising as a vehicle for removing Russia from the war.

A flurry of communications passed between Helphand and the German Government's Foreign Office at the time Lenin expressed his determination to return to Russia after the February Revolution. Helphand's motive—whether assistance to the Bolsheviks or to the German Government—has been a subject for intense historical scrutiny, but the conclusions are indecisive. It is certain, however, that he played a part in the decision to allow Lenin and his party to travel through Germany.

At that time, the aims of both Lenin and the German Government coincided: to end hostilities on the eastern front. The underlying motives, however, diverged. "I would accept the Devil's help if it would further the Revolution."

At Trelleborg, the Russians were met by Swedish Socialist Otto Grimlund who described his encounter:

> An excited Russian had told me that a group of Russian socialists were coming by boat from Sassnitz . . . He asked me to accompany him to Trelleborg to meet them and help them. "Who is coming?" I asked. 'Among them Lenin,' he said, and then whispered in my ear, 'but mum's the word.' . . . The travelers disembarked and passed uneventfully through customs, after which they set out for Mälmo where they were given hot food for the first time in four days [The restaurant car was detached at Berlin.] That same evening, we went to Stockholm. After a day there, they set off again for Haparanda and Finland to Petersburg.

Another Swedish socialist, Hugo Sillen, described events in Stockholm:

> Lenin stopped at the Regina Hotel . . . where I found him talking to some of our Swedish S-D representatives. We greeted him very cordially. He showed a keen interest in our work . . . We wanted him to stay longer, but he was anxious to return to Russia. "Every day is valuable," he said.
>
> At 7 p.m. (actually 6:37 p.m. on April 13-n.s.-1917) we were seeing Lenin off at the terminal. About 100 people had already gathered there, many of them with bouquets of flowers . . . Lenin was the center of attention. He had intelligent, sparkling eyes and made rapid, expressive gestures Then we heard the International, and little red flags appeared from the carriage windows. As soon as the train started moving, our Swedish comrades set up a wild cheering . . . which was enthusiastically echoed by the departing Russians.

Nadya's account was sparing of details. "On March 31 (o.s.) we arrived in Sweden. At Stockholm we were met by Swedish Social Democratic deputies. A red flag was hung in the waiting room and a meeting was held. I remember little of Stockholm; all our thoughts were in Russia."

Platten's version is equally sparse:

> We were given a grand reception at the Regina Hotel in Stockholm. Our journey and the terms on which it took place were immediately written up . . . Information

Emigres, Sweden 1917, enroute back to Russia

was printed on a mimeograph and sent to newspapers throughout the world . . . Despite the fact that these appeared with a bizarre assortment of misprints and interpretations, they were greatly superior to the Menshevik efforts.

(A month later, 200 Mensheviks followed the same route through Germany to Russia, necessitating a press release to explain the circumstances of their journey.)

The usual means of travel between Stockholm and Finland was by steamer to Åbo (Turku). Why, then, did the émigrés choose the lengthy train journey to northern Sweden where it joins Finland? One explanation may have been the weather. More likely, however, is that Milyukov's police were waiting at Åbo and Helsinki to nab the émigrés. This chapter of negotiations with the Provisional Government is riddled with contradictions. For whatever reason, Lenin's group left Stockholm for the circuitous route around the Gulf of Bothnia.

Despite the calendar, it was still winter in the north. After leaving the train at Haparanda, last stop on the Swedish side, they were taken by sledge—downhill and across a frozen river. Tornio, on the Finnish side, although a small frontier town, contained a railway depot of considerable importance; from there, the mainline ran south to Helsinki.

Traffic-controller Kaarlo Brusila was on duty at Tornio when the émigrés arrived. "Word had spread in the town," he related,

> and many townspeople and soldiers were gathered on the platform to meet the famous revolutionary. The express train was ready to depart. Lenin approached with quick, vigorous strides, accompanied by several men. One distinguished-looking gentleman was constantly by his side. Then Lenin stopped in the middle of the platform and greeted the assemblage. A short speech followed, in which he said: "The Revolution is accomplished, but only the Bourgeois Revolution. This is insufficient. The proletariat must take power into its own hands."
>
> He spoke in Russian. The soldiers and citizens, having command of the language, hung on his every word. Then the train was ready to leave. Lenin climbed on the step but did not go inside. 'Hyvasti soomilaiset!' (Goodby, Finns!) he said fluently in Finnish.
>
> For days afterward, the speech was hotly debated by townspeople and soldiers—a divided "party" of Mensheviks and Bolsheviks. Meanwhile, the train was on its way to Petrograd.

Contrary to his original plan, Platten was still with the group. Apparently he had undergone a change of attitude toward the Bolsheviks. Laying aside his earlier reservations, he decided to accompany them into Russia. "However," he related, "I was forced to take leave of my comrades at the Finnish frontier town of Tornio, since the Milyukov Government had refused to give me permission to enter. Most important of all, however, was that our mission had been accomplished."

Although Karl Radek, a native of Austrian Poland, had come disguised as a Russian, he too was denied entry.

After so many years spent in bourgeois, Calvinist Switzerland, it is not surprising that Nadya's version of that particular day was sentimental:

From Sweden we crossed to Finland in small Finnish sledges. Everything was already familiar and dear to us—the wretched third-class cars, the Russian soldiers. It was terribly good . . . Our people were huddled against the windows. The station platforms we passed were crowded with soldiers.

From Nadya's account, we learn that third class contained benches rather than seats. She and her husband went into an empty car where they were followed by a "defensist" lieutenant. An argument ensued, with both Lenin and the lieutenant "extremely pale."

While the train beaded south toward Uleåborg, a message was delivered in Petrograd:

Telegram No. 148
Form No.71
Received April 2, 1917 at 20 hrs 8 m.
Ulyanova
Shirokaya, 48/9 Apt.24.
From Tornio, 2. 18 hrs 12 m.
Arriving Monday 11 p.m. inform Pravda
Ulyanov.

The right-of-way was a narrow swathe carved through dense pine forests, with here and there a frozen lake glimmering through the trees. Few aboard the train slept that first night out of Tornio; and with the coming of dawn, the weary Russians watched for signs of life along the tracks. After leaving the railroad yards at Uleåborg, only an occasional clearing sprinkled with tiny, boxlike dwellings broke the monotony. From their chimneys, wisping smoke mingled with the frost-laden air, a sign that humans did indeed inhabit this Godforsaken wilderness.

As the train approached Tammerfors, Lenin was reminded of the time eleven years earlier when a group of young Bolsheviks had gathered in a paneled room of the People's House to prepare for joining the first Russian Revolution. And in a few days, he who was now affectionately referred to by his comrades as "the old man," would observe his 47th birthday. Nadya, looking past the unsightly sheds and heaps of dirt along the track to the city beyond, recollected the enthusiasm of those meetings on the street Hallituskatu. "One evening we attended a Finnish mass meeting which was held by torchlight, and its triumphant character entirely corresponded with the mood of our delegates." Nadya too was feeling her age.

At the small rural station of Riihimaki north of Helsinki, a subdued group of émigrés changed trains for Petrograd. Gone was the elation of recent days, the reckless spirit of adventure with which they had first embarked on the journey. In approximately seven hours they would face the moment of truth, and for some it must have been a chilling thought.

The charge of sedition, which had sent many to prison or exile, was a far cry from that of high treason. Nor could they expect the relative tolerance with which tsarism had treated them.

Lenin fully expected to be arrested and tried. Whether or not execution followed, would depend upon the temper of his judges. Whereas in Europe his enemies were ideological, in Russia he was considered a criminal. But as the locomotive trundled its load through forests and past granite outcroppings with what seemed exasperating slowness, he was impatient to end this interminable journey and confront whatever awaited him at Finlandski Station.

After passing through the towns of Lahti and Viborg [not the Viborg District of Petrograd], Nadya began watching for places she remembered from earlier journeys: Raivola, Jalkala, Terijoki, Kuokkala, each with its ornate wooden depot and weathered platform. The next station was Beloostrov where a surprise awaited. Standing on the platform were Lenin's sister Maria, Shlapnikov, Ludmila Stahl, "and other comrades and workers."

"Stahl urged me to say a few words of greeting," Nadya said, "but all words left me, I could say nothing. Volodya asked the comrades who sat with us if we would be arrested on our arrival, but they only smiled."

Numb with fatigue, Nadya barely noticed when the train slowed for Udelnaya on the outskirts of the Capital. With a single cryptic phrase—"Soon we arrived in Petrograd"—she ended her account of a tortuous journey.

Finlandski Station was an island amid a sea of humanity. In the side streets, on the square in front sloping down to Bolshaya Neva, it moved in a restless tide, lit here and there by torches held aloft.

From a platform behind the station, trains arrived and departed. "When Volodya came out onto the platform," Nadya remembered, "a captain came up to him and, standing at attention, reported something. Volodya, a little taken aback by surprise, saluted. Then V. and all our emigrant fraternity were led past a guard of honor which was on the platform."

After this ceremonial greeting, "Lenin," according to historian N.N. Sukhanov, "walked, or rather ran, into the Tsar's waiting-room in a round hat, his face chilled, and a luxuriant bouquet in his arms." During the ensuing speech by comrade Cheidze, Menshevik President of the Petrograd Soviet, Lenin stood awkwardly rearranging his bouquet "which harmonized rather badly with his whole figure," meanwhile gazing at the ceiling with an air of boredom and preoccupation.

Outside, several armored cars were standing near the platform with motors idling. When Lenin emerged, comrades lifted him atop one of them where he stood surveying the crowd while the other émigrés were stowed in automobiles. After his short speech, the procession began to move; a resounding cheer arose from the crowd. "Long live the Socialist world revolution!" he called out. "Long live . . " But his voice was drowned in a roar of applause and cheering.

By a zigzag route, the entourage crossed Samsonievsky Bridge over Bolshaya Neva (Neva tributary), followed Dvoryansky Street to the corner of Kronvertsky Avenue and halted. Its destination was the Palace of Kshesinskaya, première ballerina of St. Petersburg. A gift from her erstwhile lover, the Tsar, it had been requisitioned by the Bolsheviks for Party headquarters (its indignant "chatelaine" was still in residence, albeit confined to a small apartment).

The entire area was ablaze with light. From Peter-Paul, giant searchlights shone with daylight intensity upon street and bridge and river. "En route," Nadya related, "we were guarded by a chain of working men and women. At Kshesinskaya, the Petrograd comrades had arranged a comradely tea. They wanted to organize speeches of welcome, but V. turned the conversation to what interested him most, the tactics that had to be pursued."

While this sober discussion was taking place, the street outside filled with thousands who had followed the procession. "Speech! Speech!" they cried. Reluctantly, Lenin agreed to address the crowd. As he stepped out onto the second-floor balcony overlooking the river and Peter-Paul, did his mind stray toward Commandant's Wharf hidden in shadows below the searchlights? Did he envisage his brother being led down the steps one night thirty years ago? It is unlikely that the idea of poetic justice occurred to him. Looking down at the upturned faces, he spoke briefly of the tasks confronting proletarians.

Afterwards, he and Nadya "went home to our people." In the apartment on Shirokaya Street, they were given the room formerly occupied by Lenin's mother. After her death, Lenin's sister Maria who continued to live with the Yelizarovs, slept in the room she had shared with her mother during the latter's final days. She now moved to a small room beside the kitchen.

Maria Alexandrovna's room contained two small iron beds facing each other from opposite walls. Before a window overlooking the street stood a dressing table with swivel mirror; and against an adjacent wall a tall wardrobe. Beside the dressing table stood M.A.'s velvet-covered chair.

On the night in question, Gora, the Yelizarov's adopted son, hung over their beds the slogan: "Workers of the World Unite!"

"I hardly spoke to Volodya that night. There were really no words to express the experience, everything was understood without words."

Early the next morning, an exhausted Lenin was roused from sleep by the arrival of a comrade who reported that a meeting of the Petrograd Soviet was already in session. In company with Zinoviev, Lenin hurried to the meeting where he reported on the recent trip through Germany. "From there he went to a conference of Bolsheviks—of the members of the All-Russian Conference of Soviets of Workers' and Soldiers' Deputies which was in session on an upper floor of Taurida Palace." Nadya's statement indicates that the Provisional Government's authority was already being challenged by the Soviets. It also reveals that Russia's political parties were contending for control of the Soviet organizations which, as originally conceived, were non-political units representing local interests.

At Taurida, Lenin dropped a bombshell: the "April Theses" to which he had added three more. "We must prepare for it now," he said. "The date for a Socialist revolution can no longer be postponed".

While he was speaking, the stunned listeners turned to each other with surprise and dismay. Every face reflected the same question: What about the Bourgeois Revolution? Representative government? Democratic capitalism? What about the phase necessary to prepare for a future Socialist state? It was evident that the mentality of delay and gradualism was too entrenched to be forsworn at a single stroke. Conversely, Lenin perceived the February Revolution as Phase One of an uncompleted process whose moment of fruition had arrived.

On the floor below, Mensheviks were holding a meeting. Aware of what was transpiring above, they sent an emissary to request that Lenin present his theses to a joint session of Bolshevik and Menshevik delegates. This was followed by a Bolshevik motion for Lenin to repeat the report before a general meeting of all Socialist parties.

Before returning home that night, Lenin went alone to Volkhov Cemetery where he stood a long time before his mother's grave.

The joint meeting took place in a large hall at Taurida. Unfortunately for Lenin, the chairman, a former Bolshevik, had turned defensist. Bitterly debating Lenin, he accused him of advocating civil war in the midst of revolutionary democracy. (Plekhanov called Lenin's program "Delirium.") Publication of the theses in *Pravda* aroused a verbal hurricane. Kamenev published an article stating that Lenin's ideas were strictly his own and represented neither the position of *Pravda* nor the Party.

During the Bolshevik debate at Taurida, Alexandra Kollontai had been Lenin's able defender. A week later however, the members calmed down, and his program was finally accepted. This was not, however, the end of contention.

The same day Lenin's Theses appeared in print, the Petrograd Soviet voted in favor of issuing a Liberty Loan (government loan from the populace for financing the war). Now in the foreground were not only the "reckless" Bolsheviks and their Socialist Revolution, but also their stand against the war. "The Bourgeois and defensist press started a furious campaign against Lenin and the Bolsheviks," Nadya stated.

It has been said that in politics, any kind of publicity is better than none. The firestorm of words against Lenin only served to popularize his Theses. It also polarized opinion to a point where mass demonstrations replaced journalistic debate, with both sides squaring off in the streets of Petrograd.

By the end of April, the Bolsheviks had finally achieved unity within their own ranks. Henceforth, their efforts were directed toward an attempt to reorganize elections to the Soviets by replacing pro-war, bourgeois-oriented delegates with their opposites. Significant, however, was the Bolshevik statement that a present attempt to overthrow the Provisional Government would be premature. Everything depended upon the Soviets. Only through them, as a united body representing "All Russia," could an alternative to the Lvov-Milyukov government hope—not only to win power, but to retain it.

> *"Those who have not lived through revolution*
> *cannot imagine its grand, solemn beauty."*—N.K.

Inevitably, the exhilaration of recent days subsided, leaving Nadya unhappy and bored. With her husband away all day and far into the night on Party business, their former domestic life and shared interests evaporated. He returned home tired and preoccupied, only to fall into bed. Mark Yelizarov, retired from his position at the steamship company, was in and out of the apartment while busying himself with Party affairs; Anna and Maria went shopping, prepared meals, and generally supervised housekeeping. For the second time in her life, Nadya felt herself an outsider in this family circle.

Yelena Stassova, one of Nadya's fellow teachers at Sunday Evening School, had been a tireless Party worker since the League of Struggle's inception. After Lenin and his wife left Russia for Switzerland, Stassova regularly corresponded with them, conveying news about the status of Party work in the Capital. Although four years younger than Nadya, she was a close friend; and after the February Revolution she maintained an intimate relationship with the family on Shirokaya Street. As one of the dedicated "maidens" of Social Democracy, she was given the post of secretary to the Bolshevik Party's Central Committee, housed in the Kshesinskaya Mansion. Subsequently, Nadya became her assistant. "I talked to the workers who came there. Still, I knew little of the local work . . . and since no special duties were assigned to me, the absence of definite work began to pall."

On the way to work, Nadya was intrigued by conversations among groups of people gathered in the streets. "I began mingling with the crowds, listening to their heated discussions about political matters and recent events. Once I walked for three hours from Shirokaya Street to Kshesinskaya Palace, so interesting were these meetings."

Opposite the apartment was a place of rendezvous for young people, domestic servants from neighboring houses, and often a soldier or two. "Their snatches of conversation drifted up through the open windows: at 1 a.m., Bolsheviks-Mensheviks; at 3 a.m., Milyukov-Bolsheviks; at five o'clock, the same ... The white nights of Petrograd are always associated in my mind with these nightly gatherings."

By the end of July, Nadya must have wondered at her earlier mood of discontent. Beginning with the first legal May Day celebrated in Russia, events developed with astonishing rapidity as if driven by some demonic force. Coincidental with May Day demonstrations "such as had never been seen before," Milyukov dispatched a secret note to the Allied Governments promising to fight the war to a victorious conclusion, and declaring his unswerving loyalty to the Allied Cause. When this note became public, violent demonstrations erupted against him, and on May 15th he resigned.

Two days later, Kerensky succeeded him as Minister of War, and at the end of June he ordered the controversial military offensive that had bedeviled the Tsar, Prince Lvov and Milyukov. By July 19th, the offensive had collapsed, with the Germans in hot pursuit of fleeing Russian armies.

On the political front, events developed with equal precipitancy. First, the Petrograd Soviet anticipated by four days the Provisional Government's vote in favor of coalition. At this point the Mensheviks joined forces with the Social Revolutionaries, thus projecting a large majority among Socialists (not necessarily a majority in coalition government) in the present interim government, and in any future representative assembly.

As usual, the Bolsheviks were treated as pariahs—principally, but not altogether, on the war issue. Although at present they were a distinct minority nationwide, nevertheless they had become a majority in Petrograd. Lenin, as well as Party leaders, understood that it would be an uphill struggle to extend that majority beyond the Capital. Regional Soviet organizations were highly resistant to political domination by a single party.

"So far, we (Bolsheviks) are in the minority," Lenin said. "The masses do not trust us yet ... The Soviets must seize power, not for the purpose of building an ordinary, bourgeois republic, nor for the purpose of introducing Socialism immediately. The latter could not be accomplished. What, then is the purpose? They must seize power in order to take the first concrete steps toward Socialism." The power to which he referred was intended to raise the living standard of the masses—an unfortunate choice of terminology suggesting that Lenin was concerned with the aggregate of humanity rather than individuals. This impression is refuted by his private conversations with colleagues and with one-to-one relations with the rank and file from near and far.

"On May Day, I was so ill I could not get up, and so I missed hearing Volodya's speech delivered on the Field of Mars. Later that week, I had to meet him at No.3 on the Old Nevsky." New Petrograd, east of the Neva, was (and is) bisected by Nevsky Prospekt, a broad thoroughfare with the Winter Palace at one end and St. Alexander Nevsky Monastery at the other. The "Old Nevsky" was that section leading from the Monastery to Nikolaievsky (later Moskovsky) Railway Station.

A forest of ancient trees surrounded the Monastery's decaying buildings, its well-preserved cathedral and immense necropolis. In early May, the budding foliage dripped moisture that emanated from a river winding through the grounds. Outside the walls lay a mildewed working-class district, relic of an earlier time when the Monastery was the center of a small community apart from the city.

On her way to Old Nevsky No.3, Nadya saw a large workers' demonstration approaching, and from the opposite direction a procession wearing bowler hats. "Near the Nevsky Gate workers predominated, but nearer Morskaya Street and the Poitseysky Bridge (New Nevsky), bowler hats were more numerous." Among the bowler hats she overheard the following: "Lenin has bribed the workers with German gold, and now all are following him", shouted a stylishly dressed girl. "Kill all these scoundrels" someone in a bowler hat roared.

"But the workers were with us," Nadya added. "'If necessary, we'll march all night!' cried a woman worker." This simple account illustrates the all-pervasive class conflict gripping the Capital.

Nadya's boredom with work at the Secretariat was but one factor in her sense of feeling adrift in revolutionary Petrograd. The real cause was loneliness; she missed her husband's company. "I wanted to see him more often . . . He usually returned home tired, and I could not bring myself to question him about affairs."

Occasionally they went walking together late at night in some quiet street near the apartment. But Nadya's desire to be at his side also stemmed from fear for his safety: "The campaign against him was growing in fury." In Peterburgskaya District, people were now muttering the same "down with this Lenin who came from Germany," she had encountered on Nevsky Prospekt. "To hear such talk from the bourgeoisie was one thing, but to hear it from the masses was quite another." Women were often the purveyors of gossip about "German gold," and Nadya feared their remarks more than those from the bowler hats. One is reminded of the French Revolution during which women outdid men in vengefulness.

So great was Nadya's concern, that she wrote an article refuting the slander. "Volodya corrected the manuscript, and it was printed in Soldiers' Pravda on May 13, 1917."

At the end of World War II, captured German documents revealed that there was indeed "German gold." Through the agency of Dr. Helphand, substantial funds had been passed to Karl Radek, the Austrian Pole who had clowned his way from Switzerland to Haparanda on the so-called "sealed train." Radek distributed the money for propaganda purposes. Did Lenin know? Undoubtedly. But that he had no personal dealings with the German Government or with Dr. Helphand is well documented. The far-flung Bolshevik Organization, on the other hand, accepted donations from various sources, including merchant-capitalists in Russia. The rumors connecting Lenin himself with German money arose from his unhindered trip through Germany. Counterrevolution fed on the myth that Lenin was a traitor to his country, a paid agent of the German Imperial Government. However, the history of Russo-German relations during and immediately after World War I when the Bolsheviks were in power, refutes the allegations that Lenin was engaged in selling his Fatherland to the enemy.

Of primary interest to all political parties was the mood of the Soviets of Workers' and Soldiers' Deputies, whose first All-Russia Congress took place on June 16th. At the back of a crowded hall on Vasilyevsky Island, a small group of Bolsheviks watched as the S.R.-Mensheviks dominated the proceedings. Finally it was Lenin's turn to speak. And while apparently no cat-calls or jeering remarks greeted his words, the applause of his Bolshevik comrades had the earmarks of a *claque* amid the studied silence of the majority. Thus the Congress of Soviets reared its hefty bulk between proletarians and the Russia of farms and villages. In the countryside, a majority supported the Social Revolutionaries who became known as the "Peasants' Party." Representing hundreds of millions, its goals did not coincide with those of the urban workers.

The lack of trust mentioned by Lenin was mutual; he in turn mistrusted the peasantry. Nevertheless, they had to be won, and it could be achieved only through their delegates to the Soviet. "All Power to the Soviets" (*Vsye Vlast Sovyetom*) became the Bolshevik slogan which Lenin—according to his adversaries—repeated *ad nauseam.*

Aware that popular impetus for revolution was growing, the Bolsheviks planned to hold a demonstration, a move that was promptly vetoed by the Soviets. "Since we recognize the power of the Soviets," Lenin conceded, "we have no choice but to abide by their decision; otherwise, we would be playing into the hands of the enemies." Besides S.R.-Mensheviks, the latter included Constitutional Democrats, the Jewish *Bund,* a number of trade union delegates, and representatives of certain ethnic groups from the provinces. Also included were rich and middle peasants, regardless of whether or not they were affiliated with a political party.

However, the Congress decided to organize its own demonstration in order to provide the "mob" with an outlet for its passions under controlled conditions. When 400,000 answered the call, it was obvious that the days of orderly demonstrations were numbered.

Meanwhile, local (city) elections were in progress, and Nadya was voted a member of the Viborg District Council. "During the many years abroad," she recalled, "I never dared to make a speech, even at small meetings." Now thrust into the foreground, and without the presence of her husband's dominant personality, she lost her shyness and learned to speak publicly on issues to which she could relate with competence: namely, education, and sundry other endeavors for which she was particularly fitted.

Lenin reading *Pravda*

One of her tasks was that of chairman of the Committee for Relief of Soldiers' Wives, a post she assumed from Nina A-. The latter had been Nadya's fellow student at the *gymnasium* (secondary/high school) and later a teacher at Sunday Evening School. "They do not trust us," Nina said. "Perhaps you will be able to do better than we did."

The plight of soldiers' wives was personified in the following incident. "My husband is at the front. We lived well together, but I do not know how it will be when he returns ... I often think at night—Will he understand that our salvation lies in following the Bolsheviks? ... But I do not know whether I shall see him again, perhaps he will be killed. Yes, I spit blood, I am going to hospital." For a long time afterward, Nadya remembered the woman's flushed cheeks and her anxiety over a possible difference with her husband.

Besides the committee work, Nadya organized an Education Council. Its purpose was to register all illiterates in the factories, and to make arrangements with factory owners to provide space on the premises for instruction in the three R's. Then she founded a Youth League called "Light and Knowledge." Although nominally apolitical, it quickly became the domain of revolutionary-minded youth who refused to admit reactionaries to their group.

"Men should learn the domestic arts," insisted these new-age young women. "Do you (addressing male members) think that a wife is her husband's slave? No! She is his comrade."

One might have expected these matters to be postponed until the revolution was a *fait accompli*, but for years to come, the mundane and supra-mundane marched in tandem. There might be a machine gun mounted on the next corner, but its presence should not impede the progress of education—or the emancipation of women!

Lenin's chronic fatigue was a matter of concern to his family. When it became evident that he needed time for rest, they persuaded him to accept the invitation of his friend Bonch-Bruyevich who owned a *dacha* near the small village of Neuvola close to Petrograd. Since Nadya was presently involved in organizational work, Maria accompanied her brother. While they were away, a machine-gun regiment stationed in Viborg District decided to stage an uprising. Two days earlier, a committee from the regiment had been scheduled to meet with Nadya for discussion of educational matters. "Of course no one came," she said. "The whole regiment had gone." On her way to Kshesinskaya Palace, she encountered them "marching in good order" on Samsonievsky Avenue. At the Palace they halted, saluted, and marched on, followed later by two other regiments. Then a workers' demonstration came to Kshesinskaya.

The Party's Central Committee order for the uprising to be turned into a peaceful demonstration came too late. "It was the task of comrade L- to deliver the order," Nadya related, "but he lay for a long time on a couch in a room of the Viborg Council, looking at the ceiling, reluctant to go to the machine-gunners to stop them."

In the meantime, Lenin had been apprised of the situation, and cutting short his respite, he hurried back to the Capital. His overriding fear had been that an unorganized and premature uprising would provoke retaliation from the Provisional Government and thus neutralize prospects for future success. While he was cautioning against this from the balcony of the Palace, a huge crowd was already converging on Taurida. In Sadovaya Street the demonstrators ran head-on into Government military units, which opened fire. Soon the street was littered with dead and wounded. This episode had serious consequences for future relations between Viborg and the Government, resembling as it did Father Gapon's ill-fated adventure in Palace Square twelve years earlier.

Lenin was blamed for the affair, and from that moment his life was in danger. On July 19th the government ordered his arrest and that of Zinoviev as "German spies." Worse, General Polovtsev, Commander of the Petrograd Military District, ordered that if caught, Lenin be shot on the spot. Henceforth, a curious sequence of events evolved that would have fateful consequences for the future Soviet State.

Lenin was now a fugitive. Moving from place to place (seven times in all), he lodged for a time with Marguerita Fofanova, a matronly woman who had a job and was absent from her apartment during the day. This arrangement was later cited by his enemies as evidence of womanizing. Subsequently he was guided to the apartment of S.A. Alliluyev, a place of refuge not yet identified by the police. Zinoviev was already in hiding there, and Kamenev in a flat nearby.

The Alliluyevs lived on the top floor of a six-story building at No.17 Rozhdestvenskaya Street. Their apartment had both front and rear exits, thus providing Lenin with an escape route to the attic in the event of a police raid.

By this time, frustration led him to consider a move that nearly proved fatal. Hounded by the authorities, living like a vagabond first here and then there, he was on the point of relinquishing all attempts to lead the Party. Having concluded that his sole remaining option was to surrender, he trusted that a public trial—whatever the outcome for himself personally—would serve as a platform for open debate with his adversaries. As a lawyer, he knew what was involved in self-defense; as a scholar and politician, he considered himself superior in dialectics to a panel of judges. He also entertained the possibility of disappearing in the night, a nameless corpse with a bullet hole in its back. Nevertheless, he was willing to gamble his life against a public trial.

The living room of the Alliluyev flat was filled with Party leaders and cigarette smoke. Looking small and weary, Lenin was temporarily silent when his wife and sister Maria entered, having been summoned by comrades who were dismayed at Lenin's decision.

"Maria objected violently," Nadya said. "Then V. spoke to me: 'Zinoviev and I have decided to give ourselves up. Go and tell Kamenev' . . . Hastily I turned to go. 'Let us say goodbye,' Vladimir Ilyich said, stopping me. 'We may not see each other again.' We embraced."

After leaving the flat, Nadya dutifully relayed the message to Kamenev. It was not until the next day that she learned the outcome. That night two military men came to Shirokaya Street. "They searched only our room, and asked if I knew where V. was. From that I concluded that he had not been arrested." Presumably, her unemotional account resulted from years of living in crisis, when survival depended upon *sang-froid*. Was it fatalism? Or did she abhor the notion of describing in detail what must have been a shattering emotional experience? One hardly sends a beloved husband to possible death with a mere *potselui e proschaitye*—kiss and farewell!

Two days later there was another raid on the apartment. Nadya's humorous description understated the seriousness of the affair. Consistent with their present "bourgeois" life style, the Yelizarovs employed a young servant girl. "She was from a remote village, unlettered, and had no idea of who Lenin was; she didn't even know Mark's name, and when questioned by the police was unable to reply." The exasperated men began searching the kitchen, whereat the girl chided them: "Look in the oven," she said, "someone may be sitting there."

Following the search, Mark, Anna and Nadya were taken to General Staff Headquarters on Palace Square. Separated from each other and guarded by soldiers, they awaited interrogation. "Suddenly some officers burst in in a rage, ready to throw themselves at us. Had Lenin been there, they would have torn him to pieces." Fortunately, the Colonel-in-Charge intervened with "These are not the people we want ," and they were dismissed.

Because of the distance to Shirokaya Street, Mark demanded an automobile. When, despite the Colonel's promise, it failed to materialize, they were forced to take a cab. "But the bridges were up, so we did not reach home until morning."

Lift-spans on the bridges were customarily raised at night to accommodate river traffic. In times of crisis, however, this practice was useful in forestalling a surprise visit from the Viborg-Peterburgskaya proletariat. While serving the Government well, it discomfited residents on their way home from a night on the town east of Neva.

One evening Nadya returned home from the District Council to find yet a third search in progress. Entrance to the building was occupied by soldiers, and the street filled with curious neighbors. Afraid to enter, she returned to Council Headquarters only to find it closed. While walking the deserted streets, she encountered Comrade S- who warned her against returning home. "Finally we came upon Marguerita Fofanova who worked in the district, and she put us up for the night. In the morning, we found that none of our people had been arrested, and that this particular search had not been as rough as the preceding one."

Meanwhile, Nadya had been apprised of her husband's whereabouts. Following her departure from the Alliluyev apartment, comrades had persuaded Lenin not to surrender. After shaving off his beard and moustache, he donned an old coat and cap belonging to his host, and disguised as a workman, he went with Zinoviev late at night to Primorsky Railway Station where they were met by N.A. Yemelyanov. Comrade Y- was employed at the arms factory in Sestroretsk, a rural district west of Petrograd. A dedicated Party member, he had agreed to hide the men at his house in the village of Razliv.

The last suburban train left at 2 a.m. and usually carried a number of inebriated celebrants returning home. Did one of them, knowing Yemelyanov by sight, take note of a certain "Finnish" workman accompanying him? In order to avoid attention, the conspirators sat on the steps of the last coach, ready if necessary to jump off while the train was moving. However, the trip was uneventful. At 4 a.m. they arrived at Razliv Station, whose primitive log depot was buried among fir trees.

During their first days at Razliv, the men lived in the loft of Yemelyanov's barn. But when rumors reached Petrograd that Lenin was working as a fitter at the arms factory, police began searching the area. Thereafter, comrade Y- moved the pair to some property he rented in the countryside around Lake Razliv. While yet another rumor was circulating that Lenin had escaped on a German submarine, he was peacefully at work writing *The State and Revolution*—his desk and chair two blocks of wood; his abode a grass-covered hut, and on cold nights a haystack. Food and newspapers were brought by various members of the Yemelyanov family: a wife and seven children.

With the onset of autumn, however, the cold, the mosquitoes, and Russian police dogs combing the neighborhood made it obvious that Lenin and Zinoviev would have to leave Lake Razliv. Likewise, the two men had recently had a close brush with the police. A Finnish comrade described what happened:

> On a rainy day, Lenin was sitting in the hut. Suddenly a Cossack entered, cursing the weather and good-for-nothing people, and asked permission to take shelter from the rain. Lenin asked him what he was doing, whereat the Cossack said that they were hunting someone named Lenin, who was ordered to be caught alive or dead. When questioned about the crime Lenin had committed, the man could not answer. He knew only that the fugitive was 'muddled' and therefore very dangerous, that he was somewhere in the neighborhood and that he, the Cossack, had come there to suffer in the rain and cold on account of this good-for-nothing.

The Party's Central Committee decided to move Lenin and Zinoviev to Helsingfors (Helsinki).

Arrangements with the political underground were sometimes delegated to Stalin. Shortly before Lenin's return from emigration, Stalin had arrived in Petrograd (after escaping from Siberian exile), where he worked in *Pravda's* editorial department. Whether then or later, he moved to a flat on Shirokaya Street where his proximity to No.48 proved useful when a "travel agent" was needed for Lenin.

Although working under the nose of the police, Stalin's low-key personality and activities had, for the time, escaped their notice.

According to Nadya, Stalin was among those present during Lenin's initial speech from the Kshesinskaya balcony. He was also present on that fateful night in the Alliluyev apartment. "Comrade Stalin," she noted diplomatically, "and others, urged Vladimir Ilyich not to appear in court."

Stalin's freedom, however, was about to terminate. Following a police crackdown on *Pravda* offices, Kamenev and other Party leaders were arrested, whereat Stalin left Shirokaya Street for the same room in Alliluyev's flat recently vacated by Lenin. While in hiding there, he became acquainted with his host's attractive 16-year-old daughter, Nadezhda. Stalin, a widower, later married her, and the frightful termination of that union inflicted a lasting psychological wound upon the man who came to believe that he was Lenin's rightful heir.

17. The Finland Station, July 1917

In an attempt to shore up its position amid an unpopular war, the Government accelerated its pursuit of anti-war radicals. Believing, or pretending to believe, that Bolshevik collusion with Germany was responsible for military reverses, it began a local attack on the Party and its leaders. The decaying offensive against Germany provided an excuse for Government takeover of Kshesinskaya Palace and subsequent physical destruction of the *Pravda* office.

On July 20, following the collapse of Prince Lvov's government as a result of military defeat, the "Salvation of Revolution" government was formed with Kerensky as prime minister, a gesture of appeasement to the "masses" that was hardly reassuring. Despite his previous record as war minister, Kerensky was being promoted as a "man of the people" while simultaneously aligned with bourgeois militarists.

After a brief political and military alliance with tsarist General Lavr Kornilov, Kerensky fled Petrograd in an automobile commandeered from the American Embassy. With the Stars and Stripes flying beside its windshield, the car bore him through the city on a precarious ride which ended in political oblivion. Until his death in 1970 at age 89, he lived in a luxurious New York City apartment, venting his frustration through embittered attacks on the architects of the Soviet State.

During the interval before his departure from Russia, he instituted an all-out campaign against Lenin.

The police chief of Helsingfors, Kustaa Rovio, was a Social Democrat with close ties to the Russian left-wing movement. At age thirty, his hair was beginning to recede, but maturity had not dampened the revolutionary fervor of his youth. Now gainfully employed and with a wife to support, his *sub rosa* activities were necessarily limited. Nevertheless, at the beginning of August 1917, he was about to risk his career—and possibly his life—in behalf of principles.

The Rovios lived on the fifth floor of an apartment building at No.1 Hågness (Finnish 'Hakaneimi') Square in a northern district of the city. Their flat, at the front of the building and adorned with a balcony more decorative than functional, overlooked a park. Beside it, a tram line passed on its way from center to suburb. Although small, the apartment was adequate for two persons. It consisted of a kitchen-dining room, and a living area which contained two small iron beds. A short partition jutting into the room divided the sleeping area from an alcove; the latter contained a Russian tile stove, a wooden divan, and a writing table and chair before a window facing the park. The table and chair later became museum pieces.

In any season, the flat was attractive for its privacy and hominess, but this was especially true in summer when the scent of foliage, enhanced by moist breezes from the nearby Gulf, drifted in through open windows.

The square itself was large, and with the exception of one particular edifice, its surroundings were mainly residential. The exception was a massive red brick structure separated from No.1 by a narrow street leading into the square. Today it is an impressive food emporium: fish, meat, fruit, flowers. But despite present disclaimer by the natives, it resembles a police barracks and jail.

Rovio, whose wife was currently visiting her relatives in the country, agreed to hide Lenin when the Party's Central Committee found it prudent to move him from his mosquito-infested retreat on Lake Razliv.

Notwithstanding the hazards involved, a group of Finnish comrades undertook the project with energy and extraordinary skill. Finland's underground was manned by persons from various social strata. Working side by side with day-laborers were jurists, members of the Finnish Seim (parliament), professional men, socialist activists. Among them were Alexander Shotman, founder of the Finnish Social Democratic Party; and Eino Rahja, whose pointed mustachios and rakishly tilted hat conformed to his calling as an actor. Together with railwayman Guro Yalava, they devised a plan whose enormous complexity indicated the degree of danger to which Lenin was then exposed. Success depended upon the loyalty of countless other members of the Finnish "left" whose discreet hospitality would facilitate Lenin's move from village *dacha* to city along the Petrograd-Helsingfors railway.

Two options were considered: 1) walking from Razliv across the frontier to a Finnish railway station, or 2) returning Lenin to Petrograd on a local train and transferring him to another local that terminated at Raivola on the Finnish side. But sharp-eyed cadets from Petrograd's military academy on duty along the border examined passport photos with a magnifying glass. So, after prolonged consultation, the conspirators decided on Plan 2. Zinoviev would remain in Petrograd, thus eliminating the need to transport two fugitives.

Since neither Shotman nor Rahja was familiar with the swampy terrain around Lake Razliv, Yemelyanov was delegated to serve as guide. Bringing clothing and a disguise for Lenin, the trio arrived at the hut without incident.

But the ensuing night journey nearly ended in disaster. Despite his boastful self-confidence, comrade Y- lost the way. First the men fell into a small river. Finally, after wandering about the forest and working their way past an area of burning peat, they heard a train whistle. Yemelyanov and Rahja went ahead to reconnoiter. Meanwhile, the others—sodden, disgruntled, hungry—sat on fallen logs breathing acrid smoke from the nearby peat bog. Shotman discovered three small cucumbers in his pocket, "but they weren't very palatable without salt," he observed. Usually even tempered, Lenin berated Shotman for poor planning, and when the explorers returned, they too were recipients of his annoyance.

Although Yemelyanov declared that they would emerge from the woods at Levashevo Station, he was in error; the nearest village was Dibuny, "barely seven versts from the Finnish border." They had learned from railway comrades that the last train for Petrograd left Dibuny at 1:30 a.m. It was now past one o'clock. Stumbling through the underbrush, they reached the station where Lenin, Zinoviev and Rahja hid near the water tower; Shotman and Yemelyanov started toward the platform. "What are you up to?" an armed cadet asked the scruffy-looking comrade Y-, and dissatisfied with the fugitive's stuttering response, promptly arrested him.

Shotman, however, appeared to be a "gentleman." "You are taking this train, Sir?" queried the cadet, pointing to the local puffing its way to the platform. "The express is not running tonight." (Suburban tracks here joined the mainline, requiring local trains to wait fifteen minutes on a siding for passage of the express.) Under the circumstances, Shotman was forced to board the train, abandoning his three charges hiding near the water tower. Disconcerted at the sudden turn of events, he got off at Ozerki a few miles down the line, thinking it was Udelnaya in suburban Petrograd. When he discovered his error, the train had already left, and he was forced to walk the remaining distance. At three a.m. he stumbled in to the flat of comrade Kalske who served as liaison with the Finnish contingent.

I could scarcely believe my eyes," reported Shotman. "There on the floor where they had been sleeping, convulsed with laughter, lay my three *popechniki*. Having observed my dilemma at the station platform, they waited until the train was moving out and then jumped aboard, reaching Udelnaya without mishap. By the time I arrived, they had already eaten supper and gone to sleep.

Shotman, with pince-nez askew and hair disheveled, went to a comrade living on Shirokaya Street who would notify Yemelyanov's wife of her husband's arrest. (Y. eventually escaped.) Shotman's next task was to confer with locomotive engineer Yalava who lived on the Viborg Side.

The man who left Razliv was unrecognizable. Shorn of beard and moustache, and wearing a wig topped by a visored cap, he shed several years from his age. The photograph of "Ivanov" pasted to his passport was that of a much younger man with half-smile and a quizzical expression of eyes. A workman's tunic and woolen jacket completed the disguise.

Late at night after a day in Kalske's flat Lenin, Shotman and Rahja returned to Udelnaya station. At midnight, the local train to Raivola pulled in with Yalava at the throttle of locomotive No. 293.

"I came to the edge of the platform," he related, "whereat a man strode from among the trees and hoisted himself up into the cab. It was, of course, Lenin, although I hardly recognized him. He was to be my stoker. Rolling up

Lenin in disguise (passport photo)

his sleeves, he climbed to the tender and began throwing wood onto the fire."

Meanwhile, Shotman and Rahja boarded the first coach. After leaving Udelnaya, the train, with smoke belching from its stovepipe funnel thanks to the energy of "fireman" Ivanov, plowed through a jungle of fir trees. Since passport inspection was limited to coach passengers, Lenin was temporarily safe. "But as our train approached Valkeasaari (Beloostrov), our hearts were numb with fear. We anticipated a thorough search of documents, even personal search." Fortunately, Shotman's fears proved groundless. The resourceful engineer uncoupled his locomotive and headed for the water tower where he remained until the dispatcher signaled departure. "Before the third bell sounded, the locomotive was back in place, gave a whistle, and fifteen minutes later we were already on the Finnish side. At Terijoki (Zelenogorsk), Rahja and I left the coach and hurried to the locomotive where we joyously pressed Lenin's hand."

Shotman then took the next train for Helsingfors, leaving Lenin in the care of Rahja. The two men began their journey westward by a circuitous route which included stopovers, one at the rural home of Rahja's father-in-law. In the meantime, Shotman was in the Finnish capital making arrangements for Lenin's arrival "aided by Finnish delegates to the Seim," he explained. Shotman next met Lenin in Rovio's apartment.

Lenin was escorted to Hågness Square at 11 p.m. "We sat in my kitchen drinking tea and chatting until midnight," Rovio said.

Then I proposed that Lenin go to bed, but he said to me: "You go to bed; I am going to work." When I retired, he was seated at my desk, alternately writing and reading newspapers. In the morning, I found him, fully clothed (he hadn't even loosened his shirt), reclining on the hardwood divan with his head resting on his arms. Despite his uncomfortable position, he was sleeping soundly. On the desk lay a large notebook filled with handwriting and, consumed with curiosity, I began turning over the pages. It was the manuscript of his book, *The State and Revolution*.

Upon returning from work that afternoon, Rovio was confronted with a series of demands from his boarder: "You must procure all the Russian newspapers each day as soon as they arrive. And since we cannot trust the official post, you'll have to arrange for my letters to be carried secretly."

Kustaa said of his guest: "I have never met such a congenial (simpatichnovo) and charming comrade as Lenin. But although unusually modest in his personal requirements, he was very demanding about the newspapers and letters." Rovio was expected to meet the daily 6:30 p.m. express from Petrograd and return promptly to Hågness Square with his bundle of papers. Arrangements were made with a comrade in the postal van to handle secret letters. "No alibis were accepted," Rovio added. "If I failed to carry out my duties, Lenin was sharp with me."

The matter of food was discussed, whereat Lenin announced that he would pay for and prepare his own eggs and tea. "What else does a man need?" Although the arrangement for meals and newspapers appeared to be elemental, it involved a considerable amount of money.

Lenin's supply of rubles had to be exchanged for Finnish marks, and Rovio was hard-pressed to do so without attracting attention. Likewise, the ruble was rapidly deteriorating in value against other currencies, giving rise to exorbitant exchange rates. As a result, Rovio was forced to enlist the aid of Finnish comrades. Without divulging their source, Kustaa parceled out Russian banknotes to friends who exchanged them at various locations. "By doing this," he explained to them mysteriously, "you could go down in the annals of history." So cautious was Rovio, however, that no one outside the small group of Finns privy to Lenin's presence in Helsingfors ever learned of it.

The Finns, incidentally, were uncannily perceptive about Lenin's future. While fellow-Russians entertained a questionable view of his prospects, leading Finish S-D's were saying: "Within four months, you, Vladimir Ilyich, will be prime minister of your country."

The imminent return of Rovio's wife, as well a perception by the Finns that the apartment was too centrally located, made it necessary to move Lenin to a safer place. Arthur and Emelia Blumqvist, a mature childless couple, lived in a fourth floor apartment at No.46 in nearby Telenkatu. With windows overlooking a woods, the place was safe from prying eyes. Since 1905, the Blumqvists had been housing Russian and Polish political refugees, and—although apolitical at the time Lenin became their boarder—they accepted him without reservation.

Late at night, Karl Viik, jurist and member of the *Seim*, escorted Lenin to No.46 where he explained the terms: a quiet room, absolute secrecy, and financial arrangements whereby Lenin would pay for his own food. "We found him an ideal boarder," said Mrs. Blumqvist.

> He didn't smoke. And what a worker!—all day at his writing table! Once he came into the kitchen with fresh newspapers in his hand. They stated that he was hiding in Petrograd, and Kerensky was threatening to catch him. Lenin finished reading and laughed meaningfully. "It is necessary to be quick, Kerensky," he said, with a gleam in his eyes, "in order to catch me."

Weather that autumn was especially pleasant. Late on balmy evenings, Blumqvist and Lenin strolled about the neighborhood. "He went without disguise. Our only precaution was prearranged conversation in the event we encountered someone. I would revert to Swedish* (which Lenin did not understand) and deliver a monologue to mislead the ears of detectives."

The two men also attended meetings of left-wing Social Democrats which were held in the quarters of Blumqvists's brother-in-law. The flat was on the first floor of a building in Paasila Street—from Tele, a short walk to Hågness Square and across Sittasaaren Boulevard. "A public sauna was located on the premises," B- noted. "Therefore it was an easy matter to arrange visits without attracting attention. No one there knew Lenin's identity."

Nadya came to Hågness Square to visit her husband. Kustaa Rovio described her arrival. "After Lenin moved to Tele, I continued to visit him daily, bringing newspapers and letters. One day he said to me: 'Do not come tomorrow, I shall call for my newspapers at your flat.' Sure enough, the following day Lenin and Krupskaya came to my flat, walking through the large park from Tele."

Kustaa said nothing further about Nadya, but Mrs. Blumqvist was slightly more voluble. "I was in the kitchen," she said, "when Lenin's wife arrived. I went to the door and was very startled to see an unfamiliar woman, wearing a shawl over her head, standing in the entry. Vladimir Ilyich recognized her voice, and immediately explained who our visitor was. She stayed with us for a short time and then departed."

Nadya's journey from Petrograd had been hazardous. Disguised as a peasant woman, she left Primorsky Station for Razliv, where she was met by the Yemelyanovs who provided her with a fake passport and guided her on foot

---

* Finland was bilingual, a result of having once belonged to Sweden. The Blumqvists were probably of Swedish descent.

across the frontier. "I had to walk five versts through a forest from the border to Ollila," Nadya said, "a small station where I took the soldiers' train."

The next stage of her journey was routine. From the railway station in the center of Helsingfors, she went across the square and up a small rise to the main thoroughfare. A cold wind blasted the Center as she waited for a tram whose number V. had provided. His letter, written with invisible ink, contained a map of his location at Telenkatu. Unfortunately, Nadya had scorched a corner of the map when heating it over a lamp, and upon leaving the tram at Hågness Square, "I wandered through the streets for a long time before finding the street I wanted. Volodya was very glad to see me." She remembered staying in Helsingfors two days, and when she left, he accompanied her to "the last turn of the road." "He wanted very much to accompany me to the railway station. We arranged that I should come again."

The meeting must have been a shock to both: a "young," beardless husband and his "elderly" wife with shawl over her head and the bulky garments of a peasant woman!

Nadya's second trip to Helsingfors was more dramatic. The direct route, via the mainline from Finlandski Station, would have entailed legal documents for which she dared not apply. It was necessary, therefore, to repeat the trip by way of Razliv. Already familiar (as she thought) with the route across the frontier, she decided to dispense with the services of Yemelyanov. However, by the time she reached the forest beyond Razliv, night had fallen. "The moon rose. My feet began to sink into the sand. It seemed to me that I had lost my way." After stumbling through the eerie darkness, she finally arrived at Ollila where she waited a half hour for the train. "It was filled with soldiers, and I had to stand all the way."

MAINLINE RAILWAY BETWEEN ST. PETERSBURG AND HELSINGFORS
(Showing branch line Viborg-St. Petersburg following the Gulf of Finland
to Primorsky Depot in southwest of city.)

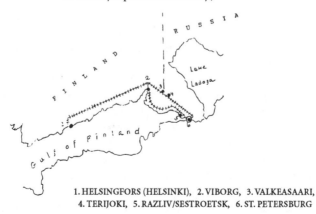

1. HELSINGFORS (HELSINKI), 2. VIBORG, 3. VALKEASAARI,
4. TERIJOKI, 5. RAZLIV/SESTROETSK, 6. ST. PETERSBURG

Their excited conversation, about politics and a possible uprising, provided her with firsthand information to convey to her husband. However, she found his responses bemused. "It was apparent that his mind was not on what she was saying, it was fixed on the rebellion and how best to prepare for it."

While in hiding, his primary source of information about developing conditions in Russia was derived from newspapers. Like a physician with a stethoscope, he monitored the collective heartbeat of the masses. Were they sufficiently aroused to seize the revolutionary initiative? And if so, at precisely what moment? And finally, who would be there to lead them?

He searched the newspapers for items more significant than reports of "unrest" here and there. Of far greater interest to him was information on the inflation rate (it was skyrocketing); the bread lines; general economic disruption; famine and chaos in the countryside. Lenin read these as symptomatic of imminent crisis, and like the former Tsar, he watched with interest the "cackling hens" of a government ministry unable to cope.

Their problem was multiple, but primarily that of inexperience in the art of governing; under autocracy their authority had been minimal to nonexistent. Likewise, the Tsar's sudden abdication had caught them unawares. But underlying these factors was a sense of indirection, of absence of a plan for the present and future state. Since February they had been muddling through a period of disorder that had become increasingly unmanageable. In their dilemma, they looked to Europe for a model, but how it might relate to the goals of their particular revolution eluded them. Russia was neither France nor Great Britain, nor—heaven forbid—Germany, whose collective and individual history in no way resembled that of the fatherland.

While they were deliberating, Marx's "historical process" outstripped them. The masses understood what the ministers failed to comprehend: that a century of socialist orientation would not yield to bourgeois capitalism and its detestable war.

Sensing that conditions for Phase Two were rapidly maturing, Lenin informed Finnish comrades that he intended moving closer to Petrograd. The city of Viborg offered both proximity and anonymity. Numerous adherents of the Russian political "left," after fleeing across the frontier, found refuge with Viborg working class families, thus establishing a pattern that was already in place when the Finns undertook to find accommodations for Lenin.

Unfortunately, the elaborate plans for his transferal to Viborg encountered a "bureaucratic" hurdle in the person of a certain Helsingfors wigmaker. This gentleman whose profession, besides theatrical work, included rejuvenating aging aristocrats, decided that his bald-headed client (escorted by Rovio) was in search of cosmetic improvement. "It will require at least two weeks," announced the man. "I am presently very busy." Likewise, with time at a premium, Lenin was told, not asked, what kind of wig to order. When he began fingering a ready-made gray wig, the wigmaker exploded: "But you are such a *young* man—not a day over forty! Now I would suggest . . ."

The ensuing argument threatened to scuttle Lenin's plan to leave Helsing-fors at the earliest possible moment. Finally, after an exasperating give-and-take, the gray wig triumphed; but for months afterward, the wigmaker regaled his clients with a tale about the young man who wanted to look old.

Lenin practiced wearing his new head-piece., "Do I have it on straight?" he repeatedly asked Rovio. "When all was in readiness," the latter concluded, "we bade farewell." This comedy of errors climaxed when the man who was a mas-ter-proponent of Marxist atheism departed the Finnish capital disguised as an elderly Lutheran pastor!

Finland: September–October 1917

Alma Raukiainen and her husband Antti were among numerous country dwellers who had moved to a suburb of the city of Viborg in search of employ-ment. "Life was hard and troublesome," Alma related. "We were starving. There was no meat, and people could obtain produce only with a ration card. But the allotment was so small I wonder how we managed to survive."

Upon the recommendation of their landlord, Antti found employment at the railroad repair shops, but his meager wages were insufficient to sustain them. So, each morning after her ten-year-old son left for school, Alma went to the city in search of work. Occasional employment in what she described as "an aristocratic family" alternated with work in a dressmaking shop.

In the evenings after work, men gathered in someone's flat where conversation was all about politics. Our landlord had worked in Petersburg where he joined the Bol-shevik Party, and, thanks to him, my Social Democrat husband absorbed the Bol-shevik world view.

One day the landlord spoke to Alma: "You are going on a little errand," he said mysteriously, "but I will say no more. The right hand must not know what the left hand is doing." With this, he handed her a ration card and directed her to a cooperative store where she was to pick up a bag of produce and deliver it to a certain address.

Late the next evening she carried the bag to Alexanderin Street, house No.15 and, as directed, entered through the kitchen. On the way she met Luli Latukka, the housewife, who appeared to be upset. "Oh, it is you," said Luli with relief after Alma had given the password. "Then," Alma related, "I noticed at one side of the kitchen a man washing at the sink. He was of medium stature, broad shouldered, and wearing a fine white shirt, the sleeves rolled up above the elbows. He was bald. He looked at me intently and, without utter-ing a word, finished washing and went to his room. He seemed to know why I had come at such a late hour."

After depositing the bag of produce, Alma returned home, puzzled by the scene she had just witnessed. "But no amount of probing satisfied my curiosity; neither our landlord nor the produce vendor, who obviously were fellow conspirators, chose to enlighten me."

The house at No. 15 Alexanderinkatu, a primitive duplex, was located in the brick-making area of Viborg. It contained two identical apartments, each with three rooms and a kitchen. On one side lived Luli Latukka, her husband Yukani and their small son; on the other, Luli's parents the Koikonens, together with their daughter Hildur and her younger brother. Mr. Koikonen was a master tile-maker. Both parents were Social Democrats, and their son-in-law Latukka a collaborator on the Finnish Socialist newspaper *Työ* (Labor).

At age twenty-seven, Luli's sister Hildur was an attractive unmarried teacher of Russian at the local school. Dark-eyed, with heavy black hair and a sweet expression, Hildur's accomplishments as a linguist were rare in a Finnish working-class family. She was among those who benefited from the Tsar's attempts to Russianize his Grand Duchy; and in September 1917, further good fortune awaited her.

The day Lenin was scheduled to arrive at the Latukka flat, Luli was in Helsingfors attending a socialist women's conference. Before leaving, she had instructed her sister Hildur to care for the guest during her absence. Lenin's name was not mentioned. "When I returned home," Luli said, "I found him at breakfast with my sister. He came forward and expressed pleasure at my return. I attempted to converse with him in Russian, but after a few halting sentences, my sister took charge of the conversation. It seemed that they (my sister and our guest) were already old friends."

Later, when they were alone together, Luli questioned Hildur: "How do you like our guest? And why did you bring him to your side of the house for meals?"

"He is an unusual man," Hildur responded. "At first, I brought his meals to your half. But then he asked to be allowed to eat here so that I wouldn't have to carry his food. But also, that he might talk with me."

Lenin's presence didn't disturb the family routine. Promptly at 8 a.m., the members—including Mrs. Latukka—left for work and the children for school. Afterwards, in his room on the Latukka side, Lenin spent his days writing articles and letters, reading newspapers in which he marked items of interest. Creative writing focused upon the immediate task of revolution. Organization of diverse and complex tactics was committed to paper with the same precision that Beethoven, for example, constructed a symphony. "Revolution is an art," said Marx.

For a working woman, mealtime was particularly stressful. Luli baked bread, prepared what she could from a meager supply of produce, meanwhile communicating in sign language with her Russian "assistant" who "swept up, pulled bread from the oven, and generally helped me with the housework. Seeing that I was uneasy about the meal and that things were not ready, let alone baked, he always praised the food, said that my buckwheat *kasha* was tasty." Luli's description of domestic matters included Lenin at the sink washing his own bed linen ("he insisted on it, even bringing wood from outside and heating water"). Lenin had become an accepted member of the family.

Like Kustaa Rovio and many other Finns, Mr. Koikonen had at one time worked in a Petersburg factory where he learned to speak Russian. On warm evenings, he and Lenin sat outside on the back steps, discussing politics. At other times, Lenin joined Koikonen in the latter's kitchen, gradually emptying the pot of coffee simmering on the flagstone hearth. "Once I was accused of drinking a whole day's supply of coffee," Lenin observed, laughing.

One morning during the second week, Hildur became ill and spent the entire day in bed.

> In the morning, as soon as everyone had gone to work, Lenin came to my room and asked with concern about my health. He was always very attentive and solicitous of me. But no one could be solicitous of him—it displeased him.

Hildur described his habit of going for a stroll after dark. "I could always sense when he was away," she said. "Once he was absent so long that I became alarmed. 'But I came back, didn't I?' he reassured me." She found his calmness "contagious." "But it is difficult to describe him to one who did not know him at close range, particularly his unpretentiousness."

Hildur seemed to him like a daughter; in coloring and temperament she resembled his sister Maria. He had longed for children of his own. "Lenin was very fond of my rascally little son," Luli remembered, "and, to the child's delight, often carried him about on his shoulder."

Repeatedly during these days, Lenin had asked the Party's Central Committee for permission to return to Petrograd, but it had been denied. Observing the rapid upsurge of revolutionary activity there and in Moscow, he feared the Party's refusal to take advantage of a fluid situation. Finally in desperation, the Committee sent an emissary, Alexander Shotman, to Viborg. A bitter argument ensued, in which Lenin accused the Finn of personally contributing to the stalemate. Mr. Latukka described the confrontation: "I remember how sternly Shotman talked to Lenin about remaining where he was for another week. The latter finally agreed, but forced Shotman to write on a small scrap of paper that he—Shotman—allegedly in the name of the Central Committee but actually on his own initiative, had issued the order. I obtained this historic scrap of paper from Shotman and sealed it in a chest of drawers, where it remained long after Lenin left and I myself had fled from Viborg when our Finnish Revolution collapsed."

Near the end of the third week, permission came from the committee for Lenin to return to Petrograd. Mrs. Latukka noted that several days earlier "he appeared to be nervous, began to go without eating, and paced uneasily up and down the room."

On Sunday October 20th, the Latukkas returned from work earlier than usual. In Hildur's words: "We had a quick supper; all of us were very serious and troubled, for we knew that Lenin was about to undertake a difficult journey."

When Rahja arrived with a clergyman's disguise for Lenin, the family knew that the moment was at hand. "I came home from work," Luli stated, "and was astonished to see a complete stranger in the room. I looked about with alarm. Then the stranger burst out laughing. The apparition was really Lenin, whom I recognized only by his voice."

Leave-taking was emotional. The family made him promise to send back word of his safe arrival. "Then we said goodbye." Mr. Latukka accompanied the two men to the tramway stop. "I wished Lenin a safe journey and success in solving the political questions. 'Follow our example' was his hearty reply, and they set off. They settled in a tram and soon arrived at the railway station. At 2:35 p.m. the train gave a whistle, and the 'October Revolution' was on the way to Russia."

Upon arrival at Raivola, they left the Petrograd Express and crossed the platform to where Yalava's "local" stood on a siding.

> On October 20, I brought Lenin back to Petrograd. He and Rahja reached Raivola only a few minutes before the train was scheduled to leave. It was midnight. Ilyich (Lenin) came quickly to the locomotive, and Rahja settled in the first coach. With me was my former stoker, so this time Lenin's assistance was not required; the fire was already burning.

Rahja described the journey in greater detail. "At Viborg Station," he said, "I bought tickets for Petrograd. We did not enter the coach, but stood in the "tambure." When people entered, I spoke to Lenin in Finnish, and he answered as agreed, *jaa* or *ei*. Never did he say *jaa* when it was necessary to say *ei*.

> We reached Raivola without incident. At Raivola, Yalava had uncoupled the locomotive and gone for firewood. While we waited, Lenin and I walked about near the pile of wood which, fortunately, was at some distance from the station. We noted suspicious-looking persons lurking about the station platform, so Lenin jumped aboard the locomotive as it began to move; I went back to the platform and entered the first coach—with two loaded revolvers in my pocket!

The coach was filled with summer visitors and a few workers, their noisy discussion of politics divided according to social class. "When the workers spoke out against the war, summer people began roasting 'German Lenin' who received millions in money to organize sedition in Russia. Bourgeois persons said that Lenin should be murdered. One of them proposed to bring Lenin in chains to Nevsky Prospekt so each could strike him and spit in his face. Then he should be burned alive. They did not know that their 'victim' was sitting nearby."

As the train approached the danger-point at Valkeasaari, Rahja became uneasy: "Would we encounter some unusual tie-up at the frontier?" In fact, Rahja's passport, in the name of a deceased army officer, was examined without question. Yalava, having uncoupled the locomotive (carrying Lenin), drove it to the water tower, waited until the first bell sounded, then steamed back into place "and we were off for Petrograd."

From suburban Lanskaya Station, they de-trained, and a comrade conducted them to a safe apartment in the neighborhood. "Already there, waiting for Lenin, was his wife, Nadezhda Konstantinovna."

The Finnish "left" was sufficiently strong to precipitate revolution. With multiparty representation in the *Seim*, and with the Russian left-wing exerting pressure on Finland's proletariat, a swing to Socialism appeared to be inevitable. Unfortunately, the presence of Russian soldiers on Finnish soil threatened to undermine what the natives considered a matter for internal determination. Unable to distinguish between the two faces of tsarism—on the one hand, its repressive military and political policies—and on the other, a proletarian-oriented Russian soldiery—the Finns confronted a dilemma.

In the Grand Duchy, no less than in Russia itself, a tenacious bourgeoisie threatened peaceful transition to a new social order. At the time Lenin departed Viborg, he was keenly aware of the problems that beset his Finnish comrades. "Follow our example," he counseled them. When questioned about the probability of Bolshevik success in Russia, he responded, meaningfully: "Wait and see."

The numerous Finns who provided asylum for Lenin offered more than mere hospitality. Unlike indifferent Switzerland, Finnish *rapport* with the Bolshevik ideal was vigorous and deep-rooted. Social Democrats considered Lenin their ideological mentor, and as such, treated him with extraordinary respect. Their care for his personal safety, at great risk to themselves, repeatedly saved him from natural disasters, and from the successive dragnets of Nicholas II, Milyukov and Kerensky.

But the terms of restrained affection with which they described him indicated a depth of feeling which, for a normally reserved people, was striking. Nor was this one-sided; Lenin himself unwittingly contributed to the *rapport.* Rather than pushing Russian Bolshevism, he listened attentively to the Finnish side of questions, discussing rather than arguing.

Curiously, in describing Lenin as a man, the most articulate were those of humble station, persons who observed him on a daily basis under ordinary conditions. Laying aside politics, revolutionary tactics and ideology, Mrs. Latukka said:

> My very limited knowledge of language allowed me to converse with him only on simple matters; therefore I chatted with him as an ordinary, simple man. They

maintain that he was a great man, destined for a great life. But all those who entered into that life felt that he was great in his soul. His humanity toward the laboring and peasant masses also extended to those who were privileged to be in close contact with him.

Observed Rovio: "It was a great honor for the workers' movement of Finland to provide shelter for the great and gifted leader of the world revolutionaries."

Lenin's personal relationships in Finland paid dividends a year later when that country petitioned for independence.

At one time, Lenin—incognito—remained overnight with Viik's mother in Lahti, then a small town on the Helsingfors-Petrograd railway. After he departed, Viik told her: "This has been the most renowned person who has ever visited our home," to which she responded, "Then it must have been Lenin!"

During negotiations with the new Soviet Government, Viik headed the Finnish parliamentary delegation to Petrograd. But when the Bolsheviks demanded dual citizenship for the Russians, the negotiations broke down. Viik's telephone call to Lenin brought immediate results. Unaware of what had been transpiring, Lenin directed the Party members to withdraw their demand; an agreement was reached, and for the first time in its history, Finland gained national sovereignty. "That was my last personal contact with Lenin," Viik added, "but I know that he always followed with interest the destiny and struggles of Finland."

Subsequently, Finnish-Soviet *rapport* managed to survive Stalinism, the bitterly fought Winter War of 1940, the post-Stalin reaction of the '60s. It survives today, albeit in muted form. Pragmatism? Perhaps. But without the legacy of Lenin, it is doubtful that bourgeois, capitalist Finland, sharing a border with Russia, would continue to exist, as it does, in a state of equanimity and internal equilibrium.

In 1966, Hildur—aged 76, long married and living in Helsinki—was interviewed by a Soviet historian who brought a television crew to her apartment. "It was my good fortune to know Lenin," she related, "to be near him for three weeks, to feel his kindness. I always felt that we were close friends." While speaking, tears came to her eyes. "I can never talk about him without emotion," she concluded.

18. Revolution, October 1917

While her husband was in hiding, Nadya became eyewitness to events following the "July Days." First, the Executive Committee of the Soviets issued a statement in which the Provisional Government was declared to be the *Government of Salvation of the Revolution*. Nadya remarked sarcastically: "On that same day, the 'salvation' began—capital punishment was introduced at the front."

A second and more significant development was Kerensky's appointment of General Kornilov as Commander-in-Chief of the army. With the front disintegrating at an alarming rate, Kerensky devised a plan for restoring discipline among the troops. The machinegun regiment held responsible for the July uprising was stripped of its arms and marched through the streets of the Capital. "I saw them as they filed into the square. While leading their horses by the bridle, one observed so much hatred in their eyes, that it was clear a more stupid method could not have been devised."

Headlines in the press were black with threats against the revolutionaries. And when the city learned that Kornilov and his troops were on their way to quell local "disturbances," the counterrevolutionary intent of Government and its Prime Minister, Kerensky, could no longer be concealed. In Viborg Sector, the "salvation of revolution" was perceived as salvation of the bourgeoisie and their tsarist supporters.

A few miles south of Petrograd, a military dictatorship was marching on the city. Immediately, Viborg sprang into action. Armed with rifles and propaganda, factory workers met Kornilov in a battle won by words rather than weapons.

Kornilov was arrested, his corps commander shot himself, and the motley Viborg army drifted back to the Capital—dusty and elated. "One of them rushed into headquarters of the District *Duma*," said Nadya, "his face flushed with excitement, threw his rifle into a corner, and began talking about chalk and blackboards (there was a shortage). Every day I had opportunity to observe how closely the Viborg workers linked revolutionary struggle with the struggle for mastery of knowledge and culture."

Although Lenin's return from Finland had been successfully accomplished, he was now at dire risk in the Capital. After his initial rendezvous with Party members, Nadya resolved not to inform anyone, including the Party's Central Committee, of his whereabouts. Her decision, based upon instinct rather than certainty, resulted from fear of a leak within the Party's own ranks; a fear that was later justified.

Marguerita Fofanova, his former landlady, resided in the Lesnoy District of Viborg at a considerable distance from "known" apartments under police surveillance. At Nadya's request, she agreed once again to hide Lenin. "Her flat was in a large house at the corner of Lesnoy Prospekt. It was particularly suitable, for most of the family had left for the summer, and even the servants had not yet returned."

Lenin went there at night, and for the next several days remained in isolation. Fofanova's mission was not only to shelter him, but also to serve as courier, carrying messages to and from the various secret "drops," delivering newspapers to him and notes from his wife. For her part, Marguerita was more fearful of Lenin's impetuosity than of discovery from without. Each morning before leaving for work, she extracted a promise; under no circumstances was he to leave the apartment. He should lock the door and open it only upon hearing the secret knock agreed on by Fofanova herself, Nadya, Lenin's sister Maria and Eino Rahja.

On one occasion he disobeyed the order. "Fofanova had a cousin who attended military school," Nadya related. "I came in the evening and saw this fellow on the staircase. He appeared embarrassed. He saw me and said: 'Someone has stolen into Marguerita's apartment, I came, rang the bell, and a man's voice answered. Then I rang and nobody answered.' I told him a tale about Marguerita's having gone to a meeting, and that I was sure he was mistaken about hearing the voice."

The man left, whereupon Nadya knocked in the agreed manner. When Lenin opened the door, she began to scold him. "The fellow might have called other people," she chided. His excuse: "I thought it was something important."

On October 24 (1917), Lenin sent Fofanova with a message to the Party's Central Committee demanding an immediate uprising. She returned home to find her boarder missing and a note lying on the table: "I have gone where you didn't want me to go. Goodbye."

Two months earlier, the Petrograd Soviet had moved from Taurida Palace to Smolny Institute a few blocks away. Located on Neva's eastern loop, Smolny—prior to the February Revolution, had been a boarding school for daughters of the aristocracy. In early September, the Bolshevik Central Committee left Kshesinskaya for Smolny where it occupied former classrooms on a second floor corridor.

As the day of reckoning approached, Lenin had become increasingly impatient. Pacing up and down in Fofanova's apartment, he came to a decision; without his presence, the Central Committee would continue to procrastinate. After sending Marguerita on an errand, he donned the gray wig, his visored cap, a heavy winter *palto*, and answered the secret knock of a comrade who would accompany him to Smolny.

Outside, wind-driven snow swirled about the cavernous streets as the two men hurried to Troitsky Bridge. Across the river they were stopped by a sentry; but presence of mind, aided by luck, saved Lenin from arrest.

One entered Smolny through a pair of gates opening to a broad avenue which ended at the portico. The landscaped grounds, with miniature shrub trees, already looked abandoned. Mud, snow, unpruned branches, unkempt borders, testified to revolution's depredation. As Lenin strode along the approach, he looked up at the lighted windows glimmering through murk. Smolny's enormous facade, an eighth of a mile unbroken stretch of granite in the Italianate style, was, on this winter night, a ghostly symbol of the past. Barely eight months earlier, proper young ladies had gathered in its classrooms for instruction in the fine art of being an aristocrat.

Lenin and his companion entered by a back door, came to the foyer where rough, bearded proletarian soldiers were lounging about, then up the ornate staircase to a corridor extending the entire north/south expanse. Proletarian mud and proletarian smells pervaded the once pristine hallway where distracted proletarian civilians scurried from room to room, carrying messages. Observing the distance to be covered, Lenin quipped: "We need roller skates."

Russia's future was determined on the night of October 10, (o.s.) 1917 in a flat at No.32 Naverezhnaya Street, an obscure byway that paralleled the Karpovski River bisecting Petersburg *storona.* The flat, located in a building not far from what is now Kirov Prospekt, belonged to N.N. Sukhanov, a Menshevik. Unbeknown to her husband, Mrs. Sukhanov was a Bolshevik, and since he was away from home, the Central Committee deemed it a safe meeting place; because of Mr. Sukhanov's moderate politics, the police were unlikely to search there for the bigwigs of Bolshevism.

In a conclave that marked "history's turning point,"* ten members— including Lenin, Trotsky, Uritsky, Kollontai, Sverdlov, Stalin, Djerzhinsky— passed a resolution in favor of immediate armed insurrection. Voting against it were the "heavenly twins," Kamenev and Zinoviev.

Lenin's insistence that the moment for action was at hand won a majority vote, but his argument was not predicated upon intuition. Besides unmistakable evidence that Russia was on the threshold of its third revolution, another factor loomed immediately ahead: the Second All-Russia Congress of Soviets, scheduled to convene on the morning of October 21st. Bolsheviks, he pointed out, had exactly eleven days in which to prove whether or not two decades of talk had been just that—talk.

Would the Congress, like the Provisional Government and Kerensky's *Salvation of Revolution,* succumb to factionalism? Would it become dominated by the Constitutional Democratic (elitist-bourgeois) Party? By the S.R.-Mensheviks? Or, in order to stave off another revolution, by a coalition of these two

---

* Trotsky's term, later borrowed by Kerensky for the title of his book *Russia, and History's Turning Point* (N.Y. 1965).

groups? Would the Bolsheviks, hesitating on the brink of opportunity, once again be chased from their homeland to languish in pockets of discontent and frustration all over the map of Europe? He was saying, in effect: If we fail now, it is the end; this moment will not recur.

Without the precondition of a completed revolution thus stiffening the backbone of the Congress, that body could easily succumb to the vacillation that heretofore had characterized Russian experiments with self-government. In such an event, "All Power to the Soviets" would become a meaningless slogan, and the Bolsheviks an international joke.

There was also another reason for seizing power before the Congress convened. Rumors had reached Kerensky's government that the Bolshevik uprising was scheduled for the day *following* the Soviets' opening session. With a preemptive date, the insurgents would thwart organized resistance by the Government.

"The alternatives to Soviet Power," Lenin stated emphatically, "are 1) military dictatorship, or 2) Russia's dismemberment by western nations." He meant, of course, Soviet Power representing the interests of proletarians and poor peasants.

The Committee majority discussed alternative dates for the uprising. Because the S.R.-Mensheviks had initially set October 21st for the Congress of Soviets, the Bolsheviks chose October 20th. Kamenev and Zinoviev betrayed their colleagues by revealing, in a press release, the proposed date. Why Zinoviev, heretofore an ardent supporter of Lenin, teamed with Kamenev, is a mystery. The union, however, proved durable, and as time went on it became, not a "loyal opposition," but one of persistent intransigence.

When the Congress was postponed to the 26th, the Bolsheviks found themselves with five extra days at their disposal, a lapse of time that could prove disadvantageous to them; hence a change of date to October 25th.

By the time Lenin arrived at Smolny, the logistics of revolution were already in place. Under Trotsky's leadership, a Military Revolutionary Committee had been formed (October 13th). "We had no money, we had no troops," he said of this embryonic Red Army. Nevertheless, a citizen force was mustered, consisting of defectors from the regular army and navy, swelled by all Viborg workers who knew how to fire a rifle. Weapons were expropriated from the Sestroretsk Arms Factory.

Trotsky had undergone an eleventh-hour conversion to Bolshevism. Was it Lenin's charm that won him? Or what? For whatever reason, he suddenly decided to regularize his commonlaw marriage with the "left." Without him at that moment, the civilian revolutionary leaders, including Lenin, might have become minor footnotes in the history of Russia.

One of the difficulties confronting revolutionary Petrograd was that of coordinating its activities with those of Moscow. The latter had been con-

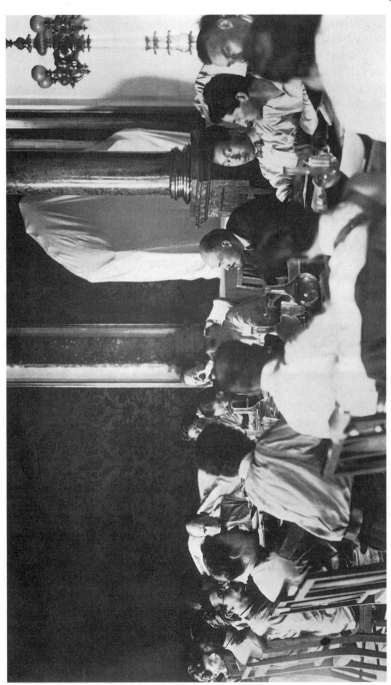

Lenin chairing a meeting. Note the many nationalities represented

ducting its own revolution and was not, at this point, ready to march in lock-step with the Capital. It required a feat of diplomacy to ensure that Petrograd, having finished what it began, did not find itself isolated from Moscow and the country at large. Certain telegraph operators in both cities worked around the clock; in Petrograd, the Nickolai Railway station was the locus of emissaries carrying messages to and from the Moscow revolutionary organization.

Trotsky's contribution to diplomacy is debatable, but his energy and com-manding personality welded together the disparate elements of a makeshift army.

Immediately after Lenin's arrival at Smolny, the women of Viborg were mobilized. "There were fifty women workers in the premises of the District Council during the entire night," Nadya related. "A woman doctor was giving them instructions in first aid. In other rooms, the workers were being armed; group after group came to the committee and received rifles and ammunition. But in Viborg, there was no one to suppress—they arrested only a colonel and several others who had come to the workers' club to have some tea. Later, com-rade Z- and I went to Smolny on a truck to see how things were going."

Meanwhile, the cruiser *Aurora*, with a skeleton crew of defectors, had steamed up the Bolshaya Neva and moored opposite the Winter Palace where Government ministers were in session.

After escaping from the Japanese Fleet in 1905, *Aurora* had wandered about the Pacific, finally seeking refuge in the Philippines. Interned there for several months, she was finally released to make her way home to Russia. This doughty vessel, on the night of October 24-25, 1917, was about to salvage her reputation from past ignominy.

Nadya did not return to Shirokaya Street that night. Excitement, like ani-mal-breath steaming in Petrograd's frigid air, pervaded Smolny's corridors and the *Aktovui Zal* where, beneath crystal chandeliers, Lenin addressed a tur-bulent mass of unshaven, unwashed proletarians. With his own chin begin-ning to sprout the familiar beard, clad in over-long trousers and the same vintage jacket he had worn in Switzerland, he resembled the lowliest among his listeners.

"I went to Smolny," wrote American Socialist John Reed in his monumen-tal account of the Revolution [*Ten Days that Shook the World*],

> its massive façade ablaze with light, and from every street converged upon it streams of hurrying shapes dim in the gloom. Automobiles and motorcycles came and went. An enormous armored vehicle lumbered out with screaming siren. It was cold, and at the outer gate Red Guards had built themselves a bonfire. At the inner gate, too, there was a blaze, by the light of which sentries slowly spelled out passes.
>
> Far over the still roofs westward came the sound of scattered rifle fire, where the junkers (military school cadets) were trying to open the bridges over the Neva, to prevent factory workers and soldiers from the Viborg quarter from joining

Soviet soldiers in the center of the city; and the Kronstadt sailors were closing them again . . .

Inside, the long, bare, dimly illuminated halls roared with the thunder of feet, calling, shouting . . . There was an atmosphere of recklessness. A crowd came pouring down the staircase, workers in black blouses and black fur hats, many with guns slung over their shoulders, soldiers in rough, dirt-colored coats, a leader or two, hurrying along in the center of the groups all talking at once, with harassed, anxious faces.

So I came to the great meeting hall. There was no heat in the hall but the stifling heat of unwashed human bodies. A cloud of cigarette smoke rose from the mass and hung in the thick air. "No smoking!" someone shouted. "No smoking!" echoed the smokers, and went on smoking. Comrade P- made a seat for me beside him. Unshaven and filthy, he was reeling from three nights' sleepless work on the Military Revolutionary Committee . . . The Committee functioned white-hot, holding in its hands the threads of insurrection and striking with a long arm . . . It was 10:40 p.m.

At 2 a.m. October 25th, revolution began with the capture of the Telephone Exchange, the Telegraph Agency, the State Bank, and arrest of two Government ministers. Chief of the City Militia, Meyer, was shot. Chaos prevailed in the streets as junkers clashed with soldiers and Red Guards. Shouts of "Peace, Bread and Land" rent the air.

Reed left Smolny around 5 a.m. and went to his room for a few hours' sleep. After dawn (between 9 and 10 a.m. at Petrograd's 60° latitude), he arose and roamed about the city, intent not only upon observing the outward manifestations of this momentous event, but of absorbing its subjective meaning for Russia and the world. A hulking man with the features of a friendly pug dog, his journalist's eye recorded with photograph exactitude the process of revolution.

The day before, he had inveigled his way into the Winter Palace where the Provisional Government was entrenched.

The place was a huge barracks, and from the condition of floor and walls, had been so for weeks. Parquetted floors were lined with dirty mattresses and blankets, upon which occasional soldiers were stretched out. And everywhere a litter of cigarette butts, bits of bread, cloth and empty bottles—French wine filched from the Palace cellars. Machine guns were mounted on the window-sills, rifles stacked between the mattresses.

Afterward, he went to dinner at the Hotel France where he was served by a liveried waiter with white napkin over his arm. Peter-Paul's cannon boomed the hour. On the Nevsky, trams were still running, restaurants and shops open, and, except for groups arguing excitedly on street corners, the populace was going about its daily business. "I heard a burst of rifle fire and saw people falling flat on the pavement; then the people lying flat stood up." While Reed was finishing his soup, the waiter returned. "Perhaps, Sir, you should go to the back dining room. The Bolsheviks are coming and there may be shooting."

"We [Reed and his wife, Louise Bryant] had tickets for the ballet at Mariinsky Theater that night, but things were much too interesting outside."

The next day he returned to the Winter Palace and found it cordoned off. "I thought you bagged all those gentlemen last night." "No, some are still inside." Red Guards were at one corner of the Square, junkers at the other. Reed walked inside and asked to interview President Kerensky. "Sorry," said a young officer in French. "Alexander Feodorvich is extremely occupied just now." Pause. "in fact, he is not here; he has gone to the front."

Reed joined the human traffic between Palace and Smolny, back and forth, one among thousands surging like a great, black tide as darkness descended over the city. "In front of Kazan Cathedral, a three-inch field gun lay in the middle of the street, slewed sideways from the recoil of its last shot over the roofs."

At Smolny, he stopped briefly outside the room where the Military Revolutionary Committee worked "at furious speed, spitting out panting couriers "The door opened, and a blast of stale air and cigarette smoke rushed out, and I caught a glimpse of disheveled men bending over a map under the glare of a shaded electric light."

Suddenly the boom of cannon from Bolshaya Neva, as *Aurora* opened fire on the Winter Palace. Although its shells glanced harmlessly off the plaster cornices, doing only minor damage to the structure, those inside recognized that Petrograd, like all of Russia, had reached the turning point, beyond which *Bog yedenui*, God, alone—or maybe the devil—knew the way ahead.

It was time to return to the Winter Palace, its red façade a fitting backdrop to revolution. "We came out into the chill night. The entire front of Smolny was one huge park of arriving and departing automobiles. A great motor truck stood there, shaking to the roar of its engines. 'Where are you going?' 'Downtown—everywhere.' We climbed in; the clutch slid home with a raking jar, the car jerked forward. As we careened down Suvorovsky Prospekt, a man tore open a bundle and began to hurl handfuls of paper into the air. Occasionally a baffled pedestrian paused to pick one up."

The papers read:

> To the Citizens of Russia!
>
> The Provisional Government is deposed. The State Power has passed into the hands of the Petrograd Soviet of Workers' and Soldiers' Deputies.
>
> The cause for which the people were fighting: immediate proposal for a democratic peace, abolition of landlord property-rights over the land, labor control over production, creation of a Soviet Government—that cause is securely achieved.

LONG LIVE THE REVOLUTION OF WORKMEN, SOLDIERS, AND PEASANTS!

Military Revolutionary Committee

Petrograd Soviet of Workers' and Soldiers' Deputies.

At the corner where Yekaterin Canal flowed under Nevsky Prospekt, the truck was halted by a cordon of armed sailors. To Reed's astonishment, he witnessed a crowd of about four hundred marching in groups of four; men in frock coats, well-dressed women, persons of various social classes. Among them he recognized members of the Provisional Government (arrested yesterday and then released), and the mayor of Petrograd. On an improvised soap-box, waving his umbrella, stood Prokopovich, Minister of Supplies in the Provisional Government. "We cannot have our innocent blood upon the hands of these ignorant men!" he shouted. Argument at the head of the column grew louder.

"We demand to pass!"

"Who are you?"

"Comrades from the Congress of Soviets."

"What is your business?"

"We're going to die with our comrades in the Winter Palace."

The sailor scratched his head. "I have orders . . ."

"We insist."

"I have orders."

"Shoot us if you wish. We bare our breasts to your guns!"

"Well, I could send someone to telephone Smolny . . ."

"What will you do if we go forward?"

"I'm not going to shoot unarmed Russian people."

"We will go forward. What will you do?"

"We will do something."

"What will you do?"

Another sailor, exasperated, stepped forward. "We will spank you," he said. "And if necessary, shoot you too. Now go home and leave us in peace."

"Whereupon," said John Reed, "the procession marched around and back up the Nevsky. I took advantage of the disturbance and slipped through the guards, then set off toward the Winter Palace."

In Palace Square he stumbled over a stack of rifles thrown down by the departed junkers. Light streamed from the Palace's open doors, "and from the huge pile came not the slightest sound." At the entrance, Red Guards were searching those who sought admittance. After showing his pass, Reed joined the crowd roaming unmolested through the corridors. At one point they were stopped. "Make way," barked a Red Guard, waving the crowd aside. Passing in single file came six frock-coated members of the Provisional Government, led by several soldiers with fixed bayonets. "First K-, his face drawn and pale, then

R-, glancing sullenly around. T- was next, glancing sharply around; he stared at us with cold fixety. They passed in silence. Outside, a few shots were fired, but the sailors brought them safely to Peter–Paul."

After traversing a maze of rooms, Reed found himself in the Gold and Malachite chamber. It resembled a corporation board room. Amid tsarist treasures stood a long table covered with green baize and flanked by rows of chairs, and before each empty place lay pen and ink and paper. Reed examined pages scribbled with plans for action, rough drafts of proclamations and manifestos. Some were crossed out and the remaining page covered with geometric "doodles," "as the writers sat despondently listening while Minister after Minister propose chimerical schemes." He picked one up and put it in his pocket.

At 11 o'clock that night, the Second All-Russia Congress of Soviets convened—under the chairmanship of Kamenev!

True to its promise, a determined group of the "left" had led the people to victory. In less than twenty-four hours, the cause of the masses, after more than a century of strife, had finally triumphed. "Yes, you won at the point of a bayonet!" cried the Opposition. Trotsky rose to address the convocation:

"You say that we, the Bolsheviki, are isolated and without support of a single other democratic group ... How is it, then, that we were able to overthrow the Government almost without bloodshed? They speak of the necessity for coalition. What sort of coalition? With those who supported the government of treason to the people? There can be only one coalition; that of workers, soldiers and poorest peasants."

A significant proclamation, signed by Vladimir Ulyanov-Lenin, stated: "Elections for the Constituent Assembly shall take place at the date determined upon—October 30 (Nov. 12 n.s.)."

Another government? And by whom? Soviet Congresses dissolved into a "democratic" parliament? The victors were trapped in their own previous commitment to convene the Assembly, although at the time, the principle of free elections did not appear to be contradictory; Lenin still hoped for a peaceful transfer of power. But has revolution ever been resolved around a conference table?

The Congress of Soviets was in turmoil, rent by the same forces that had been dividing the country prior to October 25th. Left S.R.s and a contingent of Mensheviks accepted the Bolshevik program. Others were dragged, kicking and screaming, into the new age. Stubborn oppositionists were given permission to leave.

After an all-night session, voting in the Congress had produced a number of important resolutions, among them a plan for universal social insurance, and a decree forbidding pogroms against Jews. During the last fifteen minutes, it voted to form a Council of People's Commissars "provisionally" of which Lenin was unanimously named chairman (the only title he ever held), and passed two sweeping decrees: one on peace, the other on land. Bread could not be legislated.

By the time Congress adjourned, the bleary-eyed Central Committee members (Bolshevik), had been without sleep for at least 48 hours, and many had not been to bed for over a week. Meals were snatched when time permitted. And judging Lenin's past and future practice, he probably went without nourishment, save for glasses of tea, from the time he arrived at Smolny until the morning of the 27th.

Twenty-four hours to deliver a revolution, two or three days to mop up and then back to normal: such was the expectation of those who expected immediate benefits. Alas, it was not to be. The [collective] Soviets never got the chance to exercise power, nor did the peasants receive the land promised them, at least not in the form they expected. Bread ration was cut, inflation soared out of sight, a black market reared its ugly head, the war with Germany continued. In short, conditions were worse than under the Tsar.

It was not, however, duplicity on the part of the Central Committee (Bolshevik), the Council of People's Commissars, the Congress of Soviets, or indeed any group or individual of the revolution. Nor was it absence of skill or will on their part. Conditions developed over which they had no control: first, counterrevolution; then failure of the world proletariat to rally behind Russia; and finally, world opposition to Socialism, with Western governments preparing to assault the new Soviet State. With the exception of Lenin, many of the leaders feared that their revolution might end as merely a passing phenomenon.

But in the morning hours of October 27th, the immediate concerns were law and order, the establishment of "normalcy."

"It was almost seven," Reed noted, "when we woke the sleeping conductors and motormen of the trams, kept waiting at Smolny to take the Soviet delegates to their homes. In the crowded car there was less happy hilarity than the night before, I thought. Many looked anxious; perhaps they were saying to themselves, 'Now we are masters, how can we do our will?'"

Upon returning to their apartment building, Reed and his wife were confronted by an armed House Committee. The landlady heard them come in and stumbled out in a pink silk wrapper.

"What's all this?" asked Reed.

"Protection of the house and women and children," came the reply.

"Who from?"

"From robbers and murderers."

"But suppose there came a commissar from the military Revolutionary Committee, searching for arms?"

"Oh, that's what they'll *say* they are... and besides, what's the difference?"

A "coup by robbers and murderers" was the perception of those to whom revolution was more nuisance than threat—or benefit. They were saying in effect: Kerensky and his troops are on their way to "liberate" the city, the Germans are coming. Who cares?

Observed John Reed: "Nothing is so astounding as the vitality of the social organism—how it persists, feeding itself, clothing itself, amusing itself, in the face of the worst calamities . . ."

Lenin, Nadya and Maria in car after military parade, Moscow, May 1, 1918

19. "Soviet Power"

At the end of October, Nadya packed her few belongings and moved to Smolny. On the second floor of the north wing, a classroom had been fitted with a half-partition, dividing it into bedroom and living-dining room. "One had to cross the hall to the bathroom," she said. This improvised apartment—spartan, uncarpeted, furnished only with iron beds, wardrobe lined with white Dutch tiles, a small round table, three chairs and a couch—became home to Nadya and her husband for the next several months.

Shortly after moving in, Nadya was given a decorative lady's desk containing a telephone, ink-stand and table lamp. This was her workplace. At Lenin's direction, the electric lamp was fitted with a kerosene font, since during the first months of Soviet Power, electricity was turned off before midnight in order to conserve fuel at the generating plant. "I was completely engulfed in work, beginning in the Viborg Sector, then in the People's Commissariat of Education."

Anatoly Lunacharsky, one of Lenin's close friends during the émigré period in Switzerland, had been appointed Commissar for Education. Upon coming to Smolny for instruction about his duties, he found Lenin too busy to outline a plan. "I would suggest, however," the latter stated, "that you seriously consider meeting with Nadezhda Konstantinovna. She will help you. She is deeply involved in this matter, and has in mind the correct procedure." The illiteracy rate exceeded 90%, and both Lenin and his wife were dedicated to establishing universal education.

Although Smolny's two dining halls accommodated the workers, they were crowded. Both Lenin and Nadya wished to avoid turmoil at mealtime. Therefore, arrangements were made for meals to be brought to the apartment. Their "servant," a young peasant soldier from Ufa District, was a machinegun commander delegated to guard Smolny. "Comrade Zheltuishev became very attached to Vladimir Ilyich," said Nadya, "and was ready to go through fire and water for him."

This young soldier became a valuable source of information about the couple's family life during their days at Smolny. Others were either too preoccupied, or not in position to observe their habits.

When Lenin was asked what kind of accommodations he wanted, the reply was: "As close as possible to my place of work." Someone wrote "No. 67" on a square of paper and fastened it to the door of a former classroom at the far end of the corridor's north wing, and hereafter this served as Lenin's office. Day and night, two armed soldiers stood guard outside the door.

The place was as spartan as the apartment: large desk, several bentwood chairs, a coat rack, and at one side two small desks where Lenin's secretary, Gorbunov, and the formidable Bonch-Bruyevich toiled around the clock on mounds of paper work. Behind a half-partition stood an iron bed, headed by nightstand and lamp, where during the first feverish days at Smolny, Lenin rested when sleep would have been impossible.

Alexandra Kollontai, a member of the Council of People's Commissars, described the seating arrangement at meetings in No. 67: "It was business-like. Or, to be more exact, downright inconvenient. We sat around Vladimir Ilyich and often at his back. Near the window stood Gorbunov's desk, where he took the minutes. Every time Lenin gave a direction to Gorbunov, he was obliged to turn around. But no one thought to move the desk; there were more important things to attend to. And so there were!"

The widespread belief that on the morning of October 26th, Lenin became head of state, is erroneous. Having master-minded the so-called "coup," he expected Soviet Power to assume official leadership; he never referred to *Sovnarkom* [Council of People's Commissars] and its satellite agencies as "The Government." During the initial period, his concern was to establish civil order; put an end to looting; get the trains running;. organize food supplies; establish monetary stability. With the convening of the Constituent Assembly a short time hence, the word "Provisional" (*vremennui*) inserted in the decree that established *Sovnarkom,* indicated that he considered this a temporary group. It was to be superseded by a Council of Soviets—a coalition of Left-Socialists and non-Party representatives.

The plan was disrupted when left-Mensheviks and left-S.R.s undertook to control both the transitional stage of post-October 25th and the composition of the forthcoming representative assembly, at the same time disavowing unilateral decisions by the Bolsheviks.

Initially they voted to bar the Bolsheviks from participation. Later, when it became evident that the masses were pro-Bolshevik, they relented, but with the proviso that Lenin and Trotsky be excluded. In addition to the bourgeoisie, the Bolsheviks were now confronted with two more adversaries: their own "left" co-socialists, *and the bureaucracy.* It was the beginning of civil war.

Managers and staffs of public agencies, holdovers from tsarism and the Provisional Government, promptly went on strike. Unionized railway workers refused to man the trains. Money and financial records were removed from banks. Speculators hoarded foodstuffs in order to drive up prices. The army officer corps joined the counterrevolution. Sabotage by the "Right" was rampant. When Alexandra Kollontai, newly appointed Commissar for Public Welfare, went to the Department of Charities, she found that a majority of the functionaries had gone on strike, and that Countess Panina, the former Minister, had sequestrated all the funds, leaving the poor in frightful conditions of want.

Thus untrained factory workers, soldiers, sailors, and peasants were assigned the gargantuan task of administering civil and military government. Smolny was reduced to accepting any and all persons who seemed capable of leadership.

Since Russia was still at war with Germany, reorganization of the military was imperative. A towering young sailor named Pavel Dybenko was appointed naval commander-in-chief. In addition to being a subject of derision in the anti-Bolshevik press, Dybenko also became the object of Kollontai's affection. At age 45, Alexandra, too, reached out for whoever was at hand—in this case a young man of 28 with undeniable physical appeal. Ruddy-faced, bearded, broad-shouldered, "with the clear eyes of youth, he prowled restlessly about, absently toying with an enormous blue-steel revolver, which never left his hand!"* At variance with this image of ferocity was his placid face.

However, the levity regarding his qualifications was misplaced; as early as May 11, 1917 in Helsinki, Finland, he had been elected by fellow members of the revolutionary council as chairman of *Tsentrobalt*, an organization to control activities of the fleet in Helsinki Harbor, at Kronstadt in the Gulf of Finland, and at Petrograd and Reval [now Tallinn, Estonia].

Yet another aggravation intruded. Fantastic rumors of murder, rape and pillage were being circulated, some of them self-generated, others deliberately spread to discredit the Bolsheviks. But when the Petrograd City Duma sent committees to investigate, the more lurid gossip was discovered to be unfounded. In Smolny's corridor, tables were heaped with literature refuting the rumors, armfuls of which were taken by couriers for distribution around town.

Journalistic curiosity sent John Reed to the Military Committee for permission to visit the front. In fact, there were two fronts: one with the Germans, the other where Kerensky mustered an army of Cossacks and professional soldiers for a march on the Capital. In search of the latter, Reed boarded an ambulance going south. But no one seemed to know exactly where the front was! Beyond the village of Pulkovo, where a battle had raged the day before, the driver halted beside a squadron of sailors. "Where's the front, brothers?" "This morning," one replied, "it was about half a kilometer down the road. But the damn thing isn't anywhere now. We walked and walked, but we couldn't find it."

Proceeding along the highway, the travelers heard shots. An ambush! Hastily descending from the ambulance, they crept through a nearby woods,

---

* John Reed in *Ten Days. . .*

rifles cocked. In a small clearing, three soldiers were sitting beside a campfire. "What's going on?" "Oh, we were just shooting a rabbit or two."

Although armed with a pass signed by Lenin, Reed discovered that sentries posted along the road could not read, a deficiency that nearly led to his being shot as a spy. Nevertheless, he arrived safely at *Tsarskoye Selo* [Tsar's Village] where a holiday atmosphere prevailed.

In searching village houses for spies, the victorious Red Guards had found Plekhanov ill in bed. Now sixty years old, "our Georgii" had returned to Russia after the February Revolution. It is probable that Vera Zasulich accompanied him. When questioned about his politics, he stated testily: "I am a revolutionary who for forty years has devoted his life to the struggle for freedom!"

"But you have now sold yourself to the bourgeoisie!" exclaimed a workman.

Reed was taken first to the officers' club, later to Soviet headquarters in one of the palaces. "At the center table, I found the huge Dybenko bent over a map, tracing battle lines. In his free hand he carried, as always, the enormous revolver. Anon he sat down at a typewriter and pounded away with one finger; every little while he would pause, pick up the revolver, and lovingly spin the chamber." On a nearby couch, a young workman, wounded in battle, lay dying. "Peace is coming! Peace is coming!" he gasped, his face greenish-white. At length Dybenko left his maps and typewriter, and after flinging orders right and left, climbed into a waiting automobile and was off to conquer Kerensky.

A comedic tragedy was being enacted along the roads south of Petrograd—comic in its small, human details of ordinary people caught between two political forces contending for superiority; tragic in the deadly nature of a conflict that was tearing Russia apart.

In the early dark of autumn, Reed started back to the Capital, having hitched a ride on an army truck. The vehicle, traveling without lights because of the shortage of kerosene, contended for space on a highway swarming with civilians, artillery squadrons, trucks. People stumbled along in the muddy snow, cursing all who got in their way.

"Across the horizon spread the glittering lights of the Capital, immeasurably more splendid by night than by day, like a dike of jewels heaped on the barren plain.

"The old workman who drove held the wheel in one hand, while with the other he swept the far-gleaming Capital in an exultant gesture.

"'Mine!' he cried, his face all alight. 'All mine now! My Petrograd!'"

Kerensky, mounted on a white horse at the head of his troops—Sir Lancelot, or Napoleon—was about to ride off into the sunset, a flamboyant knight-errant fleeing to Elba from his Camelot in the Winter Palace.

Smolny's response to counterrevolution was to form the Cheka, a department of internal security, a national police force whose function was political. Local militia kept order in the streets and made arrests based upon infractions of civil and criminal statutes; their duties ended at the courts of law.

This institution was used later to vilify the Bolshevik Party. Historically, such an organization, at all times and in all places, becomes a self-perpetuating bureaucracy, a government within a government with its own secret army and legal department. However in winter 1917, the Cheka's sole function was the preliminary investigation of spies, saboteurs and counterrevolutionaries.

Of all those upon whom Lenin relied, the most unlikely was chosen to head the Cheka. Felix Djerzhinsky had been brutally handled in a tsarist prison of Russian Poland where, during a savage beating, his jaw was broken, leaving the left side of his mouth badly disfigured. Emaciated, racked by a persistent cough and, as an observer noted, "his eyes perpetually swimming in tears," he appeared on the brink of death. When approached about heading the Extraordinary Commission, he at first demurred. But when it became evident that no one else was willing or able to assume the onerous task, he agreed. "I know what history will say about me," he observed ruefully.

Petrograd's hostile city government, jealous of its prerogatives, compounded other disaffections, and for a time it seemed that predictions of the Bolsheviks' imminent fall were soon to be realized. Disregarding the storm breaking over his Party, Lenin, with single-minded determination, continued the course of Peace, Land and Bread. Next on the agenda was peace.

Carnage on western battlefields was an international horror. The recent entry of the United States on the side of the Allies [Britain and France] ensured victory over Germany and Allied control of the postwar world. Thus the territorial *status quo* would not only be preserved but amplified by Germany's colonial possessions. And as punishment for having started the war, Germany and Austria-Hungary would undoubtedly suffer territorial dismemberment, giving the Allies economic, and a degree of political, hegemony over Europe.

In the far east, imperialist Japan was awaiting a propitious moment for a full-scale invasion of Russia.

The Russians broadcast by wire, and through diplomatic channels, an appeal to all belligerents for an immediate cessation of hostilities. But the terms they projected—no annexations, no indemnities, the right of peoples to self-determination—were anathema to the Western imperialists. The offer was met with stony silence. Meanwhile, Smolny's appeal to the German Government for an armistice had been accepted.

Fearing that the Bolsheviks would conclude a separate peace with Germany, the Allies began preparations for blockade and invasion of Russia.

Less than two months after Red October, a Russian delegation met with the Germans at Brest-Litovsk, a small city in Russian Poland, to discuss terms for a peace settlement. Although unable to finalize an agreement, a truce provided the Russians with time to consider Germany's offer. Meanwhile, after being released from his post at the Military Revolutionary Committee, Trotsky was named Commissar of Foreign Affairs, thus becoming chief negotiator at the second and third Brest Conferences. Unfortunately, his flawed judgment, combined with characteristic individualism, led to a disaster for Russia on both the diplomatic and military fronts.

First, the impatient Germans broke the truce and renewed their march on Petrograd. Second, the Russians lost certain territorial advantages contained in the original German offer. Third, the Russian Government was, for safety reasons, forced to move to Moscow, further exacerbating the post-October chaos. The errors of diplomacy perpetrated by Trotsky might conceivably have been avoided had Georgii Chicherin been named Foreign Affairs Commissar prior to his actual appointment in March 1918. This remarkable man, an erstwhile aristocrat and onetime close friend of Tsar Nicholas, had been attracted to Socialism in the early 1900's; later, he subscribed to Lenin's program. Endowed with an elegant mind, intellectual brilliance and personal humility, he later rendered valuable service as a diplomat. Said an observer: "Chicherin outclassed all western diplomats."

Meanwhile, at Lenin's urging, a peace treaty was finally signed ("We simply cannot fight any longer"), which unleashed an angry storm of indignation in Russia, thus adding fuel to the incipient counterrevolution. The same malcontents in the Ukraine and elsewhere who had been supporting a rapprochement with Germany, now turned on the Bolsheviks for their solution to a war already lost. When the Ukrainian *Rada* [parliament] signed a separate peace with Germany, it was "patriotic"; When Lenin's Bolsheviks, in the name of Soviet Russia, did likewise, it was "betrayal of the Revolution." "Each person views the world from his own belfry" goes the saying. Treason or pragmatism? Or mere self-interest? Dissident nationalities within Russia were trusting Germany to release them from "the stranglehold of Great Russians." Did they truly believe that predatory, imperialist Germany would liberate them?

In early January of the New Year (1918), Smolny became embroiled in controversy about the Constituent Assembly, during which it (Smolny) was accused of breaking up the convocation at the point of a bayonet .

Shifting opinion within the Social Revolutionary Party had resulted in a split which occurred *subsequent* to the election of delegates to the Assembly. Prior to Red October, a group of "right" S.R.s, together with the elitist right-wing Constitutional Democrats, comprised a powerful bloc. In many ways, the Assembly's composition, based upon pre-October delegate rolls, resembled that of the deposed Provisional Government and Kerensky's *Salvation of Revolution.*

Amid bitter debate in the Council of People's Commissars, Lenin argued that balance was presently weighted on the "right." In his opinion, "All Power to the Soviets" was about to go down to oblivion, and he was probably correct. In a contest between two representative bodies—in this case the Congress of Soviets representing the underdogs of society, and the Constituent Assembly, a coalition of socialists and bourgeoisie—history had shown that the upper classes eventually gained control. "Not so!" shouted the Opposition. The resignation of five members of *Sovnarkom*, followed (among others) by that of Kamenev and Zinoviev from the Bolshevik Party's Central Committee, was accompanied by bellicose statements about coalition. To these Lenin responded: "In the Congress of Soviets, we—Bolsheviks—hold a clear majority. It is for us, therefore, to form a government." He did *not* say: "We, the Bolshevik Party, are the government." [A huge majority of so-called Bolsheviks were adherents rather than card-carrying Party members.]

What actually transpired?

Louise Bryant came to Russia as an observer of the Revolution. Although an ardent Socialist, she at first disapproved of Lenin and was condescending in her appraisal of the Bolshevik efforts toward social innovation. A journalist like her husband John Reed, she poked about the thoroughfares, side streets and *pereyloks* of Petrograd in search of enlightenment and material for articles. On January 18th (1918), with a pass obtained from Smolny, she insinuated her way into Taurida Palace where a rump session of the Assembly had just convened. After obtaining a seat in the press gallery, she began taking notes on the proceedings. During that long night of deliberations, a declaration of the rights of the toiling masses of Russia—peace, land distribution, the validity of Soviet Power, Finland's independence, federation of the Russian (Soviet!) Republics, etc., etc. etc. etc.—was put to a vote *and defeated*.

The Bolshevik spokesman demanded the floor. "In its present state," he declared, "the Constituent Assembly is a result of the relative party power in force before the great October Revolution. The present counterrevolutionary majority of the Constituent Assembly, elected on the basis of obsolete party lists, is trying to resist the movement of workers and peasants . . . We therefore withdraw from this chamber."

Bryant observed: "Without the radical element, the Constituent Assembly was dead." After passing resolutions on peace and land distribution that resembled the Bolshevik program, it went on to proclaim the Russian State to be a Democratic Federated Republic [non-Soviet]. It also voted to bring the Allies into discussions about peace with Germany, thus negating the Bolshevik policy of unilateral dealings with the enemy.

At four in the morning, yawning Kronstadt sailors stationed at the door for security purposes, suggested that everyone go home. "We want to get some sleep," they said.

Louise Bryant's account of the foregoing would be less valid had she been a Bolshevik partisan. She followed the turbulent events as a skeptic and mere bystander; however she provided a primary source for the historical record.

The Bolsheviks' subsequent act of officially dissolving the Assembly was approved by the Third Congress of Soviets. Nevertheless, Lenin had agonized over the move. It is probable, however, that the Assembly would have disintegrated of its own political impotence; the Soviets were already performing tasks proposed by an assemblage riven with controversy and indecisiveness.

The land question was resolved by a sweep of the pen: confiscation of ecclesiastical, imperial and great private estates (without compensation), and nationalization of all land. Distribution of land among poor peasants was to be administered by land committees elected at the local level. This epoch-making edict was not a Bolshevik invention but part of the platform of the Social Revolutionary Party. It was, however, the principal factor that isolated Russia from the rest of the world. Private ownership of land was the cornerstone of capitalist societies who regarded infringement on that right as the devil's work, to be countered with the might of armies and slander of the most outrageous virulence. Forgotten in the barrage of western indignation was the fact that *personal* property—houses, furniture, anything resting *on* the land—remained inviolate. Nor was this provision transgressed, then or later, by the new government.

On the other hand, production and distribution of crops needed to feed the cities and deprived areas of the country were centrally regulated for the same reason that livestock—nominally "personal property"—was subject to expropriation. [Western society recognizes the "right of eminent domain" in the interest of the commonweal.] Under then prevailing conditions, hoarding was not only illegal but morally criminal. For a nation at war, extraordinary measures were necessary for survival.

The October Revolution had raised popular expectations, with the *narod* anticipating immediate benefits. But "my Petrograd," on paper a concrete promise, faded in the reality of civil war and invasion by foreign powers. This unfulfilled commitment nearly proved fatal to the Russian nation and its leaders.

20. Counterrevolution and Invasion

The Allies' defeat of Germany in November 1918 released their troops to launch a massive military offensive against Russia. To the civil war was now added a purpose to assault by multinational armies storming in from every direction. Even remote Vladivostok, Russia's principal port in the Far East, staggered under the blow of hostile powers. Parading through its streets with fixed bayonets, foreign troops passed before the Stars and Stripes, the French Tri-color, the British Union Jack and Japan's Rising Sun—symbols of conquest swaying in the bitter offshore wind.

In an unparalleled act of greed and malice, the Allies recruited their own allies: disgruntled Finns, Poles, Estonians, Letts, Lithuanians, Baltic Germans; and whoever held a long-standing grudge against Russia's tsarist past, or distrusted her Soviet present. Well-equipped armies struck at starving Russian workers and shivering, ill-clad peasants whose feet were bound in rags.

The Government and Bolshevik Party Headquarters moved to Moscow in March 1918. By the end of April, German armies controlled the Ukraine and the Crimea, the Japanese were advancing in Siberia from Vladivostok, and the Turks had seized Batum. Four months later, British and French troops moved into Archangel, and a French force invaded southern Russia. On August 14, the United States landed troops in northwestern Siberia. Independent right-wing governments were springing up in Siberia and the south-central provinces.

Foreign intervention operated in concert with the counterrevolutionary "White" army, now a formidable adversary led by tsarist generals and fueled by Western money and supplies. Red Russia was under deadly siege from all quarters. But a psychological blow was yet to come when the British fleet steamed into the Gulf of Finland and proceeded to bombard the Russian naval base at Kronstadt, a mere cannon-shot from Petrograd. As a result of the blockade of all her ports and other points of entry, Russia was starving.

Military and political experts abroad predicted the imminent fall of the Bolsheviks and their Soviet establishment, but they reckoned without the energy of a workers' and peasants' army mobilized by Trotsky. Clad in spotless uniform, kepi and polished boots, he traveled about the truncated Soviet state, a human tornado exhorting the exhausted *narod* to organize in defense of their revolution. And rise they did, a ragged army carrying a bizarre assortment of weapons, including spades and broom handles. Many of the "warriors" were women and young boys and girls.

Little by little, Trotsky transformed this motley company of defenders into the Red Army—disciplined, reasonably well-supplied from the Center, imbued with the determination to win regardless of personal cost.

Meanwhile, Red Finland turned White under the leadership of Baron Karl Gustav Emil von Mannerheim, Marshal of the Finnish Republic—established by Lenin and Karl Viik! The Baron's German name may have influenced his politics, but he was a national hero to the Finnish bourgeoisie. Not content with victory at home, he joined with Allied forces to invade Russia from northern Karelia.

With the collapse of Finland's proletarian revolution, many leaders and followers of the "left" fled to Russia. Among those mentioned in this narrative were Kustaa Rovio, Hildur and her family, and the Latukkas.

Rahja joined the Finnish-Russian Red Army and fought in Karelia. Karl Viik remained in Finland where, as a member of the Seim, his activities on behalf of Lenin were unknown beyond a small circle of colleagues.

Shotman died in 1937, a victim of the Stalin purges. Rovio "disappeared" during the purges, presumably another victim.

Yalava, having eluded arrest on either side of the frontier, continued to shepherd his locomotive through the evergreen forests of rural Karelia. After retirement, he lived to the age of seventy-six.

Two more years would elapse before peace came to Russia. During the interim, her history was one of fierce battles waged on all fronts of her vast domain. But despite the combined strength of White and foreign armies, Red Russia would triumph. Victory was in sight when the Allies faced defection among their own troops. First, a contingent of French mutinied after witnessing the frightful conditions under which common people were fighting for their revolution. When this perception spread to other foreign armies, the invading powers were forced to withdraw.

The most hated man in Red Russia was Winston Churchill, the wealthy British aristocrat who called Lenin "a deadly virus imported to infect the Russian people." As Secretary of War, Churchill utilized his considerable influence to bring about the Bolsheviks' downfall. But even their friends did not admire the tsarist generals. Denikin, Kolchak, Kornilov, Krasnov, Yudenich, and a "Baltic Baron" named Peter Wrangel were personally ambitious, cold and cruel. Each aspired to be military dictator of a resuscitated Russian Empire.

In Germany, defeat unleashed a revolution in which the "left," like Russia, battled against a powerful bourgeoisie. Three years earlier, Rosa Luxemburg's impassioned political prose had landed her in a German prison under "preventive custody" or "protective custody," depending upon how one interpreted the intent. "The spectacle is over," she had written.

The trains carrying reservists are now leaving in silence without the ecstatic

Soldiers, Nurses, and Lenin, 1918-19 (Lenin 4th from left, front row)

farewells of fair maidens. The crisp atmosphere of the pale rising day is filled with the voices of a different chorus: the hoarse clamor of hyenas and vultures reaping the battlefields. Ten thousand tents, regular size, high quality!! One hundred thousand kilograms of bacon, cocoa powder, ersatz coffee, immediate delivery, cash only! Grenades, lathes, ammunition pouches, matchmakers for war widows . . . serious offers only! The hurray-patriotic, widely advertised cannon fodder is already rotting in the battlefields . . . The well-groomed, cosmetic face of virtue, culture, philosophy, and ethics, order, peace, and constitution slips, and its real, naked self is exposed. The rapacious beast breaks loose . . . and the bourgeoisie's plague-infested breath spells the doom of mankind and culture. During this witches' Sabbath a disaster of world-wide magnitude occurred: the capitulation of the international social democracy.

One day before the Armistice, she was released from prison and immediately resumed her political activity. With her formerly luxuriant black hair gray and shorn, with features altered by declining health and the twilight of a prison cell, she went to Berlin. There in the vortex of revolution, she continued to inveigh against the spinelessness of German Social Democracy. She knew, however, that her days were numbered. A new "law and order" movement had arisen. The Frei-Corps, an ersatz citizens' militia, was composed of right-wing fanatics—law and order under the banner of national socialism, Nazi-ism, "death to Jews and Reds." Rosa was both Red and Jewish.

A few days after Luxemburg's release there was another: that of Corporal Adolf Hitler from a military hospital where he had been recuperating from the effects of poison gas on a Belgian battlefield. The corporal and the Frei-Corps were made for each other, and their eventual union begot the SS, Auschwitz, Treblinka.

"If the proletariat fails to make [international] Socialism a reality," proclaimed Rosa on New Year's Eve 1918, "we shall all go down to a common doom."

In January 1919 Germany's bourgeois government, playing the role of provocateur, fabricated a myth called the "Spartacus Uprising" in order to justify apprehending Rosa, her colleague Karl Liebknecht and their followers. Although heretofore negligent of personal safety, the pair sought refuge in a Berlin working-class district. Shortly afterward they were betrayed by a spy, arrested and taken to counterrevolutionary headquarters in the Hotel Eden. Upon entering, Liebknecht was struck on the head with rifle butts. Although bleeding, his request for a bandage was denied. Instead, he was taken together with Rosa before a Captain Pabst for questioning, then turned over to armed guards for transport to Berlin's Moabit Prison.

In the meantime, counter-orders had reached the hotel for Rosa and Karl to be murdered. While being dragged to a waiting automobile, Karl was again struck on the head. The car headed for Tiergarten where he was shot and his body dumped in a thicket. Later the killers brought it to a morgue. "Shot while trying to escape" was their report.

While Rosa was being escorted from the hotel under guard, she was struck on the head with a rifle butt by a trooper named Runge. Taken half dead to an automobile, she was again struck and then shot at point-blank range. As the car crossed Liechtenstein Bridge over the Landwehr Canal, its passenger door swung open and her body was tossed into the freezing waters below. Not until spring did it surface.

Franz Mehring, one of the Spartacus triumvirate, was disheartened by Rosa's death and died, a broken man, two weeks later. The Frei-Corps' next victim of note was Rosa's friend, Leo Jogiches, murdered two months after the January 15, 1919 double murder.

When the news reached Moscow, a day of mourning was declared for "Comrades Rosa and Karl."

For most of her political career, Luxemburg had been outspokenly critical of certain Lenin policies. But towards the end, having witnessed the force of counterrevolution, she relinquished her belief in "gradualism" as an alternative to armed confrontation. The *volte face* was verified when, under her direction, the Spartacus League became the German Communist Party. Her death was a deadly blow to Germany's left-wing Socialism.

Russian Marxists had long believed that in the absence of world revolution, a Russian socialist state would not long survive. Of particular interest to them was the prospect for revolution in Germany, a country whose Social Democratic Party was the most vigorous and best organized of the western socialist movements. As a result of the war, Germany was presently in ferment. When the German S-D's split into two left-wing factions [including the Spartacists], conditions appeared to be ripening for a final showdown. Marx had once stated unequivocally: "France will begin it, Germany will complete it." But in the early 1920's no one—including the Russians—could have foreseen that Germany, despite indications to the contrary, would become the principal foe of international Socialism.

Klara Zetkin was more fortunate. Residing in Stuttgart, she eluded the long reach of Berlin's right-wing fanatics and went on to espouse Rosa's legacy until forced to flee to Russia. As eyewitness to Hitler's rise, Zetkin understood what was in store for Germany, and by forswearing Social Democracy she acted with prophetic insight.

Russian life was not all battlefields and blood. Within the Kremlin walls, comrades struggled with the enormous task of building a new state apparatus. The result was a plethora of acronyms multiplying like rabbits in a congenial environment. For example, Nadya's department was *Proletkultye* [Proletarian Culture-Education], and *Sovnarkom* substituted for Soviet-Narod [People's]

Commissariat. The jargon, like the proliferation, taxed not only the memories but also the sanity of those required to deal with it. And foreign journalists, being initiated into the mysteries of a Socialist State, were particularly hard-pressed to unsnarl this word jungle for their readers back home.

Lydia Fotieva's job as secretary to *Sovnarkom* quickly became unmanageable as communications began pouring in from all quarters. When Lenin undertook to answer them, Marya Glasser and two other young women were hired on a part-time basis. Marya's expertise was shorthand, Fotieva was in charge of typing, note-taking and office organization; the other girls helped out when the load became excessive.

Some correspondents were brazenly outspoken, and had the girls been less sober-minded, they would have succumbed to mirth. One gentleman from a distant town wrote indignantly that the billeting of Red soldiers in his house had dislodged him from his bedroom and forced him to sleep with his wife. "Are you so immured in the Kremlin," wrote the man, "that you don't know what's going on out here?" To which Lenin responded: "Now wouldn't it be just too bad if you had to sleep with your wife when our brave Red Soldiers are in need of a night's rest?!"

There was often a reprimand. When Lenin discovered that a large healthy tree on state property had been chopped down, he wrote the Russian George Washington responsible for this act: "For shame! You have destroyed what belongs to the People!"

Nadya, too, received a large volume of correspondence, usually from women requesting help in some personal, domestic or financial matter. But rather than burden her husband's overworked secretaries she wrote her own replies in longhand. (Lenin wrote many personal letters by hand. Occasionally he would peck out a reply with two fingers on a typewriter with clouded type, the letter filled with crossings out and corrections above the line.)

Besides official callers, the Kremlin received a stream of visitors from among the people. War widows, workers from some distant factory; peasants in sheepskin coats often walked hundreds of miles to bring a token of appreciation. When workers at a textile mill sent a gift of suit-length cloth made there, he responded:

> I thank you heartily for your greetings and your gift. I will tell you as a secret that you ought not to send me any gifts. I earnestly request you to spread this secret among the workers as widely as possible.
>
> Please accept my best thanks, greetings and wishes.
> Yours,
> V. Ulyanov (Lenin)

Other persons came to offer suggestions, or to advise, or complain about conditions at home. None of these humble ones were turned away. When Lenin discovered that they had been kept waiting in the anteroom or downstairs, he gave orders to admit them not later than fifteen minutes after the appointed time for an interview.

On the personal side, Revolution and the lifestyle that had preceded it were beginning to take their toll. First, Nadya's friend Apollinariya died. Many other comrades who survived typhus and cholera contracted tuberculosis, often a result of the debilitating effects of malnutrition.

Lenin and Bonch–Bruyevich

And since cleanliness depended upon soap, its present scarcity or nonexistence resulted in nationwide epidemics. The Soviet Government plastered the walls of city and village with posters in which figures were depicted in the act of washing heads and clothing. "Comrades! Fight now against infection!" Government primary and secondary schools were being established from the Neva to the Pacific; but in many classrooms the heads of boys and girls were shaved in order to prevent typhus-bearing head lice.

"Dear Grandpa Lenin," wrote one little girl from a remote village, "we are learning a lot of things at school, and we wash our hands before every meal."

The insidious, creeping disease of tuberculosis spared few of the Party and Government hierarchy, causing Lenin to bombard them with stern commands to take care of their health. Nor were these reprimands intended only to preserve them for revolutionary work. To Lydia Fotieva, his "duty secretary," [term for office worker as distinct from administrator of a secretariat] he dictated countless letters offering aid to sick children, young people and adults who were strangers to him. His fear of illness became obsessive. On one occasion, Fotieva and Lenin's sister Maria were playfully throwing snowballs at each other in the Kremlin courtyard. While Lenin watched, a snowball hit Maria on the head. "He immediately rushed over," said Fotieva, "and began dusting off the snow so it wouldn't fall on her neck . . . It was his habit to fasten her galoshes, carefully questioning her on how she 'felt.'"

Under the stress of recurring crises, Nadya's health again deteriorated, and from time to time she was confined to a rest home. The building was located near a woods where pickpockets lurked. Lenin, usually on foot but occasionally by automobile, visited her daily, bringing a bottle of milk. One time the car in which he rode was held up by thieves. "I'm Ulyanov-Lenin," he said, only to meet with blank stares. Relinquishing his coat, he climbed out of the car and continued on foot, still clutching the bottle of milk.

At home, Nadya was often ill in bed. "During meetings of the Council of People's Commissars," noted Fotieva, "he would give me a key to the apartment and ask me to find out how she was feeling."

During periods of improved health, Nadya collaborated with Lunacharsky in the Department of Education. Together they went to work on an innovative curriculum in which reform of the Russian alphabet was a priority. Lunacharsky is credited with eliminating certain alphabet letters and symbols which cluttered the pages of Russian print.

As a result of the war, Russian industry was decimated, creating an acute need, not only for factories, but for skills in the technical arts and applied sciences. Some of those who formerly qualified for such positions were victims of the war; others refused to work for the new régime and vented their anger through sabotage of equipment. It was imperative, therefore, to train a new generation of technicians. Nadya played a leading role in the establishment of

Lenin, Nadya and peasants at Kashino

polytechnic institutes and supervision of their curricula. "It was she," noted Louise Bryant, "who devised the new scheme of adult education which Lunacharsky told me has proved highly efficient."

But in order to industrialize all areas of a huge country, it was necessary to provide electric power. To the slogan "All Power to the Soviets" Lenin added "Russia is Socialism plus electrification." In time, whole towns and villages abandoned their kerosene lamps.

During this period of internal reform, Russia converted to the Gregorian calendar, eliminating the 13-day lag that today confronts historians attempting to reconcile dates prior to 1918. Another innovation did little to improve the face of Bolshevism besmirched by the west. "Social Democracy," declared Lenin, "is a shibboleth both false and demeaning. Didn't Social Democrats betray us by joining the bourgeoisie? Henceforth we, the former Russian Social Democratic Labor Party shall be known as Communists. We are inheritors of the Paris Commune of 1871 and of Marx's dictum."

The Bolshevik attitude toward religion resulted from Russia's particular experience in which tsarism and the Orthodox Church had united to subjugate the masses. Lenin and Nadya were not militant atheists, but their espousal of Marxism presupposed a negative view of what they considered to be religion's stultifying influence on the *narod*. The Kremlin's sole official act, however, was to separate Church and State. "If you want the Church," it said, "you must support it privately. The State will no longer subsidize religion."

There were, however, many Bolshevik leaders and journalists who favored a broadside against Russian Orthodoxy. Lenin disagreed. "I understand," he said on one occasion, "that the newspapers carried a letter or circular about May Day, which said: expose the lie of religion, or something to that effect. This is not right. It is tactless. Just because it is the Easter holiday, we should recommend something *quite different*: not to expose the falsehood, but absolutely to avoid any affront to religion" [emphasis by Lenin].

On the other hand, the Party issued an order to expel members who practiced religion. It was the Party's hope that the demise of Russian Orthodoxy among the masses would occur through a process of enlightenment.

Substituting for the solace of religion was a plan for universal social insurance that covered unemployment, illness and old age. Countess Panina had rendered valuable service within the framework of her time. But what had formerly been charity now became a right, no longer dependent upon the sporadic efforts of a few upper-class philanthropists.

21. Peace and Transition

Lenin's removal to Moscow, together with his wife and sister Maria, had been undertaken in haste amid the threat of Petrograd's fall to the enemy. Since no preparation had been made for permanent lodging, they were taken to the National Hotel which overlooked the Kremlin and Red Square. Their rooms were located on the third floor *(deuxième étage)*. The hotel was swarming with foreign journalists, second-string diplomats, and wealthy business-men whose wives were in expensive fur coats.

Grown thin and haggard, Lenin now resembled the "old man" affection-ately referred to in his younger days. Once, on his way up in the elevator with Nadya, he apologized to the other occupants of the cage: "It's only one floor up, but I'm too tired to walk."

By virtue of intellect, dedication and organizational skill, Lenin was now acknowledged to be head of state. He was not impressed, however, and con-tinued to cling to his former title: Chairman of the Council of People's Com-missars. Still wearing the old Swiss jacket and ill-fitting suit, he went about the streets of Moscow like an ordinary citizen.

Nor did habits change when the family moved into an apartment prepared for them in one of the Kremlin buildings. Three small bed-sitting rooms, a dining room and kitchen were comfortable, if not elegant, but their air of per-manence pleased the family. Nadya decorated the place with potted plants, Maria hung portraits of her mother and elder sister Anna. Above Lenin's bed was a photograph, enlarged from a snapshot taken when he and Nadya were guests at a country gathering of peasants.

After a bloody battle between Reds and Whites, Moscow had been liberated into Soviet hands, and the city's proletarians were elated to have Lenin in their midst. Disregarding fatigue and the enormous burdens of state, he accepted numerous requests to address worker gatherings. Unattended by an armed guard, he mingled with vast crowds in the streets and factories.

The preceding January, while returning with Fritz Platten and several oth-ers from a large meeting in one of Moscow's former military establishments, a bullet whizzed through the automobile in which they were riding, barely missing Lenin but slightly wounding Platten. Was Lenin now, as earlier, too preoccupied to take account of his personal safety, or merely fatalistic?

At 7:45 p.m. on August 30, 1918, the telephone jangled on Nadya's desk. Upon lifting the receiver, she heard a distracted voice: "Vladimir Ilyich has just been shot."

Several minutes earlier, a young woman had fired a pistol at Lenin as he left the Michelson Factory after addressing a crowd of a thousand workers. With wounds in chest and shoulder, he is carried to a waiting automobile. Physicians examine him and find that his collar-bone has been splintered and the left lung punctured. No operation is performed to remove the bullet, and he is brought to the Kremlin apartment and laid on the bed of his study-sleeping room. Is he dead? No. Is he about to die? No one knows.

Meanwhile, the would-be assassin has been taken to security headquarters for questioning.

"Your name?"

"Fanya Kaplan."

"Your real name?"

"Fanya Kaplan."

"Once again, your real name?"

"Well . . . Dora Kaplan."

"What is your political affiliation?"

"Social Revolutionary."

"Ah, we understand; a terrorist."

No reply. Then Fanya bursts out: "He—*that man*—has betrayed the revolution!"

Bruce Lockhart was assistant attaché at the British legation. While technically removed from partisanship in Russian politics, he became an interested observer and eventually an activist. As a self-confessed spy for the west, and a "white" sympathizer, he was picked up by Djerzhinsky's Cheka and imprisoned pending investigation. "I was alone in my cell," Lockhart recalled,

> when the door opened and a young woman was brought in. She was not particularly attractive—dark hair and sallow skin. She passed me without speaking and went to the window. Resting her elbows on the sill with her chin cupped in one hand, she stared vacantly out. Later, when they came for her, she seemed indifferent to her fate. I never saw her again.

Together with many socialists abroad, and curious to observe what was transpiring in Russia, Angelica Balabanova came from Rome to Moscow. Because of her importance in the Italian Socialist Party, she was invited to the village of Gorki where, to everyone's amazement, Lenin was recovering from the attack.

"There was a first moment of intense emotion when I saw him with his arm in a sling. Later, I brought up the subject of the fate of the woman who had tried to kill him. He became embarrassed. 'They (indicating the authorities) will have to decide' he said. I think he would have spoken more freely if he had not been personally involved. The thought that someone should be executed for having tried to kill him was extremely painful to him."

Following an afternoon of discussion, she joined the family for supper. After the meal, Angelica urged him to rest. Before leaving, she was alone for a few minutes with Nadya. "Although I had never been on intimate terms with her, she threw her arms around me and sobbed: 'A revolutionist executed in a revolutionary country? Never!'"

In her memoir, Balabanova added: "I should describe what I have called 'supper' with them. On a little covered balcony, together with half a dozen scrawny peasant children and two cats, we ate a bit of bread, a tiny slice of meat, and some cheese—which I had brought from Sweden. He wouldn't accept the cheese until I assured him that most of it would be distributed to the children of Moscow."

She then went on to accuse Lenin, and presumably his wife, of false humility. Balabanova's journalistic style was one of "Yes, but . . .", neutralizing each positive with a negative.

Her assumption that Dora (Fanya) Kaplan was later declared to be alive and exiled to Siberia, was probably incorrect. At the time Lenin was attacked, a high-ranking Party official in Petrograd, Uritsky, was assassinated, also by an S.R. terrorist. Both acts, together with foreign intervention and the escalating counterrevolution, initiated the Red Terror. Overnight, the relaxed demeanor of the Red Guards, noted by Louise Bryant and her husband, hardened. Gone was the tolerance that had pardoned Countess Panina, the Government Ministers, the junkers and a host of other dissidents arrayed against the present regime. If what followed was indeed a "terror," the murder of Lenin would have unleashed forces of unspeakable brutality. As it was, the *Cheka* went into high gear, rounding up suspects, and meting out stern punishment.

There is scant record of public trials and official executions while Lenin was alive. Murders and executions occurred when an outraged populace took matters into its own hands. In situations where acts of terror assumed the character of mass attacks, the Government countered with military force, and countless innocent persons died in the crossfire. Likewise, house-to-house searches for terrorists netted both guilty and innocent. Zinoviev's "Red Terror" in Petrograd was described as particularly bloody.

In other instances, the Terror was perpetrated by drunken or irresponsible soldiers and sailors whose sudden liberation from tsarist tyranny unleashed pent-up emotions. In an effort to stem alcoholism, the Government stepped up a campaign that had begun in Petrograd when it discovered that the city was mined with wine cellars containing millions of gallons. Platoons were sent to smash bottles, using fire engines to pump rivers of wine into the streets. The danger of subversion by alcohol continued to threaten the Government's stability, as did outbursts of murder and looting and burning of landlord properties in the countryside.

However, the sinister reputation of Moscow's Lubyanka Prison—and by association, that of Djerzhinsky—was acquired during the Stalin years. But

Felix died a short time after Lenin. "Consider Djerzhinsky," Lenin said, referring to his deplorable state of health. "He looks like nothing at all."

Nevertheless, Lenin foresaw future abuses by the Cheka. For the present:
"They—tsarists and foreigners—all attacked us. Our only recourse was mer-
ciless, swift and instant repression. They call the *Cheka* an example of Russian
barbarism . . . But—we need to reform the *Cheka*." Djerzhinsky's organization
was largely a product of foreign intervention. Had the western powers
remained neutral, Russia would have solved her internal problems in shorter
time and with less bloodshed.

As for Lenin, the intended principal victim of S.R. terrorism, his authority
became superfluous to an organization that now perceived itself as guardian
of the Revolution. He was aware, however, that Dora's act was symptomatic of
growing popular discontent. Upon recovering his health, he began preaching
the doctrine of patience: "Under present conditions, our progress toward a
Socialist Order will be slow, painful, and fraught with errors both in planning
and implementation." But hotheads of the extreme "left" were in no mood to
wait for the millennium. Reverting to the old practice of "shoot the bastards,"
they refused to compromise with reality, with the sluggish process of change
further impeded by war, blockade and counterrevolution. Dora Kaplan's
impatience nearly altered the course of history.

The next victim of S.R. terrorism was Count Mirbach, the German Ambassador, whose assassination was intended to further provoke the Germans. A
large faction would have weocomed an invasion by Germany to save Russia
from the Bolsheviks!

Although the "Red Terror" gained worldwide attention, that of the Whites
was quietly ignored in the western press and among western diplomats and
governments. But the ferocious White Terror outdid its Red counterpart.
"Trains of death" crisscrossed Siberia with their cargoes of hapless individuals
suspected of Bolshevik sympathies, stopping only to discard emaciated
corpses. In the villages, suspects were rounded up and shot. The fate of captured Red soldiers was pre-ordained; tied to a stake, they were mowed down
by firing squad.

Among problems inherited by the Kremlin was a large contingent of
Czecho-Slovaks taken prisoner on Russia's Austro-German front. In an
attempt to divest itself of this unwanted horde, the government arranged for
its repatriation via East Siberia. But after being loaded aboard the Trans-Siberian express, they detrained and joined the Whites. They were to play a fateful
role in the life of Tsar Nicholas, his wife and five children.

After the February Revolution, the Imperial Family had been taken under
guard to the city of Tobolsk in West Siberia where they were lodged in the
Governor's mansion. Accompanying them were trunkloads of ikons and personal effects. Nicholas, happy to be relieved of the burdens of state, subsided

into a routine of domesticity, apparently forgotten by the "usurpers." Nor did his status change after Red October; for seven months the Bolsheviks likewise ignored him. But counterrevolution and foreign invasion had turned Siberia into an enemy camp. Worse, the Tsar was useful to the foes of Revolution as a symbol, a rallying point for the royalist White Army.

On May 2, 1918, as foreign and White armies advanced from the north, the Bolsheviks moved Nicholas and his family to Yekaterinburg. There was, however, no definite policy toward the Tsar, and the Government continued to improvise. Nevertheless, a tacit understanding existed between the Kremlin and Yekaterinburg officials that Nicholas should not be allowed to fall into the hands of the Whites.

> Nicholas Romanoff, ex-Czar of Russia, was shot July 16, according to a Russian announcement by wireless today.
>
> The former Empress and Alexis Romanoff, the young heir, have been sent to a place of security.
>
> The message announces that a counter-revolutionary conspiracy was discovered, with the object of wresting the ex-Emperor from the authority of the Soviet Council. In view of this fact and the approach of Czechoslovak bands, the President of the Ural Regional Council decided to execute the former ruler and the decision was carried out on July 16.
>
> – New York Times, July 21, 1918.

Who was responsible? The Council of People's Commissars? Lenin himself? Yekaterinburg was subsequently renamed Sverdlovsk. Why was Yakov Sverdlov, a small man with ribboned pince-nez and an unexceptional personality, so honored? With an extraordinary talent for organization, Yakov may have issued an order giving the Ural Soviet *carte blanche* discretion to deal with the Tsar. On the other hand, Sverdlov had been a leader in the Urals Party organization, and Yekaterinburg was the leading city of the district.

Rumors about the facts surrounding the Tsar's murder continued to circulate as late as December 1919—most, if not all of them, erroneous. Nor was the murder of the entire Imperial Family confirmed until many months later.

On December 7, 1919, relegated to page 20 of its first section, the *New York Times* printed the following curious item:

> CZAR'S JUDGE REPORTED EXECUTED BY SOVIET
> Pravda Tells of Punishment of Man Who Sent the Imperial Family to Death
> Copenhagen, Dec. 6—The Soviet Authorities in Russia have punished by death the individual held responsible for the execution of former Emperor Nicholas and his family at Yekaterinburg in June (sic) 1918, when the Czechoslovak troops were approaching that city, where the imperial

personages were then being held prisoners, according to a
dispatch to the Politiken from Kovno today.

The message quotes the Bolshevik newspaper Pravda of
Moscow as authority for this statement. The Pravda's
account states that M. Jachontoff, a member of the Yekaterinburg Soviet, has been condemned to death and executed
at Perm for ordering the execution.

Truth or falsehood? World opinion was on the side of the Tsar, now a mar-
tyr of Bolshevik barbarism. Was it an attempt to rectify a gross mistake? Or was
it merely the whitewash of a calculated, accomplished act? Future historians
would do well to seek verification of the existence of an M. Jachontoff and his
fate.

Royalist émigrés abroad wept hysterically, vowing eternal vengeance on
the "terrible man" in the Kremlin. But the Soviet Government had suffered for
its early benevolence when those pardoned joined the counterrevolution. In
war it's "them or us." Significantly, neither Lenin nor his wife referred to the
Tsar's murder.

With the interventionists in retreat and Germany finally subdued, with
counterrevolution in the final stages of defeat, a semblance of normalcy settled over Russia. Although news of the momentous events occurring there
reached the outside world in fragmentary or garbled form, it was sufficient to
attract a large number of foreigners intrepid enough to beat their way across
the border into this mysterious land of "Reds." Wild rumors continued to circulate abroad, including the one about Russian women being nationalized.
Many seeking admission to the Kremlin expected to confront a bearded monster with horns. Instead, they found an ordinary looking man with buttoned-
down shirt collar, vest and jacket, smiling amiably from his desk beside a
potted palm. Their momentary surprise was dispelled when he rose to greet
them with a vigorous handshake and motioned them to leather chairs before
the desk.

Sculptress Clare Sheridan was invited to Russia by Kamenev to carve his
bust. "It will also afford you an opportunity to see for yourself how things are,"
he said. But when she encountered her host's unfriendly wife (Trotsky's sister),
the project was abandoned. Instead, Kamenev suggested that she "do" Lenin,
an assignment that turned out to be one of the most bizarre of an already colorful life.

Clare was both beautiful and talented; she was also a cousin of Winston
Churchill.

Early one morning, armed with tools and buckets of clay, she arrived at the
Kremlin and was ushered into Lenin's "studio." Although his greeting was
friendly enough, for the remainder of the day he sat like a sphinx, his eyes
glued to a book while she worked. The silence was oppressive. Once or twice

she attempted to engage him in conversation, but after a polite response, he returned to his reading.

It was Nadya's practice to interrupt her husband's prolonged sessions in the office with a discreet tap on the door, indicating that it was mealtime. On other occasions, she added her portion of the day's bread ration to Lenin's which he kept in a drawer of his desk. From time to time he would absentmindedly reach for a piece of bread, unaware that his ration had been increased.

But at 4 o'clock, after a day in which neither artist nor subject had food or drink, Sheridan cleaned her tools, draped a moistened cloth over the bust and prepared to depart. "Tomorrow same time?" she queried. He nodded and rose from his chair with a polite word of dismissal. The following day was like the first. Hungry, puzzled and somewhat embarrassed, Clare studied him for signs of life in a face she expected to preserve for posterity. Still nothing. The silence, however, provided opportunity to view him at length and from close range, and her artist's eye absorbed details that began to appear in the clay taking shape beneath her hand.

"His expression was always thoughtful rather than commanding," she remarked. "He seemed to me the real embodiment of 'le penseur' [but not of

Lenin, 1920

Rodin's *The Thinker*] ... He looked very ill. The woman assassin's bullet was still in his body. One day his hand and wrist were bandaged; he said it was 'nothing', but he was the color of ivory."

Later, the atmosphere changed when Kalinin, President of the All-Russia Soviet, walked in. Lenin's features became animated as he talked with Kalinin. "After they had finished," Clare said, "Kalinin looked at my work and said it was 'khorosho' [good] and asked Lenin what he thought; Lenin laughed and said he didn't know anything about it, whether it was good or bad, but that I was a quick worker. When we were alone again, he seemed to unbend a little, so I took courage and showed him some photographs of my work." One of them was an idealized statue of Victory, whereat Lenin reprimanded her for making militarism—whatever the sacrifice and heroism— a thing of beauty. "War is hateful and ugly," he exclaimed. "Then," continued Clare, "hurriedly he went back to his chair in front of the big writing table as if he had wasted too much time. In another second I and my work existed no more." But when she had shown him a photograph of her son's sculptured head, "an expression of tenderness passed over his face."

When the bust was finished, he shook her hand warmly, said she had worked well, and that he thought his friends would be pleased. "Then, at my request, he signed a photograph." Lenin failed to recognize that the clay model—soon to be chiseled in marble from Clare's form—was itself a thing of beauty.

Klara Zetkin came to Russia in 1920 to discuss with Lenin the condition of German Social Democracy. After engaging in a verbal brawl with members of its Central Committee, she had resigned her position and thus found herself outside the mainstream of a movement to which she had devoted her entire adult life.

At age 63, her hair was turning gray, but the fiery spirit that had brought her to a position of leadership in Germany was unquenchable. Brimming with ideas, she almost [but not quite] talked Lenin to a standstill on the subjects of women's rights, art "bourgeois" and "proletarian," the Party, internationalism, the War.

It was during this visit that she became acquainted with Nadya. The two had met briefly in 1915 during a Women's Conference in Switzerland, but Klara's Moscow sojourn initiated a close and lasting friendship. She was unprepared for the simplicity of the Kremlin apartment; in Germany, the frock-coated leaders lived a comfortable "bourgeois" life.

"I found Lenin's wife and sister at supper which I was cordially invited to share," Klara related. "It was a simple meal in accordance with the hard times. It consisted of tea, black bread, butter and cheese. Afterward, his sister 'had to, for the honored guest,' find something 'sweet' and she discovered a pot of jam.

Lenin's family adhered strictly to living conditions of the laboring masses."

At a time when everyone's attention centered on Lenin, Zetkin's pen portrait of Nadya is unique. "Her kind face with its soft, tender eyes, showed
indelible traces of the illness that was dragging her down. Otherwise, she
remained the same, namely: the embodiment of simplicity, artlessness and a
certain chaste modesty. With her smooth hair gathered in back at the nape of
her neck in a simple knot, with her plain dress, she produced the impression
of a worker's wife . . . It would have been insulting and laughable to suppose
that she played the role of 'Lenin's wife.' She worked, carrying the worries
together with him, looked after him as she had done all her life, had done during the hard years of emigration. With sincere maternal care she transformed
the Lenin dwelling into a veritable 'hearth,' . . . in the sense of spiritual atmosphere which filled it and which reflected respect and unity among those working and living there. Their relationship was true, sincere, understanding and
warm-hearted."

When Lenin arrived, he found the three women in animated conversation
about art and education. After a "'joyous weocome" from his wife and sister, a
large cat appeared and leaped upon his shoulder, then curled up on his lap.
The setting reminded Klara of the many visits she had made to Rosa Luxemburg's apartment where a cat named Mimi was likewise a member of the family. "I immediately felt at home in the kindly, hospitable atmosphere," she said
of her first visit to the Kremlin.

Louise Bryant gained a similar impression of the apartment and its inhabitants. "Lenin adores his wife and speaks of her with enthusiasm. The first time
I told him that I wanted to meet her, he said: 'Yes, you must do that because
you will like her, she is so intelligent.'" Bryant described the apartment as spot-
lessly clean, although Nadya had no servant. There were quantities of books,
plants in the windows, a few chairs and a table. She thought "Madame Lenin"
a pale, scholarly woman, usually in poor health. "I found her both intelligent
and sympathetic. She has the same charm which Lenin has and the same way
of focusing all her attention on what her visitor is saying. When you go to his
office, he always jumps up and comes forward smiling, shakes hands warmly
and pushes forward a comfortable chair, leans forward and begins to talk as if
there was nothing else to do in the world but visit."

Male visitors, on the other hand, confined their interest to Lenin. Besides
the countless foreign journalists and socialists who sought admission were
persons driven hither by curiosity.

Kremlin apartment, October 6, 1920. The family is at supper.
"Well, Volodya, what happened today?"
"A man asked for an interview."
"Did you let him in?"

"Of course. He came all the way from England."

"Who was he?"

"H.G. Wells "

"Who?"

"H.G. Wells, a man of letters."

"What happened?"

"He told me about Socialism."

"What did you do?"

"Oh, not much, I mostly listened. He'll probably go home and write a book or something."

During the years of emigration, Nadya had involved herself in the Women's Movement. Together with Inessa, she collaborated with the "sisterhood" abroad led, among others, by Zetkin and fellow-Russian Ludmila Stahl. It was, however, a half-hearted effort on Nadya's part, and one that did not bring her the personal satisfaction she derived from educational work.

The feminism sweeping Europe never took root in Russia where the ideal was "equal" rather than "separate and equal"—a view of women's place in society far ahead of its time. Meanwhile, European women were forced to settle for their own movement in a male-dominated society.

Since Inessa was a free agent, she was able to travel about as an organizer for Socialist Feminism, but it is doubtful that she ever fully subscribed to "separate and equal."

During one of Zetkin's conferences with Lenin, she enthusiastically promoted a plan for an International Socialist Women's Congress. Although not discouraging her, he had mental reservations about its efficacy since it ran counter to his—and the Russian—perception of women as part of the social amalgam. His polite tolerance of militant feminism was neither boredom nor put-down, but resulted from a regard for women that transcended movements, conferences and feminist journalism.

After listening to Klara, he remarked:

> The true liberation of women is possible only through Communism. There is an unbroken connection between the position of women as people and members of society. We hope to fence them off from bourgeois movements like 'emancipation of women' . . . The women's question is part of . . . the proletarian class struggle . . The Communist women's movement must be "of the masses," must be part of the whole social mass movement.

He added: "It is sad, very sad that comrade Inessa is not here. She is ill and has gone to the Caucasus."

Inessa died on September 24, 1920, a victim of cholera, and her body was brought back to Moscow for burial. Chosen to give the funeral oration, Angelica Balabanova demurred "because a strange chill within me would have

Lenin, Simplest, most human, and
yet most far-seeing and invincible

John Reed

John Reed's comment on Lenin, in an album drawn up by delegates at the Second Congress of
the Communist International, July 1920

Lenin and Sverdlov watching airplanes

deprived my words of spontaneity." This mental reservation, however, did not prevent her from attending the burial, and the "strange chill" begot another kind of obituary that damaged the deceased far more than insincere words spoken at the graveside.

"I found myself in the immediate vicinity of Lenin," she wrote for posterity to scrutinize.

> Not only his face but his whole body expressed so much sorrow that I dared not greet him. It was clear he wanted to be alone with his grief. He seemed to have shrunk; his cap almost covered his face, his eyes seemed drowned in tears held back with effort. He moved forward, pushed by the crowd . . . as if he were grateful for being brought nearer to the dead comrade.

Balabanova's parting shot was another "yes . . . but": "This mood did not influence in the least his activity as statesman . . . From the funeral he went straight back to his desk."

If it is true that the quality of a life determines the degree and nature of bereavement felt by the living, then Inessa's death was indeed sad. At age 46, she had sacrificed her health to the service of the Cause. Balabanova's snide remark that Inessa had been a passive slave to Lenin and Bolshevism diminishes the value and extent of activities that were often overshadowed by more dominant personalities such as Kollontai, Zetkin and Luxemburg. Did Balabanova foresee her own death, alone in a simple apartment in New York City, unlamented by anyone?

Klara Zetkin was ill. The Russian climate had affected her lungs. One cold night after a conference with Lenin, she returned home with a fever, and for several days was confined to bed. Her room was on an upper floor of a Soviet rest home. Unfortunately the elevator was out of order, and when Lenin came to see her, he was forced to use the stairs. "How delightful!" he exclaimed sarcastically. "Another example to our enemies of our 'failed' Revolution." To Zetkin "he was solicitous as a tender mother."

"He inquired whether I was receiving medical care and suitable nourishment, asked what I needed, etc. Behind him I saw the loving face of his wife."

22. Final Journey—January 21, 1924

July 19, 1919

Nadya dearest,

I was very glad to hear from you. I sent a telegram to Kazan and, as I got no answer, sent another to Nizhny, and from there I today received a reply to the effect that the *Krasnaya Zvezda* is supposed to arrive in Kazan on July 8 . . . . I read the letters asking for help that sometimes come for you and try to do what I can.

I embrace you fondly and ask you to write and telegraph more often.

The message reached Nadya at Kazan where the vessel *Red Star* had moored during a long trip down the Volga. With hair askew and long skirt whipped by the wind, she had been dispensing propaganda along the route, talking with villagers and peasants about the aims of Soviet Russia. This thankless task had been undertaken notwithstanding ill health.

The following day Lenin received a wire from Kazan: "Arrived here today. Am well. Very much work. Are you keeping well?—Ulyanova."

In response, he wired back the same day: "We are all healthy." But despite these mutual assurances of well-being, the reality was quite different. On the 15th, she received another letter:

Nadya dearest,

I am taking advantage of K–'s visit to Perm to write you . . . Yesterday I received a letter from Molotov that you did have a heart attack; that means that you are *overworking* yourself. You must stick strictly to the rules and obey the doctor's orders . . . Yesterday and the day before I was in Gorki with Mitya and Anya [brother Dmitri and sister Anna]. The limes are in bloom. We had a good rest. I embrace you fondly and kiss you. Please rest more and work less.

The first sign of impending catastrophe appeared in Lenin's note to a colleague three weeks later: "I am not well. I have had to go to bed. Therefore, *reply by messenger.*"

As Russia's war economy and reconstruction tangled with the bureaucracy, Lenin became increasingly irascible. "*We are being sucked down* by a rotten bureaucratic swamp . . . The center of gravity of (our) activity must be a refashioning of our disgustingly bureaucratic way of work, a struggle against the red tape *which is killing all of us.*" (Emphasis by Lenin.)

He was equally annoyed by the unfocused discussions that frequently disrupted meetings of the various commissariats. "We keep sliding back to abstract theories instead of dealing with problems in a businesslike manner," he complained. "Personally, I am sick and tired of it, and quite apart from my illness, it would give me great pleasure to get away from it all. I am prepared to seek refuge anywhere."

"Anywhere" was the village of Gorki, conveniently distant from Moscow, which had been serving as a retreat from the Kremlin chaos. Close to the village stood a large manor house that had belonged to General Reinbot,* Governor of Moscow. Set on a hill amid picturesque landscaped grounds, the palatial dwelling had been expropriated by the government at the time its occupant fled to the west after Red October. When someone suggested it as a place of rest, Lenin acceded. Together with his family, he had first come here while recuperating from the bullet wounds. However, he and Nadya felt ill at ease in the opulent chambers and corridors, so they chose a cluster of small rooms in the north wing, a separate building.

For simplicity, their accommodations might have been in Smolny or even Shushenskoye. Lenin's work room was so small that it was necessary to stack books and periodicals in the windowsills. Furniture consisted of wooden beds, sofa, and a wardrobe that contained more books than clothing. Nadya occu-

House at Gorki where Lenin lived

---

* Reinbot married the widow of wealthy industrialist Mazarov who had been subsidizing the Bolsheviks. His ambivalent position "'between two stools" resulted in suicide.

pied the room next door, and an adjoining room was reserved for Maria. The "suite" also included a dining room at whose round table Lenin often worked. Each room was heated by a ceiling-high tile stove fueled with wood from the surrounding forest. "Only gradually did we get accustomed to Gorki," Nadya related. "Later on, we became acclimatized . . . Ilyich (Lenin) grew to love the balconies, the big windows."

Upon returning to Moscow in early autumn 1919, Lenin had apparently regained his health. Nevertheless, his wife and sister were alarmed by the mounting work load and his inability to sleep at night. Reluctant to nag him, they enlisted the aid of Yelena Stassova. "I decided to telephone him," Stassova said. "'Vladimir Ilyich, you should take a few days rest.' Over the wire, in a very annoyed voice, came the answer: 'Since when do you have license to order me about so freely?'"

Nadya and Maria customarily rose at 6 a.m., and one morning they found a note on the kitchen table: "Please wake me not later than 10 o'clock in the morning. It is now a quarter past four and I cannot sleep; I am quite well. If you do not wake me I shall lose another day and shall not be keeping a proper regimen."

The onset of serious illness occurred in December 1920, whereat the doctors sent him to Gorki and insisted that the family move into the central building called "The Big House." "I am so unwell," wrote Lenin to a comrade on the 30th, "that I am unable to do any work."

At the time of his present breakdown, he had been involved in reshaping the economy, and his impatience at the interruption exacerbated a physical condition that had not yet manifested the symptoms which later became identifiable. Although his illness was diagnosed as extreme fatigue, the cause was also thought to be a result of Kaplan's bullets still lodged in his body. Nevertheless, by late January of the New Year (1921), he once again appeared to have recovered. The family returned to Moscow.

In February 1921, Persia (Iran) and Soviet Russia signed a treaty of friendship which required Moscow to evacuate the province of Ghilan in northern Persia. Red troops had entered this province in 1920 in pursuit of counterrevolutionary units. Lenin favored the liberation of Ghilan. Nevertheless, Stalin sabotaged the agreement and sent arms and Soviet personnel to local chieftains in Ghilan with exhortations to organize Soviets.

The Soviet Ambassador to Teheran wrote to Lenin protesting Stalin's activities. In reply Lenin wrote to the Ambassador: "It seems to me that you are right." The Ambassador thereupon urged Riza Khan (the late Shah's progenitor), ruler of Persia, to march into Chilan and suppress the tribal leaders and particularly a certain Kuchik Khan who was supporting Stalin's policy and receiving support in return. Kuchik Khan froze to death hiding in the mountains. Riza cut off his head and displayed it in Teheran.

Among the soldiers Riza took were Russian prisoners from Stalin's Georgian province of Tula. In Moscow, Stalin was infuriated. His protégé had been killed. He blamed the Soviet Ambassador to Teheran. When the question was raised in a session of the Politburo, Stalin kept pressing his complaint.

"Good," said Lenin with a gleam in his eye, and he dictated to the stenographer. "Strict reprimand to the Ambassador for killing Kuchik Khan."

"No," someone said, 'it was Riza who killed Kuchik Khan."

"Good," exclaimed Lenin. "Strict reprimand to Riza Khan for killing Kuchik Khan."

"But we cannot reprimand Riza. He is not a Soviet citizen," Stalin objected. At this Lenin burst out laughing and so did the others. The matter was dropped." (Related by Georgii Chicherin who was present at the meeting.)

"One evening we decided to pay a visit to our young art student, Varya," Nadya remembered. "It was the famine year, but the youth were full of enthusiasm. They slept in the Commune almost on bare boards; they had no bread. 'But we have some grain,' said one student with face beaming. They cooked *kasha* for us out of that grain, although there was no salt." 'Varya' was Varvara Armand, Inessa's daughter. That year Lenin found a diplomatic post in Persia for Inessa's son, Alexander.

In March the New Economic Policy was announced: commodity exchange between proletariat and peasantry; a "tax in kind" to replace requisition of foodstuffs from the peasants. NEP's swing toward a modified form of free enterprise raised a storm of protest from Marxist purists who declared that Lenin was prostituting one of the basic tenets of Socialism. In meeting after meeting, he was forced to defend a policy dictated by prevailing conditions. Lenin correctly perceived that, regardless of Marxist theory, the people must receive immediate and concrete evidence of the benefits to be derived from Socialism.

Sovnarkom tackled another prickly issue. The backward and stubborn peasantry, wedded to primitive farming methods, resented interference from above—whether from Moscow itself or a meddlesome commissar. Collectivization (small peasant landholdings united for greater efficiency) quickly became a dirty word in the hinterlands, to be resisted by any available means. Lenin's method for overcoming peasant recalcitrance was persuasion, and it was partly for this that Nadya traveled down the Volga, talking, talking, using her prestige as Lenin's wife to convince these outlanders that they should voluntarily agree to the modernization of agriculture under state auspices and with state aid, the latter to supply machinery and agronomists. It was a program she was later forced to defend under quite different political conditions:

I talked with Zetkin about a meeting of collective farm workers. Afterwards she wrote them a letter in which she spoke about the importance of the collective arrangement and also of that which was in Stalin's speech . . . how women of the collective must enthusiastically listen and guide with effectiveness.

By the end of 1921, *Goelro* (state electrification under the direction of Gleb Krzhizhanovsky, friend of Lenin's Siberian days) and other commissariats were beginning to make inroads on social and economic problems. And on December 6th, because of impaired health, Lenin was granted a leave of absence. Once again the family retired to Gorki. "It was strange," noted playwright and novelist Maxim Gorky on a visit, "to see Lenin strolling in the park at Gorki. His image had become fused in one's mind with the picture of a man sitting at the end of a long table, competently, cleverly guiding the debates of his comrades."

As winter advanced, Nadya and Volodya considered making a trip to the Caucasus, Russia's "Riviera" where once the Tsars and now vacationing proletarians repaired for sunshine and rest. Both husband and wife agreed, however, that a visit to the Ural Mountains might be more beneficial. Neither plan materialized. In March 1922, Lenin suffered another relapse, and the puzzled doctors sent him to hospital for removal of one of the bullets. "I am sorry to delay writing," he apologized to a comrade. "I have just had surgery."

Lenin at Gorki, summer 1922

It is May 25, 1922. Gorki's birches and lime trees are beginning to bud, and along its numerous paths early wildflowers poke through the mossy turf. Encouraged by the sun, an occasional bird twitters from its perch among the quickening branches. Russia's tardy spring is slowly inching its way into the frost-bitten souls of her *narod*. But in an upper room of the Big House, Lenin lies paralyzed from a stroke that has affected his right arm and leg and impaired his speech.

To Maria falls the task of household manager and part-time nurse. And while Nadya shares the work, her primary chore is to serve as liaison between her husband and the Kremlin. Evenings are spent beside his bed where the two women reminisce about commonplace matters in the subdued tones of those who preside over a waning life.

As Lenin's condition worsened, it became necessary to inform the public, and on June 4th an official statement bluntly outlined the gravity of his illness. The physicians diagnosed arterio-sclerosis.

However, by October he had improved. Klara Zetkin, in Moscow to attend a Congress of International Communists (Comintern), has provided an emotional account of Lenin's presence at the gathering:

> A black cloud hung over my journey to Moscow because I had been informed that I would not be able to see or talk to Lenin. He who was so strong, so stoical, had been seriously ill. When I arrived at the hall, one who was apparently a gentleman of the old school approached me. "Mr. Lenin will soon be here," he exclaimed excitedly. I did not immediately react to the comical "Mr. Lenin" but jumped up and rushed to the door. Vladimir Ilyich was already there, strong as he had been before his illness. While I stood there laughing and crying like a child, Lenin reassured me. "Don't be upset," he said. "I am completely well and strong, for which I give thanks. What happened to me was a nasty trick. I can only hope that Nadya and Maria will not again be burdened with caring for an invalid. Meanwhile, world history in Russia marched forward without me. And since the comrades are overloaded with work, I am glad that I can relieve them a little." He had so far recovered that he was able to give a report on *Five Years of the Russian Revolution and Perspective on the World Revolution*.

In December another stroke ended Lenin's public career. The interval between his first attack and the Comintern gathering had been particularly stressful for Nadya. Her husband, worried about affairs of state, was demanding information ("you are keeping things from me"), and Nadya was torn between his nervous impatience and her own concern for his health. At first the doctors ordered her to withhold all business. Subsequently they allowed a few minutes each day for dictating and reading. There was a direct telephone line to the Kremlin, but its unreliability matched that of other public utilities, causing Lenin to complain vociferously. It became necessary for Lydia Fotieva to make regular trips to Gorki, bringing questions and returning with answers.

Fotieva was the prototype of an "old maid" secretary—meticulous, unimaginative, blindly devoted to her boss. Although not unattractive, her solemn face and simple attire marked her as one who had long ago relinquished any claim to a life of her own. Facts and figures were her *metier*. The exact number of letters and documents she transcribed, how many times Lenin was in his office—precisely what hour and how long he stayed—were more important than personal observations. Nevertheless, her bloodless accounts are valuable for their chronology of the progress of Lenin's illness. Notes in her journal indicated the state of his health and what he did on a given day. November 25, 1922, she wrote that Lenin was unwell and had stayed at the office only five minutes. "The doctors had ordered him to go away for one or even two months' rest. He left for Gorki at 6:15 p.m. on December 27th."

Shortly before he left for Gorki in December 1922, Fotieva reported that he was "in fairly good humor, joked, but was only worried about winding up affairs." Two days later "he found it very difficult to write; was not very cheerful; said he was feeling worse, had not slept that night; thought his illness might be final; gave directives about disposing of his books." After his first stroke, Nadya told Fotieva: "He looks all right, but then it is difficult to say . . . . He has no wish to go to Gorki."

Meanwhile, Stalin had blustered into his native Georgia with accusations of "deviationism" against local Party officials, a ploy he would later use with devastating consequences to the country at large and the Party. When this information reached Lenin, he directed the Kremlin to launch an investigation. "Just before I got ill," noted Fotieva, "Djerzhinsky told me about the Georgia incident, and this had a very painful effect upon me." Recalling an earlier incident in which Stalin, without authorization, had ordered a brutal invasion of Georgia by Red Army troops, Lenin now concluded that his Commissar for Nationalities was both erratic and dangerous.

On December 24th, he called Fotieva to take dictation. Sworn to secrecy, she typed five copies of a letter to be opened after his death. One copy he retained, three were given to Nadya, and Fotieva kept one for herself. Afterward, the rough draft was burned. This now famous document, called a "Testament," included a painstakingly worded message to the Party's Central Committee suggesting that Stalin's authority be circumscribed. It was not the first time that Stalin's character had come under suspicion, but Lenin, anticipating his own demise, recognized the power struggle that was already taking place.

In addition to several directives concerning the future of the Party, the Testament stressed the need for reorganization at the top. Speaking about the necessity for stability within the Party ranks, he wrote: "All measures must be taken to avoid a split . . . and the prime factors in the question of stability are such members as Stalin and Trotsky . . . I intend to deal here with . . . personal qualities ... Comrade Stalin, having become Secretary-General, has unlimited authority concentrated in his hands, and I am not sure whether he will always be capable of using that authority with sufficient caution."

Several days later he appended the following: "Stalin is too rude, and this defect ... becomes intolerable in a Secretary General. That is why I suggest that the comrades think about a way of removing Stalin from that post and appointing another man in his stead who in all respects differs from Comrade Stalin ... in being more tolerant, more loyal, more polite and more considerate of the comrades, less capricious, etc. This is not a (mere) detail, but one which can assume decisive importance."

Lenin has been castigated for the mildness of his cautionary statement. But a terminally ill man, separated by distance from the center of activity and concerned for the future of his Party, the Soviets, the Fatherland itself, would not in prudence have provoked a rift that could have toppled the system and precipitated another revolution. The divisive character of Russian politics in general had already begun to infiltrate the Bolshevik ranks. To preserve at least a semblance of unity within the hierarchy, Lenin devised an outwardly bland statement that would, nevertheless, send a signal to those in position to rein in the fractious and potentially dangerous Georgian. Or so he thought!

The shadow of Stalin hovered above Gorki. Upon learning of the Testament, he would panic; to be disinherited by Lenin was equivalent to ending his carefully constructed position in the Party.

But Trotsky's claim that Stalin told him that Lenin had requested poison is highly suspect; Trotsky and Stalin were already at loggerheads. First of all, Lenin was a fighter. And second, it is ridiculous to suppose that Nadya and Maria would stand by and allow him to commit suicide. His remark years earlier about the Lafargues' suicide was an abstraction. One may generalize about death during youth and health, but upon growing older, attitudes change. Lenin knew that his condition was worsening, but he would have rejected the idea of cutting short his life when there was still a chance for recovery and for useful service.

When Lydia Fotieva became temporarily ill, another duty secretary named Maria Volodicheva took over, and later the two women alternated in traveling to Gorki. Volodicheva supplemented Lydia's dry account with vivid descriptions of Lenin as his illness waxed and waned. When Marya Glasser was conscripted to assist, she too added a human touch, and together these three provided a day-to-day record of Lenin's last months.

In early February 1923, Volodicheva noted: "Outwardly he seems better—fresh and cheerful looking. As always, he dictates excellently. Without halting and seldom at a loss for words, he speaks rather than dictates. There is no compress on his head." But two days later he dictated more slowly and the compress was back on his head. Pale and obviously tired, he remarked: "It doesn't go well with me today."

When Marya Glasser saw him for the first time since his illness, she thought him paler than usual "but he looked well and cheerful." "He speaks slowly, gesticulating with his left hand and stirring the fingers of his right. No compress on his head."

"One day he was telling me an anecdote," Volodicheva said, "very gaily, laughing his infectious laugh. The next day he was pacing up and down, repeating words several times, obviously struggling with them. 'Help me,' he said, 'I seem to be stuck.' To my remark that I was his unavoidable evil for a short space of time, as he would soon be able to write himself, he said: 'Oh, that won't be so soon!' His voice sounded weary, with a hint of pain in it."

And so it went, the good days and the bad. But as the month progressed, the observant women knew that he was getting worse. Whereas he had once joked to Fotieva: "If I were at large," (at first he made a slip, then repeated, laughing) "If I were at large, I would easily do all this myself." He now complained of severe headaches. Fotieva added: "The doctors had upset him so much that his lips quivered. I said jokingly that I would treat him by suggestion and that he would have no more headaches."

Two days later he informed her that he was quite well, that he thought his was a nervous illness. "Nevertheless," she said, "he kept urging us to hurry with his requests."

The evening of February 14th, he called for Lydia; she had been working for him during the day and observed that his mind was quite clear. "That night there was an impediment in his speech, and he was obviously tired. He seemed very agitated about the Georgian problem."

At this point the entries broke off, indicating that Lenin was too ill to work. Not until March 5th did a duty secretary return to Gorki. On that day it was Volodicheva. "I came, but he put off dictating one or two letters, saying he was not very good at it just now." When she returned on the 6th, "he felt bad."

Recently he had been upset. Lenin's presentiment about Stalin was confirmed by an episode that so disturbed and frightened Nadya that she broke her usual silence about personal matters. Driven to distraction by her husband's demands for information regarding matters of state, she had been compromising the medical rules about keeping him isolated. When this information reached Stalin he called her on the telephone and, using brutal language, gave her such a dressing-down that she wept. Unwilling to tell her ailing husband, she confided in Kamenev and Zinoviev. However, they felt that Lenin should be informed.

Lydia, too, had suffered a tongue-lashing from Stalin: "Have you been telling Vladimir Ilyich things he is not supposed to be told?" He was not supposed to be told about the Georgian affair, and this may also have been the reason for Stalin's phone call to Nadya,

Upon being informed, Lenin became extremely agitated. Ill though he was, he rallied sufficiently to dictate a blistering letter to Stalin:

Top Secret

Personal
    Copy to Kamenev and Zinoviev
    Dear Comrade Stalin:
    You have been so rude as to summon my wife to the telephone and use bad language. Although she had told you that she was prepared to forget this, the fact nevertheless became known through her to Zinoviev and Kamenev. I have no intention of forgetting so easily what has been done against me, and it goes without saying that what has been done against my wife I consider having been done against me as well. I ask you, therefore, to think it over whether you are prepared to withdraw what you have said and to make your apologies, or whether you prefer that relations between us should be broken off.
    Respectfully yours,
    Lenin
    March 5, 1923

Volodicheva was then on duty, and Lenin directed her to personally hand the letter to Stalin and receive the answer from his own hands. "However," she noted, "Nadezhda Konstantinovna asked that the letter not be sent, and it was held up throughout the 6th. The next day I said I had to carry out Vladimir Ilyich's instruction. She spoke to Kamenev and the letter was handed by me personally to Stalin and Kamenev. Stalin immediately dictated his answer to me, but the letter has not been handed to Vladimir Ilyich as he has fallen ill."

Lenin's last letter, directed to comrades concerned with the Georgian affair, was dictated on the 6th.

Under the circumstances, Stalin's apology was irrelevant; Lenin was no longer able to address his contrition, the Georgian issue—or any other. On the 9th he was felled by a devastating stroke.

And what had Stalin said to Nadya? A rumor circulated in Moscow that found its way into print many years later by a woman languishing in one of Stalin's prisons. Yevgenia Ginsburg admitted that it was hearsay when she wrote: "Stalin said to Lenin's wife 'if you don't behave yourself, we'll find another widow for your husband.'"

Alternately confined to bed and a wheel chair, Lenin continued to suffer the capricious nature of his illness. Just when he seemed to be recovering, the long-term consequences of stroke reasserted themselves. Although robbed of the power of speech and of physical mobility, he was mentally alert.

Among the many physicians who regularly attended him, Nadya trusted only Dr. Guetier, a long-time family friend. Unlike the others with their false optimism and medical platitudes, Guetier answered Nadya's questions with unvarnished frankness. "What lies ahead?" "He will become increasingly fatigued." "What about his intellect?" "If he recovers physically—even partially—it will not be impaired." "How long . . . ?" (meaning how long before death). "I cannot say."

Upon meeting Lenin during the interval between his first and second strokes, Trotsky observed:

> He gave the impression of being a hopelessly tired man. The muscles of his face sagged, the gleam had gone out of his eyes, his shoulders drooped, he had a sick man's smile; even his formidable brow seemed to shrink. The expression of his face and of his entire figure might have been summed up in a word: tired. At such ghastly moments, Lenin seemed to me a doomed man . . . Without malice or mercy, the blind forces of nature were sinking the great sick man into a state of impotence from which there was no way out. Lenin could not and should not have lived on as an invalid.

After the second stroke, Nadya was aware that her husband's chance for recovery was alarmingly diminished. Nevertheless, she continued to hope as from day to day she observed the unpredictable nature of his illness. Meanwhile, the ground floor of the Big House resembled a small hospital. One room contained a telephone switchboard which was manned around the clock. Another was fitted with a medical dispensary. Several physicians, nurses and aides lived in one of the outbuildings enclosing the courtyard. Nearby was a separate building which contained kitchens, a bakery and a larder.

Family rooms were on the second floor at the front and opened on spacious balconies. In one of them Lenin lay on a small wooden bed shielded by a screen. Nadya's room was next, and the door between was never closed. While the nursing staff attended to his physical needs, his wife provided emotional support for one who was struggling against an illness, the nature of which he himself understood far better than those around him. Evenings Nadya sat beside his bed, reading aloud from works of fiction. Paralyzed, unable to communicate verbally, he signaled with a nod or movement of his good hand whether a tale was pleasing or otherwise.

One evening in late January 1924, she read him a story by the American author Jack London. "It is a very fine tale," she noted. "In a wilderness of ice, where no human being had set foot, a sick man, dying of hunger, is making for the harbor of a big river. His strength is giving out, he cannot walk but keeps slipping, and beside him slides a wolf—also dying of hunger. There is a fight between them; the man wins. Half dead, half demented, he reaches his goal." The wolf—death—stalking a dying man who wins and struggles on to his goal. "That tale greatly pleased Ilyich."

Wilhelm Pieck, a founding member of the German Communist Party, was in Moscow for a meeting of the Comintern's Presidium. These international communist leaders had been discussing the prospects for a German revolution as well as the growing threat of Fascism in Italy, Spain and Germany. Since recent news from Gorki indicated that Lenin was no worse, they had reason to hope for his eventual recovery.

At 10:30 on the morning of January 22, 1924, the telephone rang in Pieck's room at the Hotel Lux. "Is it true," an agitated colleague asked, "that Lenin died last night?" Pieck immediately phoned Klara Zetkin, but in order to avoid alarming her, his inquiry was purposely vague: had she heard any news from Gorki? No. But a few minutes later she called back. "In a voice choked with emotion, she told me that it was true."

The following morning members of the international Presidium, together with Russian leaders, boarded a train for the hour-and-a-half ride to Gorki. They found Lenin in a coffin resting on a raised bier in one of the large second-floor rooms. Reverting to the present tense, Pieck described the scene:

> His face is pale as wax, his features drawn, there is hardly a wrinkle on his face. It is hard to believe that he is no more. Silently, with tears in their eyes, people hardened in the battles of the Civil War carry out his body. And the mournful crowd follows its dead leader along a narrow path, through snow-covered fields, to the station. Numerous people, young and old, stand along the railway tracks. The melody of the Russian dead march sounds tragic in the still air.

Gerasimovo Station, a wooden miniature with decorative fretwork, lay at the foot of the hill in Gorki village. Lenin's coffin was placed in a freight car adorned with red bunting; ahead were several coaches. With steam belching from its underbody, the locomotive jolted forward, its departure unheralded by a dispatcher. The "third bell" had already sounded in a room of the Big House.

By the time the funeral train reached Moscow's Paveletsky Station, hundreds of thousands were gathered in streets leading to the center. The coffin was conveyed to the House of Trade Unions and placed on an elevated bier in the Hall of Columns. Around it stood a guard of honor. Nadya, wide-eyed with grief and shock, stood beside the coffin as thousands filed past to pay homage.

She endured those hours with characteristic equanimity. When the Congress of Soviets met in the Bolshoi Theater for a final tribute to Lenin, she sat on the stage beside members of the Central Executive Committee of the Party. The main floor and four tiers of boxes were crammed with deputies, many of them standing in the rear. Across the auditorium directly opposite the stage, the Imperial box—shorn of its double eagle—bulged with proletarian representatives of the people.

Suddenly a hush fell over the crowd. "Comrade Krupskaya says a few simple words, but they produce a tremendous effect." Following the obsequies,

Funeral procession in Gorki park

Gerasimovo Railway depot where Lenin's
casket was placed aboard train to Moscow
(author's photo).

Lenin in death, 1924

Pieck joined the workers, peasants, men and women of the Soviet as they returned to the Hall of Columns to march past Lenin's bier. "They are grief-stricken and apprehensive of the future." Nadya resumed her place beside her husband.

The procession continued uninterrupted for four days and four nights. During this time, crowds were gathered outside in the -30° temperature, attempting to keep warm from numerous bonfires blazing skyward. The funeral procession in Red Square took place on the 27th, and among the pall-bearers was Stalin, together with several others who were later to form a part of his inner circle. A mausoleum of wood had been constructed beside the Kremlin wall.

"Just at the entrance to the Square on a low platform stood a dark red coffin," noted Italian Communist Umberto Terracini. "It was still open and slightly inclined forward. Inside lay Lenin, his head resting on a red pillow. He seemed to look through his closed lids at the endless crowd of people. Only giant bonfires crackled in the icy stillness."

In early twilight of that dismal day, Klara Zetkin and three delegates to the Comintern climbed the snow-covered steps of the platform for a final glimpse of the face of one who had seemed indestructible. "His great dialogue with the world, with history and with the future has come to an end," thought Terracini as he and Klara and William Z. Foster followed Japanese communist Sen Katayama toward the steps leading from the platform. Following eulogies that managed to sound superfluous after the long period of mourning, they watched as the coffin was taken across Red Square and laid in the mausoleum.

"At 4 p.m. salvos are fired," said Pieck. "Factory whistles shriek their last salute. All of Russia is holding its breath . . . Shoulder to shoulder stand workers, peasants and Red Army men who have come from every part of the country for a final tribute. The Russian dead march, 'You have fallen, a sacrifice' rolls in a mighty wave over the Square." During his trip back to Germany, strains of the dead march continued to echo in his ears. [Pieck became the first president of the German Democratic Republic.]

Russia was indeed holding its breath. What now? Although Lenin had been absent from the scene for many months, the mere fact of his existence had stayed the hands of those inclined to political adventurism. Likewise, his ability to mediate between dissenting elements within the Party continued to be a restraining influence. With his death, the ship of state lost its helmsman.

23. The Succession in Jeopardy

Misfortunes have come on the nation—not because of
the nature of the system, but through the evil will of
those people whom chance has placed in power.
                                                    –Boris Pasternak

On October 29, 1924, revolutionary terrorist Boris Savinkov was brought
before a Soviet court charged with masterminding a plot to assassinate Trotsky, Stalin, Kamenev, Zinoviev, Djerzhinsky. The courtroom, closed to the
public, was packed with Government and Party officials who were told that
Savinkov provided the gun with which Kaplan had shot Lenin. But Lenin had
died of natural causes the preceding January; Trotsky was now on the fringes
of Party power; Djerzhinsky's political authority, at the highest level, was marginal; Kamenev and Zinoviev were merely part of the oligarchy which had
fallen into the void left by Lenin's death. At the apex of the collective leadership triangle was Josef Stalin, and it was Stalin who had most to gain from
proving that anti-government forces were out to get him.

Although Savinkov eventually thwarted Soviet justice by committing suicide, the trial was a harbinger of the future. Stalinism—with its doctrinaire
rigidity—took shape on an October evening when the balding, middle-aged
Savinkov, pleading his conversion to Bolshevism, counted on a judge's
credulity to save him. The farce was played equally by accusers and accused.

Already the post-Lenin institution, which for nine months held its breath
while awaiting the resolution of inner-Party contention, was beginning to
assume the form it would maintain for the next 29 years.

As Lenin confronted the certainty of imminent death, he was troubled by
the deficiencies of those who would succeed him. Besides his derogation of
Stalin, Lenin in his Testament had tactfully but pointedly outlined the shortcomings of his political and administrative heirs. "Trotsky," he stated, "is personally perhaps the most capable man in the present Central Committee, but
he has displayed excessive self-assurance and shown excessive preoccupation
with the purely administrative side of the work." Lenin likewise predicted that
unless Stalin and Trotsky resolved their personal rivalry, "a split will occur . . .
thus threatening the stability of our Party . . . and the possibility of its eventual downfall." He went on to rap the knuckles of Kamenev and Zinoviev for
their opposition to the October Revolution. At the same time he labeled Trotsky a "non-Bolshevik." Bukharin, a Marxist theoretician, was "outstanding
among the younger ones, the favorite of the Party . . . but, there is something

(too) scholastic about him." Lenin found that another leader "showed too much zeal for administrative work to be relied upon in a serious political matter." Krzhizhanovsky, too, came in for mild criticism.

Lenin's solution to the problem was collective leadership in which he trusted that these deficiencies would be counterbalanced by collective wisdom. A Central Committee of the Party composed of a hundred or more would, he reasoned, be in position to curb the overweaning ambitions of the few and ameliorate the weaknesses of those mentioned in his Testament.

A leitmotiv pervaded the Testament; certain of the hierarchy were too involved with the machinery of Party and Government as opposed to fluid creativity in all spheres of Soviet life. Lenin's dislike of bureaucracy and bureaucratic mentality was legendary.

The reality, however, was a small ruling group that included Josef Stalin, Leo Kamenev, Grigor Zinoviev and Leon Trotsky. Running a close fifth was Nikolai Bukharin, followed by a number of able—if undistinguished—persons who had long since paid their dues to Party and Revolution.

What sort of men were these leaders? Stalin was yet to fully reveal himself. Kamenev? Clare Sheridan had been amazed that a man who was outwardly self-assured and seemingly competent would quail before his wife's ill-temper. "With his neatly-trimmed beard, pince-nez and amiable smile," she noted, "he might have been mistaken for a bourgeois French bank manager." Said Trotsky: "Lenin's 'cold showers' [criticism] did not prevent Kamenev from loving him, even worshipping him, all of him, his passion, his profundity, his simplicity, his witticisms, at which Kamenev laughed before they were uttered, and his handwriting, which he involuntarily imitated."

Sheridan considered Zinoviev "arrogant rather than vain." "Restless and impatient, he constantly sighed and groaned. His face was thick, neck short, chest pulpy, hair curly, lips petulant, eyelids heavy. The effect was of a shrewd, fat, middle-aged woman. But he had a certain picturesque element that, exaggerated, would be turned to artistic account. His air, in contrast to Djerzhinsky, was vulgar, coarse, hard." Angelica Balabanova detested Zinoviev, and her *Memoir* is replete with personal and ideological denunciations of him.

Bukharin, the young "artist" who had visited Lenin and Nadya in Cracow was likewise shrewd, but his witty tongue and breezy self-assurance were no match for the hardy politicos who stood above him in rank, age and experience. In physical appearance Bukharin, with or without beard, was nondescript; his was not a face to remember among the portraits of that time. Side by side with Trotsky's distinctive, Mephistophelian features, Bukharin—despite his intellectual brilliance—resembled a Party functionary with duties limited to carrying out orders. But his appearance was deceiving. A razor-sharp mind, and the zeal that characterized a loyal Bolshevik, lifted him to a position of considerable authority in the Party.

Stalin, Kamenev and Zinoviev became the "triumvar" that succeeded Lenin. Trotsky, however, remained the outsider he had always been: a non-Bolshevik, a newcomer (1917) to the ranks, critical and individualistic, inclined to arrogance. Unfortunately, Trotsky was bored with routine, drumming his fingers on the table at Party sessions and surveying the ceiling with ill-concealed contempt for the slow pace of committee work.

Quoting a witticism current in 1926, Trotsky wrote: "They (the bureaucracy) tolerate Kamenev but do not respect him. They respect Trotsky but do not tolerate him. They neither tolerate nor respect Zinoviev."

Djerzhinsky—frail, emotional, devoid of personal ambition—shouldered responsibility with selfless dedication. His pale features revealed a sensitivity at odds with the wretched task of managing the *Cheka*. Indeed, there was little about him to suggest "the leader," and in this respect he resembled Chicherin. The nearly unlimited power he wielded as chief of the Soviet Secret Police was bureaucratic rather than political. Djerzhinsky, a Pole, was never a member of the Party's inner circle. Like Trotsky, he was a latterday (1917) convert to Bolshevism. Lenin accepted the services of both men without questioning too closely their past political orientation; for him it was sufficient that they serve the Cause.

In 1924 when Lenin died, Trotsky at age 47 was senior to the others, followed by 45-year-old Stalin. The "heavenly twins" Kamenev and Zinoviev were each 41 and Bukharin 36. *Sovnarkom's* only female member, Alexandra Kollontai, was a mature 52. Although possibly qualified, she was never a serious candidate for leadership. While championing the cause of equality for women [in the Leninist sense], she was barred from the one position that would have confirmed Socialist/Communist theory: women at the highest level of decision-making.

Had Lenin lived and continued in office with restored health, would Trotsky have become his eventual heir? Would Stalin have been permanently squelched by Lenin's witty and effective restraint? If Lenin had lived ... At age 53 he left the stage at a crucial time in the life of the young Soviet State. What followed was not pre-ordained, but a result of personality conflicts, great objective difficulties, and the timidity of those who failed to exorcise Stalin's weaknesses from their midst.

Psychologists, historians and Kremlin experts have long pondered the reason for Stalin's durability. The answer is, perhaps, more elementary than scholars have deduced. The rough-hewn revolutionary from Georgia was endowed with a "persona" which experience and practice further developed; a grandfather image, reassuringly solid, dependable and wise. With an Albert Schweitzer moustache and a similarly benign expression, he even looked the part. When contrasted with his more volatile and variously endowed comrades, he projected an image they totally lacked. Thus, one of the reasons for his rise to power and, to a considerable extent, how he contrived to retain it.

With the addition of a single man, the collective principle might have functioned well. Unfortunately, Yakov Sverdlov's premature death in March 1919 deprived the leadership of a steady hand and cool head.

24. Nadya, Legatee of the Socialist Ideal

After Lenin's funeral, Nadya and Maria returned to Gorki for the sad chore of packing books and personal effects for shipment to the Kremlin apartment henceforth to be their home. There was little time to mourn, to rehearse the events of previous months when they had watched husband and brother reach the point of no return.

Once back in Moscow, Maria returned to her job at the *Pravda* office where she had worked before her brother's illness. Nadya resumed her activity in the Education Secretariat [Narkompros] and took charge of long-neglected correspondence. Anna, after the death of her husband Mark in 1919, left Petrograd for Moscow to work in the Commissariat for Social Security. When it was merged with *Proletkultye* [Proletarian Culture], she found herself at odds with an assistant, possibly a result of her own abrasive personality. Her position in the united commissariat brought her into official contact with Nadya, but it did little to promote a warmer relationship than had existed in the past. Anna continued to live alone in a spacious, elegant apartment overlooking the Alexander Garden and the Kremlin Wall.

The ornate 19th Century building on Neglinnaya Street (later Manezhnaya) opposite the Kremlin's Borovitsky Gate, which had earlier housed Inessa Armand and Alexander Shotman, now became a focus for streams of visitors to Anna's "office," a kind of private commissariat in which she dispensed advice and from which she issued articles for publication. A secretary took charge of correspondence, while a maid and cook superintended household chores—a lifestyle in sharp contrast to the spartan existence of Nadya and Maria across the way. Likewise, Anna developed a following at once personal and apart from the official business of state.

The appointment of Lenin's wife and sisters to responsible posts was not nepotism. Every able-bodied, knowledgeable person was drafted into Party or government work; and in any event, few activists of that time would have settled for a life of idleness. Salaries were small but sufficient for necessities like food and clothing; housing was provided by the government.

Lenin left no estate. He had voluntarily limited his income to 500 rubles per annum, a small sum by any standards, and it is probable that—besides his penchant for acquiring books—a portion went to individuals in need. However, his family were assured support for the remainder of their lives.

Nadya was now on her own. As Lenin's widow and former close collaborator, a vast amount of work devolved upon her. To carry forward his unfinished work, to resume her own in the education sector, to write, counsel, to confer with persons of high station and low, filled a void that would otherwise have been unbearable. Perhaps she was relieved to have the bad times behind her, but the pain of separation from Volodya was like an amputation; part of her was forever lost.

Evenings after work, the two women, Nadya and Maria, found themselves involuntarily listening for the brisk step that would complete the family circle. Their own footsteps echoed dismally on the bare parquet floor; and the subdued atmosphere that inevitably follows death pervaded rooms that were once alive with Lenin's energy and sparkling wit. Since there was no further mention of the cat, one presumes that it died of grief or old age, or was left behind at Gorki. Although neither Nadya nor Maria was a "cat person" they had adapted to Lenin's fondness for animals. But after his death, the cat would have been expendable.

Nadya sorely missed her husband's counsel. Besides making speeches and chairing committee meetings, she was now expected to produce literary works, articles for publication, written statements and oral reports on education and sundry other matters; in short, to substitute for her dead husband. An earlier literary effort had been carefully edited by Lenin to such an extent that little remained of Nadya's original draft. His was a hard act to follow, least of all by a shy woman not distinguished by originality or profundity of thought. Nevertheless, she plunged into the task of being a public figure with considerable fortitude, trusting in those who were aware of her limitations to cover the weaknesses and make the best of her simple prose and lack of personal charisma.

She was saved by the aura of Lenin, which had endowed her with qualities she didn't possess. Gradually, however, she began to acquire an authority of her own, becoming a personage in her own right. Soon after Lenin's death, her dark hair turned white, and the obvious signs of age, magnified by evidence of grief, added dignity to her small figure.

A cult arose after Lenin's death that troubled his widow. On January 26, 1924, Petrograd became Leningrad, and henceforth a deluge of name changes flooded Russia. Shirokaya Street became Ulitsa Lenina. Simbirsk, his birthplace, was now Ulyanovsk. 'Leninski' and 'Ilyich' dotted the landscape. Towns and villages, factories and public buildings, parks and streets lost their former identity to a point where it seemed that the newly formed (1922) Union of Soviet Socialist Republics might become "Leninland" in a fever of tribute to the man who, during the last months of his life, was occasionally forgotten. Or, if not forgotten, at least put on hold until his possible recovery.

Nadya had intimate knowledge of his abhorrence for personal adulation, nor was she moved by accusations of power hunger, arrogance, dictatorial intransigence and a host of other epithets heaped upon him by foes and frequently by colleagues. "Lenin is not the least personally ambitious," wrote Anatoly Lunacharsky.

> I believe he never looks at himself, never glances in the mirror of history, never even thinks of what posterity will say of him—simply does his work. He does his work imperiously, not because power is sweet to him, but because he is sure that he is right, and cannot endure to have anybody spoil his work.

Nadya didn't object when, following the assassination attempt, workers at the Michelson Factory renamed their *zavod* "Vladimir Ilyich," but she may have had reservations about "Leningrad," and she certainly opposed all other manifestations of hero worship. Standing beside Lenin's bier at the memorial service, she had spoken thus:

> Comrades working men and women, peasant men and women! I have a great request to make of you: do not raise statues of him, name palaces for him, or stage pompous solemn festivals to his memory—all these were to him in life of little significance, even a burden. Remember how many are impoverished and in disarray in our country. You wish to honor the name of Vladimir Ilyich—then establish infants' homes, kindergartens, houses, schools, libraries, ambulances, hospitals, homes for invalids; and above all, create a living testament to his ideals.

Nadya, soon after Lenin's death

However, when plans were developed for the V.I. Lenin Central Museum in Moscow, she regarded the project as preservation of historical material rather than memorial—a *pamyatnik*. As memorabilia began pouring in from various sources in Russia and abroad, she threw herself into the task of verifying, placing in context, identifying the significance of this or that object. In contrast to the myth "George Washington slept here," Lenin's multitudinous sojourns were a reality, and his wife was in position to discriminate between truth and fiction. In the latter case, certain natives in the provinces, carried away by emotion, were advancing claims—"Lenin was here . . . " "I remember him when . . . "—many of which Nadya disclaimed.

Soon after Lenin's death, Nadya was urged to begin writing a memoir. Starting with her first acquaintance with him in the late 1890's, she went to work on a chronicle which has become a valuable source for historians. Its shortcomings are inherent. For, example, her need to interpose ideology into the historical and personal narrative was inevitable in view of the enormous significance of the social and political changes wrought by Lenin.

She also assisted in establishing the Marx-Engels-Lenin Institute; provided documents, explained, verified. This particular work required a re-reading of Lenin's writings, to which Nadya devoted meticulous attention.

Thus her time was monopolized by three major projects. It required, therefore, considerable self-discipline to turn her attention to the energy-consuming work of *Narkompros*. Nadya's day began at 6 a.m. and often continued until after midnight. Mornings, after a spartan *zavtrak* of bread, cheese and tea followed by two or three hours at her desk, she plodded with automaton-like regularity to the nearby Education Commissariat. A considerable portion of her work was involved with children and young people, not only supervision of textbooks and curricula, but likewise personal contacts with Soviet youth.

Two organizations had been founded during the first months of Soviet Power: Young Pioneers, similar to Cub Scouts in the west—even to uniforms and patriotic indoctrination; and Komsomol, the Soviet version of Boy/Girl Scouts. The major objective was clean living, strong bodies and healthy minds and education for Socialism. Nadya was deeply involved with both groups. "I very much regretted having had no children of my own," she said, "but now I have thousands."

In 1918 a young Rumanian girl named Vera Dridzo had come to Moscow as private librarian to a gentleman-scholar, member of the intelligentsia who had managed to survive the revolution. At age seventeen, Vera, sporting a brooch with a red star in the center, was on fire with revolutionary spirit. When a Commissariat found itself in need of additional secretarial help, Vera was co-opted to the organization where her youth and sensitivity came to Nadya's attention. Before long, she became Nadya's personal secretary.

During the year following Lenin's death, Nadya carefully concealed her grief from the public. Only the puffy, swollen eyes betrayed her sorrow, told of lonely nights when she cried herself to sleep. To Vera, however, Nadya poured out her heart—not in tearful expressions of self-pity, but in reflections on her life with Volodya: "He would often tell me .. ", "When he was in . . . " "One day we were . . . . " Reliving the past with a sympathetic listener helped Nadya to maintain emotional balance; in the telling, she lost the urge to weep. Not even Volodya's sister Maria fulfilled the need supplied by a young and attentive listener. It was as if the past were still alive, that any moment Volodya would enter the room and life would continue as before.

A shy young Party worker wished to visit Nadya in the Kremlin.

But I was afraid to look in her eyes; what would I say to her? But she herself telephoned me and I went. She talked immediately about Vladimir Ilyich, showed me his photograph. She did not display her grief. While I listened to her, I thought: "What a strong person she must be to carry herself thus." I noted that almost nothing was in her sitting-room—no new portrait of Lenin, only a single small photo on the desk. And truly Nadezhda Konstantinovna bore a heavy grief, one that

Klara Zetkin and Nadya, Moscow, ca. 1929

remained with her to the end of her days. I remember how, many years later, she said to me: "How I miss Vladimir Ilyich. Now no one telephones me at work and says, 'Come quickly, Nadyusha; without you I would not have supper!'"

To another young person, Nadya confided: "He did not say 'Darling, darling, I love you!' but he was always very gallant."

Among her youthful friends was Inessa's younger daughter Varvara. "Darling Varya" described how she and Nadya spent many hours together clipping pictures of Lenin from periodicals and pasting them into scrapbooks of various sizes. "They were for her to look at," Varya related, "which she did very frequently."

During this time Nadya's disease was taking its toll. "I look healthier," she wrote from southern Russia where the doctors had sent her to rest, "but my heart is bad." Often, in company with Maria who was also ill, Nadya returned to Gorki. The Big House was being turned into a museum, but the north wing still served as a retreat for Lenin's family, including his brother Dmitri.

It was during one of these visits to Gorki that Nadya proposed establishing a school for peasant children of the area. A site was chosen not far from the Manor House, down the hill and nestled in a grove of trees. Nearby, many years later, a small rustic museum was dedicated to Nadya, one of two *pamyatniki* bearing her name.[The other is in Moscow, the Pedagogical Institute.] The purpose was not only to memorialize her work in education, but to document the lives and careers of those first peasant students and their teachers. This humble tribute, while hardly on a scale commensurate with her contribution to education, she would have considered fitting. But like Volodya, Nadya shunned public acclaim. The Order of Lenin pinned to her blouse, the honorary degrees and high-level appointments meant nothing to her.

All of her life had been shadowed by a twilight sadness; now a heavy cloud obscured the sun of happier memories. The phrenetic pace of her existence was an attempt to flee from the lonely predawn hours in the Kremlin apartment. In pursuit of daily activity, she kept Volodya alive. But in times of solitude he was, despite the obtrusive slogan "Lenin Lives!" dead in the Red Square Mausoleum. To face that reality was more than she could bear. So talking endlessly about him to whomever would listen, immersing herself in the extension of his work, helping to perpetuate—not the personality of Lenin but his contribution to the betterment of humankind—this was her way of denying the finality of a bitter January day when she had looked upon his face for the last time, chalk-white beneath the gently falling snow, a wax doll being laid away by a grieving child.

And later: "Mine, all mine!" she exclaimed upon the occasion of her first and wrenching visit to an official gathering after her husband's death. It was a cry, not of pride, but of anguish.

About this time, a curious episode took place in Leningrad. Alma Rauki-ainen, the young Finnish girl who had delivered a bag of produce at the Latukka's and seen a stranger washing at the kitchen sink, visited the former Capital with a group of Finnish tourists. Accompanying her was Yeva, the pro-duce lady at the co-op where Alma had presented a ration card.

"At one point on the platform of Finlandski Station," Alma related, "we saw a large statue. 'Hey!' I exclaimed excitedly and seized my friend by the shoul-der. 'Yeva, that's the man I saw at the Latukka's. Was it really Lenin?' Yeva would not let me finish speaking. 'You are correct,' she said with a smile. 'But we are surrounded by tourists, and since we are living in bourgeois Finland, recalling his name might be dangerous.' The old communist was correct. Because for a long time, while I lived in Finland, no one from across the border mentioned that I saw Ilyich at such close quarters, and helped him to obtain food during the secret days of September 1917."

Except for Nadya's continuing friendship with Lydia Knippovich who was born and raised in Finland, the "Finnish Connection" was severed when she moved to Moscow. The bucolic days at Vasa and Stirsuden, the hectic period 1905-07 when she lived with Lenin briefly while he was hiding in the city of Viborg, and again in 1917 when she undertook two perilous journeys to be with him in Helsinki, were chapters in her life forever closed. It is doubtful that she often visited Leningrad after moving to Moscow.

And only once did Lenin himself return to the city of revolution soon to bear his name. It was on the occasion of Mark Yelizarov's funeral. A snapshot shows Lenin standing pensively as his weeping sister Anna looks down at the coffin. To Nadya, living in the Kremlin, her birthplace must have seemed like an orphan—without "family," without affection, almost forgotten by the rest of the country. And as if to underscore the city's neglected condition, a devas-tating flood in 1922 added to the ruin. Today, its beauty notwithstanding, the city and environs emit an air of meloncholy.

Officially, Nadya was now "Krupskaya," a concession to the fact that "Lenin" was a pseudonym. Likewise, there were three other Ulyanov women: Maria, Anna and Dmitri's wife. But Lenin himself became an "ism," some-thing that in life would have appalled him.

The official version of Nadya's life after Lenin—one of endless meetings, speeches, interviews, honors, election as representative to innumerable bodies of a dual government (Party and Soviet)—does not include mention of events transpiring within the Soviet Union and abroad, events that affected Nadya directly.

World War I, with its universal social and political disruption, spawned a new breed of national leader. Hitler, Mussolini, Franco, while professing "socialism" initiated the scourge of Fascism. In this respect, the enigmatic Josef Stalin stood apart; communism, or Russian socialism, in theory at least, was light years removed from Fascism. Thus Stalin, whatever his perversion of the Lenin program, was the enemy—not only of western capitalism, but of Fascism and all the other "isms" that grew during the postwar years.

Despite the fact that by 1929 Stalin had distorted socialist-communist democracy as conceived by Lenin, the USSR, because of certain principles built into the Soviet system, was alienated from the socio-political experiments of Germany, Italy and Spain.

Lenin's emergency wartime measures and temporary adjustments to postwar conditions had became carved in stone, to be handed down from the mountaintop by Stalin. There have been countless attempts to confuse Stalin with Lenin—and vice versa. This unfortunate misreading of the actual conditions, which dominated Western thinking and diplomacy, led to unhappy consequences for political relations between east and west: to wit—an assumption by the West that the quagmire of Stalinism was endowed with eternal life, and that the *ideals* of the October Revolution would never undergo a rebirth.

To what degree was Nadya privy to events transpiring in the Kremlin enclave? Kamenev and Zinoviev were lifelong friends and coworkers; their revelations to her would have been imparted with the sure knowledge that she would never betray them. It was rumored that for a brief time she joined the anti-Stalin opposition. However, as a woman alone, as widow of a famous man no longer around to protect her, she was frighteningly vulnerable. But in her opinion, personal safety was secondary to prudence; and with perspective in mind, with regard for the future of her husband's work, she withdrew from political activism and devoted herself to the urgent task of educating Soviet youth and promoting the Lenin principles—not an "ism" but a *living ideal* which she perceived as developing to maturity in the fullness of time.

The late 1920's and early 30's witnessed a stream of western visitors to the Soviet Union, drawn thither by rumors of the successes of the five-year plans. In addition to clergymen, journalists, creative writers, educators and the merely curious, was Harriet Eddy, professor at the University of California. Harriet was a founder of the system of rural free libraries in that state and came to Moscow for the express purpose of conferring with "Madame Krupskaya"; to exchange information and perhaps offer advice. *Narkompros* was in process of establishing what Lenin called "reading huts" in the villages.

"As I entered her study," Harriet recalled, "we shook hands, she asked me to be seated and inquired: 'What brings you to the Soviet Union?' I replied that I had a burning interest in the young Soviet State and its efforts to raise the level of education. That I would like to help in this endeavor and, I added, invite Soviet workers to enlighten us as well."

Harriet had learned that the Commission for Soviet Education was investigating teaching methods in the west, particularly the Montessori System in

Italy, the school in Batavia, New York, and the pedagogical theories of the American, John Dewey.

"Krupskaya listened to me very attentively. Since I had difficulty speaking through an interpreter, I endeavored to answer her questions as briefly as possible. She surveyed me seriously and with considerable astonishment. After all, hadn't we, the Americans, recently invaded her country through Archangel and Vladivostok? However, her face softened when I went on to explain our system in California. Afterwards, she described the Soviet system of rural libraries, mentioning the name of Ilyich (Lenin) with extraordinary warmth."

Three years later (in 1930), Eddy was invited to return to the USSR for a meeting with library workers. Upon encountering Nadya, she was greeted with "Eddy! California! Come and meet with me!" Subsequently, at a conference of Soviet educators, Eddy had the opportunity to hear Nadya speak. "There was," Eddy noted, "no interpreter present. But it was enlightening to observe with what deep attention her words were received by all listeners."

Eddy provided an interesting postscript to her account.

> Several years later my sister and I went to Cuba. On the main street of Havana we saw posters with a likeness of Lenin. We asked our hotel clerk when and where the film *Lenin in October* would be shown. "In our best theater on the next corner," he informed us. When we arrived there, we found a line extending down the block. Inside, the theater was packed with working men and women who reacted to the film with emotion. I was so impressed with this experience that I wrote to Krupskaya, describing the event. She was surprised to learn of the deep devotion to Lenin of young Cuban workers. She sent me a copy of her book, *Memories [Reminiscences] of Lenin* which I consider to be among the finest ever written by a woman about her husband.

Nadya kept to herself private opinions on the political and other horrors engulfing the land: the suicide of Stalin's wife, Nadezhda Alliluyeva; the murder of Sergei Kirov; the trials of Kamenev, Zinoviev, Bukharin and a host of others. Trotsky was murdered in Mexico, whither he had fled.

Retreating into a feminine world, Nadya confined her personal relationships to those few surviving women friends of the old Petersburg days. Otherwise, she encouraged the company of young people. Especially dear to her were Varvara and Inna Armand, daughters of Inessa.

A new addition to her own family was Olga, daughter of Lenin's brother Dmitri. This child, named for the 17-year-old Olga who died of typhoid, spent many hours in company with her Aunt Nadya, sitting beside her desk in the Kremlin apartment, plied with candy and questions about school work. Olga recorded her impressions as a teenager: "In reflecting on the life of Aunt Nadya," she related, "I remember the depth of her exceptional nature. Her intellect, tact, sagacity, vigor, and at the same time her warmth and sensibility, attracted people to her. Likewise, she had a gift for listening to others."

Physically, Nadya was rapidly deteriorating. Now in her sixties, she resembled the aged Queen Victoria of England. Her oval face was badly swollen from the Grave's Disease that had plagued her since youth. With ashen features, and beset by visual impairment, she nevertheless drove herself to the limit of endurance. Emotional breakdown, however, was foreign to her nature. From the record, only once did she openly give way to personal distress.

Maria Burdina, editor of the journal *School at Home*, came to the Kremlin apartment with articles returned for proof-reading.

> I entered the study of Nadezhda Konstantinovna and found her seated—deep, deep in an armchair. Behind a table she was hardly visible, looking attentive, with a sad face. Her hair, more than usual, was tangled on her brow and about her ears. She heard me enter but seemed indifferent. Not even looking at me, she took the packet. I asked her how she was feeling. "I feel," she said, "that I am sick and tired of hearing the doorbell, of visits and letters—all reminding me of Vladimir Ilyich. And no one would understand how hard this is for me!" Thus simply, completely, she revealed before me her great personal grief.

Otherwise, Nadya displayed a stoicism which led others to believe that she felt nothing beyond an urge to work. Occasionally, however, she was brought face to face with the real past.

Oscar Engberg, now a wizened old man, had long ago fled Finland, and because of his relationship to Lenin and devotion to the Revolution, was rewarded with the post of doorkeeper at a Soviet institution outside Moscow. One day he decided to pay a call on Nadya. She received him graciously, suggesting that this first meeting since exile days merited a photographer. The resulting picture is nostalgic—two elderly, frail persons, in profile, shaking hands. In no other photograph is her mature dignity and composure so evident. Where earlier she had attempted to hide behind others when a photographer approached, she now seemed oblivious to the camera, intent only upon pressing the hand of an old and valued friend.

There were other reminders of the passage of time. First the death of Anna Yelizarova, and finally that of Maria. Nadya's niece Olga, described the scene at Maria's funeral:

> Sadly Nadezhda Konstantinovna sat beside the coffin of Maria Ilyinichna Ulyanova in the Hall of Columns of the Trade-Union House, where thirteen years earlier she had said farewell to Vladimir Ilyich. Then, in January 1924, Maria, Dmitri and Anna were beside her. Now only Dmitri, deeply grieved, as she was, at the death of a sister ... On the day Maria died, N.K. wrote a letter to my father: "Dear family member, Dmitri! our Maria is dead. I did not phone you because it was so very sad."

Except for the housekeeper, Polya, she was now alone. There was no one to remind her to tuck in her fine, wispy hair; to rest when circles under her eyes deepened. Unfortunately, her air of self-sufficiency discouraged those who might otherwise have come to her aid. Little by little, however, Vera Dridzo filled the void left by Maria's death, and there is evidence that this devoted secretary became unduly proprietary. But there were limits beyond which even Vera dared not intrude.

Nadya continued her accelerated pace, speaking before numerous groups, attending conferences and congresses in which she was a voting delegate. And writing—always writing. When her articles and pamphlets on education were finally assembled and published, they filled eleven volumes.

One of her articles, *Anti-religious Propaganda in the Schools Under Soviet Power*, is of particular interest as an example of her style and general approach to subjects. In it, she outlines the development of such propaganda in primary and secondary schools from January 1918 to 1929, explains the transition from crude priest-bashing to what she terms "anti-religion by persuasion." The hand of Lenin, the persuader, is evident here.

"No one doubts," she wrote,

> that there is no place in the school for religion. But confusion would have arisen if, all at once, all teaching were to cease to be religious . . . The need was to re-educate or eliminate "priestly daughters"—teachers—particularly in the provinces where ignorance and superstition prevailed. It was necessary to educate an entire new generation of teachers so that, in the end, there would be no one left to propagandize. If you are religious, then seek another profession, but not the profession of teaching.

A more personal literary assignment was one of her own choosing: a biographical sketch of her friend and co-worker, Lydia Knippovich, who had recently died of tuberculosis. The material assembled for this interesting work was sufficient for a full-length biography. It contains details otherwise missing from contemporary accounts, including Nadya's own *Memoir*. One learns, for example, that Lydia, born in Finland and fluent in both Finnish and Swedish, supervised arrangements for the famous Tammerfors Conference during which Lenin first encountered Stalin; that she suffered from the same thyroid ailment as Nadya; that their friend and colleague Apollinariya had been critically ill in 1909 and forced to withdraw from all Party work.

Less inspired is Nadya's introduction to Klara Zetkin's *Recollections of Lenin*. Nevertheless, she included an account of a dramatic incident that occurred during Zetkin's last days.

> Zetkin was an elected member of the German Reichstag; she served as the oldest member of the Reichstag and (by tradition) she would have to open it. No one thought that she would have the strength to do it. She lived in a rest home near Moscow and she could hardly sit up in bed; her strength was gone and every minute she gasped for breath. But when the German Communist Party wrote that there had been a desire for her to come, she did not hesitate. She gathered her last strength and departed for Germany, laying in a store of camphor and other remedies to sustain life. She knew what danger threatened her—to catch cold and even be killed by the Fascists. This did not deter her.

Thus the 75-year-old Klara—who in her heyday had frequented the company of Engels and Karl Marx's daughter Eleanor—now nearly blind behind her dark glasses and leaning heavily on the arm of her son Konstantin, headed for Leningrad and the west. "Gathering all her strength," Nadya continued, "she opened the Reichstag with a glowing speech. Turning to the German laboring masses, she spoke to them about Russia, about the necessary struggle, about the socialist revolution." (Zetkin returned safely to Moscow where she died shortly before her 76th birthday.)

Nadya's introduction ends with emotion: "It is important and necessary for us to know that Klara, when speaking of Vladimir Ilyich, told how warmly he was loved."

Zetkin herself wrote a pamphlet about Nadya. "A person grows up to the measure of the growth of his aim," wrote Klara, quoting the German poet, Schiller. And then:

> Was Nadezhda Konstantinovna really in her 60th year? Through first impression, observing her at a convocation, one would assign to her those years. Her dignified figure, slightly stooped, bent forward as one who was accustomed to sitting for hours at a desk, writing and poring over books; her smooth white hair parted in the middle—all bespoke her years. Walking slowly, she came to the podium. At first her voice was soft and barely audible, even weary-sounding. But gradually the voice acquired strength. Precisely, calmly, lucidly, her ideas came forth, without evidence of fatigue or frailty.

In 1937, Nadya received a copy of a new book by the Webbs, co-authors of the two-volume work on trade unionism which Lenin and his wife translated into Russian during the exile days in Shushenskoye. The flyleaf contained an inscription: "To Madame Krupskaya, from her English admirers, in acknowledgment and appreciation for her 40 years of service. (signed) Sidney and Beatrice Webb."

Japanese socialist Sen Katayama dedicated a book to Nadya, as did many other foreigners connected with the international socialist movement.

But the most personal testimonials were written by compatriots who had known her on a daily basis through the years. To one of them she confided: "I loved Ilyich very much."

February 23, 1939 began with the usual routine. Nadya arose early and was joined by her secretary, Vera. Together they went over the day's program: to read and examine twenty-three letters; participate in a noon session of *Sovnarkom* and deliver a speech on political education; reply to a letter from children in Vologda District who were asking to be informed of her favorite song—they wished to perform it at school assembly on the occasion of her 70th birthday three days hence.

"All that day," Vera recalled,

Nadezhda felt herself unwell, and that evening we went with her to the suburban rest home at Arkhangelskoye. On the way she joked and laughed. The next morning, February 24th, she dictated an article on Lenin, but managed to correct only half of the copy. It was her last work.

In the evening, old friends gathered at the rest home to celebrate Nadya's approaching jubilee. Among them were Gleb Krzhizhanovsky and his wife Zinaida—the other "bulochkin." At Gleb's instigation, photographs were taken. "It was a very happy occasion," noted Vera. "Joking with old friends, reminiscing about the past, N.K. was quite lively. But on the 25th, her condition worsened. Nevertheless, she said that, if the doctor permitted, she would attend the Party Congress on March 10 and deliver a scheduled address."

Birthday greetings had been pouring in from all parts of the country. The following article appeared in *Pravda*:

> The Central Committee of the Party and the Council of People's Commissars send you —"Old Bolshevik" and friend of Lenin—our warm greetings. We wish you good health and many more years of fruitful work for our Party and the laboring people of the Soviet Union.

Late that night Nadya's condition became critical and she was taken to the Kremlin hospital. While the nation celebrated her birthday, February 26, she lay in a state of semi-consciousness with Vera by her side, holding her hand. Once she rallied sufficiently to ask; "What is going on out there in the world?" "I told her," Vera said, "about the greetings of the Central Committee, about the congratulations. She began to close her eyes and did not again regain consciousness."

Meanwhile, Nadya's brother-in-law Dmitri had been summoned. "Before leaving home," stated his daughter Olga, "he told Mama and me to send our farewells by him. Shortly we came to Aunt Nadya's ward, and at length the doctor came out and said: 'Go in to her. Nadezhda Konstantinovna wishes to see you.' But at this point we felt that the secretary, V.C. Dridzo, would not allow Mama and me to say farewell to her."

The following day Nadya, like Volodya and Maria before her, lay in the Hall of Columns. Among the mourners filing past her open coffin was a new generation who looked upon her face as that of a beloved grandmother. After the ceremonies, her body was cremated and the ashes placed in an urn to be buried alongside the Kremlin Wall in a mass grave that contained the ashes of Inessa, Klara Zetkin, John Reed, and many "Old Bolsheviks" who had preceded her in death.

"The death of Comrade Krupskaya," noted Pravda, "a woman who has given her entire life to the work of communism, is a great loss for the Party and the sorrowing Soviet people."

In a remote prison, Yevgenia Ginsburg decried the article's brevity and coldness. With simple words untainted by officialdom, Yevgenia produced a fitting obituary:

> We were depressed and profoundly shaken by the death of Lenin's widow, Krupskaya. We wept bitterly as we looked at the small photograph in the newspaper—I believe it was the first time we had cried since we arrived at Yaroslavl. The obituary was cold and matter-of-fact. The 'boss' [Stalin], of course, did not like her. We gazed at her kind face, her school-ma'm collar, her straight, smooth, gray hair. Everything in her appearance was familiar, close and dear to us. Her death was like the final act of a tragedy; the last decent, honorable figures were disappearing from the stage, dying or being destroyed.

Gleb Krzhizhanovsky, longtime friend and colleague of Lenin and Nadya, penned a verse to her memory:

> *In our souls you do not die,*
> *Your time of trial is not to be feared,*
> *There is no threat of your being forgotten*
> *Whose person with Lenin was so completely fused.*

The recent words of Olga Dmitrievna Ulyanova bridge the years since her Aunt Nadya died—years of war, injustice, betrayal of all for which she labored:

> From 1929 until the end of her days, Nadezhda Konstantinovna worked on behalf of education. She wrote articles for future government and Party use which are recognized even in our own day. In particular, of great interest to the present time is a work by Krupskaya *Quantitative and Qualitative Calculation*, (taking stock), an article which came to light in the newspaper *Evening Moscow*, November 11, 1988. The article is amazingly contemporary. She seems to be speaking, not from long ago 1926, but presently—in the time of *perestroika*.

How does one characterize such a life? "Educator"? But she was more catalyst and organizer than innovator. "Friend of children and young people"? What does that say about the thousands of personal letters she wrote to them and about them; the meetings and interviews during which she listened to their comments, offering counsel and encouragement? "Devoted wife"? She was more than that.

Better than any other, Nadya herself summarized it. "My life," she said, "has been one of exceptional good fortune—to witness, to be at the center of events, when all of life was in the process of change."

Reference Notes

Preface

1. Vospominaniya, O., *Vladimir Ilych Lenin*, B 10 tom. T. 2, M. , c. 367

Chapter 2

1. Note 75, Vol.37, Lenin: Collected Works [1967].
N.K. wanted her sentence reduced in order that she and V.I. might leave exile together. He had already fulfilled one year of his term.
2. See L #267, 268, 269, 270 and K-#17, 20, 22, 27, 29 in Vol.37 (Lenin's *Collected Works*).

Chapter 3

1. The following were written or translated and published under the authorship of "V.Ilyin" during exile:
   1. The *Development of Capitalism in Russia*
      a) Excerpts published in successive issues of the periodical *Nachalo* 1897.
      b) Published in book form March 1899.
      c) Second enlarged edition pub. 1908 St. Petersburg.
   2. *The History of Trade Unionism* - Sidney and Beatrice Webb (translation).
   3. *Industrial Democracy* - Sidney and Beatrice Webb (translation; edited by V.I.).
   4. *Economic Studies and Essays* - published in book form 1898.
   5. Reviews of current books - published in various issues of *Nachalo* .
   6. Miscellaneous articles and translations, mainly dealing with economic/agrarian questions.
Nadya collaborated in the work of translating (2) and (3) above. She also did much of the work on fair [hand-written] copies and proofreading of the shorter works.
Money from these publications accumulated in the bank account of Anna Ulyanov-Yelizarova. Because of delays by some publishers in paying, rather large sums of money reached the author after he had left Russia.

Chapter 6

1. Kurnatovsky, following his arrest in Tiflis, was exiled. At the expiration of his term, he returned to St. Petersburg where his involvement in the first Russian Revolution (1905-07) ended in another arrest, after which he was sentenced to penal servitude for life. In 1906 he escaped abroad where he lived until his death six years later.

Chapter 16

1. Itinerant "holy man," confidant of the Tsaritsa. Although notorious as a lecher, he remained close to the Imperial family because of his seeming ability to heal the Tsarevich, heir to the throne, who suffered from hemophilia.
2. Year 1919.
3. Nihilism—destruction (of the existing order) for its own sake, without regard to consequences.
4. Anarchism—rebellion against any authority. Nihilism and anarchism are not synonymous.
5. Lenin was a voluntary emigré abroad.
6. Bolshevism was not synonymous with either nihilism or anarchism.
7. No documents were found.
8. The Yelizarov apartment on Shirokaya Street, Petersburg.
9. The Austrian coins, remaining from Yelizaveta's inheritance, that Nadya brought from Switzerland.

Bibliography

Krupskaya, Nadezhda Konstantinovna

Klyuchi ot schastya zhenskogo; vstrechi i besedi N.K.Krupskoi so rabotnitsami Moskvi: sbornik (sost. Bliskovskaya, N.Z.). Moscow 1986

Krupskaya, Kunetskaya and Mashtakova (series "Molodaya Gvardiya"). Moscow 1973

Krupskaya, Nadezhda Konstantinovna, o nei, Dridzo, Vera. Moscow 1958

Lenin, Krupskaya, Ulyanovi: Perepiska. Moscow 1981

Moya Zhizn (Autobiography for Young People). Moscow 1959

Nadezhda Krupskaya, Dridzo, Vera. Moscow 1966

N.K.K., Lebidova and Pavlotskaya. Moscow 1962

N.K.K., Biblio. trudov i literaturi o zhizn i deyatelnosti. Moscow 1973

N.K.K., Biografiya, Dridzo, Vera Moscow 1978 (with Manbekova et al). Moscow 1978

N.K.K., Biografiya, Obichkin, G.D.; Dridzo, Vera; Manbekova, C.Y. Moscow 1988

N.K.K., Bibliograficheskii ukazatel. Moscow 1959

N.K.K., Collection of pedagogical writings 11 Volumes (in Russian). Moscow 1959

N.K.K., Deyatelnost, ped. idei, Litvinov, S.A. Kiev 1970

N.K.K., Pisma iz Ufi 1900-01. Moscow 1984

N.K.K., Sbornik dokumentov i vospominanii. Perm 1969

N.K.K., Zhizn i deyatelnost vo fotografiyakh i dokumentakh. Moscow 1974

N.K.K., Zhizn i pedagogicheskaya deyatelnost, Konstantinov, N.A. Moscow 1948

O Nadezhda Krupskoi Vospominanii, ocherki, stati sovremennikov (several authors incl. Dridzo). Moscow 1988

Podarki detei V.I.Leninu i N.K.Krupskoi. Moscow 1985

Ryadom so Leninim (Recollections of N.K.K. by contemporaries) . Moscow 1969

Slavnye Bolshevichki (N.K.K. and others). Moscow 1958 (translation by Mary Hamilton-Dann in Library of Congress).

Strastnii propagandist, Leninskovo ucheniya (o N.K. Krupskoi), Zamislov, Yuri V. Moscow 1986

Svetloye imya: Nadezhda. Ulyanova, Olga Dmitrievna. pub. in Moscow Pravda Feb.24, 1989

Vospominanii o N.K.K., pod.red., Arsenyeva, A.M. Moscow 1966

Vo to dalekiye godi: V.I. Lenin i N.K. Krunskaya vo pismakh ko rodnim, Deich, G.M. Moscow 1982

Lenin, Vladimir Ilyich

Kabinet i kvartira V.I. Lenin vo Kremle. Moscow (n.d.)

Lenin, V.I., Aksyutin and Martunshuk. Moscow 1987

Lenin vo vospominanyakh Finnov (full translation with annotations and graphics by Mary Hamilton-Dann. MS in U. of Rochester Library). Moscow 1979

Leninskiye mesta vo Finlandii. Helsinki 1981

Muslitel i revolutsioner, Krzhizhanovski, G.M. Moscow 1985

Na povorotye, Lepeshinski, P.N. Moscow 1985

Neissyakamaya energiya, Fotieva, L.A. Moscow 1985

Pamyatniye Leninskie mesta Moskvi i podmoskovya, (Fotoputevoditel). (pictorial)

Rasskazi o Lenine, Lunacharski, A.V. Moscow 1985

"Sarai" i "shalash" vo Razlive. Leningrad 1985

Sibirskaya ssilka V.I. Lenina. Moscow 1984

Smolny (Lenizdat). Leningrad 1986

Uchitel i drug, Stassova. E.D. Moscow 1985

Vospominanii o Lenine, Zetkin, Klara (Full translation with explanatory preface by Mary Hamilton-Dann. MS in U. of Rochester Library.) Moscow 1958

Zdes zhil i rabotal Lenin. Moscow 1966

Days With Lenin, Gorky, Maxim. N.Y. 1932

Impressions of Lenin, Balabanova, Angelica. U. of Michigan Press 1964

Lenin, V.I., *Collected Works* 45 volumes (4th Edition 1964); 57 volumes (5th Edition in Russian). Moscow 1964, 1970

Lenin Memorial Places in USSR. Moscow 1983

Lenin on Religion (Little Lenin Library Vol-7). N.Y. (n.d.) International Pub., Inc.

Lenin-museo, Tampere, Finland, archival material

Lenin: Notes for a Biographer, Trotsky, Leon, N.Y. 1971

Lenin, the Man and His Work, Williams, Albert Rhys

Memories of Lenin, Krupskaya, N.K.,. London 1932

Revolutionary Silhouettes, Lunacharski, A.V., Moscow 1923

They Knew Lenin: Recollections of Foreign Contemporaries, USSR 1968

General

Adolf Hitler, Toland, John. N.Y. 1977

(A) *History of Finland,* Jutikkala and Pirinen, N.,Y. 1962

An Ambassador's Memoirs (3 vols.), Paléologue, Maurice, N.Y. (n.d.)

An Essay in Political Criticism, Malraux, André, Harvard U. Press 1967

An Ideology in Power, Wolfe, Bertram D., N.Y.1969

Assassination of Trotsky, Mosley, Nicholas, London 1972

Before the Deluge, Friedrich, Otto, N.Y. 1972

Behind the Veil at the Russian Court (Yekaterina Radziwill), Vassili, Count Paul, N.Y. 1914

(*Bolshaya Sovietskaya Entsiklopediya*) articles on Krupskaya, Kollontai, Inessa Armand, Klara Zetkin

Boris Godunov, Platonov, Sergei F., Leningrad 1921

British Agent, Lockhart, R.Bruce, N.Y. 1933

Bukharin and the Bolshevik Revolution: A Political Biography,1888-1938, Cohen, Stephen F. N.Y. 1971-73

Comrade and Lover, Ettinger, Elzvieta (ed. and trans.), MIT Press 1979

End of the Romanovs, Alexandrov, Victor, N.Y. 1966

Feliks Dzerzynski and the SDKPiL: A Study of the Origins of Polish Communism, Blobaum, Robert, Columbia U. Press 1984

Feudalism to Communism, Okey, Robin, U. Minnesota press 1982

(The) *Finnish Revolution 1917-1918,* Upton, Anthony F., U. Minnesota Press 1980

(The) *First Russian Revolution 1825,* Mazour, Anatole, Stanford U. Press 1937

History and Russia's Turning Point, Kerensky, Alexander, N.Y. 1965

History of the CPSU, Little Stalin Library Vol.7

History of the Russian Revolution (3 vols.), Trotsky, Leon, U. Michigan Press 1957

Imperialism and the Accumulation of Capital, Bukharin, Nikolai, Boulder CO 1978

In War's Dark Shadow: Russians Before the Great War, Lincoln, W. Bruce, N.Y. 1983

Ivan the Terrible, Payne and Romanoff, N.Y. 1975

Karl Marx, the Essential Writings, Bender, Frederic L., (ed.). N.Y. 1972

Karl Radek, the Last Internationalist, Lerner, Warren, Stanford U. Press 1970

Khruschev Remembers, Khruschev, Nikita, Boston 1970

Lenin, Possony, Stefan T. Chicago 1964

Let History Judge (The Stalin Years), Medvedyev, Roi, N.Y. 1972

Letters of Rosa Luxemburg, Bonner, Stephen E. (ed.), Boulder CO 1978

Letters of Rosa Luxemburg, (incl. in Bukharin, see above)

Letters of Tsar Nicholas II to Empress Alexandra, N.Y. 1924

Letters of Tsar Nicholas II to Dowager-Empress Marie, N.Y. 1924

Lost Splendour, Youssoupoff, Prince Felix, N.Y. 1954

Marx's Daughters, Florence, Ronald, N.Y. 1975

Mein Kampf, Hitler, Adolf, N.Y. 1939

Memoirs, Eden, Sir Anthony, Boston 1965

Memoirs of a Terrorist, Savinkov, Boris, N.Y. 1931

Mirrors of Moscow, Bryant, Louise, N.Y. 1923

My Life, Trotsky, Leon, N.Y. 1930

(*The*) *Naked Truth,* Sheridan, Clare, N.Y. 1928

Once a Grand Duke, Alexander, Grand Duke of Russia, New Jersey 1932

(*The*) *Paris Commune,* Mason, Edward S., N.Y. 1967

Recollections of Romanovs and Bolsheviki (Julia Grant), Cantacuzène, Princess, Boston 1919

(*The*) *Red Heart of Russia,* Beatty, Bessie, N.Y. 1918

Rosa Luxemburg, Frohlich, Paul

Rosa Luxemburg, Ettinger, Elzvieta, Boston 1986

Russia and the Weimar Republic, Kochan, Lionel, Cambridge, England 1954

Russia, 1917; the February Revolution, Katkov, George, N.Y. 1967

(*The*) *Sparticist Uprising of 1919,* Waldman, Eric, Marquette U. Press 1958

Stalin, Trotsky, Leon, N.Y. 1941

Ten Days that Shook the World, Reed, John, N.Y. 1960

Through the Russian Revolution, Williams, Albert Rhys, N.Y. 1921

Tovarishch Inessa (in Russian), Podlyashuk, Pavel, Moscow 1985 (complete translation.

MS by Mary Hamilton-Dann in Penfield, N.Y. Library and Library of Congress)

Weimar, A Cultural History, Laqueur, Walter, N.Y. 1974

(The) Weimar Chronicle: Prelude to Hitler, De Jonge, Alex, London 1978

Writings of Leon Trotsky 1934-35. N.Y. 1971

Germany and the Revolution in Russia 1915-1918. Documents from the archives of the German Foreign Ministry captured after WW II. London, Oxford U. Press

Essays, Hamilton-Dann, Mary, (manuscript): *The Russian Dilemma: Quest for Oceans; Nationalism and the Elastic Boundaries of Eastern Europe,* both 1987-89.

Chronology of Lenin's major writings

What the "Friends of the People" Are and How They Fight the Social-Democrats, multigraphed, 1894

The Development of Capitalism in Russia, publ. 1899

What Is To Be Done? March, 1902

One Step Forward, Two Steps Back, May, 1904

Two Tactics of Social-Democracy in the Democratic Revolution, May, 1905

Materialism and Empiro-Criticism, April–May, 1905

Imperialism, the Highest Stage of Capitalism, 1916, publ. 1917

The Tasks of the Proletariat in the Present Revolution (April Theses), 1917

The State and Revolution, 1917, publ. 1918

Left-Wing Communism, an Infantile Disorder, 1920

Newspapers and Periodicals Lenin founded, edited, and/or wrote for

Iskra (The Spark), 1900–1903

Vperyod (Forward), Dec 1904–May 1905

Proletary, (Workers), May 1905–from Geneva. Fall 1906 also publ. abroad

Novaya Zhizn, (New Life), Oct–Dec 1905

Zvezda (Star) 1910

Pravda, (Truth), 1912

Soldatskaya Pravda (Soldiers' Truth), April, 1917

Biographical Index

Adler, Viktor *(1852-1918)*. Leader of Austrian S-D Party. *134, 155, 156*

Alexandra, Empress of Russia, *1872-1918*. German-born wife of Tsar Nicholas II. Granddaughter of England's Queen Victoria. *179, 180*

Alliluyev, Sergei A. *(1866-1945)*. Russian revolutionary. Joined S-D Party in 1896. Mechanic and locomotive engineer in Tiflis. Moved to St. Petersburg 1907 where his apartment became a "safe" h.q. 1912-17. Held managerial posts in Soviet Government, Father of Nadezhda Alliluyeva who, at age 17, became Stalin's second wife. *205*

Armand, Inessa *(1874-1920)*. French-born revolutionary feminist. Children: Alexander b. 1894, Fedor 1896, Inna 1898, Varvara 1901, Andrei 1903. *141-145, 153, 159-61, 174, 175, 262, 283*

Axelrod, Paul *(1850-1928)*. Russian. Marxist theorist. Co-founder first Russian S-D Party. Menshevik leader. Editorial member *Iskra*. Opposed Bolshevik Revolution. Supported Provisional Government of Lvov and (presumably) Kerensky. Colleague of Plekhanov. *15, 70, 72-74, 78, 79, 87, 95, 96, 116, 174, 187*

Balabanova, Angelica *(1878-1965)*. b. in Ukraine to upper-class parents. Left home at age 19 to join revolutionary movement. In Italy worked for socialist journal *Avanti*. Was named secretary to the leadership of the 3rd International, 1919. Was propangandist for Russia, later "disillusioned" with Bolsheviks. Author of MY LIFE AS A REBEL, 1938. *157, 160, 161, 169, 174, 254, 255, 264, 280*

Bebel, August *(1840-1913)*. German. Leading political figure in history of W. European socialism. Co-founder German S-D Party. *145*

Blumqvist, Arthur *(1878-1951)*. Emelia his wife d. 1968. Finnish non-activist S-D's. Sheltered Lenin and Nadya in Helsingfors during underground period. *213, 214*

Bogdanov, Alexander A. *(1873-1928)*. Russian. Medical school graduate, economist, philosopher, author of books on experimental science. Grad. U. of Kharkov. Joined S-D 1896. Organized Institute of Gerontology and Hematology 1921. Died as result of blood transfusion performed on himself. *115-117, 120, 126, 134*

Bonch-Bruyevich, Vladimir D. *(1873-1955)*. Russian. Doctorate degree in history, scholar and journalist. Joined S-D 1895. Active in Marxist circles. Emigrated to Switzerland 1896 and established contact with Emancipation of Labor group (Plekhanov, Axelrod, Zasulich). Wrote for Lenin's *Iskra*. After 1918, director of State Museum of Literature and Museum of History of Religion and Atheism. *107, 204, 234, 236*

Bryant, Louise *(1890-1936)*. American journalist; wife of John Reed. Born to wealthy family, but sympathetic to Russian Revolution. Visited Russia 1917 and again 1920-21. Met Lenin, Kalinin, Djzerzhinski, Chicherin. Wrote about her experiences in *Mirrors Of Moscow* and *Six Red Months In Russia*. *241, 242, 261*

Bukharin, Nikolai *(1888-1938)*. Russian. Bolshevik leader and theorist. Son of a teacher. S-D from 1906. Met Lenin and Nadya in Cracow 1912 while a fugitive from tsarist police. Replaced Zinoviev as president of Communist international. Executed Mar. 13, 1938. *150, 151, 161, 279-281*

Chekhov, Anton *(1860-1904)*. Russian novelist and dramatist. *7*

Chicherin, Georgii *(1872-1936)*. Russian politician; later, Soviet Commissar of Foreign Affairs. *240, 281*

Churchill, Winston *(1874-1965)*. Twice Prime Minister of England. Conservative member of Parliament. *244, 258*

Denikin, Anton *(1872-1947)*. Russian general of counter-revolutionary army. Fled to U.S. after defeat. Died in Ann Arbor, Mich. *244*

Deutsch, Leo G. *(1855-1941)*. Russian. b. of merchant family. Leader Russian S-D. Arrested 1901, fled abroad, joined *Iskra* staff. Later joined Mensheviks. Lived in USA 1911-16 where he published "Free Word" in N.Y. Returned to Russia 1917. Pensioner from 1928. *86, 87, 95*

Djerzhinski, Feliks *(1877-1926)*. Polish. S-D. Latterday convert to Bolshevism. Became head of *Cheka* (secret police) and Commissar of Transportation. Administered relief for children of USSR. *113, 225, 239, 255, 256, 271, 279, 281*

'Dominika'. Wife of Vaneyev. *19, 22, 25, 31, 49, 52*

Dostoyevski, Feodor *(1821-81)*. Russian author. *5, 6*

Dridzo, Vera, b.1902 Rumanian. Became Nadya's private secretary. *x, 286, 287, 292, 295*

Dubrovinsky, Yosef F. *(1877-1913)*. Russian. Member Narodnaya Volya Movement. Later Marxist. Exiled 1898. Was agent for *Iskra* after joining Bolsheviks 1903. Long career of exile, release, escape. Contracted T.B. Final arrest 1910. Hopelessly ill, he committed suicide by drowning himself in the Yenisei River. *115, 120, 125, 126, 130*

Eddy, Harriet Gertrude *(1877-1967)*. Ass't. Prof. Agricultural Extension, U. of Cal. at Berkeley. 1909-1918 worked at Cal. State Library where she organized system of rural free libraries in 40 of 58 counties. To Russia in 1926 for 5 mos. on sabbatical from U. of Cal. Again to Russia 1930-31 to visit rural libraries. Afterward, a Soviet Women's Library Org. visited Cal. rural libraries. *290, 291*

Engberg, Oskar *(1874-1955)*. Finnish S-D. Fellow-exile in Shushenskoye, of Lenin and Nadya. In old age, a pensioner in Moscow. *34, 37, 40, 44-47, 52, 54-56, 292*

Engels, Frederick *(1820-1895)*. German Socialist; collaborator with Karl Marx. *74, 76*

Fedoseyev, Nikolai E. *(1871-98)*. Russian. Among first propagandists of Marxism in Russia. Expelled from Kazan Gymnasium for spreading Marxism. Organized a Marxist group which included Lenin. Exiled to East Siberia 1895. Committed suicide. *40, 42*

Fofanova, Margarita *(1883-1976)*. Russian. Daughter of an office worker. Studied at St. Petersburg Institute of Agriculture. Joined Bolshevik Party 1917 and engaged in extensive party work. Pensioner from 1934. *205, 206, 224*

Foster, William Z. *(1881-1961)*. American. Socialist. Outstanding labor organizer. Later chairman of American Communist Party. *278*

Fotieva, Lydia *(1881-1975)*. Russian. Emigrated from Russia 1904. Assisted Nadya with correspondence "abroad." Long history of Party work. Joined staff of V.I. Lenin Central Museum, Moscow, 1938, where her experience as Lenin's principal "duty" secretary was a professional asset and brought her many honorary awards. Pensioner from 1956. *248, 250, 270-272*

Gapon, Georgii *(1870-1906)*. Russian. Former priest Russian Orthodox Church. Born to

family of well-to-do peasants. Studied St. Petersburg Theological Academy 1898-1903. Founder of police-sponsored workers' organization. Ordered by Okhrana (tsarist secret police) to infiltrate S.-R. Movement. Unmasked as a spy, condemned by group of workers at village of Ozerki, near St. Petersburg, and hanged. *105-107*

Ginzberg, Yevgenia *(1906?-1977)*. Russian. Author of REAP THE WHIRLWIND, based upon her 18 years in a Soviet prison.

Gorky, Maxim (pseudo. of Alexei Maximovich Peshkov) *(1868-1936)*. Russian novelist and playwright. Son of a joiner and cabinet-maker. Father's early death left family dependent upon the mother's small income from her own father's dye works. During 1888-89 and 1891-92 "I wandered about Russia," Gorky remembered, "working as a stevedore, baker and at other trades. It was a hard life." Arrested 1889 for participating in outlawed political circles. Became on-and-off supporter of Lenin. Died in Gorki (Nizhny-Novgorod). *2, 108, 109, 117-119, 126, 127, 131-134, 150-151, 269*

Grant, Julia (Princess Cantacuzène). Author of a memoir castigating Lenin. *179-182*

Grimm, Robert. Swiss. *(1881-1956)*. Chairman Swiss S-D Party to 1919. Leader of Second International. Deputy to Swiss Parliament. Opposed idea of a united working-class movement. *187, 188*

Guèsde, Jules *(1845-1922)*. French socialist leader. *157*

Hanecki (Fürstenburg), Jakob S. *(1879-1937)*. German. From 1896 member of Lithuania/Poland S-D. Became commissar finance post-October 1917. *187*

Haarala, Hildur, Finnish. b.1890 Befriended Lenin while he was in hiding at Latukka apartment. Sister of Luli. Interviewed by Soviet T.V. 1966. *218, 219, 222, 244*

Hardie, James Kier *(1856-1915)*. Scottish. Co-founder with Ramsey MacDonald of British Labor Party. *157*

Helphand, Alexander *(1869-1924)*. *191, 192, 201, 202*

Hitler, Adolf *(1889-1945)* *75, 246, 289*

Huysmans, Camille *(1871-1968)*. Belgian. Socialist writer and statesman. Secretary of Socialist International. *157*

Jaurès, Jean *(1859-1914)*. French socialist leader. *157*

Jogiches, Leo *(1867-1919)*. Polish. S-D, Colleague and lover of Rosa Luxemburg. *74, 247*

Jordania, Noah, Russian. Early leader of Russian S-D. *90*

Kalmukova, Alexandra M. *(1849-1926)*. Russian. Graduated from "gymnasium" as school teacher. Taught in Sunday Evening Schools in Kharkov and St. Petersburg. Joined populist *Narodnik* Movement, later *Emancipation of Labor* group and finally (St. Petersburg) *League of Struggle*. Served on editorial boards of "legal" Marxist papers *Novoe Slovo* and *Nachalo*. Ran storehouse 1889-1902 for popular literature in St. Petersburg. Gave money to *Iskra* and *Zaria*. 1902 exiled abroad, continued to finance Bolsheviks. Post-1917 worked in public education and at Ushinskii Pedagogical Institute, Leningrad. *70*

Kamenev, Leo *(1883-1936)*. Russian. Colleague of Lenin and member of leadership after Lenin's death. *107, 125, 136, 143, 152, 153, 198, 205, 206, 208, 225, 226, 232, 241, 258, 273, 274, 279-281, 290, 291*

Kaplan, Dora (Fanya), Russian. Terrorist member Social-Revolutionary Party. Tried to assassinate Lenin. *254, 256, 279*

Karpinski, Vyacheslav A. *(1880-1965)*. Russian. Doctorate in Economics. S-D 1898. Connected with publishing Bolshevik literature in Switzerland. *125, 161, 189*. Olga (Sophia) *(1859-1957)* his wife. *278, 294*

Katayama, Sen *(1859-1933)*. Japanese. Son of a peasant. Typesetter in Tokyo 1881. To U.S.A. 1884. Graduated Yale U. 1895. Returned to Japan, organized first Japanese trade union 1897. Helped organize Jap. S-D Party. Opposed Russo/Japanese war. Arrested 1911 for organizing strike in Tokyo. Imprisoned. 1914 forced to emigrate to U.S.A. Joined American socialists, later became a communist. Died in Moscow, buried in Red Square. *278, 294*

Kautsky, Karl *(1854-1938)*. German. Socialist, luke-warm Marxist who pursued theoretical disputes with Lenin and Russian S-D Party. *128, 134, 157, 159*

Kerensky, Alexander *(1881-1970)*. Russian. Head of Provisional Government following abdication of Tsar Nicholas II. *185, 186, 200, 209, 221, 223, 226, 230, 238*

Kirov, Sergei *(1886-1934)*. Russian. Leningrad Party boss, assassinated Dec. 1934.

Knippovich, Lydia *(1857-1920)*. Russian. Daughter of a physician; born in Finland. Was Narodnik Populist end of 1870's. Joined League of Struggle (St. Petersburg) 1889. Arrested and exiled. S-D member 1890 traveling throughout European Russia as Propagandist. Attended famous Tammerfors Conference. 1911-13 again exiled. Her health ruined, she died in the Crimea. *11, 19, 54, 65, 96, 119, 128, 289, 293*

Kolchak, Alexander *(1873-1920)*. Russian. Son of naval artillery officer. Commanded destroyer at Port Arthur—Russo-Japanese war. Commanded Baltic Fleet WW I. Minister of War and Navy in "Siberian Government." Defeated 1920. Turned over to Red Army, tried and shot. *244*

Kollontai, Alexandra *(1872-1952)*. Russian. A leader of International Women's Movement. Successively Soviet Ambassador to Norway and Sweden. *136, 140, 141, 160, 161, 198, 225, 236, 237, 281*

Kornilov, Lavr *(1870-1918)*. Russian General; a leader of counterrevolutionary armies. Led troops in march on Petrograd Aug. 1917 for purpose of establishing a military dictatorship. Killed during military encounter with Red Army. *209, 227, 244*

Krasnov, P.H. *(1869-1947)*. Russian. A leader of counterrevolution. After defeat of Germany WW I, emigrated to that country and continued anti-Soviet activity. During WW II, cooperated with Hitlerites, forming army units composed of "White" émigrés from Russia. Captured by Soviet troops; returned to Russia; sentenced as a traitor and hanged. *244*

Krupskaya, Yelizaveta *(1842-1915)* Mother of Nadezhda.

Krzhizhanovski, Gleb *(1872-1959)*. Russian. Power engineering specialist. Colleague of Lenin. "Journeyman" poet, technical expert. Vice President USSR Academy of Sciences 1929-1939. Noted for involving scientists in solving economic problems of the country. Zinaida Nevzorova his wife *(1869-1948)*. Daughter of a teacher. Grad. Chemistry, St. Petersburg Advanced Courses for Women. Taught Sunday Evening School. Joined League of Struggle. Held supervisory post in *Iskra* Organization. Worked in public education as deputy chairman of a commission post-1917. *16, 19, 22-25, 30-32, 36-38, 40, 47, 53, 65, 66, 94, 269, 280, 295, 296*

Kurnatovski, Viktor *(1868-1912)*. Born in Riga. Son of a physician. He was exiled to Minusinsk District of Siberia where he met Lenin and Nadya. Later traveled to Georgia where he organized an *Iskra* center. Died in exile in Paris. *88, 89, 92, 93*

Lafargue, Laura *(1845-1911)*. Daughter of Karl Marx. Activist in French socialist and workers' movements. *131, 132, 145*

Lafargue, Paul (1842-1911). French. Husband of Laura. Son-of a French wine merchant who lived in Cuba. Medical student in Paris. Met trouble with authorities over political activity. Finished medical education in England. mar. Laura 1868. Both committed suicide because of age and in irmity. *131, 132, 145*

Latukka, Luli *(1886-1938)*. Finnish. Working woman who, with her husband, gave sanctuary to Lenin while on his way to Russia 1917. *218-221, 244*

Lepeshinski, P.N. *(1868-1944)*. Russian. Son of a priest. While a student at St. Petersburg U., was arrested and exiled to Siberia where he became acquainted with Lenin and Nadya. Later fled abroad to Geneva where he renewed contact with Lenin, also in exile. Post-1918, worked in Commission of Education. Became in 1927 director of Moscow Museum of History. *42, 49, 55, 88, 89, 106*

Olga his wife *(1871-1963)*. b. to well-to-do family. Grad. Medical School 1915. Married 1897, followed him into exile. Worked as physician. Author of several scientific/medical works.

Liebknecht, Wilhelm *(1826-1900)*. A leading German socialist of 19th Century. *123*

Karl his son, *(1871-1919)*. Colleague of Rosa Luxemburg and Franz Mehring in forming Spartacus League, an offshoot of German S-D Party. Murdered in Berlin. *123, 136, 158, 177, 246, 247*

Lockhart, R.H. Bruce *(1887-1970)* British diplomat, journalist, self-styled "British Agent" (spy). In Moscow at time of Dora Kaplan's attempt on the life of Lenin. Wrote interesting first-hand accounts of his experiences in USSR while a diplomat. *254*

Lunacharsky, Anatoly V. *(1875-1933)*. Russian. Joined S-D 1903. Author dramatist. U. degree in science and economics (Zurich). Soviet statesman, writer, critic, art historian, lecturer on socialism. Close friend of Gorky. First Soviet Commissar Education and Culture. Clashed with Stalin. Was eased out of his post, sent as ambassador to Spain. Died on the way at Menton, France. *106, 136, 235, 250, 285*

Luxemburg, Rosa, *(1870-1919)*. Polish. Distinguished journalist and socialist theoretician. Wrote books on political economy, philosophy, literature, art. Editor of *Saxon Arbeit-*

erzeitung. Co-founder with K. Liebknecht and F. Mehring of Spartacus League. Murdered 1919 in Berlin. *74, 75, 118, 123, 124, 136, 141, 145, 150, 160, 177, 244, 246, 247*

Lvov, Georgii (Prince) *(1861-1925)*. Russian. Lawyer by education, large landholder. Member of Cadet Pary (Constitutional Democrats). Headed 2 cabinets of Provisional Gov. Emigrated from Russia and became active anti-Bolshevik abroad. d. in Paris. *199, 200, 209*

MacDonald, James Ramsey *(1866-1937)*. Scottish. First Labor Party Prime Minister of England. While nominally attached to socialism held ambivalent views of certain socialist trends. Became a disappointment to many who elected him, and disappeared from the scene as Britain succumbed to increasing conservatism. *157*

Malinovsky, Andrei, Russian. Bolshevik deputy to tsarist, Duma (parliament). Discovered to be spy for tsarist secret police. Ensuing scandal forced him from office and he fled abroad. Later returning to Russia he was executed as a traitor and spy. *144, 150, 152, 154*

Mannerheim, Karl Gustav Emil—Baron von. *(1867-1951)*. One of the 'Baltic Barons'; active in Finnish/Russian affairs. Grad. U. of Helsingfors and Nikolai Cavalry School, St. Petersburg. Until 1917 served in Russian Army. Led anti-socialist forces in Finland, 1918. Marshal 1933, Pres. of Finland 1944. Commander Finnish Army during "Winter War" 1939-1940. Forced into retirement 1946. *244*

Martov (Zederbaum), 'Yuli' *(1873-1923)*. b. Constantinople, son of a merchant. Vacillating member of S-D Party. Advised various approaches to socialism. Eventually forswore revolutionary Marxism. d. in Berlin. *31, 32, 40, 50-53, 63, 70-73, 80, 83, 86, 94, 96, 129, 136, 174, 187*

Marx, Karl *(1818-1883)*. *7, 62, 76, 84, 107, 123, 124, 218, 247, 252*

Mehring, Franz *(1846-1919)*. German. b. to a wealthy family. Ph.D. university 1882. Philosopher, historian, literary critic. Joined S-D Party 1891. A leftist and Marxist leader German S-D Party. *123, 136, 158, 177*

Milyukov, Paul *(1859-1943)*. Russian. Historian and politician. Served in Prince Lvov government post-February Revolution 1917. Opposed Kerensky policies. *187, 200, 221*

Nevzorova, Zinaida, (see Krzhizhanovski)

Nicholas II *(1868-1918)*. Last Tsar of Russia. Executed, together with his wife and five children, at Yekaterinburg in July 1918. *1, 2, 27, 57, 98-100, 103, 105, 115, 153, 157, 176, 183-185, 221, 256-258*

Pieck, Wilhelm *(1876-1960)*. German. Son of a worker. Prominent in German S-D Party from 1895. Left wing socialist. Post-WW II worked for de-nazification of Germany. One of founders of German Communist Party. President German Democratic Republic from 1949. *275, 276, 278*

Platten, Fritz *(1883-1942)*. Swiss. Son of a worker. From 1912, secretary of Swiss S-D Party. Organized Lenin's trip through Germany. Arrested many times. A founder of C.P. of Switzerland, 1921. Moved to USSR 1923. Senior research worker at International Agrarian Institute Moscow. Taught at Moscow Institute of Foreign Languages. *174-176, 187-190, 194, 253*

Plekhanov, Georgii *(1856-1918)*. Russian. b. of petty gentry. Theoretician and Marxist. Founder of Emancipation of Labor group. Expelled from St. Petersburg Institute of Mines for revolutionary activity 1876. Émigré in Switzerland, Italy, France 1880-1917. Post-October 1917 became Menshevik. Noted for history of philosophy and social thought. Died in Terijoki (now Zelenogorsk) Finland May 3, 1918. Buried in Leningrad's Volkhov Cemetery. *15, 70-75, 78, 79, 86, 87, 90, 94-96, 106, 107, 117, 118, 136, 157, 198, 238*

Potressov, Alexander N. *(1869-1934)*. Russian. Grad. Natural Sciences, St. Petersburg U. Studied Law to 1893. Joined Marxists early 1890's; later League of Struggle. Arrested, exiled. Helped found *Iskra*. 1903 joined Mensheviks. Social chauvinist during WW I. Post-October 1918 was anti-Bolshevik. Emigrated, wrote for Kerenski's journal DNI. *70, 80, 86, 94, 96*

Prominsky, I.L. *(1859-1923)*. Polish. Political exile, friend of Lenin and Nadya in Siberia. *33, 37, 45, 47, 51, 52, 55, 56*

Pushkin, Alexander *(1799-1837)*. Russian. Poet. Anti-tsarist. Bell-weather of various Russian revolutionary movements. Killed in a duel. *5*

Radek (Sobelsohn), Karl *(1885-1939?)*. b. in Ukraine. Joined S-D of Poland/Lithuania. Pro-Lenin. Succeeded Luxemburg and Liebknecht in leadership of German Party. Eventually clashed with Stalin who called him a "Trotskyite." Recanted views 1929, stayed in favor. One of those who escaped

execution during the 1930's trials, but was sentenced to 10 years in prison. Probably died there. *174, 189, 194, 201*

Rahja, Eino *(1886-1936)*. Finnish. Socialist. Served as 'underground' emissary between Finland and Petrograd during critical days of 1917. Fought on the Karelian Front WW I. *210-212, 219, 224*

Rasputin, Grigor *(1871-1916)*. Russian. "Holy man"; friend of Empress Alexandra in connection with her ailing son. Murdered by members of anti-court faction in effort to "save the monarchy." *6*

Raukiainen, Alma *(b. 1890)*. Finnish. Aided Lenin during his underground period in Finland. *217, 218, 289*

Ravich, Olga (see Karpinski)

Reed, John *(1887-1920)*. American. Journalist. Sympathetic to Russian Revolution. Author of TEN DAYS THAT SHOOK THE WORLD, a classic first-hand account of October 1917. Died in Moscow, buried in Red Square. *228-34, 237, 238, 263, 295*

Reinbot, last tsarist governor of Moscow District. *266*

Roland-Holst, Henriette *(1869-1952)*. Dutch. Socialist and writer. Joined S-D 1897. Edited Dutch left-wing newspapers. Joined Dutch Communist Party 1918. In 1927 left it to become Christian Socialist. Member Dutch resistance during Nazi occupation 1940-45. Wrote poetry with socialist overtones, biography of Garibaldi, drama, studies on socialism. *157, 159, 174*

Rosenburg, A.M., Russian. Sister of Gleb Krzhizhanovski. Married Basil Starkov. *19, 22, 25, 30-32, 37, 40, 44, 47, 52, 55*. Elvira (E.E.) her mother.

Rovio, Kustaa *(1887-1938)*. Finnish. "Underground" member Finnish S-D. Sheltered Lenin in Helsingfors. Took active part in workers' revolution, Finland, 1918; fled to Petrograd. *209, 213, 217, 222, 244*

Savinkov, Boris *(1879-1925)*. Polish. *279*

Sheridan, Clare *(1885-?)*. English sculptress cousin of Winston Churchill. Visited Moscow to do a bust of Lenin. Wrote account of her experiences in USSR. *258-60, 280*

Shotman, Alexander *(1880-1937)*. Russian. b. in village of Alexanarovskoye near Moscow, son of a worker. Occupation: lathe operator. Joined League of Struggle. Member Helsingfors Finnish S-D Party 1911-1912. Arrested, exiled to Siberia 1913. Lenin's contact when he was hiding in Razliv. Post-1917 served in

Commissariat of Postal and Telegraph Services USSR. *210-212, 219, 244, 283*
Silvin, M.A. *(1874-1955)*. Russian. Son of a civil servant. S-D from 1891. Joined League of-Struggle 1893. That same year enrolled in Law School of U. St. Petersburg. Arrested 1896, exiled to Irkutsk, Siberia. Fled abroad 1904. Returned to Russia 1905. Leaned toward Menshevism. Withdrew from political activity 1908. Post-October 1917 worked in Soviet institutions. After 1932 a pensioner. Wrote articles on League of Struggle. *36, 52, 55, 62, 65.* Olga his wife.
Stahl, Ludmila *(1872-1939)*. Russian. Daughter of a factory owner. S-D from 1897. A leader of International Women's Movement. Arrested several times and exiled. Emigrated 1907. Active in Paris Bolshevik section of S-D and French Socialist Party. 1912-14 contributed editorials to *Pravda*. Post-1918 held prominent posts in various Party and literary/Party organizations. *145, 153, 160, 196, 262*
Stalin, Josef V. *(1879-1953)*. Succeeded Lenin as General Secretary of CPSU. Took a leading role in development of the socialist economy and the Soviet state and the victory over Hitler, 1941-45. Committed theoretical and political errors and gross violations of socialist laws, departing from Leninist standards and practices. These were later condemned by the CPSU as alien and harmful to Marxism-Leninism. *26, 88, 91-93, 151, 207, 208, 225, 267, 268, 271-74, 279-91, 289-291*
Starkov, Basil *(1869-1925)*. Russian. Son of an office worker. Grad. 1889 from St. Petersburg Technological Institute. Helped found League of Struggle. Arrested 1895, exiled 1897. Worked at various jobs in Siberia during exile. Released, became dir. of electric power plant in Baku. Post-1917 worked in Commissariat of Foreign Trade. 1921 USSR trade representative in Germany. d. in Berlin. (mar. to Krzhizhanovski's sister: see Rosenberg). *19, 22, 24, 30-32, 36-38, 40, 55*
Stassova, Yelena *(1873-1966)*. Russian. Revolutionary. "Elder Stateswoman" who tended Party records and guarded Party ideology before and after October 1917. Grad. gymnasium. S-D from 1898. Joined League of Struggle. Taught Sunday Evening School. Agent of *Iskra* from 1901. Member Comintern 1921. Anti-war and anti-Fascist delegate to W. European meetings. Buried in Red Square. *199, 267*
Sverdlov, Yakov *(1885-1919)*. Russian. Son of

artisan-engraver. Apprentice in a pharmacy 1900. S-D from 1901. Arrested, imprisoned, exiled several times. His organizational skills evident at an early date and he occupied important posts in the Party, eventually becoming titular head of state post–1917. "Virtually controlled Party Organization and State bureaucracy" (Soviet Encyclopedia). Buried in Red Square. *114, 225, 257, 263, 282*
Tolstoy, Leo *(1828-1910)*. Russian. Russian novelist and social reformer. *6, 52, 137*
"Tonechka" (see A.M. Rosenberg)
Troelstra, Pieter *(1860-1930)*. Dutch. Educated as a lawyer. S-D from 1893. During WW I his frequent mind-changing on the role of socialism elicited the following from Lenin: "A typical specimen of the venal, opportunistic leader." Troelstra also wrote poetry and contributed to Frisian literature. *157*
Trotsky, Leon *(1877-1940)*. Member of revolutionary movements from 1897. A leader of opportunist trends in the RSDLP, Menshevik from 1903; Bolshevik, 1917. Split repeatedly from Lenin's policies and headed a faction. Expelled from CPSU in 1927, exiled abroad in 1929 for continued opposition. Fled to Mexico, murdered there in 1940. *86, 94, 126, 134, 149, 174, 225, 226, 240, 243, 272, 275, 279-281, 291*
Turati, Filippo *(1857-1932)*. Italian. Political figure, publicist. Helped found Italian Socialist Party 1895. During WW I anti-war for Italy. After Fascist coup, fled to France and continued anti-fascist work. Died in Paris. *157*
Ulyanov, Vladimir Ilyich (Lenin) *(1870-1924)*
    Anna (sister) *(1864-1935)*
    Alexander (brother) *(1866-1887)*
    Olga (sister) *(1871-1891)*
    Dmitri (brother) *(1874-1943)*
    Maria (sister) *(1878-1937)*
    Maria Alexandrovna (mother) *(1835-1916)*
    Olga Dmitrievna (niece, daughter of Dmitri) *b. 1925*
Vaillant, Paul *(1892-1937)*. French socialist. *157*
Vander Velde, Emile *(1866-1938)* Belgian Socialist leader. President International Socialist Bureau. *157*
Vaneyev, Anatoly A. *(1872-1899)*. Russian. Family were civil servants. Student St. Petersburg Technological Institute 1893-95. Helped found League of Struggle. Worked on newspaper publicity for Lenin. Arrested 1895, exiled 1897. Died in exile of T.B. *25, 27, 31, 32, 49, 50*
Vetrova, Maria *(1870-1897)*. Russian. Daughter

of a peasant woman. Brought up in orphanage. Completed secondary school. Worked as a teacher 1889-94. Enrolled in Advanced Courses for Women 1894, St. Petersburg. Became involved in *Narodnaya Volya* movement. Arrested 1896. Imprisoned in Trubetskoi Bastion of Peter-Paul Fortress. Burned herself to death (see text). Two hectograph proclamations issued in protest. Five to six thousand students demonstrated in front of Kazan Cathedral Mar. 4, 1897; routed by police. Also 'Vetrova Demonstrations' in Moscow and Kiev. *21*

Viik, Karl *(1883-1946)*. Finnish S-D. Member of Seim (Finnish Parliament). Sympathetic to Russian Revolution. Friend of Lenin. *214, 222, 244*

Webb, Sidney *(1859-1947)*. Beatrice his wife *(1858-1943)*. Worked as a team in behalf of British Socialism. Writers, journalists, inluential members of British Labor Party. *24, 38, 294*

Wells, H.G. *(1866-1946)*. British novelist and journalist. *262*

Wrangel, Peter (Baron Wrangel) *(1878-1928)*. One of the "Baltic barons" of ambiguous national heritage (German/Russian). General counter-revolutionary army. Commanded "White" Army of the Crimea. Was defeated. Fled abroad 1920; d. in Brussels. *244*

Yakubova, Apollinariya *(1870-1917)*. Revolutionary; early close friend and colleague of Nadya. Later broke with Lenin and his wife. *11, 14, 16, 19, 22, 41, 52, 62, 63, 83, 249*

Yelizarov Mark T. *(1863-1919)*. Russian. Political activist. Husband of Lenin's sister Anna.

Yudenich, Nikolai *(1862-1933)*. Russian. General of counter-revolutionary army. After defeat, fled abroad. Died in France. *244*

Zasulich, Vera *(1849-1919)*. Russian. Born a member of the gentry. Grad. boarding school in Moscow 1867. Qualified as teacher. Moved to St. Petersburg, became involved in revolutionary movement. Imprisoned and exiled 1869-71. Acquitted by jury in the Trepov Case. Fled abroad. Became foreign rep. Red Cross and *Narodnaya Volya*. In 1883 shifted to Marxism and joined Emancipation of Labor group (Plekhanov, Axelrod). Translated works of Marx and Engels. Member editorial staff of *Iskra*. Later defected to Mensheviks. Opposed October Revolution. Wrote history of International Workingmen's Association; also works on Rousseau and Voltaire. Died in Petrograd May 8, 1919. Buried near

Plekhanov in Volkhov Cemetery. *15, 70-74, 80, 83, 86, 87, 94, 96, 238*

Zetkin, Klara *(1857-1933)*. German. Born in Saxony, daughter of a village schoolmaster. Attended private teachers college in Leipzig. Married a Russian fellow-student, Osip Zetkin. Joined S-D 1881. From that period, was actively involved in the movement and became closely associated with all leading socialists of her day. Outspoken, militant, well-informed, Zetkin maintained her position of leadership until the day of her death. Her internationalist position and activities resulted in her being accepted as an outstanding personality on "both sides of the aisle" in an era of great male chauvinism. Died in Moscow rest-home, buried in Red Square. *74, 75, 136, 141, 158, 160, 247, 260-262, 264, 270, 276, 278, 293-295*

Zinoviev (Radomyslski) Grigor *(1883-1936)*. Russian. Born to lower, middle-class Jewish family in Ukraine. No formal education but attended lectures in law, Bern U. 1901 joined S-D and *Iskra* org. After Party split, 1903, joined Bolsheviks. Returned to Russia on "sealed train" 1917. Vacillation vis-a-vis Lenin policies. Post-Lenin, same with regard to Stalin (first anti-, then pro-Trotsky). Expelled from Party, 1934. Accused of Complicity in murder of Kirov. Shot Aug. 25, 1936. His political career paralleled that of Kamenev. *108, 125, 136, 143, 147, 151, 152, 160, 175, 177, 197, 205, 207, 211, 225, 226, 241, 255, 273, 279-281*